LEGITIMIZING THE ARTIST:
MANIFESTO WRITING AND EUROPEAN MODERNISM
1885–1915

In the late nineteenth and early twentieth centuries, the production of literary and cultural manifestoes enjoyed a veritable boom and accompanied the rise of many avant-garde movements. *Legitimizing the Artist* considers this phenomenon as a response to a more general crisis of legitimation that artists had been struggling with for decades. The crucial question for artists, confronted by the conservative values of the dominant bourgeoisie and the economic logic of triumphant capitalism, was how to justify their work in terms that did not reduce art to a mere commodity.

In this work Luca Somigli discusses several European artistic movements – decadentism, Italian futurism, vorticism, and imagism – and argues for the centrality of the works of F.T. Marinetti in the transition from a *fin de siècle* decadent poetics, exemplified by the manifestoes of Anatole Baju, to a properly avant-garde project aiming at a complete renewal of the process of literary communication and the abolition of the difference between producer and consumer. It is to this challenge that the English avant-garde artists, and Ezra Pound in particular, responded with their more polemical pieces. Somigli suggests that this debate allows us to rethink the relationship between modernism and post-modernism as complementary ways of engaging the loss of an organic relationship between the artist and his social environment.

(Toronto Italian Studies)

LUCA SOMIGLI is an associate professor in the Department of Italian Studies at the University of Toronto.

Luca Somigli

LEGITIMIZING THE ARTIST

Manifesto Writing and European Modernism 1885–1915

UNIVERSITY OF TORONTO PRESS
Toronto Buffalo London

Reprinted in paperback 2014

ISBN 978-0-8020-3761-9 (cloth)
ISBN 978-1-4426-5773-1 (paper)

Printed on acid-free paper

Toronto Italian Studies

National Library of Canada Cataloguing in Publication

Somigli, Luca
Legitimizing the artist : manifesto writing and European modernism, 1885–1915 / Luca Somigli.

(Toronto Italian studies)
Includes bibliographical references and index.
ISBN 978-0-8020-3761-9 (bound)
ISBN 978-1-4426-5773-1 (pbk.)

1. Modernism (Art) – Europe. 2. Modernism (Literature) – Europe. 3. Futurism (Art) – Europe. 4. Futurism (Literary movement) – Europe. 5. Avant-garde (Aesthetics) – Europe – History – 19th century. 6. Avant-garde (Aesthetics) – Europe – History – 20th century. 7. Revolutionary literature – History and criticism. I. Title. II. Series.

N6758.5.M63S64 2003 700'.94'09041 C2003-904838-1

This book has been published with the help of a grant from the Canadian Federation for the Humanities and Social Sciences, through the Aid to Scholarly Publications Programme, using funds provided by the Social Sciences and Humanities Research Council of Canada.

University of Toronto Press acknowledges the financial assistance to its publishing program of the Canada Council for the Arts and the Ontario Arts Council.

University of Toronto Press acknowledges the financial support for its publishing activities of the Government of Canada through the Book Publishing Industry Development Program (BPIDP).

Contents

Acknowledgments

I would like to thank the numerous friends and colleagues who have been most generous with their support, and who have read and commented on various drafts of the chapters of this volume. Material in chapters 1 and 3 was first developed as part of my doctoral dissertation at SUNY-Stony Brook; I thank the thesis director Hugh Silverman, and the members of the dissertation committee Krin Gabbard, Luigi Fontanella, and Sandy Petrey, for their help and guidance. As the project developed, I greatly benefited from the critical insights, the comments and suggestions, and above all the patience and encouragement of Ken Bartlett, Rocco Capozzi, Manuela Gieri, Francesco Guardiani, Elizabeth Legge, Michael Lettieri, Ernesto Livorni, Francesco Loriggio, Jay Macpherson, Mario Moroni, John Picchione, Lucia Re, and Max Statkiewicz. I also thank the two anonymous readers of the manuscript for the University of Toronto Press for their useful and perceptive advice. My most heartfelt gratitude goes also to Jason Blake, Paolo Chirumbolo, Elana Commisso, Patrizia Di Vincenzo, Franco Gallippi, and Marisa Ruccolo, who at different times were my research assistants. Special thanks to my brother Paolo and to Chiara for their invaluable help in musical matters.

I would also like to acknowledge the generous financial support given to this research project by the Social Sciences and Humanities Research Council of Canada and by the Connaught Fund. The Humanities Research Centre of Oxford Brookes University provided much welcome logistic support during a research trip to England; I am especially grateful to Steven Matthews for his friendly advice and for bringing the Visiting Scholar Programme to my attention. At the University of Toronto Press, I was very fortunate to work with an outstanding and experienced professional team, in particular Ron Schoeffel, Anne Laughlin, and Ruth Pincoe. Finally, I am grateful to the community of Victoria College for providing the best collegial environment in which to do research and write.

On a personal note, this book could not have been written without the love of my parents, and without Arthur, who helped just by being there.

The book is dedicated to Sue, with love.

LEGITIMIZING THE ARTIST:
MANIFESTO WRITING AND EUROPEAN MODERNISM
1885–1915

Introduction: The Artist in Modernity

Haloes and Auras

'*Il faut être absolutement moderne*': few sentences in the history of literature seem to have the prophetic and injunctive force of Arthur Rimbaud's famous dictum, so often invoked as the emblem of the literature that by breaking with the conventions of Romanticism, opens up the space of what is labelled – precisely – as 'modern.' But is Rimbaud's pronouncement to be read merely as an exhortation, or does it not also carry a more problematic – even foreboding – inflection that might rather recall its apparent opposite, Alexander Pope's admonition 'Moderns, beware'?[1] In other words, isn't the sense of obligation that '*il faut*' carries profoundly ambiguous, as it configures the modern as both a new dimension to embrace completely and without reservations, and simultaneously, as a destiny to which the human subject is consigned, and where one must – whether willingly or not – learn to dwell and make a home? Being modern, then, is from the beginning a Janus-like condition, in which the thrust forward toward the utopian future imagined by the strong ideologies of modernity – the worker's paradise of Marxism or the perfectly self-regulating world of free enterprise of capitalism – is balanced by a backward glance that, like that of Walter Benjamin's angel of history, perceives what is smashed and trampled by the march of 'progress': not only past modes of existence, but also needs and desires that do not find a place in the narratives of modernity.

What I intend to consider in this book is how artists have responded to Rimbaud's injunction, or, to put it differently, how they have attempted to renegotiate and re-legitimate their role in a landscape characterized by profound and radical social and cultural transformations that, among other things, implicitly or explicitly called into question many traditional assumptions about the arts and their place in society. I focus on the genre of the manifesto because I believe that it is here, in a textual space ambiguously poised between the aesthetic and the political, between the work of art and propaganda, between practice and theory, that we can both trace the shifting terms of the broader debate of what artists are and do, and follow the development of the increasingly antagonistic relationship between artists and their audiences that characterizes much of modernism and, to a certain extent, of post-modernism. The thirty or so years with which this study is concerned – from the mid 1880s to the mid 1910s – constitute a crucial phase of self-examination in European cultural history that begins with the decadent funeral of art, buried under the rubble of a supposedly decayed, degenerate, and crassly mercantile Western civilization, continues with the emergence of the avant-garde as an attempt to clear the ruin and re-invent the very notion of what constitutes art, and culminates with the re-appropriation of and accommodation with tradition of high modernism. Moving from France to Italy to England, *Narratives of Legitimation* thus seeks to re-construct the European context of literary modernity.

The widespread use of the term 'post-modern' to indicate the current cultural and social 'condition' of Western societies suggests that 'modernity' itself no longer refers simply to the contemporary, as its origin in the Latin adverb *modo* (recently) implies. Rather, modernity has become a thoroughly historicized category against which can be set a whole constellation of other notions, which establish with it a network of relations of contiguity and opposition: modernism, avant-garde, and of course post-modernism itself.[2] There is a general agreement that the nineteenth century not only marked the high point of modernity, but also saw the rise of those cultural experiences for which labels such as modernism and avant-garde try to account. The nineteenth century is represented as a phase of difficult and often tumultuous transition and dislocation, a 'maelstrom' (Berman 16), a 'black hole' (Karl 4), or a period of turmoil (Eysteinsson 6) in which the consolidation of capitalist economy, the formation of the European nation-states, the advances in science and technology, and the influence of the positivist paradigm of knowledge production profoundly transformed the social institutions, the economic structures and the communal ideologies that had governed European cultural and political life until the

French Revolution. If there is anything that the different aspects of this mutated social and cultural horizon have in common is a utopian dimension: the suggestion that they can ultimately offer better models of integration between the individual and the social, whether that is accomplished by letting the invisible hand of free enterprise do its work, by constructing new homogeneous communities of blood and/or culture, or by trusting the enlightening power of science and its practical applications. In this sense, nineteenth-century positivist modernity is indeed the heir of the Enlightenment. Even Marxism, the major strain of critical thought of the social effects of modernity, is oriented by a utopian impulse even while identifying, in Hegelian fashion, conflict rather than linear progress as the engine of history. Another way to formulate this is to consider Jean-François Lyotard's articulation of the fracture between modernity and post-modernity in terms of the legitimating function of what he calls metadiscourses. For the French philosopher, modernity is defined not by the ultimately positive or negative attitude toward the contemporary cultural milieu but rather by its recourse, in both affirmative and critical instances, to a series of grand narratives, from 'the dialectic of the Spirit' to 'the emancipation of the rational or working subject' to 'the creation of wealth' (xxiii), which endow with coherence and above all with a teleological trajectory – a conclusion, as in a story – the social and ideological discourses that constitute modernity itself.

Yet, as we have already noted, the discourse of modernity is from the beginning split and divided. Marxism itself may be easily seen as a sort of linchpin between these two ensuing conceptions of modernity: if on the one hand it is characterized by an ultimately positivist faith in progress, at the same time it also rejects the cultural and social values, and in particular the instrumental and utilitarian logic, of bourgeois modernity. The anti-bourgeois thrust of the cultural movements with which this book begins (decadentism and symbolism) is an aspect of this second, 'critical' modernity, which articulates a series of responses to the modernity that one *must* inhabit and to which one is destined whether or not one shares its beliefs and ideological imperatives. This second modernity, then, is what will be later defined – as a historiographic and critical category – as 'modernism': 'an attempt to *interrupt* the modernity that we live and understand as a social, if not "normal," way of life' (Eysteinsson 6). Eysteinsson's definition, which is echoed in much of the critical literature, interprets the culture of modernism as a culture of rupture and alienation that brings into relief the social and cultural experiences that are repressed or swept away by the unfolding of the narratives of modernity. A rhetoric of fragmentation and inversion orients the discourse of decadentism and symbolism, as if those cultural movements aimed precisely at both questioning the coherence of the metanarratives of bourgeois modernity and at giving a voice to – or at least showing the persistence of – experiences that could not be easily accommodated within its story. The artist, the dandy, the aristocrat, the *flâneur,* the street performer, the inept – and the avant-garde adds its own peculiar characters, such as the madman/woman or the criminal – are the figures that populate the counter-narratives of modernism. Under their pressure, the apparent unity of the grand narratives shatters into a series of local discourses that articulate their own alternative 'truths' – that is, the alienation and marginalization of those who do not conform to the principles of efficiency and productivity which power the social and economic engine of modernity and who reject its ensuing moral and ethical values. To be sure, this fragmentation is quite different from the free play of language games that orients the post-modern condition in Lyotard's account, since it is modernism in the first instance, and not only the contemporary critics of post-modernism, that is haunted 'by the paradisaic representation of a lost "organic" society' (Lyotard 15). The century of positivism closes with the rise of those psychological, philosophical, and scientific theories that question its very premises, from the solidity of the subject to that of the social institutions and the system of moral values underlying bourgeois society, and even – with Einstein's relativity – of the very structure of the natural universe. In other words, modernism, begins to explore what we might call (using a term that would gain currency at the dawn of the twentieth century) the 'unconscious' of modernity, in the sense that it articulates and brings to light its underlying but repressed (or unrepresented) assumptions and gives form to its ensuing social and personal 'dis-eases.' The Nietzschean 'death of God' names the collapse of the belief in a transcendental principle governing the natural and social order and inaugurates a series of fractures, of fissures within structures of experience that had hitherto appeared unitary. Thus, morality finds its repressed other in the will to power, and comes down from the heaven of metaphysics and into the fallen world of material history (with Nietzsche it becomes the object of a 'genealogy'); the Cartesian subject appears merely as the surface expression of drives and impulses unknowable to the subject itself; and even language, far from making reality immediately accessible, as the realist novel had seemed to do through the rhetorical strategies of what Roland Barthes has called the 'reality effect,' finds itself divided from the world, its inaccessible double, and infinitely divided within itself, a system built on differences and deferrals rather than on identities.[3]

In an ideal genealogy of the bifurcation between modernity and modernism, between the triumph of capitalist economy and positivist science on the one hand and the resistance to the utilitarian logic and the bourgeois values governing social modernity on the other, Charles Baudelaire's works constitute one of the central nodes: his poems and his prose writings represent the first fully articulated reflection on the subject of modernity, a term which he introduced into aesthetic discourse and legitimized, but which, at the same time, also brought into the horizon of experience of the artist the alienation and solitude that modernity itself fosters. As Walter Benjamin realized in his dazzling essays and fragments on the poet, Baudelaire's works provide the anatomy of a society that finds itself in the midst of an epochal transformation – a paradigmatic shift in which the capitalist system of production and its ensuing social and cultural transformations begin to find a vocabulary through which to represent and thematize themselves and, at the same time, to bring their contradictions into view. Baudelaire's very definition of modern art (to which I will return in chapter 2) is symptomatic of this transition, as it seeks to hold together, in a balance that the aesthetic movements to come will find most precarious, two apparently contradictory notions: 'l'éternel et l'immuable' [the eternal and the immovable], which characterizes the discourse of art as the literary and artistic tradition formalizes into institution; and 'le transitoire, le fugitif, le contingent' [the transient, the fleeing, the contingent] (*Œuvres complètes* 2: 695; 'The Painter of Modern Life' 403), which characterizes the discourse of modernity itself, with its emphasis on production and on the overcoming of obstacles of nature, human and otherwise, that stand in the way of the march of progress.[4]

Among Baudelaire's works, the prose poem 'Perte d'auréole' ('Lost Halo,' 1865), one of the compositions of *Le spleen de Paris* initially rejected by the publisher and published only after the poet's death, stands out for the richness of its allegory. This veritable 'primal modern scene,' as it has been called,[5] articulates a series of contradictions that will haunt literary modernity – contradictions to which the artists and movements that I will consider in the rest of this book sought to provide a solution. The prose poem, as the reader will recall, takes the form of a brief exchange:

> 'Eh! quoi! vous ici, mon cher? Vous, dans un mauvais lieu! vous, le buveur de quintessences! vous, le mangeur d'ambrosie! En vérité, il y a là de quoi me surprendre.
>
> – Mon cher, vous connaissez ma terreur des chevaux et des voitures. Tout à l'heure comme je traversais le boulevard, en grand hâte, et que je sautillais dans la boue, à travers ce chaos mouvant où la mort arrive au galop de tous le côtés à la fois, mon auréole, dans un mouvement brusque, a glissé de ma tête dans la fange du macadam. Je n'ai pas eu le courage de la ramasser. J'ai jugé moins désagréable de perdre mes insignes que de me faire rompre les os. Et puis, me suis-je dit, à quelque chose malheur est bon. Je puis maintenant me promener incognito, faire des actions basses, et me livrer à la crapule, comme les simples mortels. Et me voici, tout semblable à vous, comme vous voyez!
>
> – Vous devriez au moins faire afficher cette auréole, ou la faire réclamer par le commissaire.
>
> – Ma foi! non. Je me trouve bien ici. Vous seul, vous m'avez reconnu. D'ailleurs la dignité m'ennuie. Ensuite je pense avec joie que quelque mauvais poète la ramassera et s'en coiffera impudemment. Faire unheureux, quelle jouissance! et surtout un heureux qui me fera rire! Pensez à X, ou à Z! Hein! comme ce sera drôle!' (*Œuvres complètes* 1: 352)
>
> ['Hey what! You here, dear fellow! You, in a house of ill fame! You, the drinker of quintessences! You, the ambrosia eater! Really, this takes me by surprise.'
>
> 'My dear fellow, you know my terror of horses and carriages. Just now, as I was crossing the boulevard, and hopping in the mud, in quite a hurry, through the shifting chaos where death comes galloping from all sides at once, my halo slipped off my head, in one abrupt movement, into the mire of the macadam. I didn't have the guts to pick it up. I considered it less disagreeable to lose my insignia than to break my bones. And anyway, I said to myself, misfortune is good for something. Now I can walk about incognito, commit foul acts, and indulge in debauchery like ordinary mortals. So here I am, just like you, as you can see!'
>
> 'At least you should put out a notice for your halo, or have the police advertise for it?'
>
> 'Good God no! I'm fine here. You're the only one who recognized me. Besides, dignity irks me. And I'm glad to think that some bad poet will pick it up and insolently stick it on his head. Make someone happy, what

a delight! and especially a happy someone I can laugh at! What about X, or Z! Right! Wouldn't that be funny!' (*The Parisian Prowler* 113)]

Benjamin, who noticed the neglect of this *poème en prose* in Baudelaire scholarship, was the first to underscore its significance as a poignant testimony of the crisis of art in modernity; in 'On Some Motifs in Baudelaire' he relates it to the question of the loss of the aura of the work of art. In 1977 Fausto Curi provided a superb reading of 'Perte d'auréole' in the introduction to his collection of essays programmatically entitled *Perdita d'aureola*. Curi's interpretation of the prose poem articulates certain symbolic oppositions that underlie it and, more in general, the whole tradition of literary modernity. Central to this argument is the image of the brothel where the poet has retired when he is recognized by his friend. 'The brothel,' Curi writes, 'is the metaphorical site of poetic truth, just as the market and the museum are the real site of the artistic lie' (vii).[6] In the brothel, in other words, the artist is metaphorically and literally naked: he takes off the robes of office and the social persona assigned him by the bourgeoisie, and moreover, he listens not to the dictates of decorum but to the needs and desires of his own body.[7] As the futurist poet Aldo Palazzeschi was to put it in his poem 'E lasciatemi divertire!' almost half a century later, 'i tempi sono molto cambiati / gli uomini non dimandano / più nulla dai poeti, / e lasciatemi divertire!' [times have changed / people no longer ask / anything of poets, / so let me have fun!] (*L'incendiario* 68). The loss of the halo, the symbolic insignia of the poet's social status and function, is the result of a transformation that pushes him to the margins of capitalist economy; and this loss of function results in both absolute freedom – going to the brothel, 'having fun' – and absolute uselessness – that is no longer being asked to play any role in the self-representation of the bourgeois order.

The fallen condition of the poet in modernity is thus articulated through the comparison between art and prostitution – a comparison that indeed Baudelaire himself made explicitly in one of the notes collected in *Fusées*, where he wrote pointedly: 'Qu'est-ce que l'art? Prostitution' [What is art? Prostitution] (*Œuvres complètes* 1: 649; *Intimate Journals* 3).[8] The artist is a producer who sells his products on the marketplace, just as a prostitute sells her body and a worker sells his or her labour.[9] The poet thus reveals the inescapability of the process of commodification in capitalist society, in which everything, including sentiments such as love and 'spiritual' products such as works of art, becomes inscribed into the marketplace and turned into a commodity to be bought or sold. But paradoxically it is in this moment of revelation that the poet is able to communicate the truth about the ideological foundations of the social, political, and cultural structures of bourgeois society, and thus recuperate for himself a new and potentially revolutionary function: 'visibly countering the brothel to the halo, that is, making manifest in an irrefutable way his condition of individual forced to prostitute himself which the bourgeoisie sought to keep hidden, the poet violates the pact imposed on him by the dominant class and the norms of bourgeois morality to such an extent that his insubordination is irreversible, and the social function of the art that he practices is completely useless to the bourgeois' (Curi ix).

A remarkable similarity between Baudelaire's parable and a slightly earlier passage by Marx and Engels in the *Communist Manifesto* offers other motives for reflection.[10] Marx and Engels write: 'The bourgeoisie has stripped of its halo every occupation hitherto honoured and looked to with reverent awe. It has converted the physician, the lawyer, the priest, the poet, the man of science, into its paid wage-labourers' (476). If the bourgeoisie can strip the artist of the halo, that means that the halo itself is not an 'eternal' characteristic of the artist, as the idealist tradition might want to suggest. This raises the question of where the 'halo' comes from, a question that points to the historicity and the constructed nature of the halo itself. The halo is an instance of what Roland Barthes would call a 'myth' – that is, a narrative that 'transforms history into nature' (*Mythologies* 129). By assigning a transhistorical character to the work of the artist – the 'work of art' – it conceals the relationship between the artist himself and the other producers that the visit to the brothels brings back to light. The halo is itself a product of capitalism, a kind of mask that disguises, behind the celebration of art's timeless and placeless essence, the artist's ties to the dominant class. If there may be a degree of exaggeration in Curi's description of the artist as the 'salaried celebrant [*vate*]' of the bourgeoisie,[11] it is certainly true that the parameters for the definition of who and what is an artist are thoroughly historical ones. The author, as Michel Foucault has famously argued, is not a simple biographical figure, but rather a 'function of discourse' (124) whose structures and operations are different in different historical moments. Thus, Foucault has demonstrated that the conception of author that still guides our understanding of the notion arose in the seventeenth and eighteenth centuries and inverted the terms of the previous horizon: scientific discourse, validity of which was ensured by the authority of the author, detached itself from the 'biographical' presence of its utterer and found a new principle of validation in the objective parameters of independent observation and testing, while the author's name became the validating principle of 'literary' discourse for reasons that are not totally foreign to the rising dominance of the capitalist mode of production and the ensuing need to regulate the circulation of symbolic goods in the marketplace.[12] Furthermore, the transition from sacral to courtly art results in a transformation of production from collective and therefore anonymous to individual – that is, from craft to art. Courtly art, as Peter Bürger writes, 'is representational and serves the glory of the prince and the self-portrayal of courtly society' (47). While it partially liberates the artist who now 'produces as an individual and develops a consciousness of the uniqueness of his activity' (47) – and it is this uniqueness which precisely constitutes the halo – it also places the artist in the position of '*vate*,' a position he will continue to occupy with the rise of the bourgeoisie.[13]

The halo was the insignia of the poet, his badge of office, and its loss is not without a traumatic dimension. In spite of the mocking attitude of the poet in 'Perte d'auréole,' another passage in Baudelaire shows the difficulty of completely letting go of the halo. A note in *Fusées* relates the same anecdote, but with a different ending:

> Comme je traversais le boulevard, et comme je mettais un peu de précipitation à éviter les voitures, mon auréole s'est detachée et est tombée dans le boue du macadam. J'eus heureusement le temps de la ramasser; mais cette idée malheureuse se glissa un istant après dans mon esprit, que c'etait un mauvais présage; et dès lors l'idée n'a plus voulu me lâcher; elle ne m'a laissé aucun repos de toute la journée. (*Œuvres complètes* 1: 659)

> [As I was crossing the boulevard, hurrying a little to avoid the carriages, my halo was dislodged and fell into the filth of the macadam. I luckily had time to recover it, but a moment later the unhappy thought slipped into my brain that this was an ill omen; and from that instant the idea would not leave me alone; it has given me no peace all day. (*Intimate Journals* 13)]

This variation on the theme of the lost halo may even present a more nuanced picture of the situation of the modern artist: the halo may not in fact be totally lost, but its radiance shines less brightly; or, to use the terms of Baudelaire's allegory, the halo may be precariously balanced on the poet's head, in danger of being shaken off by the pressures of modernity. In both anecdotes, it is the traffic on the modern boulevard that hurries the poet along and causes him to drop his halo: thus, the loss is also the result of a transformation in the rhythm of lived experience, now accelerated by the invention of new modes of conveyance (the carriages are the ancestors of the automobiles celebrated by the Futurists), which move along both goods and people and transform the subject's relationship to space and time.[14] Whether abandoned to its fate or recuperated at the last minute, the halo can no longer function as it did before: once it has been knocked into the mud of the macadam, it has become visible; it is no longer something whose presence can be taken for granted, something that emanates directly from the office of the poet. Rather, it is now recognized for what it is, an artificial glow that can be removed just as easily as it was bestowed. In plain terms, its ideological function becomes evident. For this reason, even after recovering the halo the poet is obsessed by the thought of its loss: he now knows that it *can* be lost, and that once this happens he will have to work through that loss either to find a new badge of office or to understand how to operate within a crowd that no longer recognizes his difference.

The thought of the lost halo haunts modernism, which tells unrelentingly, like Coleridge's ancient mariner, the story of its vanishing. The two possible endings of the incident on the boulevard also present us with two options for the poet, options which describe in broad terms the space within which this self-conscious interrogation regarding the status of the artist is articulated. On the one hand, we have the artist who was quick enough to pick up the halo: but the swift gesture of putting it back on his head may not have gone unnoticed by the passersby, and even if it has, the artist himself, as we have already pointed out, is nonetheless aware of the accident. Thus, the artist can no longer go about his business as usual, but instead must justify, to himself and to his audience, the presence of the halo. The gesture of putting the halo back on, which he performed so adroitly while running across the boulevard, is thus repeated compulsively, over and over, as he insistently represents his otherness from 'ordinary mortals,' polishing the halo so that he cannot be mistaken for a common man by his observers, let alone be able to travel incognito. Decadentism, in both the French and Italian declensions, for instance, belongs to this horizon: Joris-Karl Huysmans's *À rebours* and Gabriele D'Annunzio's *Il piacere*, to mention but two of the most salient results, narrativize the quest for the halo. According to the father of Andrea Sperelli, the protagonist of *Il piacere*, the 'fundamental maxim' in which lies 'true superiority' is that 'Bisogna *fare* la propria vita, come si fa un'opera d'arte' [one must *fashion* one's life the way one fashions a work of art] (D'Annunzio 37), and this could well be the emblem of nineteenth-century aestheticism. In this sense, I would suggest that Baudelaire's allegory also represents the crisis in the structure of literary communication that Bürger associates with aestheticism: the transformation of the distance between art and life into the content of the work of art.[15] The halo is lost to 'life' – to the chaos of the modern city in which the individual has to renegotiate his relationship to the environment and to others[16] – and moreover its loss has made it possible for the poet to mix with that other phenomenon of urban reality, the crowd, to merge with it, to let his individuality melt with and hide in the multitude.[17] Thus, in the case of the decadent hero, the recovery of the halo entails a reconstruction of the distance between him and the masses, and the halo often becomes a prison, an enclosed space like Des Esseintes's home or, metaphorically, the obsessive-compulsive sexual-sentimental behaviour of Sperelli.

At the other end of the spectrum we find the emphatic rejection of the halo, which now becomes an object of scorn and ridicule. The halo comes to be identified with the institution; that is, it is the result of the acceptance of a series of norms and regulations imposed by the bourgeois audience on the artist. Baudelaire points to this solution, too, when his now un-haloed poet mockingly imagines that his lost halo, which is associated with dignity and decorum, may be picked up by some bad poet who will happily deck himself with it. Berman's gloss on this passage is illuminating: 'the halo [...] may, by virtue of its very obsolescence, metamorphose into an icon, an object of nostalgic veneration for those who, like the "bad poets" X and Z, are trying to escape from modernity' (162). This escape is precisely what the decadent artists – the Des Esseinteses and Sperellis of *fin-de-siècle* literature – seek. The halo is, on the other hand, happily abandoned by the avant-garde, at least in some configurations such as Dada, which in fact demotes the poet to a mere assembler of words (I am thinking, for instance, of Tristan Tzara's famous 'recipe' for composing poems in his 'Dada Manifeste sur l'amour faible et l'amour amer'). Between these two extremes there are several other options, some of which will be explored in the course of this study. The Italian futurist avant-garde, for example, wavers between the two poles, and its sarcastic desacralization of art and the artist, accompanied by a call to merge with the crowd and enter the chaotic flux of modern life, will eventually turn upon itself in a process that returns the artist to an uneasy but ultimately accepted subjection to political power.[18] The English avant-garde, on the contrary, engages in a critical dialogue with futurism precisely to reconstruct the distance separating the artist and the audience and to reconquer, along with the halo, a hegemonic function for the artist.

However, we are not quite done with the discussion of the elusive and evanescent elements that characterize literary communication. If the artist is defined – at least until the moment when it slips off his head – by the halo that sets him apart from other men and women, the work of art is also endowed with an ineffable quality that distinguishes it from other forms of commodity. I am referring of course to what Benjamin, writing once again about Baudelaire, has called the 'aura.'[19] In one of his best known essays, 'The Work of Art in the Age of Mechanical Reproduction,' Benjamin discusses the effects of modern technologies of reproduction on the 'authority' of the aesthetic object. Benjamin initially defines the concept of the 'aura' through a comparison with the observation of a natural phenomenon: 'We define the aura of the latter [natural objects] as the unique phenomenon of a distance, however close it may be' (222). He then points out that, for the work of art, this distance is the result of its original sacral value, which lingers, once art becomes secularized, as 'authenticity.'[20] The aura is finally the supplement that allows one to differentiate between the work of art and the commodity, and, as Benjamin further observes, its withering in the age of mechanical reproduction is the result of the substitution of 'a plurality of copies for a unique existence' (221). For the German critic, mechanical reproduction, by bringing the work closer to the masses and therefore diminishing the distance characteristic of the auratic work of art, engenders a transformation not only in how the work is perceived, but also in the relationship between producer and consumer. Indeed, in certain contexts, such as the newspaper and, in Benjamin's overly enthusiastic appreciation, Russian cinema, such an opposition comes to vanish.[21] Benjamin's account remains an important element in the reconstruction of the modernist crisis that we are attempting to delineate because it emphasizes the question of the reception of the work of art. The transformative effect of mechanical reproduction is due not only to the fact that it calls into question the relationship between original and copy and the authority of the former, but also to the fact that it transforms the very reception of the work. In Benjamin's words, mechanical reproduction 'enables the original to meet the beholder halfway, be it in the form of a photograph or a phonograph record. The cathedral leaves its locale to be received in the studio of a lover of art; the choral production, performed in an auditorium or in the open air, resounds in the drawing room' (220–1). The significance of the metaphor of the work meeting its beholder halfway becomes clearer if we consider Bürger's important addition of the role of art as institution to Benjamin's reflection. In bourgeois society art maintains a semi-independence from the norms regulating the marketplace by claiming to be separate and autonomous from the praxis of life. Yet once the work of art begins to meet its beholder halfway, the ideological implications of the discourse of autonomy become visible, since fruition is no longer mediated through a series of institutional sites such as the museum or the concert hall, but instead becomes inscribed in the sphere of private choices, something to be chosen among a multiplicity of options, like any other market product.

Fredric Jameson has rightly criticized Benjamin's vagueness in invoking 'mechanical reproduction' as a technique that can liberate the revolutionary potential of modern media, writing that 'technical reproducibility as such had existed at least since the invention of printing during the Renaissance' (*Aesthetics and Politics* 108). The question of reception – that is, of the encounter of the work with a determinate horizon of expectations – however, can allow for a reformulation of Benjamin's argument that brings the theme of the decline of the aura into sharper focus. Granted, techniques of mechanical reproduction had existed before the nineteenth century, but it is at the height of the industrial revolution that the spread of literacy and the expansion of readership – along with technological inventions ranging from the rotary press and pulp paper to new means of transportation – made it possible for mechanically reproduced works to be mass produced and to reach a vast audience. It could be suggested that the *feuilleton*, often written by eminent authors but distributed through the mass circuit of the newspaper, is the first example of the mediation between high and low culture made possible by the expansion of mechanical reproduction, which then affected other arts, and even forms of aesthetic production such as cinema, which could not exist without mechanical reproduction itself.[22] *Feuilletons* are a particularly good example of the always narrowing gap between the work of art and the commercial product, since by the time of their insertion in newspapers the revenues generated by the latter were due mostly to advertising rather than to actual sales, and the popular appeal of the serialized narratives served in its turn to broaden the readership of the newspapers, and, simultaneously, of their commercial messages.[23]

Thus, the status of the work of art, like that of the artist, becomes problematic. The presence of works constructed according to the principles of commodity production calls into question the very validity of the category of the work of art. In this case, too, the responses vary along a broad range that occupies the whole spectrum of modernism: from an even more obstinate attempt to resist turning the work into 'culinary' art by widening the gap between the work and the horizon of expectation of the readers,[24] to the blatant dismissal of the aura itself as the ground for the surplus value of the work of art, and the overturning of the logic of the field of cultural production through the polemical insertion of mass produced objects (Marcel Duchamp's famous urinal, for instance) into the realm of the aesthetic. As was the case with the halo, we will see that Futurism and the English movement articulate more contradictory and less radical responses that nevertheless entail a confrontation with the new conditions of fruition of the work of art in modernity.

The Baudelairian poet remains the best emblem of the condition of dislocation and alienation characterizing the artist in the second half of the nineteenth century, as he can recall what it is like to have a halo and to live in the empyrean of poetry feeding on ambrosia, but, having abandoned his halo, he must also confront the horrors of the capitalist metropolis, insistently thrust into the foreground in both *Le fleurs du mal* and *Le spleen de Paris*.[25] This transitional condition between the memory of the prophetic and guiding mission that characterized the poet in the conception of Romanticism and the contemporary reality of the artist's growing integration or marginalization in the capitalist system of commodity exchange reflects a wider shift in social and cultural paradigms that is well described by Perry Anderson in his essay 'Modernity and Revolution.' Late nineteenth-century and early twentieth-century bourgeois society is itself the node in which the tensions determined by the persistence or emergence of different social structures of social organization converge – tensions that Anderson defines in terms of three coordinates: the lingering presence of an aristocratic and landowning class, the emergence of the technologies of the second industrial revolution, which are still substantially novel, and the prospect of social revolution with the rise of socialism and the organization of the first mass parties. 'European modernism [...] thus flowered in the space between a still usable classical past, a still indeterminate technical present, and a still unpredictable political future' (326). These three coordinates account for much of the variety of responses that are classified under the label of modernism, from the isolation of the aristocrat-aesthete in the ivory tower of aestheticism, to the futurist celebration of technology and the surrealist attempt to unite aesthetic and political revolution. Each of these three factors inflects, in different ways, the different articulations of modernism: thus, for instance, the question of how (or whether) to integrate the artist with a mass audience is equally central to the decadent project of Anatole Baju and to the futurist program of Filippo Tommaso Marinetti.

It is significant that, of the three parameters that delineate the space of modernism in Anderson's account, the one linked to the present has to do with technology rather than with class. If there is anything that links the different tendencies of modernism, in fact, it is the rejection of values associated with the contemporary articulation of the social order of bourgeois modernity, and in particular with the means-ends rationality. Even technology is fascinating (or frightening) because of its transformative potential: the futurist celebration of the machine is due in great part to the fact that it is characterized by the energy, vitality, and love of danger that constitute a counterpoint to the staid, narrow, and calculating utilitarianism of a middle-class whose heroic phase has long past. Thus, if above we have outlined a series of different responses to the loss of the social function of the artist in modernity, here we can point to their elements of continuity, in particular the 'oppositional' stance that characterizes artists and their production. Modernism, in its different configurations, thus positions itself in the terrain of what Zeev Sternhell has defined as anti-materialism, which expressed itself in a rejection of both liberal democracy, seen as the political expression of the individualism of free-market economy, and classical Marxism, whose positivist foundations and emphasis on class struggle seemed to run counter to the desire to reconcile the social divisions wrought by modernity at a collective level. Sternhell's description of the aims of Fascism as a product of this complex process of anti-materialist rebellion are interesting. He writes: 'Fascism wished to rectify the most disastrous consequences of the modernization of the European continent and to provide a solution to the atomization of society, its fragmentation into antagonistic groups, and the alienation of the individual in free market economy' (6). While I do not wish to imply an all too easy identification of modernist aesthetics and fascist politics,[26] I do want to suggest that the two phenomena are faces of a similar anti-materialist debate, which in both aesthetics and politics could assume different configurations (hence the radically different politics of two equally antibourgeois aesthetic movements such as futurism and surrealism, and conversely, the different aesthetics of two closely related irrationalist political movements such as fascism and Nazism). In other words, when dealing with modernism we are in the presence of not merely an 'aestheticization of politics,' in Benjamin's famous formulation, or its counterdiscourse, 'a politicization of art' (cf. Benjamin, 'The Work of Art' 241–2), but rather a contamination of the two domains, in which certain forms of artistic and political discourse construct themselves by means of the same rhetorical and tropological strategies. The question that both modernist aesthetics and modernist politics have to confront is one of legitimation: given the anti-institutional thrust of their programs, on what basis can they found the legitimacy of their own counterproject? We know from Lyotard the importance of narrative strategies in addressing the problem of legitimating new forms of authority. Lyotard has in fact demonstrated the contiguity between the legitimating narrative of positivism and that of liberal democracy, which he sums up in these terms: 'the name of the hero is the people, the sign of legitimacy is the people's consensus, and their mode of creating norms is deliberation' (30). Modernist politics intervene by attempting to replace this particular narrative with new narratives, such as the one that turns the hero from the people into the producers (a move linking syndicalism to fascism), or the one that identifies the collective hero with the charismatic individual, replacing deliberation with direct interaction between the leader and the people. In any case, this process entails the adoption of strategies derived from the domain of the aesthetic, which shore these legitimating narratives in the imagination of their audience. The attention paid by fascism, Nazism, and soviet communism to the ritualistic dimension of public life and the performance of the myths of the regime is too well-known to need rehashing here, but if politics realize the importance of the aesthetic for its legitimation, the opposite is also true. The resistance to commodification that characterizes modernist art forces it to deal with the problematic dimension of its autonomous status in bourgeois society. If, as Fredric Jameson has written, 'legitimation becomes visible as a problem and an object of study only at the point in which it is called into question' (Foreword viii), it is at the precise moment when the legitimacy of the artist and of the work of art as a type of producer and product operating in a domain free of the laws of the marketplace is challenged that new narratives of legitimation have to be articulated. In other words, art can no longer simply proclaim its otherness from the socio-economic sphere and expect to find in its autonomous status its function and its salvation; in fact, as we will see in chapter 1, decadentism, which in my account constitutes the phase that heralds and brings into focus the problematics engaged by the avant-garde, is precisely the result of the acute awareness of the failure of the aesthetic as a realm autonomous from the social and the economic. The commodification of the work of art is itself already a denial of the autonomous status of art, which would then be defined through the same parameters that determine other forms of commodity production. Against this 'bad' integration of art and life, modernism reacts with its own counternarratives, which in the first instance seek to undermine the legitimating narrative of capitalism itself.

There are, of course, a number of ways in which this 'oppositionality' can be articulated. One, for instance, may lead to the further detachment of the artist from the praxis of life – that is, in the direction of the vanishing of the author and the self-production of writing theorized by Stephan Mallarmé. Another may involve the formation of a collective discourse that seeks to bring art back into life so as to transform it according to its principles. In this second instance, artists attempt to make use of and saturate with their discourse the very sites of mass communication of the bourgeoisie, and to find their way into newspapers, advertisements, the popular theatre, and so on. At the very limit, instead of the vanishing of the author, we witness to the transformation of everyone into a potential producer of art, thus calling into question the division of productive functions in capitalist society, the mechanisms of the institution of art, and the separation of art from the other institutional spheres of bourgeois life. In one instance, the recovered halo consumes the poet; in the other, it is picked up by everyone and thus belongs to no one.

In an essay on the historiographic category of modernism, the Italian Anglicist Giovanni Cianci proposed its identification with the 'historical avant-garde.'[27] While attractive, this superimposition has certain limitations that we should address at this point. As it has become institutionalized in literary history in England and the United States, 'modernism' has a much broader field of applications and includes figures ranging from the 'high modernists' of the Anglo-American tradition (Pound, Eliot, Joyce, Stein) to European writers such as Kafka, Proust, or Pirandello, to name just a few, who can be described as avant-garde only in the very broad sense of 'innovative' or 'anti-traditionalist,' but whose relationship with the historical avant-garde, understood as a series of organized groups and movements with specific projects articulated in programmatic documents, is tenuous at best. Thus, the distinction between modernism and avant-garde remains useful to understand and account for the complexity and variety of experiences that characterize the period. Within a broadly constructed anti-institutional and oppositional modernism, the historical avant-garde may then be seen as a more radical moment, whose adversarial stance involves not only the specific sites of the institution of art or literature but also, in the words of Raymond Williams, 'beyond these, the whole social order.' Williams continues: 'Thus the defence of a particular kind of art became first the self-management of a new kind of art and then, crucially, an attack in the name of this art on a whole social and cultural order' (51).[28] The distinction becomes important, as we will see, once we address the attempt on the part of artists such as Pound to appropriate the instruments developed by a movement such as futurism without accepting in full its anti-institutional thrust. But the differentiation is also functional to the aims and purposes of this project. The greater radicalism of the avant-garde aims not only at transforming the institution of art from within but also at negating art altogether and reintegrating it into the praxis of life. As Bürger has pointed out, this involves a complex re-articulation of the function of the work of art, its production, and its reception – in other words, the constitutive elements of the institution itself. The avant-garde is thus characterized by a series of practices aimed at transforming the process of literary communication, which artists integrated in the marketplace take substantially for granted, to elaborate new forms of authorship (for instance, through collective authorship), new forms of work (the free-word poem, the *objet trouvé*, the collage, etc.), and new modes of reception of the work (the insertion of the spectator into the work of art). It is in this context that the manifesto, which will constitute the central genre of our enquiry, becomes crucial, as it quickly turned into one of the central sites in the avant-garde debate on the role of art and the artist. In other words, it is precisely through manifestoes that avant-garde artists and writers confront their audience with the problem of the loss of the halo and attempt to articulate new strategies of legitimation of their activity.

What Do We Talk about When We Talk about Manifestoes?

In the summer of 1999 the *International Herald Tribune* published in its editorial page what turned out to be a rather minor and inconsequential footnote to a much more widely covered and controversial event, namely the conflict of the previous spring between the military juggernaut of NATO and the Republic of Yugoslavia, or at least its modern-day rump, Serbia and Montenegro. The piece, written by the Crown Prince Alexander of Yugoslavia, was entitled 'A Manifesto to All the People of Yugoslavia' and was addressed directly to the Prince's 'countrymen,' the people of Yugoslavia itself. The manifesto contains the expected calls to 'a process of national regeneration,' to a 'national unity government,' to 'stand[ing] up to the dictator that is now destroying us and cast[ing] him out.' It also offers, albeit sketchily, a political program. But most of all it constitutes a rallying cry, a call to arms (metaphorical, in this instance), and – given the fact that its issuer, the 'heir to the throne of Yugoslavia,' is apparently excluded from the actual levers of power in the country whose people he appeals to – a bid for a transformation in the distribution and exercise of power. At a textual level, this pronouncement mobilizes discursive strategies that are typical of manifesto writing. For instance, the geographic and political distance, separating the prince from his audience is rhetorically bridged by the play of pronouns. The author uses the first person plural 'we' when he first addresses his countrymen, in name of a common national identity in which are reconciled the antinomies – noble/common; leader/follower; individual subject/plural masses; myth ('the country my ancestors created ...')/history ('we are now a pariah state, our economy is broken') – that stand at the base of the article, and that are represented by the opposition between the 'I' of the manifesto writer and the 'you' through which the countrymen return to be the Prince's followers: 'There is nothing in our history that prevents us from achieving the transformation accomplished by many other former communist countries. [...] I pledge myself to help you in this great effort to achieve democracy and human rights for one and all.' If it lacks the drive, scope, and imaginative grandeur of Marx and Engels's *Communist Manifesto*, that lightning summary of human history and prophecy of its future, it is nonetheless clear that the Prince's manifesto is the latest in a genealogical line of which the Marxist contribution is one of the (deservedly) more famous and influential instances. Both call for a radical transformation, and in both cases their authors are ready to place themselves at the service of the people for the coming revolution. Manifestoes and political upheavals appear inextricably linked. If the last two centuries have been an age of revolutions – from those that shook the British and the French empires at the turn of the eighteenth century to those that, in the nineteenth century saw the birth of European nation states such as Italy, to the great upheavals of the twentieth century (certainly not least, that of 1968) – then they have also been an age of manifestoes, the texts that have accompanied and sought to provide a discursive ground for these traumatic transformations.

Today manifestoes are certainly alive and well, enjoying renewed life through the Internet, which has kept texts such as the 'Unabomber's manifesto' in circulation well beyond the time in which the version distributed by the *New York Times* and the *Washington Post* was in print, and through such comparatively sober examples as Cary Nelson's *Manifesto of a Tenured Radical*, in which the usual immediacy and pithiness of manifesto writing becomes somewhat lost in the large-scale architecture of a book. Writing manifestoes remains a privileged way for dissenting or marginalized voices to speak out, to affirm their presence, to reach out to like-minded individuals and invite them to band together for a common cause. It is, as Mary Ann Caws has argued, the 'deictic genre par excellence,' a sort of verbal gesture that, at the most basic level, simply says 'LOOK! [...] NOW! HERE!' (xx). And yet, by now the gesture has perhaps become all too common: were it not for the fact that it came in the wake of three deaths and a seventeen year campaign of mail-bomb terror, it is unlikely that the Unabomber's manifesto would have inspired much interest or received so much exposure on the part of mass media. Certainly it would not have been followed by the scale of debate that ensued for instance after the publication of Filippo Tommaso Marinetti's 'Le Futurisme' on the front page of the Parisian daily *Le Figaro* on 20 February 1909, even if the Unabomber had had the not inconsiderable advertising skills of the futurist leader. In fact, it could even be argued that in the case of the Unabomber, the actual 'manifestoes' were the acts themselves, the practice of literally assaulting the institution against which his revolution should have been fought: as a call to action, the manifesto is a kind of textuality that seeks to reach for its other beyond the boundaries of the text itself, a revolution in the symbolic representation of everyday life that desires to spill out into its practice, to close the gap between the domain of writing and that of life – which is why the manifesto became so useful to the avant-garde. It is in this ambiguous position between theory and practice, between the realm of the proleptic program ('what is to be done') and the actual performance of the action, the translation into deed of the project, that the manifesto lies. It is also because of this ambiguous position that the manifesto has been notoriously so difficult to define. In the words of one of its most astute analysts, Claude Abastado, 'The manifesto is therefore Proteus – mutable, multiform, unseizable. [...] The search for *one* definition is deceiving; that of an essence, illusory. The manifesto does not exist as an absolute' (3).

This elusiveness is ascribed by Daniel Chouinard to the 'extra-literary' character of the manifesto, which posits it in an indeterminate space between word and world, between text and act. This argument is confirmed by some of the attempts to provide a definition for the genre. Bruno Traversetti describes the manifesto as a document that 'by defining a program of poetics and indicating its inspiring principles, establishes the operative horizon of a literary tendency, the formal status of a school, the aesthetic or ideological hypothesis linking together an already constituted group of writers, or tends to attract to itself and to formalize in its act of self-consciousness a section of the contemporary literary experience' (157). But this general definition, which seems to emphasize the self-conscious and programmatic nature of the manifesto, is quickly qualified. Other types of texts may assume the role of manifesto either because they seek to articulate, theoretically or practically, a normative paradigm, or because they are perceived *a posteriori* as the 'synthesis' of a series of motifs and formal solutions that best embody or even anticipate and in some way foster the principles of a movement or school. (Traversetti mentions Huysmans' *À rebours* as an example of this latter type.) Vincent Fournier addresses the same question. For him, in spite of a few scattered occurrences before that date, the manifesto 'acquires the right of citizenship' in literary terminology only with the publication of Jean Moréas's 'Manifesto of Symbolism' in 1886. Therefore, the manifesto 'would finally constitute a restricted nomenclature if literary historians did not bring under [its] rubric several texts which were not designated as such' (7570). This opening up of the category allows Fournier to define as manifestoes 'theoretical works or prefaces' that are in the main produced by writers and are therefore 'professions of faith.' Thus, for the French critic any public declaration, any piece of polemical writing on literary matters can be classed as a manifesto.[29]

In his 'Introduction à l'analyse des manifestes,' the preface to a special issue on manifestoes of the journal *Littérature,* Abastado was the first scholar of the genre to identify the pragmatic function of the text as its fundamental characteristic. Noting the difficulty of elaborating a structural description of the manifesto, he suggests that the constant elements that can be isolated are best described as discursive strategies that serve the polemical and antagonistic function of the genre. In manifestoes, he pointedly notes, 'writing is first of all doing' ('Introduction' 9). Abastado's essay, however, also demonstrates the difficulty of delineating the boundaries of the genre once its definition relies on merely pragmatic criteria. His five levels of classification range from what he calls a '*stricto sensu* application of the term,' – that is, texts that openly assume the label of manifesto (and that Abastado defines contrastively in terms of their difference from other related genres such as the declaration or the appeal) – to the designation as manifesto of spectacular acts through which one or more individuals seek to 'make their voice heard' ('Introduction' 5). Indeed, certain acts – for instance, a terrorist act – require, along with other types of investigation, a rhetorical reading, an interpretation in which the protagonists of the event and its consequences are read as if they were linguistic signs and as if they worked according to the semiotic procedures that govern discourse. For example, in one of the most traumatic events in recent Italian history, the kidnapping of Aldo Moro in 1978 by the Red Brigades, the figure of the statesman had both denotative and connotative value in that he not only signified directly his own policies and programs, but also stood metonymically for the 'system,' for the state apparatus, the party to which he belonged, and so on.[30] It is not by chance that we use a linguistic metaphor to define such acts: their purpose is 'to make a statement.' Thus, certain cultural products and certain acts are interpreted as manifestoes not by virtue of any structural homologies that may link them, as semiotic objects, to written manifestoes, but rather because these written texts or proclamations on the one hand, and paintings, jazz compositions, literary works, or even terrorist actions on the other perform a similar function. The *manifestaire* dimension of any such 'texts' cannot be determined in isolation but only in terms of the relationship they establish with their audience: we are, in other words, in the presence of what Paolo Bagni has called 'the *relational* character of the concept of genre' (102) – that is, the inscription of the process of genre attribution in the broader process of reception of the work, which situates it in relation to the other textual products that form the tradition.

An example of this dynamic is offered by the putative first literary manifesto. Trying to identify such a progenitor is, of course, a slightly more interesting version of the old chicken and egg conundrum, since once the term began to gain some degree of legitimacy within the literary debate, suddenly other texts could be retrofitted as manifestoes. In any case, the first text on literary matters to bear the label of manifesto is, to my (and, as mentioned, Fournier's) knowledge, Moréas's so-called 'Symbolist manifesto,' published on 18 September 1886 by *Le Figaro*, which thus began its long association with literary polemics. But Moréas's piece is interesting precisely because of the ambiguity of that gesture of classification, which was in fact the result of an editorial decision on the part of Auguste Marcade, the editor of the newspaper, who had invited the poet to write a contribution to the debate on 'decadent' poetry. It was in fact Marcade who prefaced the text with a short note under the heading 'a literary manifesto' (cf. Moréas 29). The choice of word struck Anatole France, one of its earliest commentators, as curious. On 26 September he wrote in *Le Temps*: 'Un journal, qui reçoit d'ordinaire les manifestes des princes, vient de publier la professione de foi des symbolistes' [A newspaper, which usually receives the manifestoes of princes, has just published the profession of faith of the Symbolists] ('Examen' 45). That France should remark on this transition of the genre from the domain of politics to that of aesthetics is important because it emphasizes the originality of the gesture, and at the same time it points to its "mediatic" dimension. Marcade's choice of generic label, whatever his intentions, reorients the perception of the text from a statement of poetics to a polemical stand – perhaps beyond the intent of the author himself who in a letter to the novelist carefully responded to his objections by professing his respect for the tradition[31] – and inserts it squarely within the debate on decadent poetry, which is openly recalled in the introductory note. Interestingly, this debate, too, is presented as a media event: 'Depuis deux ans,' Marcade writes, 'la presse parisienne s'est beaucoup occupée d'une école de poètes et de prosateurs dits "décadents"' [for two years, the Parisian press has been very concerned with a school of poets and prose writers called 'decadents'] (Moréas, *Les premières armés* 29). The press has given legitimacy to a dispute that is otherwise eminently internal to the milieu of the poetic avant-garde, and Moréas's essay is a manifesto of the new school precisely because of the intertextual relations that link it to other statements and articles, such as Anatole Baju's copious manifestoes of decadentism/*decadisme* or René Ghil's recently published *Traitè du verbe*, in this public debate.[32] This suggests that manifestoes are not simply 'machines to generate desire' ('Introduction' 7), to use another of Abastado's formulas, but that they are first and foremost *machines to generate discourse*: the manifesto, in other words, cannot be cut off from the public discourse that arises around and as a result of its issuing (hence, the extreme case of the terrorist act, characterized by the attempt to divorce the action from its practical results, and to turn it into a purely discursive gesture).

This editorial reorientation of Moréas's 'Le symbolisme' has consequently played an influential role in the interpretations of the text itself. Abastado, for instance, both follows the critical tradition by labelling the text as a manifesto, and sets it, as an example of the genre, in opposition to the declaration arguing that the latter 'states its position without demanding that its addressees adhere to it' (3). And yet, Moréas avoids the injunctive rhetoric of political manifestoes such as that of Marx and Engels, and even presents symbolism not as a moment of rupture but of continuity in the unfolding of the literary history of France, as the inevitable result of the decay of the previous schools, writing that 'Il serait superflu de faire observer que chaque nouvelle phase évolutive de l'art correspond exactement à la décrépitude sénile, à l'inéluctabile fin de l'école immédiatament antérieure' [It would be superfluous to observe that each new evolutionary phase in art corresponds exactly to the senile decrepitude, to the inevitable end of the school which came immediately before it] (29–30). If anything, Moréas displays the tranquility of someone who sees himself as the destined heir of the cultural tradition. The author is concerned with the defence and legitimation of a cultural project already in progress and of his own role within it *vis-à-vis* other competing schools such as naturalism, which comes under censure at the end of the text. Ultimately the reader is addressed with an eye to his seduction, rather than his enlistment in the movement.[33] This, as we will see in chapter 1, is coherent with the overall thrust of the fin-de-siècle poetic avant-garde, which finds itself at a complex moment of transition and has to mediate between the need to re-legitimate its function by appealing to its bourgeois audience through the media that are proper to it (in particular the newspapers) and the simultaneous and related need to re-articulate its distance from its audience, or, as we put it in this introduction, to recuperate its halo.

The classification of a text as a manifesto thus depends upon the pragmatic results that its insertion within a certain field of (political, aesthetic, religious, etc.) relations provokes. In other words, a manifesto need not explicitly call for change as long as its function of rupture becomes evident as a consequence of the effects it has upon the field itself. For instance, to call Verlaine's sonnet 'Langueur' a manifesto of decadentism is to emphasize its foundational function in articulating a series of tropes and themes which then become characteristic of a cultural situation that clearly distinguishes itself from the dominant Parnassian group and coalesce into a school with its principles and its leaders. In any case, a text is usually classified as a manifesto when it seems to point to a rupture, whether foregrounded or not, within the unfolding of a certain field; as Janet Lyon has cogently argued, 'the manifesto both generates and marks a break in history: it is both a trace and a tool of change' (16).[34] Thus, if the manifesto situates itself in the space between art and life, it is perhaps possible to consider it as a genre that questions the contours of that boundary, and that calls for a more complex understanding of the text as event and of the textuality of the event.

Recent studies of the genre have brought into relief the complexity of the theoretical issues raised by this most ambiguous of genres, which often disguises as merely local cultural or social polemics debates that in fact involve broader issues of agency, power, and identity. Janet Lyon's important monograph has shown its inextricable links with the social and political discourse of modernity, and in particular with the discourse of universality which has characterized the post-Enlightenment political rhetoric. In this sense, the manifesto is a constant reminder of 'the exclusions and deferrals experienced by those outside the "legitimate" bourgeois public spheres of public exchange' (3); but at the same time it opens up the space through which marginalized voices and experiences can attempt to make the voice of their diversity heard. Jeanne Demers and Line McMurray have delineated an anatomy of the genre focusing on the question of power. Their discussion of the institutional function of the manifesto is particularly important for this study. They distinguish between manifestoes of imposition and manifestoes of oppositions arguing that: 'Their fundamental difference is [...] in the fact that one represents the group in power, and the other does not. That this power may rather be symbolic as in the case of literature does not change in any way the fundamental fact: the relationship with the institution is inevitable. It is a question of striking a blow, of fulfilling/invalidating an explicit or implicit contract with the partner/adversary, of strengthening/displacing the law, eventually to control/displace the site of the word of the other' (53–4). The two scholars clearly point out the defining function of the manifesto: that of symptom of an institutional crisis, or rather, of the presence, within an institution of one or more legitimating discourses competing for dominance.[35] This is of course true of both political and aesthetic manifestoes: Marx and Engels's *Communist Manifesto*, for instance, counters the bourgeois discourse of free enterprise with the principle of 'free development of each' as 'the condition for the free development of all' (491). In the case of the institution of literature, the legitimation crisis is even more profound because the very figure of the artist is called into question. The thread running through the three chapters of this volume is precisely the analysis of the strategies of legitimation employed by the artists of the avant-garde in order to redefine their social role. Initially, with the decadents, this entailed the recuperation, as the legitimating discourse, of an aristocratic understanding of the work of the artist. The movements that follow – in our study, futurism and imagism – represent two examples of the articulation of alternative narratives that lead either in the direction of a complete renewal of the process of literary communication and, at the limit, the abolition of the very difference on which the institution itself rests – namely the difference between producer and consumer or artist and audience – or to the adoption of the legitimating discourse of other, more powerful, institutions as a means to re-assert that very same constitutive difference.

Chapter One

Strategies of Legitimation: The Manifesto from Politics to Aesthetics

A HISTORY OF THE MANIFESTO (1550–1850)

From the Prince to the People: The Voice of Authority and the Voice of Resistance

'L'etimologia,' Alberto Savinio writes in *Dico a te, Clio* (74), 'è la sirena degli animi semplici' [etymology is the siren of simple souls]. Without completely falling prey to its enchantments or accepting too uncritically its suggestions, we can take an examination of the origins of the word 'manifesto' as a useful starting point for the historical reconstruction to be articulated in the first part of this chapter. As most dictionaries agree, the word 'manifesto' likely derives from the Latin adjective *manifestus*, from *manus* [hand], and a conjectural adjective **festus*, related to the root **fend¬re* (cf. Latin *of-fend¬re* or *de-fend¬re*), and thus with a primary sense of 'taken by hand,' or 'palpable.'[1] Metaphorically, the word then takes at least two meanings: on the one hand, it becomes a synonym of 'evident, obvious,' as in 'manifest destiny' (cf. *Oxford English Dictionary*, ad loc. 'manifest'); on the other, it comes to imply a sense of discovery or unconcealment: The *Dizionario etimologico della lingua italiana* offers 'preso sul fatto' as a translation for *manifestus*, while the *Grand Larousse* has 'pris en flagrant délit' – both equivalent to the English 'caught red-handed.' This double connotation can be found, for instance, in the first canticle of Dante's *Divina Commedia*: in the famous episode of the pilgrim's encounter with the leader of the Florentine *Ghibellini* Farinata degli Uberti (*Inferno* X), Farinata correctly identifies Dante's nationality by recognizing his language, and addresses him thus:

'O Tosco che per la città del foco
    vivo ten vai così parlando onesto,
    piacciati di restare in questo loco.
La tua loquela ti fa manifesto
    di quella nobil patria natìo
    alla qual forse fui troppo molesto' (vv. 22–7)

Here the word 'manifesto,' in its adjectival sense, implies that Dante's language both reveals and puts on display his identity for Cavalcanti, that it gives something away (namely, the fact that the pilgrim is, like his unexpected listener, a Florentine) and that, once made evident, the truth which has been displayed is irrefutable.

In any case, while the adjectival form is already present in Latin, the noun *manifesto/manifeste/manifest* is peculiar to the modern languages. According to Daniel Chouinard, in French the noun was first used with the meaning of, in F. Godefroy's words, 'un état détaillé de la cargaison que le capitaine doit remettre à la douane à son arrivée' [a very detailed list of the cargo that the captain must deliver at customs upon his arrival] (*Dictionnaire de l'ancienne langue française*, 1888; qtd. Chouinard 22–3), a usage which, though exceptional, is attested before 1550,[2] and which is still common both in English (in the form 'manifest') and in French.[3] After the mid sixteenth century, the term came to acquire the more familiar meaning of 'public declaration or proclamation' (*OED*) with which we are concerned here. The Italian 'manifesto' is usually listed as the source of the nominal usage, but the dating of the earliest instance remains doubtful. Chouinard partly quotes the definition given by Salvatore Battaglia's *Grande dizionario della lingua italiana* to support his argument that the French noun was a calque from the Italian. In Battaglia, a manifesto is described as: 'Foglio di carta manoscritto o stampato, di vario formato, che si affigge per lo più in luoghi pubblici, con scopi propagandistici o pubblicitari; per divulgare fatti riguardanti la collettività e notizie che si vogliono rendere di dominio comune' [handwritten or printed sheet of paper, of various format, displayed mostly in public places for propaganda or publicity to divulge matters of interest to the collectivity and news of which the public must be informed] (ad loc. 'manifesto'). This acceptation, however, is not attested before 1574, the year in which it first appears in French.[4] Rather, what we find in Italian is a meaning that the *Grande dizionario della lingua italiana* defines as restricted to the code of chivalry: 'documento indirizzato alla pubblica opinione per difendersi da un'accusa' [document addressed to the public opinion, to defend oneself from an accusation] (ad loc., def. 4). This usage is found as early as 1551 in a work by Fausto da Longiano, *Il duello regolato alle leggi de l'onore,*[5] and, as we will see in a moment, is closely linked to the meaning that predominates after the seventeenth century, namely that of a proclamation in which a certain party justifies its conduct. The passage reported by Battaglia from da Longiano and a subsequent instance of this specific acceptation from Scipione Maffei's *Della scienza chiamata cavalleresca* (Venezia, 1716) are of some interest. Da Longiano writes:

> Due essere le maniere di uno scrivere principalmente. L'una si dice manifesto, l'altra cartello. Questi due modi sono tra sé differenti. Che 'l manifesto s'indrizza a l'università de gli uomini per sgravarsi da un'imputazione generale o particolare contro autore incerto. Il cartello si mette fuori contro persona certa.

> [The are two main manners of writing. One is called *manifesto,* the other *cartello.* These two manners are different from one another. The manifesto is addressed to all people to deliver oneself from general or specific accusation of uncertain authorship. The *cartello* is issued against a known person.] (Battaglia, ad loc. 'manifesto,' def. 4)

Maffei further clarifies: 'Bisogna che tu consideri che, immaginario essendo ... il foro di queste cause, le prove che in esse altri vuole addurre non altramente far si possono che divulgendo e spargendo manifesti e scritture' [You must consider that, insofar as the tribunal for these suits is imaginary, the proofs that others want to bring forth in them cannot be brought forth in any other way than by divulging and spreading around manifestoes and written texts]. The domain of the manifesto is therefore the arena of public opinion and public discourse, and this characteristic will remain a fundamental element of the genre in all the permutations of its usage. What makes this acceptation especially interesting, however, is the fact that it hinges on the question of how the individual subject is to define one's own identity. Clearly, in these definitions the issuer of the manifesto does not speak *ex cathedra,* as it were, as the vessel of a certain kind of (political) power, as is the case with the definitions that we will consider in a moment, but rather invokes the written word to take back the power to define himself and his actions. In the passages by da Longiano and Maffei, the individual is called to defend himself from the words of an enemy whose identity is not known and who cannot be called upon to account for them. In Maffei's definition in particular, we can recognize in the virtual 'tribunal' (*foro*), the 'forum' of public opinion, in whose presence the accused has no better way to defend himself than to send forth equally public declarations to an audience that is both undefined and diffuse. The purpose of the manifesto, in other words, is to oppose a certain dominant discourse with a counter-discourse designed to replace it, and to shift the power to define the subject to the subject himself.

In its broadest application, however, the manifesto as a genre of discourse belongs to the pragmatic realm of politics. Between the seventeenth century and the moment when it penetrates the domain of literary theory in the nineteenth century, the term is normally associated with some form of political struggle.[6] Since the dictionary definitions from the period all agree, it may be helpful to consider a brief selection.

> *Vocabolario degli accademici della Crusca* (1611): 'quella polizza, o relazione, che fanno i ministri del pubblico, e i sergenti della giustizia: onde Fare il manifesto' [that bill or report which is issued by public ministers and sergeants of justice; hence, to issue a manifesto]

> Cotgrave, *A Dictionaire of the French and English Tongves* (1611): 'A manifestation, or declaration'[7]

> Richelet, *Dictionnaire françois* (1679): 'Écrit où l'on découvre son dessein, & où l'on se justifie de quelque chose. [Publier un manifeste]' [Text in which one unveils one's design, and in which one justifies himself for something (to issue a manifesto)]

> Furetière, *Le dictionnaire universel* (1690): 'est une declaration que font des Princes par un escrit public, des intentions qu'ils ont en commençant quelque guerre, ou autres entreprises, & qui contient les raisons & moyens sur lesquels ils fondent leur droit & leurs pretentions. On le dit aussi de pareils escrits que font pour la deffense de leur bien, ou de leur innocence, les Grands Seigneurs qui sont accusez. Ce que les Princes appellent *manifeste*, les particuliers l'appellent *Apologie*' [It is a declaration issued by princes by means of a public writing regarding their intentions upon commencing a war or some other enterprise, and that contains the reasons and means upon which they found their right and their claims. The writings that are issued by great lords in the defence of their welfare or of

their innocence are also called thus. What princes call a *manifesto* is called a *justification* by private individuals.]

Grand dictionnaire de l'Académie françoise (1694): 'Écrit par lequel un Prince, un État, un parti, ou une personne de grande qualité rend raison de sa conduite en quelque affaire de grande importance' [Writing through which a prince, a state, a party, or a person of great standing accounts for his conduct regarding some business of great importance]

A certain drift can be detected in these definitions, although naturally the changed cultural and linguistic context must also be kept in mind in accounting for divergences in meaning. The earliest vocabulary definition, that of the *Accademia della Crusca,* emphasizes the referential, informative function of the manifesto, reflected by many of the examples reported by Battaglia, such as that from Galeazzo Gualdo Priorato's *Storia del ministerio del cardinale Giulio Mazzarino* (1677): '[f]u eziandio affisso per tutte le cantonate delle contrade principali un manifesto della suddetta assemblea, il contenuto della quale era che i buoni servitori e sudditi del re ivi radunati non altro oggeto avevano che di ristabilire la pace nella città' [finally, in all the street corners of the major boroughs was displayed a manifesto of the aforementioned assembly whose content was that the good servants and subjects of the king gathered therein had no other objective than to re-establish the peace in the city] (ad loc. 'manifesto,' def. 1). In this sense, the purpose of the document is to make known to the general public the effects of an event that has already taken place and, like the declaration to which Cotgrave relates the manifesto, it does not offer the possibility of a rebuttal. It is a one-way form of communication validated by the status of the issuer (the ministers and sergeants, that is, the holders of civil and military power) and by the content of the text, which must be of public interest.

There is not, in any case, a clear line of demarcation between manifesto and declaration, two terms that are used essentially as synonyms in several contemporary documents. For instance, they are clearly linked together in George Rákóczi [Racokzkie] I, Prince of Transylvania's 'Declaration or Manifesto to the States and Peers of Hungary' (1644), a text that otherwise falls quite nicely within the parameters of the definition provided by *Le dictionnaire universel,* since the prince is here concerned with justifying to his peers the military mobilization undertaken to defend the interests of the Protestant churches. The polemic with the emperor and his laxity in protecting Protestants (5) shows how the manifesto is already a textual space in which to articulate an 'eccentric' political position, an alternative political position to that of the principal seat of power.

The later definitions – supported by several earlier examples – shift attention away from the constative dimension of the text, namely the distribution of information, and toward the performative. Now the manifesto no longer simply informs the public of the results of the actions of its rulers, but instead begins to play a suasive function: it aims at convincing its audience of the justness of the issuer's cause, and therefore, in some cases, it must precede the actions that it is meant to justify, almost as a preemptive strike on public opinion in order to control that opinion once action is taken. Thus, in Cardinal Guido Bentivoglio's *Della guerra di Fiandra* (1645), for instance, we find the following occurrence: 'Pubblicò egli [il re di Francia] ... contro il re di Spagna la guerra; e con un manifesto acerbissimo procurò di concitare, quanto più fieramente gli fu possibile, tutti i suoi sudditi a farla. Né tardò poi molto ad uscire di Fiandra un altro manifesto contrario, nel quale dal re di Spagna si procurava di giustificare le azioni succedute dalla sua parte, in ordine alle cose di Francia' [He (the King of France) made public the war against the King of Spain; and with a very bitter manifesto he sought, as fiercely as he could, to excite his subjects into making it. Nor did it take long for another opposed manifesto to come out in Flanders. In it, the king of Spain endeavoured to justify all the actions that had occurred on his side, as regarded the matters of France] (Battaglia, ad loc. 'manifesto,' def. 3). The shift is significant, as it marks a transformation in the discursive relationship between the issuer of the manifesto and his addressees: although nominally the power relation between the two poles of the communicative process has not changed, since the manifesto is still promulgated by those who hold political office and the addressees are still denied the possibility of responding, now their presence is itself significant and remarked upon. While the declarative manifesto described by the *Accademia della Crusca* finds its legitimacy in the authority of its issuer, the manifesto of the King of France seeks legitimacy from precisely those who will be affected by it; it seeks to constitute them into what the declarative manifesto assumes them to be, namely loyal subjects, ready and willing to obey the word of the Authority. With the response of the King of Spain, the battleground shifts away from Flanders, and moves into public opinion – however narrowly that public may be constituted – and the manifesto becomes a weapon in the struggle for political legitimacy.

Chouinard offers a lengthy example from François-Eudes de Mézeray's *Abrégé chronologique de l'histoire de France* (1678), in which, as he suggests, one can find one of the earliest 'restricted and systematic use[s] of the term' (22) undeformed by the retrospective uses that led to its application, *a posteriori*, to numerous texts that do not otherwise invoke the label. The passage, taken from the records for April 1562, details an episode at the beginning of the religious wars between Catholics and Huguenots under the reign of Charles IX and the regency of his mother Catherine de Medici. As is well known, Catherine de Medici had initially adopted a conciliatory policy toward the Huguenots in order to protect the authority of the sovereign from the influence of the powerful Guise family. This policy culminated with the issuing of the edict of January 1562, which granted Protestants freedom of religion outside walled cities. However, as the hostility between the two factions escalated into open war after the massacre of Vassy (1 March 1562), the regent eventually sided with the Catholics and returned the king to Paris under the protection of Francis, Duke of Guise. Let us now turn to Mézeray's account.

> En effet le Prince de Condé, en partie de dépit d'avoir été trompé par une femme, (car il le croyoit ainsi) en partie de colere de voir ses ennemis maîtres de la personne du Roi, & de crainte aussi de demeurer à leur misericorde, & de laisser refroidir l'ardeur de ses amis & du parti Huguenot, s'en courut à bride abatue avec deux mille chevaux à Orleans [...].
>
> Ce fut là comme la place d'armes & le siege capital de son Parti. Or pour le faire subsister dans l'unité & dans la discipline, qui sont les liens nécessaires de tout établissement, il prit serment de tout ceux qui se trouverent là; qu'ils demeureroient unis pour la défense de la personne du Roi & de celle de la Reine, pour la réformation & le bien de l'Etat; qu'ils méneroient une vie sans reproche & chrétienne, observeroient les Loix du Royaume & Reglemens militaires, & auroient soin d'avoir des Ministres pour leur prêcher la parole de Dieu; qu'ils le reconnoîtroient pour Chef, se soumettroient à tous ses orders, le serviroient de leurs personnes, & lui fourniroient armes & argent.
>
> Il écrivit ensuite à tous les Princes d'Allemagne, les sujets qu'il avoit eus de prendre les armes, & leur envoya les Lettres originales de la Reine mere a fin de les persuader à lui prêter secours pour la tirer de captivité le

> Roi & elle. Il fit en même tems publier un Manifeste par toute la France à même fin, & peu de jours après fit courir la copie d'une ligue, soit vraie, soit supposée, faite entre le Pape, le Roi d'Espagne & les Guises pour exterminer tous les Sectateurs de la nouvelle Religion. (Mézeray 3: 265–66)
>
> [In fact the Prince of Condé, partly vexed at having been deceived by a woman [Catherine de Medici] (or so he thought), and partly angry at seeing his enemies masters of the person of the king, and believing also that he abided there at their mercy, and that the ardour of his friends and of the Huguenot party would cool, rode at full gallop to Orleans with two thousand horsemen.
>
> The city was like the fortress and the main headquarters of his party. Now, in order to make it fare in unity and discipline, which are the necessary bonds of all concourses, he made all those who were there swear that they would remain united for the defence of the king and the queen, for the reformation and the welfare of the state; that they would lead an irreproachable and Christian life, observing the laws of the kingdom and military regulations, and that they would take care to have ministers to preach to them the word of God; that they would acknowledge him as leader, submit to all his orders, serve him with their person, and provide him with arms and money.
>
> He then wrote to all the princes in Germany the reasons why he had taken arms, and he sent them the original letters of the queen mother, in order to persuade them to offer his aid to free the king and her from captivity. At the same time, he had a manifesto issued throughout France with the same purpose, and a few days later he circulated the copy of a pact of confederacy, real or forged, between the pope, the king of Spain, and the house of Guise, for the elimination of all the members of the new religion.]

Chouinard remarks that this passage brings into particular relief the importance of reception for the manifesto. Perhaps more interestingly, however, the presence of several types of discourse in Mézeray's account also makes it possible to outline the specific mode of reception invoked by the manifesto *vis-à-vis* that of other forms of political proclamation. In the second and third paragraphs, the opposition between oath and manifesto is established in terms of the relationship between the emitter and the addressee. The oath, we may recall, is one of the primary examples of the performative in J.L. Austin's *How To Do Things with Words*: the oath makes something happen outside the realm of language; it binds those who take it to a common program or goal, but naturally it presupposes a previous agreement among those who enter into it. In the case of the episode reported by de Mézeray, the oath is instrumental in transforming a commonality of interests and concerns into a clear program with a specific platform, carefully detailed by the Prince of Condé. It does not, however, seek to change the convictions of its audience, and instead puts them publicly on display. The text almost emphasizes the centripetal, inward-looking nature of this procedure: the oath simply replicates at a political and legal level the physical coming together of the Prince of Condé and the members of the Huguenot faction in the city of Orleans. On the contrary, the manifesto looks outside and beyond the city walls; it is addressed to those who are not currently and actively engaged on the Huguenot side and must be convinced to do so, with – should the rhetoric of the manifesto prove not to be sufficient – the addition of possibly forged diplomatic documents. The purpose of the manifesto, along with the other documents sent to the German princes, is to *persuade* them to join the Huguenot cause, 'to bring [them] to his side,' as the chronicler puts it – in other words, to effect a transformation in their allegiances. If the oath binds, thus consolidating and formalizing a state of facts and ensuring the status quo against dangerous transformations, the manifesto seeks to change the status quo, to shift allegiances and loyalties, and ultimately to facilitate a transferral of power.

The distinction between 'manifesto' and 'declaration' also hinges on the question of power, although, as we have already noted, early attestations of the former do not always make a distinction between the two, and the opposition is certainly less constant than Chouinard suggests. De Mézeray's passage supports Chouinard's superimposition of the two terms on two other fundamental oppositions: that of 'quest for power' *versus* 'power' and that of 'declaring oneself' *versus* 'declaring.' While the Prince of Condé addresses the other princes to convince them of the righteousness of his struggle, and thus performs an act of suasion in which the other is interpellated as an equal from whom one seeks support – a support that can be freely given or withdrawn – in the case of the 'declaration' of the royal council, the issuing of the document is an exercise in power, addressed to the subjects of the king as subject *to* his power and therefore coerced into obedience. The prince speaks to his equals, whereas the council hands down directives to the representatives of the law, the bailiffs, and their underlings who are charged with executing the King's power. In the pure exercise of power of the council's declaration we can see the workings of what Louis Althusser has called the Repressive State Apparatus, while the manifesto, like the system of mass media that Althusser uses as one of his examples (143), functions as an 'Ideological State Apparatus,' interpellating its addressees as subjects capable of carrying out their own choices but also inscribing them within an ideological horizon in which the struggle for power is constructed as a moral and ethical battle for the defence of religious freedom. Thus, while the declaration presupposes a hierarchical system and re-enforces the relative position of the different social subjects within that vertical structure, the manifesto cuts across that structure; the manifesto is addressed to one's equals or, as in some of the examples that follow, even to one's 'betters,' and seeks a re-organization of the social system that accounts for the requests of the issuer. The power sought by the manifesto writer is, in the first instance, that of responding to the authority and authoritativeness of the dominant discourse, and thus of making oneself visible. It is in this sense that the manifesto is always a 'self-declaration,' as Chouinard has suggested: it interpellates its addressee and constitutes him or her as the subject of a new ideological discourse, and it simultaneously defines its issuer as the spokesperson of the new authority upon which this counterdiscourse founds its validity. In doing this, it also questions the authority of the power against which it sets itself, and forces that power at least to reconsider and redefine the ground of its legitimacy. Thus, for instance, Rákóczi's manifesto involves its interlocutor in a dialogue with the rebel prince, as Emperor Ferdinand III accompanies his military response to the rebellion of the Prince of Transylvania with his own 'Declaration or Manifesto Wherein the Roman Imperial Majesty makes known to the States & Peers of *Hungarie*, what reasons and motives have compelled him to proceed in open Warre against the Prince of Transylvania' (cover).

Thus, since at least the sixteenth century the manifesto documents the experience of a rupture within a society or a culture that had hitherto considered itself cohesive. If at the end of the eighteenth century the rupture will be articulated along class lines,[8] the religious wars of the sixteenth and seventeenth centuries divide Europe in a way that is no less traumatic or generalized. In England also the rise of the manifesto as a genre of political discourse resulted from both social and religious conflict, as Janet Lyons's reconstruction of the manifesto production during the struggle between 'Diggers' and 'Levellers' makes clear. She writes, 'manifestoes and related forms appear most often in clusters around those political crises which involve definitions of citizenship and political subjecthood' (16).

Furthermore, the validity of definitions from late-seventeenth-century lexicons is partly belied by other examples. Once it becomes the textual site in which those who are on the periphery in the struggle for power make their voice (and reasons) heard, the manifesto can be appropriated by groups and authors other than the princes, states, or persons of great standing named in Furetière's dictionary or the *Académie française* definition – the political and religious leaders who speak on behalf of other political subjects. In other words, the manifesto is a symptom of a double crisis: First, it makes evident – manifest, as it were – the fragmentation of Christian Europe with the end of the monopoly of Catholicism, which nominally at least provided cohesion to the continent over religious matters. This loss of a common faith dissolves the last glue, the last common discourse, linking the nascent nation states, and religious differences come to superimpose and in a number of cases to subsume and summarize, all other cultural, linguistic, and political differences. Second, this religious crisis also leads to a political crisis insofar as the clash between divine and earthly law is no longer conducted at the level of religious and secular authority – pope and emperor – but affects the life of the faithful, who are now able to have a say, through their religious leaders, in how the two types of authority relate to one another. It is no surprise, then, that one of the first manifestoes not issued by a political authority appears on the eve of the Civil War in England. In this manifesto the political struggle between king and parliament dovetails with a symbolically much more powerful struggle between two opposing religious identities. The author of the anonymous pamphlet entitled 'A Declaration sent to the King of France and Spayne From the Catholiques or Rebells in Ireland' issued in Paris on the eve of the Civil War (the text is dated 24 April 1642) and later published in London in the English translation of a certain 'R.C. Gent.' remarks on the collapse of ethno-cultural and religious difference:

> [The Earl of Tyrone] tooke armes for the maintayning of the liberty of the Catholicks against the Protestants in that great and universall subject of division which the diversity of religion had caused to arise throughout Christendome, [... which] added to the first and greate difference which arrose in that countrey between the naturall *Irish* and those who were

> called *English-Irish,* that is to say descended from the *English* and the Inhabitants of *Ireland,* another difference to it of Catholickes and Protestants, which now is growne so strong as to make them forget their antient quarrell, and to recombine all those into the same body which are found of the same belief. (3)

The pamphlet also evidences the ongoing transformation in the use of the term manifesto, which is not without ambiguities. The explicative subtitle of the pamphlet, 'Wherein is discovered their [of the Catholics] treacherous practizes under the pretence of Religion and their bloody Actions full of Cruelty and Barbarisme' (1), leaves little doubt as to the propaganda nature of the publication, which is best displayed in the 'Manifesto of the Covenant or Oath they [the Catholics] have made and taken for the defence of the Catholique League against the Protestants in that Kingdome' (1). Here the term 'manifesto' is not synonymous with the 'covenant' whose eighteen articles and concluding oath take up the bulk of the publication, but rather seems to be applied to the text because it has the function of revealing a truth concealed 'under the pretence of Religion.' If we recall the adjectival meaning of the term, the purpose of the 'manifesto' is to 'catch red-handed' the Irish Catholics in the performance of their supposed deceitful and traitorous practices. As was the case with the description of the Prince of Condé's actions in de Mézeray's account, the oath binds together a preexisting community, while the manifesto reveals its program to the world, although here – the example is notable because of this peculiarity – the issuer of the manifesto and the author of the program are not the same person, and the manifesto is used as a weapon against the latter. In any case, what is significant is the fact that the manifesto is well established as the textual site in which a struggle for (self)-definition is carried out, and in which, with the disappearance of a common religious discourse on which is founded the legitimacy of political power, opposing parties stake out the new ground upon which they can legitimate their program.

Once the authorship of manifestoes is no longer limited to the holders of political office, the content also greatly expands beyond 'business of great importance.' We find, among the specimens published in the 1680s, 'The Earl of Castlemain's Manifesto' (1681), issued by the author, Roger Palmer, Earl of Castlemain, as a justification for his own conduct and a pledge of his loyalty to the Crown, and the 'Manifesto of Near 150 Knights, and Eminent Merchants and Citizens of London,

Against the Jews now in England' 'presented to King and Parliament' in 1689 by Samuel Hayne, a document that witnesses to the shift of battleground from politics to economics, thus paralleling a similar shift in authorship from the feudal class to the bourgeoisie.[9] Other examples, such as the 'Manifesto or Declaration' issued by the founders of a new church in Boston in 1699, show that the semantic field of the term 'manifesto' remains to a certain extent quite broad and ill-defined; in this case the text is not meant to justify present or future action against another party, but rather to set down the 'Undertakers'' 'Aims and Designs [...] together with those Principles and Rules [they] intend by GOD'S Grace to adhere unto' (*Manifesto or Declaration* 1). This kind of manifesto, however, constitutes a key link in a chain that connects the 'informative' document of the type first defined by the *Accademia della Crusca* to the specifically programmatic manifestoes that proliferate with the avant-garde: the various 'technical' manifestoes of futurism or, parodically, texts such as Tristan Tzara's Dada 'Antimanifesto.' The manifesto no longer hands down a rule to be enforced by the officers of the law, but instead a political, social, religious, or, ultimately, cultural program in which the reader can participate. Even in this case, conquest is the ultimate aim of the manifesto, but the object is now the reader.

The definition in the *Encyclopédie* (1757), which reiterates those given by late sixteenth-century lexicographers such as Furetière, implicitly points out the legitimacy crisis to which the manifesto witnesses.

> MANIFESTE: s.m. (*Droit polit.*) déclaration que font les Princes, & autres puissances, par un écrit public, des raisons & moyens sur lesquels ils fondent leurs droits & leurs prétentions, en commençant quelque guerre, ou autre entreprise ; c'est en deux mots l'apologie de leur conduite.
>
> Les anciens avoient une cérémonie auguste & solemnelle, par laquelle ils faisoient intervenir dans la déclaration de guerre, la majesté divine, comme témoin & vengeresse de l'injustice de ceux qui soutiendroient une telle guerre injustement. [...]
>
> Les puissances modernes étalent à leur tour, dans leurs écrits publics, tous les artifices de la rhétorique, & tout ce qu'elle a d'adresse, pour exposer la justice des causes qui leur font prendre les armes, & les torts qu'ils prétendent avoir reçus.
>
> Un motif de politique a rendu nécessaires ces *manifestes*, dans la situation où sont à l'égard des uns des autres les princes de l'Europe, liés ensembles par la religion, par le sang, par les alliances, par des ligues

offensives & défensives. Il est de la prudence du prince qui déclare la guerre à un autre, de ne pas s'attirer en même tems sur les bras tous les alliés de celui qui l'attaque: c'est en partie pour détourner cet inconvénient qu'on fait aujourd'hui des *manifestes*, qui renferment quelquefois la raison qui a déterminé le prince a commencer la guerre sans la déclarer.

[MANIFESTO, m. n. (*political law*) declaration made by princes and other powers, by means of a public writing, regarding the reasons and means upon which their rights and their claims are founded, when starting a war or some other enterprise. It is, in a word, the justification [*apologie* is a term also used by Furetière] for their conduct.

The ancients had a stately and solemn ceremony through which they sought the intervention of the divine power as witness and avenger for the injustices of those who conducted such a war unjustly.

The modern powers display in turn, in their public writings, all the artifices of rhetoric and all the skill one possesses to make public the justice of their causes, which leads them to take arms, and the wrongs which they have supposedly received.

A political motive has made these *manifestoes* necessary, given the situation in which the princes of Europe are in relation to each other, linked together by religion, by blood, by alliances, by defensive and offensive leagues. It is prudent for the prince who declares war to another not to draw upon himself at the same time all the allies of the one he attacks: it is in part to avoid this inconvenience that nowadays one makes *manifestoes*, which sometimes conceal the reason which led the prince to start a war without declaring it.] (7: 37–8)

The disappearance of a transcendental authority, the 'divine power,' as the guarantor of the justice of the enterprise of the worldly powers leads to a proliferation of competing discourses that find their justification in themselves, or rather in the effectiveness of their rhetorical strategies. In the century framed by the Glorious Revolution and the French Revolution, the manifesto is one of the symbolic sites that witness to the emergence of the bourgeoisie as the class that legitimates political power. Thus, the two manifestoes by James II – one directed to the Catholic princes and one to the Protestant princes – are met with scorn on the part of the author of a point-by-point rebuttal (*The Late King James' Manifesto Answer'd* and *The Late King James's Second Manifesto, Directed to the Protestant Princes, Answered*), who, in the conclusion of the second text, notes that the late king 'has lost all hope to be Restored by the free Consent of his Subjects, since he would ingage both Protestant and Catholick Princes to Restore him by Fire and Sword. But we need not to be afraid of the Effect his Arguments may have upon them, for they are the weakest that can be imagined' (32). Authority now rests with the subjects of the sovereign, who is such only by virtue of their 'free consent,' as both James II and his successor William III knew well. The sovereign's appeal to the other princes of Europe, the very act of issuing of a manifesto, is in fact the sign of his impotence and loss of authority, as he finds himself in the same position as those groups striving against the dominant discourse 'to make their voice heard.'

An exchange of manifestoes between the sovereign and the nobility following the French Revolution brings into further relief the centrality of the question of authority. On 20 November 1791 a group of exiled French noblemen issued a *Nouveau Manifeste des Princes émigrés, et leur profession de foi sur la Costitution françoise,* in which they protested against Louis XVI's acceptance of the constitution. This 'code monstrueux,' in their view 'a non seulement dénaturé la forme du Gouvernement, mais même détruit ses bases, & jusqu'à son essence' [has not only distorted the nature of the form of government, but has destroyed its very basis, and even its essence], insofar as it 'anéantit le contrat de la Nation Françoise avec ses Monarques' [annuls the contract of the French nation with its sovereign] and 'romp les anciens fermens' [breaks the ancient oaths] (Xavier et al. 4). Louis's response, in his *Grand Declaration du Roi* – significantly addressed to 'all the French' – invokes the inappellability of the king's authority – 'vous osé, MM., manifester des volontés contraires à la mienne' [you dare, gentlemen, manifest wills opposed to mine] (2) – but also grounds it on its identification with that of the people: 'je vous répete, MM., aucune considération ne peut l'emporter sur la volonté générale, qui est aussi celle de votre Roi' [I repeat, gentlemen, no consideration can prevail over the general will, which is also that of your King] (3).

The French Revolution – as the period of rupture *par excellence* in modern European history, the upheaval that projects the bourgeoisie to the centre-stage of history and heralds the rise of the modern political episteme – is fertile ground for manifestoes from both sides of the barricades. The abrupt hortatory opening to Poissonnier des Perrieres's manifesto to the French, 'Français, depuis plus de deux ans vous êtes couverts d'opprobre & d'infamie aux yeux de l'univers' [Frenchmen, for over two years you have been covered with disgrace and infamy in the eyes of the universe] (3), already looks forward to the vehement appeals of the avant-garde manifestoes; in the *Manifeste de la ville et état d'Avignon* the deputies of the city, liberated from 'le double joug du despotisme ultramontain et de l'aristocratie de sa Municipalité' [the double yoke of ultramontane despotism and of the aristocracy of its municipality] (1), agree to the reunion of the city to France and enjoin the population of that other papal seat, Rome, to welcome 'les grands jours de la vérité' [the great days of truth] (40) and to recover their freedom from the temporal rule of the Pope. If manifestoes had become an instrument for political propaganda as early as the sixteenth century, the political manifestoes of the great bourgeois revolutions of Europe witness to a more general 'mental' upheaval, to use Alain Meyer's category, as they call for a reorientation in the way in which the very foundations of the social structure are represented: feudal oaths and bonds of loyalty linking the king to the nobility to the general population – the third estate – are replaced by a social pact in which the power of the sovereign is the expression of the will of the people.[10]

But the question of what the contours of that 'people' might be is also addressed by manifestoes. The issue is confronted by the 'Manifeste des Égaux' (1796), which was written by Sylvain Maréchal to propagandize the ideals of the underground 'conspiracy of equals' led by Gracchus Babeuf after the Thermidorean reaction and the ratification of the 'Constitution of the year III,' which scrapped the (never enacted) democratic rights of the constitution of 1793 and defined the right to suffrage on the basis of census. The manifesto opens by appealing to the 'PEOPLE OF FRANCE!' but this addressee, which the manifesto seeks to represent as a unitary body since the innate equality of all men is precisely what is at stake in it,[11] appears immediately divided since the people of France include 'les ennemis d'un ordre de choses le plus naturel' (199) [the sworn enemies of a truly natural order of things (94)] who oppose the establishment of the Republic of Equality for which the manifesto calls. There are in fact two addressees in the manifesto. Initially, using the familiar 'tous,' the text adresses 'the people,' the subjects of an unequal, unjust, and repressive social order: 'Pendant quinze siècles tu as vécu esclave' (197) [For fifteen hundred year you have lived in slavery (91)]. Quickly, however, another addressee – the bourgeoisie whose counter-revolution has trampled over the aspirations of the first 'tous' – emerges: 'Législateurs, gouvernants, riches propriétaires, écoutez à votre tour' (198) [Men of high degree – lawmakers, rulers, the rich – now it is your turn to listen to us' (91)]. Thus, through a symmetrical translation, the speaking subject also changes from the 'we' who harangue the people and who are defined by their adversaries as a group of mere destroyers and instigators of mob violence (in other words, the conspirators themselves, a political avant-garde whose task it is to show the people the way to the future) to a universal subject which identifies with the people itself, the 'us,' whom the rich are advised to fear. It is this collectivity that becomes the subject of a future in which 'nous prétendons désormais vivre et mourir égaux comme nous sommes nés' (197–8) [we shall live and die as we have been born – equal (91)]. There is clearly a partial superimposition between the referents of the pronouns: the 'we' who 'shall live and die [...] equal' includes the 'you' who are invoked at the beginning of the manifesto. Thus, the manifesto seeks to perform rhetorically what it professes as its aim, the transformation of 'the people' into the subjects of their own history. Once again, we must recall the pragmatic function of the genre: a discussion of the revolution is obviously not the same thing as the revolution itself, and the manifesto will have performed its function effectively only if and when it manages to translate its program into action, and word into deed. Hence, at the close of Marechal's manifesto the articulation of the program comes not to a conclusion but rather to a moment of transition from written text to revolutionary practice: 'Ouvre les yeux et ton cœur à la plénitude de la félicité. Reconnois et proclame avec nous LA RÉPUBLIQUE DES ÉGAUX' (201) [Open your eyes and hearts to full happiness: recognize the REPUBLIC OF EQUALITY. Join us in working for it (95)]. Initially 'the people' is recognized in its fundamental unity and equality, in its shared subjection, by the author of the manifesto, but something more is needed for the manifesto to perform its function felicitously, to use Austin's term. In this shift of the people from addressee to addresser – from 'tous' to 'nous' – lies the utopian dimension of the manifesto, since it envisions as its result a transformation in the relations of power that will allow the undefined 'people' to define itself and to take hold of its own destiny, to become subjects of its future history.

As Janet Lyon has argued in analysing the mechanisms of the play of pronouns in manifestoes, 'the manifesto provides a foothold in a culture's dominant ideology by creating generic speaking positions; the nascent audience interpellated by "we" is then held together as a provisional constituency through a linguistic contract' (24). However, if on the one hand this 'we' can indeed be understood as 'an inherently colonizing construction' (26), it also makes visible and available subject positions that the institutions against which it rails have either suppressed or which those same institutions are unable or unwilling to conceive because they question the legitimacy of the existing structure of power, whether political or symbolic. Indeed, the figure of the spectre evoked at the beginning of the paradigmatic political manifesto of the nineteenth century, Marx and Engels's *Communist Manifesto*, metaphorizes precisely the mobile and shifting dimension of the subject of the manifesto. Through a kind of circular movement, the end of the text returns the reader to its initial situation, with the Powers of old Europe quaking before their adversary. There is, however, at least one significant difference between the two stagings of this scene of conflict. In the famous opening of the manifesto – 'A spectre is haunting Europe – the spectre of Communism. All the Powers of old Europe have entered into a holy alliance to exorcise this spectre: Pope and Czar, Metternich and Guizot, French Radicals and German police-spies' (473) – communism is a spectral presence, a 'nursery tale' (473), a myth, while the Powers of old Europe are embodied by the institutions and figures that uphold them – monarchs and presidents, political and religious institutions, parties and police spies. At the closing of the manifesto, on the contrary, we are confronted with something more fundamental and substantial: 'Let the ruling classes tremble at a Communist revolution. The proletarians have nothing to lose but their chains. They have a world to win' (500). The manifesto reveals the fundamental division that bourgeois institutions and ideologies and their representatives, in all their diversity, conceal – namely class struggle. The spectre has coalesced into the proletariat, whose identity as a class the manifesto details with great care. However, the emergence of the proletariat, its recognition of itself as a class, also allows for a reinterpretation of the whole of human history as nothing other than 'the history of class struggle' (473). In other words, by making it possible for a certain subject to emerge, the manifesto argues for a complete reorientation of a field – culture, politics, history.

The Manifesto and the Making of the Intellectual

The second half of the nineteenth century, as already mentioned, is characterized not only by a proliferation of political manifestoes but also by the appropriation of the genre on the part of the artistic avant-garde. An established critical tradition, in fact, sees the period between the two great revolutions of nineteenth-century France (the 1848 Revolution and the revolt of the Commune) as the moment in which the metaphor of the avant-garde, which had hitherto been limited to the sphere of the political, found its way into the aesthetic debate and took root there, even after the end of the alliance between the political and the artistic avant-garde.[12] The dialogue between the 'two avant-gardes,' as Renato Poggioli calls them, was not necessarily an easy one, and it is significant that, in *Mon coeur mis à nu*, Baudelaire remarked ironically on the use of the term in the literary domain:

> Les poètes de combat.
> Les littérateurs d'avant-garde.
> Ces habitudes de métaphores militaires dénotes des esprits, non pas militants, mais fait pour la discipline, c'est-à-dire pour la conformité, des esprits nés domestiques, des esprits belges, qui ne peuvent penser qu'en société. (*Œuvres complètes* 1: 691)

> [The fighting poets.
> The literary vanguard.
> This use of military metaphor reveals minds not militant but formed for discipline, that is, for compliance; minds born servile, Belgian minds, which can only think collectively. (*Intimate Journals* 39)]

Baudelaire's scorn points to two different problems that developed fully in the decades leading up to the turn of the century: on the one hand, it suggests that freedom of thought and freedom of expression, unconstrained by the demands of political commitment, are the values that regulate the self-understanding of those involved in intellectual labour; on the other, it indicates one of the consequences of the loss of the halo, namely the fact that artists are engaged in a process of renegotiation of their social role in a now fully developed bourgeois society. Indeed, the very notion of avant-garde implies a division within the field of cultural production among – at the very least, since the available positions are in fact much more fluid and articulate[13] – those writers and artists who are integrated within the economic structures of the dominant (economic) field, and those who find themselves in an economically subaltern position that at the same time allows them a greater degree of expressive freedom. It is for this reason that in the 1880s and 1890s – at precisely the moment when, for Renato Poggioli, the political and the artistic avant-garde part ways – we see, in fact, a partial convergence between politics and art under the aegis not of socialism but of anarchism, which could be linked to the artistic avant-garde by the common rhetoric of absolute freedom.[14] When Marinetti wrote in his manifesto of foundation of Futurism 'Noi vogliamo glorificare [...] il gesto distruttore dei libertarî' [We want to glorify the destructive gesture of the libertarians] (*TIF* 11),[15] he was simply reiterating the close relationship between the political and the artistic avant-garde, which in France at least dated back over twenty years.

The situation of the market of symbolic goods in the second half of the nineteenth century has been analysed in a more complex and articulated way for France than for any of the other countries that constitute the focus of this study, thanks mostly to the work of Pierre Bourdieu and his school, and in particular to the extensive examinations of the formation of the intellectual class conducted by Christophe Charle.[16] If on the one hand France offers a case study of cultural trends that traverse the whole of Western culture (for instance, in terms of the transformations wrought by technological innovations or the autonomization of the sphere of the aesthetic), it is also important to emphasize the specificity of the French situation. The Parisian avant-garde and its forms of cultural intervention comes to constitute an example for other movements (the case of futurism is paradigmatic); however, by exporting such forms into different socio-cultural milieus, these movements are forced to confront the contradictions of their model.

The later decades of the nineteenth century witness a profound transformation in both the production and the reception of symbolic goods, especially in the literary domain. Charle has remarked that this radical alteration in the market is to be imputed to several parallel and complementary factors. First, we witness a sharp decrease in the price of printed books thanks to cheaper production costs, and as a consequence, the appearance of what can easily be called the first 'best sellers,' such as Zola's *L'assommoir*, which reached 100,000 copies in its first five years. However, this expansion of the market for what has been called 'industrial literature' (the expression, as we will see when discussing Anatole Baju, was already common among its contemporary denigrators) also necessitated an increase in demand, fostered by the movement of scholarization that characterized the end of the Second Empire and the first years of the Republic, and which affected not only the younger strata of the population, but also the adults, whose attendance to adult courses grew six-fold between 1863 and 1869.[17] Technological innovations in the printing process, and in particular the invention of the rotary press and the replacement of cloth paper by much cheaper pulp paper, affected the popular press even more extensively. Lower production costs, the introduction of advertisement, and the institution in 1881 of more liberal legislation regulating the press (which, among other things, further reduced the initial financial investment for a publishing venture by lifting the need for a security deposit) all contributed to the expansion of newspaper and periodical production, which saw its apogee in the decades characterized by the birth of the first avant-garde groups, that is, the 1870s and 1880s.[18] The synergetic relationship between the press and the new literary market is well described by Charle, who points out the mutual support between the two media. In particular, journalism offered writers a space in which to test their work, a means to increase their audience and, not least, a steady source of income, while newspapers themselves began to play an increased role in the process of diffusion of literary products: 'The deluge of production makes critical mediation an obligation, while traditional instances, salons, the Academy, etc., become inefficient for certain categories of readers as a result of the democratization of the public' (*La crise littéraire* 47). But the press was not simply the handmaid of the literary domain: rather, through the mediating function of the critic, it became an influential force in shaping the literary debate and, most importantly, in drawing that debate outside the narrow sphere of the 'industry insiders.' Thus, for example, when Moréas published the article 'Les Décadents' in *Le XIXe Siècle* in August 1885, he was responding to the public controversy on the *succès de scandale* of the parodic collection of decadent poems *Les déliquescences* by Adoré Floupette (the pseudonym behind which hid the poets Henri Beauclair and Gabriel Vicaire), which had been stirred and amplified by the press. The term 'manifesto' has not been applied to this earlier text by Moréas, which indeed lacks the programmatic and injunctive tone associated with the genre; however, this text also recalls some of the earlier instances of the manifesto since its function was to provide a justification to a popular audience for a poetics that ap-peared in itself mystifying. But the article in turn provided more fuel to the discussion on the notion of decadence itself, forcing Moréas to enter again the public arena with his essay on Symbolism, at the invitation of the editor of *Le Figaro*, as we have seen in the introduction.

The growing public dimension of the work of the intellectual finds however its counterpoint in a more and more noticeable disarticulation of the relationship between artists and writers on the one hand and social and political institutions on the other. The autonomization of the field of cultural production, as we will see in greater detail in the second part of this chapter, is both a consequence of this process and the completion of a parcelling out of human experience into a series of compartmentalized domains that characterizes bourgeois society. In France the transition from the Empire to the Republic had a powerful role in completing this process of autonomization, since it marked the disappearance of traditional forms of patronage and their replacement by reliance on market forces. Charle notes the conflictual relationship between artists and the new political class of the Republic:

> The hostility towards politics, which means, in reality, to parliamentarism and to the political personnel, is considerable in the literary milieus, and it easily spills beyond the narrow circles of the avant-garde. A structural datum is at the origins of this dislike. By their function and their position in social space, the political and the literary field are in competition. Writers, like politicians, need newspapers and magazines to gain renown or to disseminate their beliefs. On the other hand, the democratic system does not foster the mecenatism or patronage on which depended traditionally, under the monarchy or the empire, the authors who practised the less financially rewarding genres. The new personnel, derived from a more recent bourgeoisie characterized by more traditional tastes, is further and further removed from the growing audacities of the avant-garde. (*Naissance des 'intellectuels'* 99–100)

But if politicians and artists compete for visibility in the public sphere, clearly the legitimating rhetoric invoked by each group is quite different. While politicians are legitimated in their public role by the electoral process itself, and therefore ultimately by their function as representatives of the 'people,' for the intellectuals the problem of legitimation is much more complex. It is interesting, in this context, to see the emergence of a form of manifesto writing that, as with the manifestoes of princes and personages of great standing of the definition in the *Grand dictionnaire de l'Académie françoise*, is completely self-referential and serves only to legitimize the social role of its issuer(s).

Two episodes in the debate on the role of intellectuals are especially interesting. In 1889, the naturalist novelist Lucien Descaves published the antimilitaristic novel *Sous-offs*, and was quickly brought to court by the Ministry of War for insulting the army and offending morals. On 24

December *Le Figaro* published a notice, signed by fifty-four writers (including Alphonse Daudet, Georges Ohnet, Emile Zola, Edmond De Goncourt, and Paul Bourget), in which the signatories lay claim to the freedom of the intellectual from political constraints. The short text reads:

> Des poursuites sont intentées contre un livre, sur la demande du Ministre de la Guerre, à la veille d'une discussion législative sur la liberté d'écrire. Nous nous unissons pour la protester.
>
> Depuis vingt ans nous avons pris l'habitude de la liberté. Nous avons conquis nos franchises. Au nom de l'indépendance de l'écrivain, nous nous élevons énergétiquement contre toutes poursuites attentatoires à la libre expression de la pensée écrite. Solidaires lorsque l'art est en cause, nous prions le gouvernement de réfléchir.
>
> [Certain proceedings have been instituted against a book, on demand of the Minister of War, on the eve of a legislative debate on freedom of writing. We come together to protest.
>
> For twenty years we have been used to liberty. We have conquered our freedoms. In the name of the independence of writers, we rise forcefully against all hostile proceedings against the free expression of written thought. Joined when art is at stake, we request the government to reflect.] (qtd. Charle, *Naissance des 'intellectuels'* 111–12)

In 1893, *L'Ermitage* conducted a survey of ninety-nine intellectuals on the question of the best social organization of society and the degree of freedom of the writer within it confirms the position held by the signatories of the defence of Descaves. About a third (twenty-three) favoured some kind of social constraints, whether of a socialist, authoritarian, or aristocratic nature; a further twenty-four were either undecided or indifferent. When confronted with the issue of censorship, however, the respondents showed unanimity in calling for complete freedom for the artist.[19] What these two documents show is the formation of a new self-understanding of intellectuals (and in particular, of artists) as a class, which, like art itself, comes to be defined by its autonomy from the economic and political realm, and therefore, almost reciprocally, by its freedom from the constraints of that realm. Glauco Viazzi has remarked that the futurist movement was the first cultural group to organize itself like a modern party, with a clear propaganda strategy and a centralized 'secrétariat' in charge of organizing group activities. If this is true, the organization of intellectuals in France at the turn of the century can be described as a less structured and yet no less political form of association – a lobby or labour union, that is a federation of groups and individuals brought together by the necessity of reaffirming and legitimizing their social role.[20] Intellectuals – that ill-defined class gathering writers, artists, critics, and academics that begins now to perceive its general and common interests – thus follow the general trend of collective organization or professions and classes, but with one important difference: instead of specific interests, they lay claim to 'disinterested interests, universal values, and general institutions' (Charle, *A Social History of France* 215).

But the self-referential function of the manifesto on behalf of Descaves is also remarkable if we further consider the tone of the argument. For the signatories, the point is not whether Descaves's novel was antimilitaristic – a question that, in fact, is not even addressed directly. Rather, Descaves's social role is the stake, since that role grants him the immunity that is claimed for the writer; that social role, however, is sanctioned by the signatories themselves, who identify with him and consider him one of their own. Notice, for instance, how the attack on Descaves is an attack against 'our' free expression – the plural pronoun coming to include not only Descaves, whose 'free expression' is after all the only one directly on the line, but also the signatories. The manifesto thus plays an important double role: on the one hand, the symbolic value of the names appended to the text endows the demand with legitimacy and dignity. On the other hand, the claim to 'immunity' from any restrictions in the circulation of their ideas constructs precisely that difference upon which the intellectual class grounds its identity and its status. In other words, the manifesto simultaneously defines and legitimates a new social function for writers and artists.

The public dimension of the clash between political power and the rising intellectual class is also not to be underestimated. By publicly displaying their protest against the threat of repressive measures against the world of cultural production, the signatories turn their remonstration into a performance of their symbolic power, of their authority to administer and police their own domain. If the explicit addressee of the manifesto is the government, the implicit addressee is the general (bourgeois) public of *Le Figaro*, for whose benefit also this display of defiance is executed. Thus, the gesture of opposition to political power in the name of the specific and distinctive role of the intellectuals within bourgeois society aims at establishing the intellectual class as a legitimate interlocutor of politcal power in the court of public opinion, and constituting it as a unified formation with its own specific social functions. The loss of the halo, of the privileged status that characterized the individual artist, is addressed through a procedure that on the one hand organizes intellectuals as a pressure group – or, to use the term already employed, a lobby – along lines compatible with the mechanisms regulating competing interests in bourgeois society, and on the other hand re-articulates the difference of their offering from other goods on the market.

The position of the artist in the network of social and economic relations in the second half of the nineteenth century, however, is a complex and contradictory one. The vigorous defence of intellectual freedom occasioned by the threat to Descaves's novel or the proclamation of that same value as the only unifying factor, across political and poetic lines, in the *enquête* of *L'Ermitage*, offers a sort of 'zero degree' of the new intellectual field, bent upon recuperating certain of the traditional privileges of the artist and the man of letters.[21] The issuing of a manifesto or a proclamation, in this case, serves to unify and to give coherence to the disparate forces of the field, regardless of their own perception of their identity *vis-à-vis* that of other practitioners. But while this minimal agreement is enough to differentiate the intellectuals, as a body, from other classes and interest groups, it also suspends the question of the ground on which, precisely, the individual figures can claim their membership within the field itself. The presence, among the signatories of the Descaves petition, of a member of the symbolist movement such as René Ghil and of one of the veritable *bêtes noires* of the avant-garde, the popular bourgeois novelist Georges Ohnet, demonstrates how the competing principles of legitimation that divide the field of cultural production can be set aside when it comes to defending the general principle of the freedom owed to the intellectual class as a whole. Manifestoes can thus play a role in defining the relationship between the field of cultural production and other competing fields such as that of political power, and can simultaneously articulate a series of positions within the field itself, thus accounting for its diversity and for the concurrent presence, within it, of various ideological and poetic stances.

The formation of this 'restricted field' dovetails with another phenomenon, the rise of the literary groups, the various schools and movements that dot the landscape of late nineteenth- and early twentieth-century European culture. The formation of literary groups witnesses to the need for artists to redefine their social role, although in ways that oppose the dominant ideology of productivity and financial profit. Charle remarks that the rise of the group as organizational principle of the cultural field is a result of the autonomization of the sphere of the aesthetic, since 'when the dependence of literature on the rest of social life was stronger and more direct, a literary group had no reason to exist. The writer was the spokesperson of a social, religious, political or ideological group, or at least tried to play that role' (*La crise littéraire* 18).[22] But if this is true, then the loss of the halo noticed by Baudelaire might be seen as a recognition – under a suitable ideological guise – of the loss of this role, which precipitated the artist into a condition comparable to that of any other producer of goods. Thus, the gesture of recovery of the halo entails the elaboration of another narrative or series of narratives to validate the artist and his work, and to re-establish a relationship with the audience. In the transition from the collective reception of the work in sacral art to the individual fruition in bourgeois society, in which both the moment of production and that of reception are reduced to a purely private level, the group – the coming together of a number of artists in the name of a common aesthetic program – turns into a fundamental strategy to resist the assimilation of the work of the artist to that of any other producer. But this difference now has to be itself produced. We are in the presence of a crucial legitimation crisis: in the absence of a socially shared notion of what a work of art is and does, it is up to artists themselves to engage in the process of renegotiating such a function.

The literary group is thus the institution through which the individual artist negotiates his relationship with the broader field: groups and schools articulate a series of possible positions and legitimation strategies within the field – strategies that are on the one hand in competition with one another but on the other are joined by their common opposition to the principles of legitimation of bourgeois society. Manifestoes are crucial instruments in this struggle because, by virtue of their ambiguous positioning in a space between the creative domain (they are issued by the producers themselves) and the sites of mediation and reception of the works (they appear in journals and in the popular press, participate in critical and public debates, and do not claim an autonomous status like the work of art), they function as a kind of bridge between the two fields. In other words, the formative function of manifestoes is carried out simultaneously on two levels. First, as already discussed, they serve to differentiate the field of cultural production from other social domains, and to legitimate its autonomy. Second, within the restricted field of artistic production, they serve to articulate the identity of the various groups of individuals who, by either signing the manifesto or assuming the name which it proposes, explicitly affirm their allegiance to it, and bring to it the symbolic capital associated with their names (and, in turn, share in the symbolic capital of the group).[23] It is for this reason that the recognized masters of the major tendencies of poetic and literary life – Verlaine, Mallarmé, Zola – are not themselves the issuers of manifestoes even when their names are invoked by their decadent, symbolist or naturalist followers or when, as in the case of Verlaine (which we will discuss below), the established author explicitly gives support to a given school or movement: they have no need for the publicity or the public recognition that would derive from their association with a group.

In this sense, Mallarmé's remark on schools in Jules Huret's *Enquête sur l'évolution littéraire* is symptomatic. Expectedly, Mallarmé emphasizes the necessary independence and individuality of the artist: 'J'abomine les écoles, [...]; je répugne à tout ce qui est professoral appliqué à la littérature qui, elle, au contraire, est tout à fait individuelle' [I hate schools; I abhor anything professorial applied to literature which, on the contrary, is absolutely individual] (Huret 104). Likewise, in a later *enquête* published in 1905, the decadent novelist Catulle Mendès answered the question posed by Georges Le Cardonnel and Charles Vellay on the function of schools by denying their utility and voicing a critique of avant-garde groups that would become almost canonical: 'ils passent leur vie à rédiger des proclamations, et ils oublient de faire des œuvres' [they spend their life writing proclamations, and they forget to make works] (Le Cardonnel and Vellay 33). On the other hand, Saint-Georges de Bouhélier, the founder of the naturist school, remarked on the strategic function of groups: 'On a toujours ri des écoles, [...] toutes les plaisanteries ont été faites à ce sujet. En réalité, il ne s'est rien produit de grand dans la littérature, en dehors d'elles. [...] Et c'est tout à fait compréhensible: dans toute société, il est indispensable aux écrivains, surtout novateurs, de se grouper, et de combattre contre ce qui leur est hostile' [People always laugh at schools, every possible joke has been made on the subject. In fact, nothing in great literature has been made outside of them. And this is understandable: in every society, it is necessary for writers – especially innovators – to come together and to fight those who are hostile to them] (Le Cardonnel and Vellay 136–7). The question is not whether the group and its propaganda activities in themselves stimulate the productivity of a given author; rather, groups serve as a means of controlling at least in part the discourse in and about the artistic field, and a means of bringing into relief the work of the individuals who comprise them. If not all artists can take advantage of the buzz created by scandalous or controversial works such as *À rebours* or *Sous-offs*, which had gone through thirty-two editions by 1890,[24] the collective project can constitute a suitable alternative, as the debates within the artistic field spill, through the press, into the broader sphere of public life and gain visibility.

Of course, any discourse of identity is simultaneously a discourse of difference. To issue a manifesto is not only a way for a group to consolidate itself around certain principles, goals, or even poetic fathers, but it serves to remark the differences of that group from other competitors. The proliferation of schools that began in the late 1870s with the foundation of the first poetic circles, such as the *Hydropathes* and the *Zutistes*, is symptomatic of the institutionalization of a series of strategies – the foundation of a group, the issuing of one or more manifestoes, the demarcation of one's poetic project versus those of the competitors – in the struggle for symbolic capital.[25] This is not to say that such groups *only* serve as a kind of instrument of propaganda: the aesthetic and ideological differences among such groups are often very real, and, as we will see once we discuss futurism, they may involve a complete re-articulation of the process of poetic communication. Rather, the point is that in the half century between the 1870s and the 1920s the dynamics governing the 'restricted field' – the space in the field of cultural production that resists the commodification of the work of art – are codified in ways that become fully visible only at their waning, when Dada is able to hollow out their content and construct a kind of 'empty' avant-garde in which the performance of by now traditional gestures and procedures serves to reveal the bankruptcy of the very project of defending the autonomy and difference of 'art.' In the next section, we will examine the broader political and cultural implications of the formation of avant-garde groups by examining a specific example of fin-de-siècle Paris, the self-proclaimed 'Decadents' or 'Decadists' led by Anatole Baju.

HOW TO BE A DECADENT: ART, POLITICS AND SOCIETY IN THE MANIFESTOES OF ANATOLE BAJU

A Crisis in Communication

When in 1891 the cultural journalist Jules Huret carried out for the *Écho de Paris* his survey of the contemporary literary situation *Enquête sur l'évolution littéraire* (later collected in a volume) the echoes of the conflict that, in the second half to the 1880s, had divided symbolists and decadents had already begun to abate, to the point that he could treat the two groups as variations of a single symbolo-decadent movement (99), of which Paul Verlaine was, along with Stephane Mallarmé, one of the main precursors. Questioned about the meaning of the two terms, however, Verlaine was evasive. Of symbolism he said: 'Vous savez, moi, j'ai du bon sens; je n'ai peut-être que cela, mais j'en ai. Le symbolisme? ... comprends pas ... Ça doit être un mot allemand ... hein? Qu'est-ce que ça peut bien vouloir dire? Moi, d'ailleurs, je m'en fiche. Quand je souffre, quand je jouis ou quand je pleure, je sais bien que ça n'est pas du symbole' [You know, I have some good sense; maybe that's all I have, but I do have it. Symbolism? ... I don't get it ... It must be a German word ... uhu? What could it mean? Me, I don't give a damn. When I suffer, when I am happy or when I cry, I know very well that those are not symbols] (109). When asked how he could accept the epithet 'decadent,' and what the term might mean for him, Verlaine was more forthright:

> C'est bien simple. On nous l'avait jetée comme une insulte, cette épithète ; je l'ai ramassée comme cri de guerre ; mais elle ne signifiait rien de spécial, que je sache. Décadent! Est-ce que le crépuscule d'un beau jour ne vaut pas toutes les aurores! Et puis, le soleil qui a l'air de se coucher, ne se lèvera-t-il pas demain? Décadent, au fond ne voulait rien dire du tout. Je vous le répète, c'était plutôt un cri et un drapeau sans rien autour. Pour se battre, y a-t-il besoin de phrases!
>
> [It's simple. This epithet had been thrown against us as an insult; I took it up as a battle-cry. But as far as I know it doesn't mean anything specific. Decadent! Isn't the twilight of a beautiful day worth as much as any dawn? But then, doesn't the sun which seems to set also rise the following morning? In the end, decadent meant nothing at all. I repeat, it was rather

a rallying cry and a flag with nothing around it. In order to fight, one needs slogans. The three colours confronted by the black eagle, that's enough, one fights!] (112)

Verlaine had of course been instrumental in the appropriation, on the part of those artists who set themselves in opposition to naturalism and the bourgeois novel, of the term 'decadent.' His sonnet 'Langueur,' which opens with the famous line 'Je suis l'Empire à la fin de la décadence' [I am the Empire at the end of decadence], was first published in the review *Le Chat Noir* in 1883. This poem had removed the term 'decadence' from the realm of literary criticism and turned it into a badge of honour, a term around which a group of artists would seek to delineate not only a poetic program but, most importantly, a wholesale redefinition of the relationship between art and life. Verlaine's almost cavalier attitude toward the term and what it had represented could thus easily be taken for a wholesale dismissal of the polemic that had held the attention of the literary public for the past few years.

Indeed, Verlaine was not the only protagonist of the literary debate on decadence and symbolism to consider the conflict with a certain historical detachment. In the *enquête*, Jean Moréas was still careful to defend his claim to the role of founder of the symbolist school, declaring that 'c'est moi le premier qui ai protesté, dès 1885, contre l'épiphète de *décadents*, dont on nous affublait, et c'est moi qui ai réclamé en même temps celle de *symboliste*' [it was me who first, since 1885, protested against the epithet of *decadents*, the grotesque mask with which we were decked, and it was me who at the same time made use of that of *symbolists*] (116). His leadership seemed confirmed by the banquet in the spring of 1891 in honour of his collection of poems *Pèlerin passionné*, and yet, a few months later Moréas too distanced himself from the movement. On 14 September 1891, in an open letter to *Le Figaro* he called for a return to the 'Gallic chain' that flourished from the troubadours to Racine and La Fontaine, and which the movements of the late eighteenth century and the nineteenth century – 'le Romantism et sa descendance parnassienne naturaliste et symboliste' [Romanticism and its Parnassian, naturalist, and symbolist lineage] (Mitchell 47) – had shattered. If 1891 might have been considered 'the auspicious date' of symbolism, as Ernest Raynaud has called it (*La mêlée symboliste (1890–1900)* 7), it was also a year in which, in several circles, the demise of the movement was seriously contemplated. And its rival of half a decade before was in no better shape. Only a year later Anatole Baju, who from the columns of his journal *Le Décadent* had sought to articulate the principles of the literary and cultural movement that he eventually dubbed, as an alternative to the ethically overdetermined decadentism, '*décadisme,*' proclaimed its end. In *L'anarchie littéraire,* a pamphlet written in 1892, he concluded his survey of the literary landscape by writing: 'Le Décadisme est mort et enterré: Le Décadent est un homme tellement parfait qu'il n'y en a plus. Presque personne aujourd'hui ne se réclame de cette école que le ridicule paraît avoir tuée. Il n'y a guère que Verlaine qui ne l'abandonne pas' [Decadism is dead and buried: The decadent is such a perfect man that there are no more examples of it. Nowadays practically no one refers to that school which seems to have been killed by ridicule. Only Verlaine does not abandon it] (34).

Decadentism and symbolism are dead: long live decadentism and symbolism ... In spite of their original proponents' somewhat premature obituaries, both of these early 'isms' of modernity have in fact enjoyed a long and prosperous life in literary histories. Thus, when the terms are now invoked it is not uncommon to make a distinction between narrowly conceived 'decadent' or 'symbolist' movements, with their journals and manifestoes, their leaders and polemics, and decadentism and symbolism as broad cultural tendencies with variable chronological and aesthetic boundaries, period terms that rival in scope what in the Anglo-American tradition is indicated as modernism. This problem is analysed by Laurence Porter in *The Crisis of French Symbolism*. Among the various 'criteria of periodization' that have been invoked to delimit symbolism (but a similar argument is also valid for decadentism), Porter identifies at the narrowest level of definition 'the publication of formal artistic manifestoes proclaiming a new school of writing,' and at the widest 'general current ideas; the zeitgeist' (14). Quite rightly, he finds both approaches (and the intermediate alternatives) lacking: the first would focus attention on a minor figure of symbolism, Moréas himself, and on a very limited period of time, the 1885–91, during which the poet consciously claimed the title of *caposcuola*. The second approach, exemplified by René Wellek's definition of symbolism as 'the broad movement in France between Nerval and Baudelaire to Claudel and Valéry' (qtd. Porter 16), would make it impossible to find a series of defining features encompassing the poetic production of all the figures inscribed in it.[26] Porter suggests an alternative interpretation: symbolism is the continuation and radicalization of the romantic questioning of the circuit of cultural communication. The romantics challenged the existing social, artistic, and linguistic institutions but not the very possibility of establishing alternative ways of communicating with their audience. For the symbolists, on the other hand, it was the very possibility of an effective communication that became dubious: 'Instead of challenging the audience's preconceptions regarding what poetry should say, and how, Symbolism disrupted the very communicative axis linking sender to message to receiver, thus calling into question the possibility of any communication whatsoever. The French Symbolist movement, then, was neither a coterie nor a system, but a crisis' (Porter 20). Such an interpretation of turn of the century poetry seems unexceptionable. And yet, isn't this 'symbolist crisis' part of a larger crisis in European letters that cuts across national traditions and generic boundaries, and that is characterized by a general questioning of the function of the artist and his relationship with his audience?

The point is not so much to determine, once and for all, the semantic field covered by the term symbolism, but rather to note the consonances, the overlappings, and the fruitful intersections between it and other terms that have been used to map late nineteenth- and early twentieth-century culture. Thus, for instance, in Italian literary historiography, it is decadentism that comes to define the crisis described by Porter. The term, introduced by Vittorio Pica in a series of articles dedicated to French literature in *La gazzetta letteraria*, entered the critical vocabulary as a concise (and negative) summation of the subjectivist turn of romantic and post-romantic poetry; through Benedetto Croce's mediation and its subsequent inscription in Italian historiography with the pioneering work of scholars such as Walter Binni it has come to indicate, although from a different theoretical perspective, the same crisis of representation that Porter identifies at the core of symbolism.[27] A similar inward turn is identified by Peter Bürger as the defining feature of what he prefers to call 'aestheticism,' a term that, by unifying the culture of the period under a label not invoked by the artists themselves, bypasses the whole debate over the relationship between decadentism and symbolism. In Bürger's reconstruction of the development of bourgeois art, aestheticism is the moment at which bourgeois art reaches 'the stage of self-reflection,' the moment when autonomy – 'apartness from the praxis of life' – is no longer only the condition characterizing the way art functions in bourgeois society, but also becomes its very content (Bürger 47–8).

The model of communication elaborated by Roman Jakobson will help to clarify what seems to be the common theoretical perspective of these different ways of accounting for the aesthetic production at the turn of the century. This model identifies six fundamental factors in language, summarized by the following diagram:

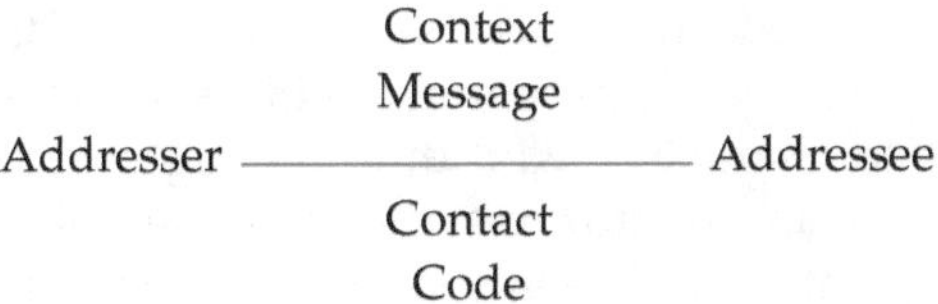

If we consider the type of communication that is postulated by the readings of fin-de-siècle literature we have discussed, we will be able to understand more clearly the features of its 'communication crisis.' On the one hand, there is a blockage in the relationship between addresser and addressee that is located at the level of the code. Many of the verbal experiments of fin-de-siècle poetry go in the direction of a renewal of language in which the decoding of the poetic message is not a function of the addressee's knowledge of a series of socially constituted rules, from those related to mere linguistic competence to those deriving from one's level of proficiency in the specific field of literary communication, but rather results from acquired competence in the system of signification elaborated by the addresser. I am thinking, for instance, of projects such as the one articulated in René Ghil's *Traité du verbe* (1886), which seeks to orchestrate the relationship between phonetic sounds, colours, and musical instruments, thus turning into a structured system Baudelaire's intuition of a synaesthetic relationship among different realms of sensory experience, best expressed in the sonnet 'Correspondences,' and Rimbaud's theorization of an associative relationship between colours and sounds in 'Voyelles.'

A further blockage can be observed at the level of the context – that is, in the referential function of language. As the content of the work of art becomes the self-fashioning of the artist himself, as in Huysmans's *À rebours* or D'Annunzio's *Il piacere*, it becomes more and more difficult to use language to bridge the gap between the space of the subject and the world of lived experience. The autonomy of the work of art that Bürger describes in terms of the transformation of the social status of the artist and of the work of art, unfolds itself, at the level of aesthetic communication, in a withdrawal of the artist within himself, and within the possibilities of a linguistic code unmoored from its socially constituted foundations.

Symbolism, decadentism, and aestheticism all name aspects of this general crisis, which involves not only the relationship between poet and audience, but also that between the aesthetic experience and the lived experience of modernity. Art, in modernity, finds the moment of its greatest freedom at the price of the loss of its dimension of collective experience that had characterized it until the eighteenth century, when it was organic to social institutions and was the object of a collective fruition.[28] The formation of the autonomous sphere of the aesthetic is one of the effects of the rise of bourgeois society: art, as Terry Eagleton has put it, becomes 'autonomous [...] of the various social functions which it had traditionally served' (9), but also loses its privileged status, its products becoming commodities whose value is ultimately determined by the marketplace. From this derives the peculiar double bind of the modernist artist, caught in this play between the absolute freedom of an aesthetic discourse that can reject all forms of traditional constrictions of code and content,[29] and the need to circulate his products in a social environment dominated by the rules of capitalist exchange. This is, as we will see, the contradiction against which the project of the decadents runs aground: on the one hand, the individual becomes the only validating principle of any aesthetic project, and the artist is thus absolutely free to articulate his program; on the other, that individual project must at least have the potential to become the seed for a social project – indeed, to acquire a mass following – in order for it to become visible in the market of symbolic goods, and this entails that the severed bond between artist and audience be somehow re-established. Freedom and invisibility go hand in hand, as the artist's marginality is both his triumph and his defeat. After the loss of his halo, the poet of Baudelaire's parable is both absolutely free ('I can walk about incognito, commit foul acts, and indulge in debauchery like ordinary mortals,' he says) and absolutely marginalized and invisible ('You're the only one who recognized me,' he tells his interlocutor) (445).

Here is the dilemma of modernism, which the movements that arise in the second half of the nineteenth century can only begin to thematize: how can artists bridge the gap between the social and the aesthetic without renouncing autonomy or surrendering completely to the commodification of their products? The dichotomy of modernism and mass culture – what Andreas Huyssen has influentially called 'the great divide' – has its origins in this crucial moment when the paradigmatic shift in the structuring of knowledge that gives rise to aesthetics, ethics, and science, all within the integrative horizon of the capitalist mode of production,[30] is accompanied, as we have noted above, by specific social and technological transformations within the ambit of the production and circulation of knowledge, such as the development of Linotype and the rotary press, the decrease in the price of newspapers (thanks to advertisements), and the increase in readership. By the 1880s, the commodification of the literary product was not simply a theoretical possibility, a threat on the horizon of the artist, but rather a present-day reality, made evident by the rise of popular literature, which in many cases was diffused by the first mass medium of modernity, the daily newspaper. Thus, the struggle for the autonomy of art waged by the poetic movements of that decade was already, to a certain extent, a rear-guard battle against a *de facto* transformation of the market of literary products that pushed the producers of 'high art' toward its economic margins. In other words, the literary product is already a Janus-like creature, which on the one hand seeks consecration according to the laws endogamous to it (such as publication by certain journals or publishing houses, reception by critics and other producers, etc), and on the other is an object of exchange regulated by the laws of offer and demand of the capitalist marketplace. Pierre Bourdieu has clearly described the tensions that structure the artistic field, which is, as he writes, 'the site of struggle between the two principles of hierarchization: the heteronomous principle favourable to those who dominate the field economically and politically (e.g. "bourgeois art") and the autonomous principle (e.g. "art for art's sake")' (40). Autonomy thus comes to constitute a kind of refuge from the pressures and regulations of the broader field of power, which includes, in a dominated position, the artistic field. In other words, within the field of power relations that structure capitalist society, artists, as a group with common interests, find themselves marginalized. However, the artistic field and the products within it remain illuminated by a sort of afterglow of the lost aura, and retain a degree of 'symbolic capital' that makes it possible for the subfield itself to be structured according to its own internal rules.

Two opposing principles of legitimation structure the artistic field in the second half of the nineteenth century. On the one hand, we have legitimation on the basis of economic profit and popular acclaim, which is the measure of the success of such products as the popular novel and theatre (the *feuilleton* and the vaudeville, for instance) and of bourgeois art. This type of legitimation obeys the general rules of the broader field of power, in which economic capital is the measure of the effectiveness of any productive enterprise. On the opposite side of the field are located works that find their legitimacy and their success in terms that invert those of the economic field: here we are confronted with the 'economic field reversed,' as Bourdieu has put it, since a key component of what measures the success of the producer is precisely his minimal or even non-existent margin of profit. In this case, other institutions come into play to evaluate the work of art and to determine the success of the artist: first and foremost, the other producers already endowed with symbolic capital, but also avant-garde publishers, and merchants who invest in the future reputation of this or that artist.[31] In any case, this articulation of the field ensures that an antagonistic relationship with the public is turned into a sign of innovation and seriousness: *épater les bourgeois* entails not only flaunting one's disdain for middle class moral and social values, but above all denying the validity of its foundational principle, the authority of the marketplace in determining success.[32]

The opposition between economic and symbolic capital reproduces, at the level of the artistic field, that between a literary production that does not call into question the relationship between addresser, addressee, and referent, and therefore presumes that it can provide a representation of reality that can be effectively decoded by its audience, and a literary production that makes no such claims, and that in fact affirms the incommensurable distance separating the artist from the public and art from the world. And yet, it is in the world that these works must also operate, and it is only through an audience that they can perform their function. This begins to explain an otherwise curious phenomenon: it is precisely at the moment when a writer's legitimation is inversely proportional to success that we witness a proliferation of extra-literary texts that discuss, explain, justify, and promote the literary and aesthetic project of this or that group. Furthermore, this debate often spills outside of the confines of the section of the field occupied by the avant-garde groups and into the popular press. In other words, if the works of the artists do not overtly seek an audience,[33] and at the furthest limit aim at a closed circuit of communication in which the artist himself constitutes the whole of his public, what becomes public is the discourse around the functions of art and the role of the artist carried out by both the specialized and the popular press.[34] In this context, the production of manifestoes and revues is functional to increasing the visibility of a certain group, while the work, in its splendid isolation, can turn into the virtue of increased symbolic capital the necessity of the limited circulation of the poetic production of the avant-garde.

The journal *Le Décadent* offers an interesting example of the role played by what we might call, with an expression taken from Gerard Genette, the 'epitextual' production of manifestoes and articles in shaping the public discourse on art and in re-establishing, through a new system of communication which flanks that enacted by the work of art, direct contact with a broad audience.[35] In fact, I would suggest that between aesthetic product and aesthetic discourse a kind of double loop is established whereby the latter both proclaims the values asserted by the work itself – that is, the autonomy of the work of art and of the artist *vis-à-vis* the social and economic norms regulating bourgeois life, the divorce of the language of art from the language of everyday social interaction, etc. – *and* simultaneously supplies to the *lack*, the gap or void in the communicative process resulting from the withdrawing of the artist in the space of his subjectivity. In this sense, the manifesto operates as the 'supplement' famously described by Jacques Derrida in *Of Grammatology*. While the work of art is itself a plenitude, a self-contained unit that finds in itself its own justification (and, as we have already seen, at the limit requires no audience – only a producer), the manifesto as supplement, while not invoking the identity of work of art, 'super-adds' something to the work from outside, it 'intervenes or insinuates itself *in-the-place-of*; it fills, it is as if one fills a void' (Derrida 145) – the void resulting from the breach in the relationship between artist and audience.

Anatole Baju, the Impresario of Decadence

Le Décadent was founded in 1886 by Anatole Baju, the son of a miller from Confolens, in the department of Charente. In 1884, at the age of twenty-three, Baju moved to Paris where he found employment as an adjunct schoolmaster in Saint-Denis.[36] Bonner Mitchell writes of Baju that 'he did not have the ambition of becoming a great poet but [...] was deeply interested in issues of literary theory' (15), a not too ungenerous description if one considers his limited output as a creative writer, which has contributed to the formation of an image of Baju as a kind of parasite of the main players of the literary arena (particularly Verlaine, who supported and frequently contributed to Baju's journal, and even applauded his coinage of the term *décadisme*), best summarized in Laurent Tailhade's scathing epigram

> Ce noble délire,
> Dieu! que ne l'ai-je eu?
> Je voudrais tant lire
> De vers de Baju! (qtd. Raynaud, *La mêlée symboliste (1870–1890)* 76)[37]

Baju's adoption of the term 'decadent' as the title for his literary paper has also been seen as an opportunistic move that allowed Baju to put himself in the position of theorist of decadence in spite of the fact that by 1886 the term was already in wide circulation as a label for certain antitraditionalist literary tendencies. Noël Richard has remarked that Baju and his disciples simply sought to exploit decadence after the notion itself had acquired cultural legitimacy with the publication, between 1880 and 1885, of its central texts, including Verlaine's 'Langueur,' Huysmans' *À rebours* and 'Adoré Floupette's' parodistic poems *Les déliquescences*, which became a literary event. Baju's journal thus seems to mark the culmination and even the beginning of the decline of the notion of decadence, a notion soon to be replaced as a general term for the poetic production of French avant-garde poets by that of symbolism. Michaud makes this suggestion clearly: '*Le Décadent* [..] proves that the idea has not died and [...] consecrates the term once and for all. But already at this moment other forces have come to the fore – forces of construction and synthesis which would quickly overcome the negative stage of decadence' (2: 262). And yet, the mediating function played by Baju and his journal is of interest here, and in this respect his role in the literary field was more positive and productive than is generally recognized, as his attempts to define the different elements that had coalesced into the notion of decadence both contributed to the further diffusion of the notion and to its formalization and *normalization* into a school, no matter how ephemeral. Furthermore, with the launch of the rival journal *Le Symboliste*, directed by Gustave Kahn with Moréas as editor in chief,[38] the opposition between the two schools – the decadents and the newly named symbolists, each faction well provided with its manifestoes and journals, its own flags for which to fight, to return to Verlaine's metaphor[39] – helped in turn to legitimize the two terms as major competitors in the struggle for the definition of modern poetry. While the terms of the confrontation may indeed have been subtle and more significant to the contributors of the two journals than to the public at large,[40] it is precisely the repeated circulation of the words that helped to project them into the consciousness of the public, not as the labels of two schools, but rather as broad poetic and even politico-cultural categories.

But do Baju's articles, for all their pretended authoritativeness, amount to a coherent program?[41] Even Baju himself characterized his *décadisme* as a purely negative movement, whose aim was not to articulate a new poetic theory but rather to clear the way for the literature of the future – a statement that indicates the very real uncertainties of Baju and his associates in translating their vague ideas into a clear policy. Already in the first issue of the journal, in an article signed 'Louis Villatte,' Baju had written: 'Nés du surblaséisme d'une civilization schopenhaueresque les Décadents ne sont pas une école littéraire. Leur mission n'est pas de fonder. Ils n'ont qu'à détruire, à tomber les veilleries et préparer les éléments fœtusiens de la grande littérature nationale du XXe siècle' [Born of the over-blasé offspring of a Schopenhauerian civilization, the decadents are not a literary school. Their mission is not to found one. All they have to do is destroy, topple all old things, and prepare the fetal elements of the great national literature of the twentieth century] ('Chronique littéraire' 3). The negativity of the decadent project was reasserted in the 1892 pamphlet *L'anarchie littérarie,* in which Baju, bitterly reflecting on the failure of bringing together the different strands of the literary avant-garde, wrote: 'L'école décadente, négative de sa nature, n'existait que comme force de destruction' [The decadent school, negative by its own nature, only existed as a force of destruction] (5).

And yet, week after week, in the editorials that opened the journal during its initial run, Baju outlined not so much a literary theory as an existential type, the decadent, thus helping to bring this figure down from the empyrean of the nobility of blood and taste to which its influential model, Huysmans's Des Esseintes, had consigned it and into everyday life. In this sense, and *contra* Baju's own initial statements, this turned out to be an eminently constructive and even political project, since it sought to articulate a response to the social and political questions raised by modernity. Like Des Esseintes, Baju's decadent finally had to acknowledge the impossibility of an existence *sub specie aesthetica,* in which the subject can find in art a refuge and a shelter from the strife of modern life.

Le Décadent lived through two incarnations, for a total of seventy issues neatly divided in two series of thirty-five each. The first series, entitled *Le Décadent littéraire & artistique* (though the second adjective was dropped after issue 18), first appeared on 10 April 1886 and was published until 4 December of the same year. The second series began after a one year hiatus in December 1887. Retitled *Le Décadent. Revue littéraire bi-mensuelle,* the publication had changed more than just its periodicity; it abandoned its previous newspaper format for that of the traditional literary review. This transformation was also reflected in Baju's rhetoric, which now avoided the pugnacious and polemical tone of his previous articles in favour of the more detached attitude of the critic. Significantly, with issue 33, the review was retitled *La France littéraire. Philosophie - critique - sociologie*; however the change did little to improve circulation and the journal ceased publication with issue 35 (May 1889).

The first series of *Le Décadent,* on which we will focus because of its more militant nature, was produced almost single-handedly by Baju, often writing under different pseudonyms such as Louis Villatte or Pierre Vareilles.[42] Among his collaborators, the most important and influential was by far Verlaine, who remained a sort of patron of Baju's enterprise throughout the three years of its life, but the most productive were Verlaine's friend, the painter Frédéric-Auguste Cazals (who used the pseudonym Georges Huguet) and the poet and critic Albert Aurier. The failed merger with the group of *La Vogue* made the participation of many of the younger symbolist poets in Baju's journal impossible, but Gustave Kahn, Rachilde, Rané Ghil, and some future members of the *École romane,* such as Maurice Du Plessys and Ernest Raynaud, occasionally contributed with poems, prose works, and critical articles. The four-page publication had a newspaper format, and was initially printed by Baju himself, with the help of his younger brother who had some experience as a typographer. It was rather spartan publication, and the 'homemade' nature in the first few issues was evidenced by frequent misprints. It opened regularly not with a literary text but, like a newspaper, with an editorial, a programmatic statement usually by Baju (though not always under his name) in which the journal took a position on a specific issue. This strategy of 'a manifesto every week,' as Joachim Schultz has described it (86), anticipated the intense manifesto activity of the historical avant-garde, and in particular of the Italian futurist movement, and had, most importantly, a key strategic function in the construction of the decadent movement and of the ideal type it publicized. If the disengagement of the artist from the practices of every day life carried the risk of making him and his products invisible in the literary field, the obsessive accumulation of texts that belong to the area of the field closer to a mass audience, journalism, made it possible to endow their author with another kind of visibility, that due to a cultural mediator rather than to a producer. Evidently, this strategy worked, as is witnessed by the at times impatient accounts of Baju's status in the mass-media as a spokesperson for decadence in the years in which his journal was published. Raynaud's recollections are again instructive. Summarizing Baju's contribution to the literary debate, he wrote:

> Furthermore, he did a great service to the new writers, because more than anyone he contributed to creating around them a profitable agitation. Let us not forget that all his articles were picked up and commented by the great press. During the polemic over Boulanger, the very powerful *Figaro* did not hesitate to oppose him to Maurice Barrés. It must be acknowledged that being able to give others such an illusion of oneself witnesses to more than an ordinary character. (*La mêlée symboliste (1870–1890)* 77–8)

As previously mentioned, the terms of the debate over decadence had already been delineated by the time that Baju decided to appropriate the term for his own program.[43] As early as the second half of the previously century, Edward Gibbon's *History of the Decline and Fall of the Roman Empire* (1776–88) had provided one of the most influential and powerful narratives guiding nineteenth-century historiography. Indeed, as Paolo Giovannetti has remarked, decadentism is first and foremost, 'an actual *philosophy of history*' (14), and even its identification with a theory of style, with a practice of literary production and reception, functions because style and literary production can be framed in terms of a diachronic narrative that traces their evolution toward the climax of contemporary refinement and formal elegance. Style itself is memory: on the one hand, it is the last remnant of past greatness, the polished surface that both conceals and redeems the decay of a civilization; on the other, it links the present to other moments of over-cultivation (Hellenism, the late Roman Empire, the rococo) and constructs the present as a repetition of the past, as its continuation and its destiny. The notion of decadence (and the term itself) was first linked with the domain of literary production by the French critic Désiré Nisard in his study of the poetry of the late Roman Empire *Études de mœurs et de cri-*

tique sur les poètes latins de la décadence (1834), in a context that revealed its ambiguous nature as both a historical marker and an aesthetic judgment. The poets of late Latinity belonged to the historical horizon of the decline of the Empire, but their poetic production was also the first to exhibit a series of traits that recur in other periods of decadence – a 'style of decadence' symptomatic, for Nisard, of an 'unusual state of exhaustion in which the richest imaginations can do nothing for true poetry, and are left with only the power to destroy language scandalously' (qtd. Calinescu 160). But it was Bourget, who, building upon Théophile Gautier's introduction to *Les fleurs du mal*, took Baudelaire's poetry as the foundation of a full-fledged 'theory of decadence,' as he entitled a section of his essay on the poet collected in the first volume of his *Essais de psychologie contemporaine*. With Bourget, decadence becomes a clearly delineated aesthetic category. In Bourget's theory, Nisard's exhausted cultural body is replaced by one riddled by disease, albeit a disease that is finally positive and even productive:

> Une société doit être assimilée à un organisme. Comme un organisme, en effet, elle se résout en une fédération d'organismes moindres, qui se résolvent eux-mêmes en une fédération de cellules. L'individu est la cellule sociale. Pour que l'organisme total fonctionne avec énergie, il est nécessaire que les organisme moindres fonctionnent avec énergie, mais avec une énergie subordonnée. [...] L'organisme social n'échappe pas à cette loi. Il entre en décadence aussitôt que la vie individuelle s'est exagérée sous l'influence du bien-être acquis de l'hérédité.
>
> [A society must be compared to an organism. Like an organism, in fact, it divides into a federation of minor organisms, which in turn divide into a federation of cells. The individual is that social cell. In order for this organism to function energetically, it is necessary that the minor organisms themselves function energetically, but with a subordinated energy, and in order for these minor organisms to function energetically, it is necessary that the cells that form them function energetically, but with a subordinated energy. The social organism does not escape this law. It enters into a state of decadence as soon as individual life is exaggerated under the influence of acquired well-being and of heredity.] (14)

Social and biological bodies share the common tendency towards decline, and this decline, inborn (hence the reference to heredity) and yet triggered by external factors (in this case, the achievement of a 'state of well-being,' of the sense of self-complacency of an imperial power or a bourgeois society at the peak of its development), is the result of a fragmentation of the body into its individual constituents, into shards of the once powerful unitary subject. Decadence is, finally, the severing of the connection between the individual and the social compact, the impossibility of integration of the inner life of the subject and the public affairs of the nation, which now become irreconcilable alternatives. Imagining the analysis of the 'social mechanism' on the part of a future 'pure psychologist,' Bourget writes:

> Voici à peu près comment il résonnera: 'Si les citoyens d'une décadence sont inférieurs comme ouvriers de la grandeur du pays, ne sont-ils pas très supérieurs comme artistes de l'intérieur de leur âme? S'ils sont malhabiles à l'action privée ou publique, n'est-ce point qu'ils sont trop habiles à la pensée solitaire?'
>
> [Here is how he will reason: 'If the citizens of a decadence are inferior as makers of the greatness of the country, aren't they much superior as artists of their own souls? If they are unskilled in private or public action, isn't it that they are too skilled in solitary thought?'] (15)

The antinomy between material and spiritual life, or action and thought, is marked by the very sharp distinction – made even more evident by the syntactical and lexical repetitions in the passage – between the *ouvriers*, the workers, on the one hand and the artists on the other. While the former work in and on the material world, the latter take the self, the inner space of their own subjectivity, as the material out of which to refine the quintessence of the work of art. Bourget sets not only the terms, but the very metaphorical arsenal for the discourse of decadence, so that, for instance, Paul Verlaine's 'Langueur' appears almost as a poetic re-articulation of Bourget's argument. Not only do we find the obvious opposition between the *ennui* of the 'Empire at the end of decadence' and the energy of the invading hordes, the 'great white Barbarians,' which Bourget shared with Nisard (though through an overturning of the latter's condemnation),[44] but we are also confronted with the complete disjunction between the life of the 'soul all alone' (*l'âme seulette*) and that of the world, whose echo arrives as a report of something hardly relevant and in any case occurring in a space perfectly foreign to that in which the soul carries on its existence: 'L'âme seulette a mal au cœur d'un ennui dense, / Là-bas on dit qu'il est de longs combats sanglants' [The soul, all alone feels in its heart the pain of a thick *ennui*. / They say that down there are taking place long bloody battles] (370–1).

Is this inward turn nothing more than a reaction formation to the shock of France's defeat in the Franco-Prussian war in 1870, which had resulted in the very real decline and fall of an empire, and to the self-inflicted wound of the Commune and its bloody suppression, as a number of commentators have suggested?[45] Certainly, the connection between the military defeat and a more insidious cultural colonization was easily made, so that when almost three decades later Saint-Georges de Bouhélier issued his own manifesto in *Le Figaro* (27 January 1897) to announce the foundation of naturism, a movement with very emphatically nationalistic overtones, he could write that 'Le triomphe de ces étrangers [Wagner, Nietzsche, and Ibsen] sur la littérature ethnique de nos pays nous semble plus terrible et mauvais que l'invasion des conquérantes armées allemandes' [The triumph of these foreigners on the autochthonous literature of our country seems to us more terrible and injurious than the invasion of the conquering German army] (Mitchell 57). And yet, the discourse of decadence also allowed the poets of the seventies and eighties to ground the transformations at work *within* the confines of the field of cultural production in terms of a general theory of history: just as the body appeared marked with signs that could allow the scientist to chart the evolution of the species, so cultural production could offer to the careful observer the symptoms that pointed to the transformations of the social body, the nation.

This short-circuit between biology and history constitutes the starting point of 'Aux Lecteurs!,' the text that opens the first issue of *Le Décadent*. 'Aux Lecteurs!' has traditionally been identified as the 'manifesto' of Baju's decadent group, even though Baju himself did not label it thus.[46] A comparison with Bourget's essay is instructive to understand the mechanisms of what we can call, using Claude Abastado's theory, a 'manifesto-like text' (*texte manifestaire*) (3), that is, a text which, even though it may not explicitly invoke that category, is related to the manifesto in terms of both structure and reception.[47] Bourget's tone is detached and analytical, and his vindication of decadent art and of Baudelaire in particular is cast in the form of a scientific investigation (an 'essay in contemporary psychology'), even going so far as to take the persona of the future social scientist charged with accounting for a phenomenon that, from his perspective, is of merely historical interest. Baju, on the contrary, assumes the role of the propagandist: he does not assess the state of things, but calls for an active, transformative practice that involves the reader directly, that calls him to take a position. He announces the presence of a plural subject on behalf of whom he speaks with assertions such as 'Nous ne nous occuperons de ce mouvement [decadence] qu'au point de la littérature' [we will not be concerned with this movement except than from the point of view of literature] or 'Nous serons les vedettes d'une littérature idéale' [we will be the scouts of an ideal literature] (1). Most importantly, the text seeks to establish that dialectic between margin and centre, which is a recurrent feature of manifesto writing.[48] The function of this text, in fact, is not only to establish the program of the group, which even becomes a secondary question, but rather to provide a map of the cultural landscape in which the relationship between the movements and figures endowed with symbolic capital and those, like Baju and his decadents, without it is clearly laid out. By proclaiming their otherness from and marginality in relation to the dominant discourses of the literary field – an operation of self-definition that becomes clearer and more explicit with later issues of the journal, in which Baju polemizes against both the naturalists and the bourgeois writers – the decadents endow their own program, no matter how indeterminate, with the solidity and the coher-ence deriving from the opposition to the common enemy. What does remain ambiguous, however, is the position of the reader, who is appealed to in the title but for whom there seems to be no place within the structure of the text: divided between the critical analysis of the situation and a description of what the decadents aim to achieve, Baju's opening salvo never quite decides whether to address the reader as an adversary, whose conventional good taste must be flogged, or as a potential ally and future decadent. This is an early instance of that ambiguous relationship between artist and audience, between the desire to re-assert and validate the autonomy of art, and the need to legitimize a cultural project through the formation of a specific audience within the larger body of 'mass' readership, which will also characterize futurism and the formations of the English avant-garde.

Baju first qualifies the more negative implications of the notion of decadence by identifying it with the 'transformation inéluctable' [inevitable transformation] that affects all human institutions – 'religion, mœurs, justice' [religion, morals, justice] ('Aux Lecteurs' 1) – but then moves on to define the specificities of modern decadence. In fact, the original aspect of Baju's appropriation of the notion is that it becomes disconnected from the historical precedent of the decline and fall of the

Roman Empire to become a definition of modernity *tout court*. As was the case with Bourget, Baju sets up a binary opposition in which the individual and society are the two mutually exclusive poles in the process of what he calls 'social evolution': the refinement of the individual, the transformation of everyday life into a work of art, is thus carried out at the expense of the solidity and integrity of the social compact, which breaks down and fragments into its constitutive elements, the individuals themselves: 'La société se désagère sous l'action corrosive d'une civilisation déliquescente' [Society disaggregates under the corrosive action of a deliquescent civilization] ('Aux Lecteurs' 1).[49]

The opposition of the individual and society is redoubled by that between the artist and the 'masses' as, issue after issue, Baju and his collaborators denounce the rival contemporary schools, and Zola's naturalism in particular, because of their accessibility to a mass public. In the third issue of *Le Décadent* Baju published an article (signed with the pseudonym Pierre Vareilles) that under the programmatic title 'Décadence,' openly declared the elitist nature of the movement:

> Parlons du mouvement littéraire. [...] Que dire de la littérature industrielle de MM. Zola, Ohnet et Co.? N'y a-t-il pas là les signes manifestes de la plus visible des décadences? A quelle époque avait-on jamais abaissé l'art au niveau des masses? Est-il indispensable qu'il soit à la portée de tout le monde.
>
> Non.
>
> Il doit être le partage d'une élite d'esprits éclairés, une sorte de sacerdoce inaccessible au vulgaire sous peine de n'être plus l'art.
>
> [Let us discuss the literary movement. It is known that it always follows a social movement. What can we say of the industrial literature of MM. Zola, Ohnet, & c.? Does it not display the most obvious signs of decadence? In what period has art ever been lowered to the level of the masses? Is it necessary that it be accessible to everyone [?]
>
> No.
>
> It must be the lot of an elite of enlightened spirits, of a sort of priesthood inaccessible to common people [*au vulgaire*] under pain of no longer being art.] (1)

Ultimately, the question at the core of the elitism of Baju's *décadisme* is a redefinition of the relationship between aesthetics and society in antithetical terms. This brings into relief the ambiguity of the very notion of decadence: what is destructive for the social fabric turns out to be beneficial for the individual, who can thrive and refine his tastes and desires in the face of a society that can no longer offer moral and ethical standards. Confronted by a decayed civilization, by a democracy ruled by the merely mathematical logic of 'numbers' and which therefore prefers 'se faire gouverner par vingt imbéciles que de se laisser conduire par un homme de génie!' [to let itself be governed by twenty imbeciles than to let itself be led by one man of genius!] (Baju, 'Quintessence' 1), the artist can escape its materialistic logic only through the cultivation of the self. The terms of Baju's socio-cultural polemic can be articulated through the following semiotic square:

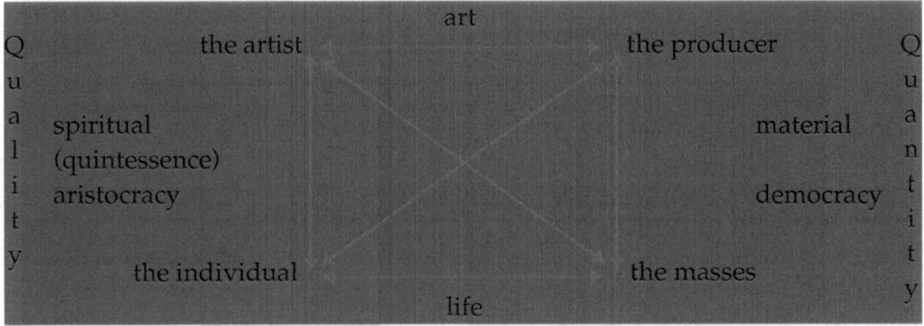

The work of the decadent artist finds its contrary in those of the naturalist and of the bourgeois writer (the novelist Georges Ohnet in particular had the dubious distinction of being singled out as the archetypal example of the latter group), the representatives of a literature accessible to a broad public and more generally, of a rising popular literature that brings the logic of industrial production into the aesthetic domain.[50] As Baju clarifies elsewhere, the decadent poet 'n'est pas un producteur. Il peut perpétrer un sonnet environ tous les six mois, ou quelque autre piécette de longueur analogue. Dans chacun de ses mots il met une portion de son âme immarcessible et on s'imagine inhaler en le lisant les spires d'une vie humaine' [is not a producer. He may commit a sonnet about once every six months, or some other little piece of similar length. In each of his words he puts a portion of his incorruptible soul and one imagines that in reading it one inhales the whorls of a human life] (Vareille, 'Le poète décadent' 2). The associative chain is clear and unambiguous: the writer of 'industrial literature' writes for a mass public, and is concerned with the material rewards offered by the literary field: a large readership and financial success. The decadent writer on the other hand obeys the internal laws of artistic production, in which the 'beautiful' object finds its justification within itself, so that public success is both unnecessary and potentially dangerous insofar as it brings into the precinct of art the laws of its other.

Quintessence or Institution? Language and the Autonomy of Art

In widening the trench – *'l'infranchissable fosse,'* as he himself puts it in 'Deux littératures' (1) – between the artist and the mob, however, Baju underscores the contradictory situation of the aesthetic experience in modernity. Indeed, there is a close relationship between this fracture and that of art and life, since it is precisely with modernity that aesthetics arises as an autonomous sphere of experience. Terry Eagleton explains this transformation clearly in *The Ideology of the Aesthetic.* While in pre-modern 'organic' societies the 'three mighty regions of the cognitive, the ethico-political and the libidinal-aesthetic' (366) were integrated within the horizon of theological discourse, and found in it and in each other the furthest limits toward which they could pursue their enquiry, with modernity these three spheres of experience become autonomous of each other and develop their own rules of legitimation, which are mutually incompatible.[51] Eagleton even formulates the 'exasperated' – yet profoundly convincing – argument that aesthetics arises at the moment of the death of art – not in the Hegelian sense, but rather in the more practical sense of its 'demise as a political force' (368). In other words, art becomes more and more integrated in the capitalist mode of production, its products turning into a form of commodity, yet the aesthetic promises to offer a realm of experience in which the constitutive aporia of capitalism is suppressed, if only momentarily. This, in Eagleton's reconstruction, is the power of the Kantian theorization of aesthetic judgement:

> The universal quality of the taste cannot spring from the object, which is purely contingent, or from any particular desire or interest of the subject, which are similarly parochial; so it must be a matter of the very cognitive structure of the subject itself, which is presumed to be invariable among all individuals. Part of what we enjoy in the aesthetic, then, is the knowledge that our very structural constitution as human subjects predisposes

> us to mutual harmony. It is as though prior to any determinate dialogue or debate, we are always already in agreement, *fashioned* to concur (96).

Thus, the pleasure of the aesthetic experience lies not only in its opening up of a territory apparently free of the purely instrumental logic that structures all other forms of experience in capitalist society – in other words, in offering 'a sphere that does not fall under the principle of the maximization of profit prevailing in all spheres of life,' as Bürger puts it (42) – but also, and perhaps most importantly, in constructing that sphere as the true grounding of human nature.[52] In a famous passage in *The Communist Manifesto*, Marx writes: 'The bourgeoisie, wherever it has got the upper hand, has put an end to all feudal, patriarchal, idyllic relations. It has pitilessly torn asunder the motley feudal ties that bound man to his "natural superiors," and has left remaining no other nexus between man and man than naked self-interest, than callous "cash payment"' (475). It is this atomization of society that the aesthetic seeks, at least in part, to heal. The transition from a feudal to a bourgeois society pivots on the 'invention' of the individual subject, whose relationship with the social body is determined not by the vagaries of birth and lineage, but by the individual achievements, quantifiable in economic terms, in the public arena. The individual entrepreneur becomes the hero of the narrative of capitalism, and, as Marshall Berman has remarked, one of the great bourgeois successes 'has been to liberate the human capacity and drive for development' (94). But if all social bonds are turned into economic relations, and pure and unmitigated antagonism becomes the only mechanism governing society, then bourgeois society carries within itself, in its very practices, the germs of its dissolution. The aesthetic provides the model for a form of experience that mediates between the subject and the universal, between individual freedom and a general rule, the normative power of which is all the more effective since it is not imposed from an outside source, but derives from lived experience itself. The aesthetic thus becomes a blueprint for all the forms of social relations that promise to reconcile individual self-interest and collective practice that can counter the centripetal force driving capitalism. The family, religion, academia, the legal system – the institutions that Louis Althusser has called 'Ideological State Apparatuses' – function, like the aesthetic, by offering a mediation between the individual and the collective by means of a law that has its roots not in the injunctions of a power extrinsic to the self, but in the free acceptance of customs and practices that experience inscribes in the individual. The individual subject thus becomes the source of its own subjection to the socially constituted structures that regulate its inscription within bourgeois society, and that serve to hold together that society itself.[53]

It is my claim that decadentism emerges as both a consequence and an acknowledgment of the failure of this integrative project. Bürger has pointed out that the ultimate result of the Kantian theorization of the aesthetic is the severing of the bond between art and the praxis of life, and 'the (erroneous) idea that the work of art is totally independent of society' (46). But this complete autonomization of the sphere of the aesthetic finds its counterpart in the formation of a new kind of cultural product whose relationship with the work of art is ambiguous since it shares with the work of art a number of formal characteristics, and yet is profoundly integrated in the marketplace. Industrial art is even the necessary correlative of 'high' art since the relative autonomy of the *soi-disant* work of art depends on the complementary presence of a fully commodified form of cultural production, against which it can claim its autonomous status.[54] In a sense, the question of what constitutes a work of art is addressed, at least partially, by the parallel question of what constitutes a cultural product as pure commodity, which would be its subjection to the laws of the marketplace. Thus, *a contrario*, the work of art is that cultural product which sternly refuses to obey those same laws. This, at least, is the self-understanding that dominates those sectors of the field – such as that occupied by avant-garde poetry – which find themselves in a dominated position in economic terms, and which thus invert – inversion being, after all, 'the master trope of decadence'[55] – the legitimating principle of the dominant field of production, and associate symbolic capital with lack of financial and popular success. Baju repeatedly describes this double articulation of the field of cultural production, most notably and coherently in the aptly titled 'Deux littératures:'

> Avec l'instruction profusée comme elle l'est aujourd'hui, dans vingt ans tout le monde saura lire. Il n'y aura plus d'ignorants: les ânes deviennent les animaux les plus rares de la nature : ils seront de phénoménales exceptions. Tous les plombiers de France et de Navarre sachant lire et écrire s'estimeront assez forts pour juger les oeuvres d'art. [...] On ne comprendra pas, c'est égal, on n'en formulera son jugement qu'avec plus d'assurance. C'est la mode au moment ; ce qu'on ne comprend pas on le déclare

incompréhensible, idiot, c'est plus tôt fait.

[With education as widespread as it is today, in twenty years everyone will be able to read. There will no longer be any ignorant people. Asses will becomes the rarest animals of the world; they will be exceptional phenomena. Since every plumber in France and Navarre will be able to read and write, they will believe themselves well equipped to judge works of art. If one does not understand, no matter, he will express his opinion with even greater assurance. It's the fashion of the times: what one does not understand, one declares incomprehensible, stupid, and that's readily taken care of.] (1)

Baju seems oblivious to the irony of a school master whose literary pretensions were fostered by the spread of literacy and the ensuing expansion of the market for periodicals blasting the nefarious results of universal education. And yet this is the symptom of a more widespread sense of uneasiness on the part of an intellectual class that refuses to adapt to the new market conditions, but remains otherwise unable to justify or legitimate its social function. For the romantics, poets could be, in the famous Shelleyan expression, 'the unacknowledged legislators of the World' (140), capable of giving shape, through their creative activity, to human thought and human relations. At a slightly lower level on the creative scale, they could perhaps be the 'avant-garde' of a social project elaborated by the philosophers but made tangible, communicable, and ultimately popularized by means of the 'weapons' peculiar to the artists, which strike directly 'the imagination and feelings of people,' as the Saint-Simonian Olinde Rodrigues had proposed in his dialogue 'L'Artiste, le savant et l'industriel' (qtd. Calinescu 103). The common element of these two alternative legitimation strategies lies in the fact that they both assign the artist a function that is at once critical and integrative. By the second half of the century, both options, far from justifying the work of the artist, have come to constitute the two different explanations of his marginalization. Shelley's 'unacknowledgment' becomes Baudelaire's loss of the halo. In this transition, the poet himself figuratively and literally joins his audience in questioning the social relevance of the work of poetry, and can at best become a mute witness to the ravages of capitalist society, which he can neither alleviate nor redeem.[56] On the contrary, Rodrigues's ideal coordination of the work of the artist with that of the ideologue ultimately results in the transformation of the former into a propagandist: since the power of art that Rodrigues describes is independent of its content, the sensuous appeal of the work of art can function equally well to buttress the existing power structures as to question them.

Decadent 'inversions' are thus only the counter-move to a more global process of inversion that diametrically re-arranges the network of relations linking the artistic and the socio-political spheres. Not only is the intellectual forced to renounce the claim to a guiding role in the evolution of society – a claim that linked both the Shelleyan and the Saint-Simonian declensions of the theme of the artist as prophet[57] – but he is also confronted with the invasion of the legitimating principles of the social and political spheres into that of the aesthetic. In other words, artists risk losing their guiding role even in the field that should be of their competence, namely that of aesthetic judgment, because the value of the work of art will be determined by the 'bad' consensus formed by the marketplace and embodied by the choices of the mass audience, the 'plumbers' from the provinces who, in Baju's account, having shelled out their hard-earned money in the purchase of a cultural product, have the gall of expressing their opinion on the subject.

Thus, the emergence of mass production and mass reception – and finally of mass media, of which industrial literature is the herald – also signals a profound transformation in the notion of the aesthetic as a unitary experience that connects the subject to the community. We are, in other words, in the presence of what Gianni Vattimo has defined 'aestheticization as an extension of the domain of mass media' (56): '[t]he mass media do not provide a means for the masses which is at the service of the masses; it is the means *of* the masses, in the sense that the masses as such are constituted by the mass media as a public realm of common consensus' (55). Industrial literature thus both fulfills and perverts the Kantian project: it connects the individual to a collective experience, but it does so not by eliciting free consent, but rather by carefully delimiting the individual subject's freedom. Horkheimer and Adorno have provided a classic account of this dynamic in their *Dialectic of Enlightenment*: 'Kant's formalism still expected a contribution from the individual, who was thought to relate the varied experiences of the senses to fundamental concepts; but industry robs the individual of his function. Its prime service to the customer is to do his schematizing for him' (124). The decadent artist refuses to become integrated into this system, but his solution, as articulated by Baju, is quite simply that of pulling up the draw bridge connecting the artist with the audience, and of seeking refuge in the citadel of Art, besieged by commercial products but – within its walls – free of their contamination.[58]

The question of the autonomy of the aesthetic thus returns to be central, although in the inverted form that we have seen above. It is no longer a question of the aesthetic offering an experience free of the instrumental logic of the economic sphere and 'providing the affective bonds which traverse the alienations of human life' (Eagleton 98–9); rather, it comes to define the impossibility of the dialogue between art and life, so that art, in order to retain its independence, renounces *a priori* to engage the sphere of experience, and in particular that of economic relations, which threatens to turn its products into commodities. Bürger summarizes well the double-edged nature of this notion of autonomy: 'Only after art, in nineteenth-century Aestheticism, has altogether detached itself from the praxis of life can the aesthetic develop "purely." But the other side of autonomy, art's lack of social impact, also becomes recognizable' (22). Autonomy becomes institutionalized not as the defining characteristic of the aesthetic experience, but more specifically of art and of the artist. The decadent artist no longer even considers the possibility of engaging an audience, and the perceived impossibility of acting in the present is sublimated by a projection of the distinctive truth carried by the work of art into the future. This explains one of the peculiarities of Baju's description of decadence, which is presented as *both* a decline and a rebirth, most especially in 'Le fumisme' (4 September 1886):

> Le progrès est lent mais éternel. L'humanité ascendra jusqu'à ce qu'elle s'identifie avec la Divinité. Hélas! une partie des hommes seulement ascend, la partie intelligente, l'autre, la plèbe a pu progresser jusqu'à ce jour et se dégager de ses plus grossiers instincts de barbarie primitive, il arrive fatalement une époque ou elle ne peut aller plus loin, où elle est forcée de s'arrêter et de stagner, clouée au sol par l'ignorance. Alors les classes supérieures continuent seules à se paraffiner et vont victorieusement à la conquête des secrets de la Science et de la Nature.
>
> [Progress is slow but eternal. Humanity will rise to the point of identifying with the Divinity. Alas! only one group of men rises, that of the intelligent; the other, the plebs, has been able to progress until now and to liberate itself of its coarser instincts of primitive barbarism – a time will inevitably come when they will not be able to go any further, when they will be forced to stop and stagnate, fixed by ignorance. Then the superior

classes alone will continue to refine themselves and will triumphantly move to conquer the secrets of Science and Nature.] (1)

Unlike later avant-garde experiences such as futurism, which envision a future resolution of the dichotomy between artists and audience through a series of practices aimed at blurring the two sides of artistic communication, Baju's decadent project sees in the widening of the gulf the validation of its radical separation from the public. In 'Deux littératures' he formulates a similar prediction:

> Les tendances égalitaires de notre époque auront produit ce résultat. Au lieu de l'égalité sociale et intellectuelle rêvée par le nivellement à outrance, on aura, avec les débris de toutes les castes détruites, formé deux classes nouvelles parfaitement délimitées et entre lesquelles aucune fusion ne sera possible à l'avenir.
>
> [The egalitarian tendencies of our age will produce the following result. Instead of the social and intellectual equality dreamed of by excessive levelling, there will form, along with the debris of all destroyed castes, two new classes perfectly delimited and between which no fusion will ever be possible in the future.] (1)

The rejection of the rules governing the circulation of commodities leads to a further 'inversion' in the structure of the decadent work of art as a communicative act. Thus, the model of production outlined by the semiotic square above can also function as a model of reception, in which the non-productive and non-for-profit (*economic* profit, of course) nature of the decadent work of art is carried to its limit in a short circuit that identifies producer and receiver, artist and audience: 'Il [the poet] a quelquefois douze lecteurs et, s'il n'en a pas du tout, il écrit pour lui seul. Il fait de l'art pour le plaisir de l'art' [Sometimes he has a dozen readers and, if he doesn't have any at all, he writes for himself. He makes art for the pleasure of art] ('Le poète décadent' 2). The circle is closed, and the 'deliquessence' of society finds its counterpoint in its cognate, 'quintessence' – the refinement of thought which is the aim of decadentism and which, Baju suggests, could even provide a more accurate label for the decadent school.[59] But this also solves the more pressing problem of where art must be situated in modernity. Granted, there are two types of artistic production, but the 'real' – or, to use Baju's term, 'official' – art, the one that rises above the contingency and materiality of life, is the art that peremptorily refuses to engage the world, and in particular rejects any immediate political practice. Thus Baju, the future socialist candidate, can recoil in the face of the Republic – whose legitimacy, however, the decadent writer does not dispute, as that too would imply an engagement with the practical world – finding instead refuge in the aristocracy of the mind that must seek its justification elsewhere.[60]

Language becomes the instrument for the re-articulation of the relationship between the artist and his audience, and for the reconstitution of a hierarchy of cultural production in which poetry returns to occupy a pre-eminent role, alternative to that of prose fiction.[61] As described by Baju, language is the ground on which the disgregation of the social body and the refinement of the individual reveal themselves. The language of the naturalist and bourgeois novel is oriented toward the direct and immediate apprehension and appropriation of the world through the deployment of words that are meant to signify reality in its adulterated materiality, through the rhetorical procedure that Roland Barthes has called 'the reality effect' whereby the 'useless details' of the text are invested with the function of signifying reality, of saying *'we are the real'* (148), thus short-circuiting, through a kind of 'referential illusion,' the distance between sign and referent, and flattening the plurivocity of language. Barthes concentrates on a functional analysis of the power of this procedure; however, its effectiveness lies in the moment of reception, to which Barthes also alludes when he discusses the 'reality effect' in terms of its relation to rhetoric. In other words, the relationship between words and things, between the domain of signs and extralinguistic reality is established at the moment when the text undergoes the process of interpretation. Umberto Eco's collection of essays *The Limits of Interpretation,* which further elaborates his theses on reception formulated as early as *Lector in fabula,* can be helpful in clarifying the problem. As Eco argues, the process of interpretation is the result of a dialectic relationship between what he calls the *'intentio operis'* – the 'the way in which the text foresees and directs [the reader's] interpretative operation' (45) – and the *'intentio lectoris'* – the structures of reception and the horizon of expectations that the reader brings to the text. It is within the narrows established by these two sets of parameters that the work of interpretation moves. But Eco's most important contribution to the debate is the affirmation of the profoundly social and intersubjective dimension of this process. He quite willingly acknowledges the theoretical validity of the Derridean critique of the metaphysics of presence – the well-known argument that signs do not reveal things but only refer, potentially *ad infinitum*, to other signs in an inexhaustible procession of metaphors (signs only point to and replace other signs). However, he also sets pragmatic limits to the semiotic drift implicit in the non-permeability between the order of language and the order of reality. Such limits lie not in the nature of things, but in the community of users of (a) language as 'guarantee of a nonintuitive, nonnaively realistic, but rather conjectural notion of truth' (39). In other words, even in the absence of a transcendental truth – which becomes at best merely a postulated 'possible and transitory end of every process' (41) – the process of semiosis itself produces 'a socially shared notion of the thing that the community is engaged to take as if it were in itself true' (41).

Thus, referentiality is the product of a social compact, and it becomes the first casualty in the decadent attack against socially constituted institutions. It is on the ground of language itself that the Bajutian artist articulates his difference from the crowd: while what speaks through everyday language is the collective voice of a community, to which it links the individual, what speaks through poetic language is rather the irreconcilable otherness of the poet, whose experiences cannot be contained within the boundaries of institutionalized language. In 'Aux lecteurs!' Baju had already asserted the centrality of language as both sign of and antidote to modern decadence. On the one hand, in fact, 'C'est dans la langue surtout que s'en manifeste les premiers symptômes [of decadence]' [It is in language above all that the first symptoms manifest themselves] (1). And yet on the other hand, the result is a renewal of language, as poetry becomes the expressive tool to voice the experience of modernity: 'A des besoins nouveaux correspondent des idées nouvelles, subtiles et nuancées à l'infini. De là nécessité de créer des vocables inouïs pour exprimer une telle complexité de sentiments et de sensations physiologiques' [New ideas, subtle and infinitely nuanced, correspond to new needs. Hence, the necessity to create unprecedented words to express such complexity of feelings and of physiological sensations] (1). The world becomes consumed by the book by being jettisoned from the scope of the poet, who surveys and gives voice not to the world, but rather to his own subjective experience, as Baju further explains in 'Quintessence:'

> N'est-ce pas leur but [the poets'] de chercher la quintessence des choses, d'en extraire le parfum le plus intense, pour produire en quelques instants une sarabande de visions frappantes donnant la sensation de la

manière des faits?

[Isn't their aim to seek the quintessence of things, to extract from them the most intense perfume, in order to produce, in a few instants, a saraband of striking visions giving the sensations of the manner of facts?] (1)

Thus, the poet articulates what everyday language forces into silence because it does not belong to its collective patrimony. The *de facto* ineffectuality of literary production in the realm of social and political life becomes, in Baju's articulation of the decadent program, its badge of honour, the mark of its alternative status to the materialist logic that permeates all domains of activity in capitalist society – in a word, its new *aura*. The artist sums up within himself the whole process of literary communication: he is the producer of an *œuvre* – himself – which finds in self-contemplation the moment of its reception.

To summarize, then, the semiotic square sketched above helps to lay out the implications of what are fundamentally two mutually incompatible models of (literary) communication. The popular artist writes for a mass audience, and aims at reaching it as broadly as possible. He performs successfully if he can translate his success in quantitative terms, but precisely because of this necessity to reach a broad audience he has to treat language as a social tool, in which consensus constitutes the foundation of the process of signification and the condition for the reception of the work. On the contrary, in the model proposed by Baju language is a private code that the artist can manipulate at will to bend it to the unseizable form of his emotions and sensations. The artist is his own subject, and at best his work can be approached by those who, like him, are willing to distill it of its socially constituted relation with referents outside of itself. For Baju/Vareilles, the thought of the decadent poet

n'apparaît pas toujours clarissime au premier coup d'œil, elle est souvent énigmorphe. Pour la tourbe lecturière, c'est du volapuk, mais pour l'aristocratie littéraire c'est un élixir désordinaire bon pour démorboser par ces temps de banalité splénétique.

On finit toujours par le comprendre et la satisfaction intime qu'on éprouve à deviner ses sphinxités nous dédommage amplement de notre laboriosité.

[will not always appear very clear at first, it is often enigmorphous. For the reading mob it is gibberish, but for the literary aristocracy it is the extraordinary elixir for demorbifying in these times of spleenetic banality.

One always ends by understanding it, and the intimate satisfaction one feels when fathoming its sphinxities fully repays us of our labour.] ('Le poète décadent' 2)

Baju's prose even attempts to perform what it asserts, deploying 'words unheard of,' the '*vocable inouïs*' already mentioned in the first issue of the journal: the '*enigmorphe*' thoughts of the decadent poet are represented by means of a neologism that actually bends language to take the shape of a mysterious, slippery concept – a new word corresponding to a new idea. Likewise, the work of the poet expresses '*sphinxités*,' a word which evokes a relationship between the reader and the text in which signs are equivocal and fundamentally undecipherable; only the individual acuity and ability to manipulate words – as in the encounter between Oedipus and the Sphinx – can provide an escape from the labyrinth of language.

It is in the attention to the formative power of language that we can also find an important point of contact between Baju's decadent program and the poetic project of symbolism, in spite of the personal differences among the members of the two schools. Mallarmé, in particular, distinguished between an instrumental use of language and an 'anti-nominalist' one in which language is returned to its 'virtuality,' to its capacity of signifying through allusions and indirect- ness, and thus of creating an experience that is consumed in language itself.

Narrer, enseigner, même décrire, cela va et encore qu'à chacun suffirait peut-être pour échanger la pensée humaine, de prendre ou de mettre dans la main d'autrui en silence une pièce de monnaie, l'emploi élémentaire du discours dessert l'universel *reportage* dont, la littérature exceptée, participe tout entre les genres d'écrits contemporains. [...]

Je dis: une fleur! et, hors de l'oubli où ma voix relègue aucun contour, en tant que quelque chose d'autre que les calices sus, musicalement se lève, idée même et suave, l'absente de tous bouquets.

Au contraire d'une fonction de numéraire facile et représentatif, comme le traite d'abord la foule, le dire, avant tout, rêve et chant, retrouve chez Poëte, par nécessité constitutive d'un art consacré aux fictions, sa virtualité. ('Crise de vers,' *Œuvres complètes* 368)

[Telling, teaching, even describing, that's all very well and yet all that would be needed perhaps for each of us to exchange our thoughts as humans would be to take from or leave in the hand of another a coin, in silence, but the elementary use of speech serves the universal reporting in

> which all the contemporary written genres participate, with the exception of literature. [...]
>
> I say: a flower! And from the oblivion to which my voice relegates all contours, as something other than the unmentioned calyces, musically arises, the idea itself, and sweet, the flower absent from all bouquets.
>
> Contrary to the facile numerical and representative functions, as the crowd first treats it, speech which is above all dream and song, finds again in the Poet, by a necessity that is part of an art consecrated to fictions, its virtuality.] ('Crise de vers,' *Mallarmé: The Poet and His Circle* 233)

This distinction clearly recalls the one articulated by Baju between the materiality of industrial literature and the ineffability of a poetic product that refuses to be 'accessible to everyone,' which we have seen in 'Decadence.' If anything, Baju is more open about the ideological implications of the divarication between instrumental and poetic language, as it is clearly presented as a sublimation of the poet's anxiety over the social role of the intellectual class. In ordinary communication, words are exchanged 'in silence' like coins; but coins are, of course, a peculiar kind of commodity, whose only function is to be exchanged for – translated into – something else. The poetic word can be preserved by withdrawing it from circulation, so to speak, and entrusting it to the artist who alone can endow it with its fullness of meaning. In this process the word is removed from language as a system of exchange: it no longer exists in syntagmatic and paradigmatic relation to the other elements of the system, in which identity is defined negatively, as a function of difference, of lack; instead, it shines in supreme isolation, pointing not to the materiality of social reality, but to the ideal plenitude of the poetic Absolute.

The Unrecoverable Halo: The Aristocrat and the Clown

In the previous sections I have sought to demonstrate that the 'crisis in communication,' (the terms of which were discussed above, pp. 57–65) is the result of the radical reorientation of the field of cultural production that follows the consolidation of capitalist economy and of the commodification of the work of art. We have seen that, as a consequence, the very notion of autonomy, which had characterized the discourse of aesthetics since its Kantian formulation, shifts from defining the integrative role of art between the individual and society to assuming the disjunctive function of separating the artist from the crowd. I want to return to this question to suggest that it is precisely at the point where Baju ends his blistering indictment of contemporary society that we can begin to perceive the discursive space in which the historical avant-garde will arise.

Consider for a moment Baju's comparison of art and politics. Although Baju had specifically renounced politics in 'Aux lecteurs!,' the subject reappears quite regularly in his manifestoes, if only so that the author could proclaim its incommensurability with art. In the fifth issue of *Le Décadent*, for instance, Baju opens his lead article 'Chronique' with the pointed statement that art and politics are two absolutely incompatible things. He then clarifies: 'Je ne veux pas dire la haute politique des Richelieu et autres hommes d'état: celle-ci se confie presque à l'art' [I don't mean the high politics of Richelieu and other men of state. That practically borders on art] (1). Needless to say, the opposition between seventeenth- and nineteenth-century politics reflects that between 'high' and industrial art. In the former, the elite endowed with symbolic or political capital defines itself in qualitative terms: the criterion by which the political class designates itself makes it impermeable to other social classes, insofar as its authority comes not from a worldly investiture but rather reflects the divine order. On the contrary, there is no qualitative difference between the representatives and their electors in the Republic that the decadents so vituperate: access to the governing body is determined, as in the case of success in popular literature, by quantitative means, that is, by votes in an election. Thus, the mechanism governing artistic production, the superior aesthetic quality of the work of art, is diametrically opposed to the quantitative principle that determines success in the political realm. That a politician may also be qualified to exercise power is not a matter that interests Baju, since he is concerned not with the domain of practical politics but rather with the rhetoric that governs the self-understanding of the political and the artistic system. In other words, from Baju's perspective the qualifications of elected officials are uninfluential insofar as they are not what guarantees their position. Likewise, the decadent leader does not even contemplate the possibility that a 'serious' artist may also encounter popular favor, since that would prove that the artist has compromised himself to popular taste. As he writes in August 1886, taking up the metaphor of art as priesthood that we have already seen at work in other manifestoes:

> Ils s'imaginent, ces démocratiseurs, avec leur esprit de nivellement à outrance, démocratiser l'art ce qu'il y a de plus aristocratique par sa nature,

de plus inaccessible à la profanité des tourbes. Ils ne savent pas que c'est un sacerdoce réservé à quelques initiés et que les tendances égalitaires de notre époque sont impuissantes à lui porter la plus légère atteinte.

[These democratizers, with their excessive levelling, imagine that they can democratize art, which is, by its own nature, the most aristocratic thing, the most inaccessible to the desecration of the mobs. They do not know that it is a priesthood reserved for a few initiates, and that the egalitarian tendencies of our age are powerless to strike the slightest blow against it.] ('Eux' 1)

Significantly, the article is entitled 'Eux' [Them]. The opposition between 'them,' a pronoun behind which the author ranges all the adversaries – in mass politics and mass culture – of his movement, and 'us,' used here and elsewhere in Baju's programmatic texts to designate himself and his companions is an uncompromising antinomy that cannot be recomposed because the rules governing successful performance in the two camps are incompatible.[62]

But the identification of artists and aristocrats in which Baju likes to indulge opens *décadisme* to a moment of insight. The question that Baju can only thematize indirectly is whether 'high' art, like the aristocracy, has not *already* lived through its phase of dissolution. Baju's opposition of high and industrial art rests on the premise of the coexistence of two mutually exclusive but equally viable principles of validation: that of the field of cultural production and that of the field of economic relations. The example of the aristocracy, however, is indicative of the unevenness of the relationship between the two fields and their respective principles of legitimation, since the residual presence of the aristocracy as both an economic and political element is a function of the ability of its individual members to conform to the rules of the game of bourgeois democracy and capitalist economy. Likewise, in the literary domain the proclamation of art as a religion whose rituals are performed by a selected and self-selecting cadre of initiates is effective only as long as it can be more than an endogamous ceremonial, and can be inserted into the cultural debate via the channels that are proper to it. Such channels include the same popular press that made journals such as *Le Décadent* possible, which turned, however briefly, people like Baju into national figures, and which initiated and continued on its pages the debate on decadentism, symbolism, and other fin-de-siècle 'isms' (here that assiduous arena for manifestoes, *Le Figaro*, played a key role). In other words, the recovery of the aura as the distinctive characteristic of the work of art in relation to the commodity can occur at precisely the moment in which the aura itself has turned into a form of commodity.

Eagleton has written that '[f]rom Romanticism to modernism, art strives to turn to advantage the autonomy which its commodity status has forced upon it, making virtue out of grim necessity' (370). This formulation is both icastic and convincing, and yet it only partially accounts for the modernist crisis. He continues: 'Autonomy in the worrying sense – social functionlessness – is wrenched into autonomy in a more productive sense: art as a deliberate turning upon itself, as a mute gesture of resistance to a social order which, in Adorno's phrase, holds a gun to its head. Aesthetic autonomy becomes a kind of negative politics' (370). And yet, the 'worry' never quite goes away, a 'mute gesture' is always dangerously close to not being seen or heard, and if a work is to seek an audience, to point out to *someone* an alternative to the capitalist logic of productivity and profit, then it must be able to engage its public, to establish the link that the decadents reject *a priori*. Baju is better suited to diagnosing the disease and forecasting its potential complications than to indicating a cure: clearly, the danger is to turn the artist into a producer, to submit the 'other' truths of art (disinterestedness, pleasure) to that of the market; and yet, is the splendid isolation of the ivory tower, the nostalgia for a nobility of blood, a valid alternative?

Thus, the aristocrat becomes the vehicle for Baju's metaphoric representation not of the isolation and superiority of the artist, but of his contradictory condition. The clearest formulation of this insight is the piece that opens issue 9 of *Le Décadent*, 'Zim Boum!'

> Entrez Mesdames, entrez Messieurs! le spectacle n'est pas ordinaire et vaut la peine qu'on s'y arrête. Entendez-vous les sons d'un orchestre colossal? Ceux qui soufflent dans ces cuivres ne sont pas de vulgaires musiciens ramassés dans l'écume des villes.
>
> Ce sont des virtuoses, des talents, des génies, des gens du monde, tout ce qu'il y a de select. Ils daignent d'offrir en pâture à vos regards inassouvis du beau, parce que vous même êtes un public choisi e capable de les apprécier.
>
> Entrez Messieurs, entrez Mesdames, surtout. C'est pour vous que ces fils de nos preux se sont emmaillotés dans des habits de clowns. C'est pour procurer quelques rares et précieuses sensations à votre existence blasée et épuisée par la nérvosité moderne.

ZIM-BOUM! C'est le cirque de Molier. Entrez, c'est commencé.

> [Come in, Ladies and Gentlemen! This is not an ordinary show, and it is worth your while to stop. Do you hear the sound of a colossal orchestra? Those who blow into this brass are not vulgar musicians scraped together from the scum of the city.
>
> These are virtuosos, men of talent, geniuses, men of the world, everything of choice that one can find. They condescend to offering themselves as fodder for your gazes unsatiated of beauty, because you are yourself a select audience who can appreciate them.
>
> Come in, Gentlemen, and above all, come in, Ladies. It is for you that the children of our heroes are swaddled in clown suits. It is in order to stir something rare and precious in your blasé existence, enervated by modern nervousness.
>
> ZIM-BOUM! It's the Molier circus. Come in, it's about to begin.] (1)

The circus performer was not a wholly new metaphor for the decayed condition of art in bourgeois society, having previously been used by, among others, Baudelaire – who once again turns out to be the most insightful anatomist of the transformation of the aesthetic discourse in modernity – on several occasions (for instance, in one of the *Fleurs du mal*, 'La muse vénale,' which even in its title thematizes the question of the commodification of art).[63] Like Baju's decadent discourse, the poem is structured around the opposition of the aspiration for the ideal, which is the way in which poetry as an institution – the muse – understands its mission and the necessities of living in the material world. Thus, while the muse is 'amante des palais' [in love with palaces] and yearns to glean 'l'ór des voûtes azurées' [gold out of the azure vaults], she finds herself forced either to perform empty rituals, singing, like an altar boy, *Te Deums* in which she does not believe or, like a 'saltimbanque à jeun' [a starving mountebank], to sell its charms '[p]our fair épanouir la rate du vulgaire' [to bring amusement to the vulgar crowd] (*Œuvres complètes* 1: 15 / *Flowers of Evil* 27). However, in Baju's version of the scene, the performers have become the decayed descendants of an ancient aristocracy of blood and deed: the equestrian Mlle X, whose nobility 'dates back to the crusades' and whose very face reveals the 'majesty' of her lineage; or the Count of Z., descendant of generals and ministers, whose 'forms of an uncommon virility' serve him to perform exercises at the horizontal bar. Baju's noblemen and noblewomen, still circumfused by the glow of their titles and in spite of their condescension, find themselves on display like clowns and entertainers, engaged in the same act of audience seduction that is characteristic of modern politicians and popular writers.

Finally, then, 'Zim Boum!' is the moment of recognition – albeit one that is quickly repressed in the official discourse of the movement – of the failure of aestheticism as a project of redemption of art through its removal from the engagement with the audience, and through the closure of the circuit linking the producer to the consumer by folding the institution within itself and identifying the two roles. As we will see in chapter 2, it is precisely by thematizing the question of the position of the audience in the process of aesthetic communication that the movements of the avant-garde will articulate their response to the problem of how to bridge the gap between art and consumption.

Chapter Two

A Poetics of Modernity: Futurism as the Overturning of Aestheticism

On 20 February 1909 the Parisian daily *Le Figaro* published on its front page a three-column piece by Filippo Tommaso Marinetti that was destined to become one of the central documents of the avant-garde: the manifesto best known by its Italian title, 'Fondazione e manifesto del futurismo,' but which on its first appearance carried the much more sober headline, 'Le Futurisme.'[1] It was preceded by an editorial note that questioned its supposedly disruptive potential: 'Le *Figaro* qui a déjà servi de tribune à plusieurs d'entre elles [literary schools], et non des moindres,' says the jaded editorialist, 'offre aujourd'hui à ses lecteurs le manifeste des "Futuristes"' [*Le Figaro*, which has already provided a forum to numerous literary schools, and not the least important, offers today the manifesto of "Futurism" to its readers] (Caruso, *Manifesti* 0).[2] Although, as the note makes clear, futurism was by no means the first literary movement or the first 'ism' to appear on the scene of European culture, much has been written about the foundational role of this manifesto, indicated by several commentators as a pivotal point in the history of the avant-garde and of twentieth-century aesthetics. For Luciano De Maria, one of the Italian scholars most closely associated with the critical re-discovery of futurism in the 1960s, futurism was 'the first movement [...] with an artistic and extra-artistic global ideology' ('Il ruolo di Marinetti' 34), the pattern of which was to be followed by Dada and surrealism.[3] Charles Russell calls futurism 'the first fully formed' and 'the first truly international avant-garde movement,' establishing 'a pattern of personal and artistic behavior that would shape many contemporary and subsequent avant-garde and modernist movements' (87–8); Giovanni Lista goes so far as to proclaim the front page of *Le Figaro* of 20 February 1909 as 'the true act of birth of this century' (*Futurisme* 79). Even a scholar such as Alberto Asor Rosa, who is ideologically distant from futurism – and not always generous in his consideration of the movement – has indicated in this originary quality its important contribution to European culture, suggesting that it represents the first Italian intellectual and artistic movement to have continental and even world-wide resonance since the seventeenth century.[4] Such readings may be amply justified by the future articulations of the historical avant-garde and precisely by the practice of manifesto-writing, which constantly returns the founders of new movements back to the discourse of absolute innovation and of rupture with the past that Marinetti's 'Le Futurisme' certainly foregrounds. And yet, they perhaps also accept too unquestioningly Marinetti's own representation of his cultural project as an absolutely new beginning, as the point of origin of a new (cultural) age. Marinetti's ambition stands out in few places as clearly as in the introduction to the 1925 volume *I nuovi poeti futuristi*:

> Le parole in libertà spaccano in due nettamente la storia del pensiero e della poesia umana, da Omero all'ultimo fiato lirico della terra.
>
> Prima di noi paroliberisti, gli uomini hanno sempre cantato come Omero, con la successione narrativa e il catalogo logico di fatti, immagini, idee. Fra i versi di Omero e quelli di Gabriele D'Annunzio non esiste differenza sostanziale.
>
> Le nostre tavole parolibere, invece, ci distinguono finalmente da Omero poiché non contengono più la successione narrativa, ma la poliespressione simultanea del mondo.
>
> [Words in freedom clearly cleave in two parts the history of thought and of human poetry, from Homer to the last lyrical breath on earth.
>
> Before us *paroliberi* [free-word poets], men have always sung like Homer, with a narrative succession and a logical catalogue of facts, images, ideas. There is no substantial difference between Homer's verses and those of Gabriele D'Annunzio.
>
> On the contrary, our free-word tables finally distinguish us from Homer because they no longer contain narrative succession, but the simultaneous poli-expression of the world.] (*TIF* 187)

The 'aesthetics of rupture' underlying the first manifesto of Futurism and the rhetorical and formal strategies through which the movement is constructed as a radical break with the cultural past will be discussed in detail in this chapter. However, the discourse of origins and originality is a tricky business; it is first necessary to question the historical narrative implicit both in Marinetti's account of futurism and in that of some of its commentators. In fact, the very notion of a linear historical progression underlying the experience of the avant-garde may in the end be problematic: thus, it will be more useful if, instead of a history of the avant-garde starting around 1909, we consider the possibility of reconstructing a genealogy of futurism that will also serve to suggest a possible trajectory for the futurist project after its inception. The different perspective entailed by a genealogical enterprise is clearly delineated by Paolo Valesio: 'Genealogy distinguishes itself from the usual historical chain of connections because of its lack of abstraction and rationalistic ambition. Its logic is, in fact, that of "*x* son of *y*," and not that of "*x* effect of *y*." When we grasp any historical relation as a concrete personal relation, we have grasped a genealogy' (14). A genealogical perspective will thus bring to light the return, in the manifestoes and as a result in futurism itself, of a series of repressed anxieties over the roles of the artist and the work of art that characterize nineteenth-century culture – anxieties that futurism will recast in terms of an agonistic program of renewal, better to elaborate the avant-garde project of transforming the relationship between art and life.

In this sense, the question of origins will remain significant only if we rethink the notion not as an absolute beginning, although that is precisely how futurism will present it, but rather as a node that in fact, in Walter Benjamin's words, has 'nothing to do with genesis': 'The term origin is not intended to describe the process by which the existent comes into being, but rather to describe that which emerges from the process of becoming and disappearance' (*Origin* 45). In other words, the origin of futurism can be read as the result of a powerful dialectical process that forces Marinetti to confront and discard a series of options regarding the place of the intellectual in modernity, and to forge out of these possibilities a new project that seems to offer an effective escape from the strictures of the models handed down by the symbolist and decadent traditions. Thus, the text that most bears witness to this process, the first manifesto, will present the traces of what has been discarded – left behind in the whirlpool of the originary moment – and at the same time will open up space for the emergence of a new project whose features remain, at least initially, undefined. Futurism thus aims as much at closing a certain historical experience as at opening a new one, and in this fundamental instability lie both its originality and its originary quality: if futurism inaugurates the twentieth century, it is perhaps most importantly because it seeks to provide closure to the nineteenth.[5]

FROM DECADENTISM TO FUTURISM

Marinetti 1898–1908: Portrait of the Futurist as a Young Decadent

The question of the origin of the movement returns obsessively throughout Marinetti's futurist *œuvre*. Undeniably, after the consolidation of the fascist regime and the return of the futurist leader within the fold of the party, assertions about the primacy of the artistic movement over Mussolini's party seem to have had little more than a consolatory function, as if the fact that it had played St John the Baptist to the fascist Messiah could provide a kind of vicarious function to a movement whose political ambitions had been clearly curtailed and which, in spite of its rhetoric, had been forced to retreat on the terrain of the aesthetic. Thus, it is not surprising to find that on the very same page of *Futurismo e Fascismo* – a text published in 1924 that represents a very public recantation of the doubts and suspicions regarding the revolutionary nature of fascism that had pushed the author outside of the party in 1920[6] – Marinetti makes a claim to primacy writing that the First World War victory at Vittorio Veneto and the advent of fascism 'costituiscono la realizzazione del programma minimo futurista' [constitute the realization of the minimal program of futurism] and simultaneously acknowledges the marginal role of futurism itself within the regime: 'Il Futurismo è un movimento artistico e ideologico. Interviene nelle lotte politiche soltanto nelle ore di grave pericolo per la Nazione' [Futurism is an artistic and ideological movement. It intervenes in political struggles only in the hour of direst danger for the nation] (*TIF* 494).[7] But in 1915, at what he perceived as another turning point – the entrance of Italy into the European conflict – Marinetti had already prefaced the collection of manifestoes entitled *Guerra sola igiene del mondo* with a text that attempted to take stock of the situation of Futurism and to outline a first micro-history of the movement.[8]

The text opens with a recollection of the moment of foundation of futurism itself. It is not, as we will see, the first time that Marinetti recalls this turning point, but here, instead of projecting it onto a mythopoetic level, as in the manifesto of foundation, he clearly localizes it in time (and, in practice, also in space, since the reference to *Poesia* links it to Marinetti's editorial activities in Milan):

> Il giorno 11 ottobre 1908, dopo aver lavorato per 6 anni nella mia rivista internazionale «Poesia» per liberare dai ceppi tradizionali e mercantili il genio lirico italiano minacciato di morte, sentii ad un tratto che gli articoli, le poesie e le polemiche non bastavano più. Bisognava assolutamente cambiar metodo, scendere nelle vie, dar l'assalto ai teatri e introdurre il pugno nella lotta artistica.

> [On 11 October 1908, after having worked for six years on my international journal *Poesia* to free the Italian lyrical genius, under the threat of death, from its traditional and mercantile blocks, I suddenly felt that articles, poems, and polemics were no longer enough. We must absolutely change method, go into the streets, assault theatres, and introduce the fist into the artistic struggle.] (*TIF* 235)

Marinetti presents this moment of transition as a sudden illumination, comparable to the state of intuition described in the coda to the 'Manifesto tecnico della letteratura futurista,' the 'Risposte alle obiezioni': 'Per *intuizione,* intendo dunque uno stato del pensiero quasi interamente intuitivo e inscosciente' [By *intuition* I mean therefore an almost entirely intuitive and unconscious state of thought] (*TIF* 56). But a more careful consideration of the decade between Marinetti's first introduction into the milieu of fin-de-siècle poetry and the foundation of futurism offers a more complex picture of his artistic maturation, and suggests that futurism was the result of a long period of gestation and of confrontation with the poetics of decadentism and symbolism that constituted the horizon within which it was conceived.

Marinetti was born Emilio Angelo Carlo Marinetti in 1876 in the Egyptian city of Alexandria, where his father Enrico had relocated in 1873 to practice law and to escape the problems surrounding his unusual familial situation, since his companion (and the mother of the future poet), Amalia Grolli, was already married.[9] Marinetti's cultural formation was from the beginning open to diverse influences. While his mother, an enthusiastic and discerning reader of poetry, introduced him to Italian and European classics, Marinetti's formal education at the Jesuit college Saint François Xavier, which catered to the foreign elite of the Egyptian city, was in French, the language to which he also turned for his earliest literary efforts, published between 1894 and 1895 in a small self-produced magazine *Le Papyrus: revue bi-mensuelle littéraire, artistique, fantaisiste et mondaine,* of which he issued 21 numbers. The articles published by the young Marinetti in his eclectic periodical show a keen interest not only for literary issues but also for social and political ones, and an early fascination with anarchism that also marked his later writings, including the first manifesto of futurism. After being expelled from Saint Xavier, Marinetti completed his *baccalauréat* in Paris, where he lived from April to July 1894, and then rejoined his parents who in the meantime had returned to Milan. In November of that year, he followed his father's wishes and enrolled at the University of Pavia to study law, eventually completing his studies at the University of Genoa in 1899 with a thesis on the role of the sovereign in a parliamentary government. If his enthusiasm for a legal career was less than whole-hearted – 'Pur adorando mio padre odio tutti i problemi giuridici e i divieti della legge' [although I love my father I hate all juridical problems and all legal proscriptions], he was to write in his memoirs *Una sensibilità italiana nata in Egitto* (206) – his enthusiasm for poetry remained on the contrary as lively as in his Egyptian youth, and was further fostered by recurrent, if often short, sojourns in Paris, where he frequented the literary salons and became acquainted with many important figures of the turn-of-the-century artistic milieu. In 1898 his poem 'Les vieux marins' was awarded first prize in the poetry competition of the *Samedis populaires* organized by the symbolist poets Gustave Kahn and Catulle Mendès; and, in the following years, Marinetti began a fruitful and frequent collaboration with several of the periodicals associated with the symbolist movement (*La Vogue, La Plume, La renovation esthétique,* etc.), through which he established himself both as a poet and as a cultural liaison between Italy and France, regularly writing on Italian poetry for French reviews, and on French poetry for Italian publications.

Marinetti also had the opportunity to demonstrate his considerable organizational skills quite early on in his career. In April 1898 he replaced Renzo Ermes Ceschina (future founder of the homonymous publishing house) on the editorial staff of the journal *Anthologie-Revue de France et d'Italie,* founded in Milan by the poet Edward Sansot-Orland with the financial support of the Triestine expatriate Ernesta Stern, whose Parisian salon Marinetti frequented. The initial aim of the periodical was to provide a point of encounter and mediation between French symbolist culture and contemporary Italian poetry. In January 1898, however, the *Anthologie-Revue* marked the departure of its editorial line from its earlier eclecticism by adding the subtitle 'Organe de la Renaissance Latine,' and thus openly entering the debate on what Michel Décaudin has famously called 'the crisis of symbolist values.' In the notion of 'Latin Renaissance' converged throughout the 1890s a series of cultural movements and projects that found a common denominator in the rejection – or at least the critique – of the cultural and literary values associated with the decadent/symbolist *koiné,* interpreted as a deviation from the national traditions of the Latin countries as a result of the influence of Germanic and Slavic culture.[10] As we have already seen, in 1886, the erstwhile theoretician of symbolism, Jean Moréas, founded the 'école romane' with the intention of returning contemporary poetry to the principles of harmony and order in the classical tradition, the development of which had been interupted by the advent of romanticism and its late-nineteenth-century naturalist and symbolist offshoots. More influentially, Eugène-Melchior de Vogüe published an essay entitled 'La Renaissance Latine' in the *Revue des deux mondes* on January 1895 in which he predicted the advent of a cultural renaissance of Latin countries, of which the works of Gabriele d'Annunzio were the earliest and most significant example. In Italy, too, the project of rebirth had great resonance: it was, for instance, one of the central issues debated by Ugo Ojetti with his interlocutors in his *enquête Alla ricerca dei letterati* (1895); it was also the topic of a survey sponsored by the Florentine periodical *Il Marzocco* (which at the turn of the century was close to the D'Annunzio's circle) and published in the issues from 26 December 1897 to 30 January 1898.

The idea of a Latin Renaissance also had clear political implications, as was the case with one of its most original formulations, the naturist movement. Founded by the young essayist and future playwright Saint-Georges de Bouhélier, *naturisme* had made itself known to the public through a gesture that should be by now familiar: the publication of a manifesto in *Le Figaro* (10 January 1897). As was to happen with Marinetti's first manifesto, Saint-Georges de Bouhélier's was introduced by an editorial note that, in spite of its ironic tone, allows us to isolate quite clearly the concerns of the new movement: 'Où vont ces jeunes gens – ou plutôt où retournent-ils?' it asked. 'Ils le disent: à la simplicité, à la clarité – à la nature. Ils sont contre Ibsen pour Zola, contre Nietzsche pour Diderot, et contre Wagner pour Jean-Jacques ... Après les hallucinations et les névroses du symbolisme, il paraît d'assister à une sorte de convalescence des esprits' [Where are these young people going – or, rather, where are they returning? They say: to simplicity, to clarity – to nature. They are against Ibsen for Zola, against Nietzsche for Diderot, against Wagner for Jean-Jacques ... After the hallucinations and neuroses of symbolism, it seems that we are about to witness a sort of convalescence of the spirit] (Mitchell 55). Indeed, as we have mentioned in the previous chapter, the program outlined in the manifesto mixes a nationalist rhetoric, in which it is not difficult to perceive the still smarting wound of defeat in the Franco-Prussian war, with the intention of returning to a classical conception of art that is the heritage of Latin nations.[11] Another element of interest in the manifesto of *naturisme* is the appeal to a poetry that will be capable of returning poets to mix 'aux tribus' [with the tribes] (60): a poetry, in other words, that will rediscover its social function by taking as its object not the individual but the community. That the particular target of the critique is decadentism is clear from the examples that illustrate Bouhélier's program: 'Au lieu d'évoquer de charmantes amantes et de sauves seigneurs chimériques,' he writes, 'nous chanterons les hautes fêtes de l'homme' [Instead of evoking charming lovers and chimeric lords, we will sing the high festivals of men] (59–60). The naturists solve the ever-present question of the relationship between art and life by imagining an organic society composed of 'les marins, les laboureurs nés des entrailles du sol et les pasteurs qui habitent près des aigles' [sailors, labourers born of the bowels of the earth, and shepherds who live near the eagles] (60), free of the contradictions and social conflict that characterizes capitalism, in which the poet can return to play his sacral role of spokesperson for the collective practices of the tribe (not surprisingly, the poet who is put forward as model, namely Hesiod, casts de Bouhélier's discourse back into the space of myth).[12]

The debate thus proceeded along two parallel lines: on the one hand, the affirmation of the necessity of a return to tradition that, in Latin cultures, is supposedly founded on the principles of harmony and simplicity; on the other, the intention of finding a positive solution to the artist's condition of alienation that symbolism had eloquently articulated. Marinetti, who published his first poem in the March 1898 issue of the *Anthologie-Revue*, appears significantly out of synchrony with the 'Latin' program of the journal. Not only did his poetic production demonstrate a close allegiance to symbolism; even his critical writings seemed to defend those very figures and values which the Latin Renaissance called into question. In a review of Lorenzo Perosi's oratorio *La resurrezione di Lazzaro* (September 1898), for instance, Marinetti openly expressed his admiration for Wagner. More significantly, in an insightful critical appraisal of the work of the critic Vittorio Pica, the future leader of futurism articulated an eloquent defense of decadentism, of the 'anarchy of form' and *vers libre* (invoking his *maître* Gustave Kahn), mustering as relevant examples *L'après-midi d'une faune* of the 'sublime poet' (132) Mallarmé and, once again, Wagner's opera.[13] What is finally most striking about the article is the fact that its symbolic structure already looks forward to the manifestoes of futurism, but with an inverted polarity. Consider a particularly telling passage in which Marinetti, following Pica, argues that contemporary literary schools are but a reflection of the age:

> Nous portons sans doute, un poids considérable d'ancêtres et notre sang a charrié à travers les siècles trop de désirs, de joies et de douleurs! La littérature doit reproduire nécessairement nos angoisses frissonantes nos sanglots et nos trébuchantes ivresses, «nos maladies» si vous voulez. Se plaindre des modernes écoles avancées c'est se plaindre d'un miroir parce qu'il reproduit exactement un visage qui nous déplait.
>
> [We carry, without a doubt, a considerable weight of ancestors and our blood has conveyed down the centuries too many desires, joys and pains! Literature must necessarily reproduce our quivering anguishes and our heavy inebriations, 'our illnesses,' if you will. To complain of the modern advanced schools is to complain of a mirror because it reproduces exactly a face which displeases us.] ('Vittorio Pica' 131)

The weight of the past and of the exhaustion ensuing from its pressure on the present is of course one of the structuring themes of the manifesto of foundation of futurism, and more in general, of the rhetoric of the movement, but in this early phase of his career, Marinetti declines it, coherently with the discourse of decadentism, in terms of an inevitable destiny to which modern literature is consigned.

The *Anthologie-Revue* ceased to exist as an independent journal by merging with *La Vogue* in April 1900. The following year, Marinetti implicitly declared the failure of the project of a Latin Renaissance in one of his most important pre-futurist statements of poetics, a review of Pietro Mascagni's opera *Le maschere* published in *La Plume* on 15 February and significantly entitled 'Mascagni contra Wagner.'[14] The opening night of the opera on 17 January – a complex event that, in an unprecedented publicity stunt, was presented simultaneously in six different Italian cities[15] – constituted the culmination of a long process of gestation that had begun as early as August 1896. Mascagni's correspondence with the librettist Luigi Illica shows that, in spite of the difficulties in completing the project, the composer was convinced from the beginning of the validity and the positive outcome of his attempt to return to the Italian tradition of the *commedia dell'arte*. Indeed, in an interview published by *La Perseveranza* on the occasion of the 1907 revival of the opera, Mascagni described his work as a renewal of 'i simboli dello spirito italico, sano, autentico' [the symbols of the healthy, authentic Italian spirit] (Morini 1: 335), of the serenity of the Italian tradition forgotten since the days of Gioacchino Rossini. While the identity of the adversary against which this struggle for health and serenity was to be fought was left unspoken on that occasion, the composer was more forthcoming in two public speeches delivered around the time of the completion of *La maschere*. Speaking at the Teatro Goldoni in Venice early in 1900 on the topic of the evolution of music, Mascagni had distinguished two musical genres: the symphonic, charac-terized by 'poche idee e molta scienza' [few ideas and much knowledge] (Morini 2: 134) and the dramatic, which conversely displays little knowledge and many ideas. These, however, are not merely two stylistic options: rather, they are two national styles, that divide between them the 'peoples' of Europe, and explain the tendency of Italian composers towards opera.

> La musica, come l'idioma, è lo specchio fedele del carattere di un popolo. Nel melodramma è sintetizzata mirabilmente tutta la vita delle genti latine, e del popolo italiano in specie. La musica sinfonica rispecchia l'indole pensosa, dialettica, austera dei popoli del nord.
>
> [Music, like language, is the faithful mirror of the character of a people. The life of the Latin populations, and of the Italian people in particular, is admirably synthesized in melodrama. Symphonic music mirros the thoughtful, dialectical, austere attitude of the peoples of the north.] (Morini 2:134)

For Mascagni, as for de Bouhélier, the 'people' – which, as is typical of the rhetoric of both romanticism and the Italian Risorgimento, is identified with the 'nation' *tout court* – is the repository of the true and authentic cultural values of a tradition. Thus, the return to a formula and a series of situations that are perceived as popular, the *commedia dell'arte*, serves precisely to free art of the incrustations of the pernicious influence of a foreign culture, which is by definition alternative to and incompatible with the autochtonous tradition, and which has swayed it from its legitimate path of development. This is the foreign influence that *Le maschere* was designed to confront, as if Mascagni were correcting a historical error, and resetting the clock of Italian opera back to pre-Wagnerian days.

That Wagner and, more specifically, his influence on Italian music are the ultimate target of Mascagni's polemic becomes clear in another conference, also held in 1900, in which Mascagni was called to commemorate the composer Nicola Piccinni. In the conference, Mascagni again articulated a binary opposition in which Rossini, with his motto 'melodia semplice e varietà nel ritmo' [simple melody and variety in rhythm], was invoked as the archetypal figure representing the Italian tradition, now openly opposed to Wagner, who represented the opposite tendency in which music is subordinated to the necessities of dramatic action. Significantly, the Rossinian lineage is specifically Italian and includes Alessandro Scarlatti, Nicola Piccinini, and Giuseppe Verdi, while the representatives of the other fundamental inclination are French and German: Jean-Baptiste Lully, Christoph Willibald Gluck, and of course Wagner himself. In fact, Mascagni did not deny the importance of Wagner; in an *enquête* sponsored in 1902 by the Committee of the Press Exhibition in Copenhagen he referred to Wagner as 'un riformatore dell'arte musicale' [a reformer of musical art] (Morini 2: 150), albeit one whose grandiose *œuvre* Mascagni saw as destined to remain isolated. Rather, he questioned the effect of Wagner's propensity for theoretical statements and formulations, which had led to a purely scientific or philological approach on the part of his less talented Italian disciples, as he further argued at a 1903 conference. Hence, Mascagni's return to Rossini and to the Italian tradition was a return to music that 'si indirizzava al sentimento e non alla convinzione, che parlava al cuore piuttosto che alla mente' [addressed feelings and not convictions, that spoke to the heart rather than to the mind] (Morini 2; 148). And if Mascagni does not make use of the language of decadence and renaissance to characterize his own enterprise, his argument still belongs to that horizon, as can be seen in the conclusion of his conference on Piccinni, in which he called for a true and sincere art – *arte vera e sincera* – that would set aside all the recipes and theoretical formulations that 'questo secolo neurotico ha imposto agli esangui' [this neurotic century has imposed upon the weak]. Once more, the polluted, diseased body of national culture, which has succumbed to the epochal disease of the fin-de-siècle, needs to be purged and made healthy again.[16]

Contrary to its author's expectations, *Le maschere* flopped on opening night, enjoying a degree of popular success only in Rome, where it was directed by the composer himself. Marinetti relates the events of the momentous night:

> Dans la soirée du 17 janvier, à la rampe de six principaux théâtres, à Milan, à Venise, à Turin, à Gênes, à Rome, à Vérone, Pietro Mascagni livrait une bataille audacieuse contre la polyphonie allemande en donnant son opéra *Le maschere.*
>
> L'auteur de *Guillaume Ratcliff* et de *Iris*, avait annoncé un peu partout la prochaine résurrection de l'antique mélodrame italien. Tout en s'inclinant devant le génie prodigieux de Wagner, il dénonçait le péril d'asservir l'opéra italien aux complexités orchestrales modernes, et voulait revenir aux proportions harmonieuses de la musique de Rossini.
>
> [On the evening of 17 January, on the stages of six major theatres, in Milan, in Venice, in Turin, in Genoa, in Rome, in Verona, Pietro Mascagni engaged a daring battle against German polyphony by staging his opera *Le maschere.*
>
> The author of *Guglielmo Ratcliff* and of *Iris* had announced everywhere the coming resurrection of ancient Italian melodrama. Even as he bowed to the extraordinary genius of Wagner, he denounced the danger of subjecting Italian opera to modern orchestral complexities, and wanted to return to the harmonious proportions of Rossini's music.] (127)

In a remarkable example of 'simultaneity' *avant la lettre*, Marinetti juxtaposes the local failure of the opera in Milan to that of the other cities, from which hourly telegrams reported on the proceedings of the evening. The total debacle led Marinetti to question not so much the reasons for the defeat, but more in general, whether the battle 'contre la polyphonie, le complexe, le raffiné, pouvait-elle être gagnée' [against polyphony, complexity, refinement could be won at all] (127), that is, whether a simple return to tradition could offer a solution to the sense of cultural crisis represented by the success of decadent culture.

Marinetti's answer, and his ensuing analysis of the significance of Wagner, takes as its starting point Nietzsche's interpretation of the composer as cultural symptom. Indeed, the very title of the article is an echo of Nietzsche's *Nietzsche contra Wagner,* and the German philosopher is here openly invoked for the first time in Marinetti's *œuvre.* Berghaus has already pointed out that Marinetti probably began reading Nietzsche in his student years, noting convincingly for instance, the parallelisms between a number of the poems collected in the 1904 volume *Destruction* and both *Zarathustra* and *The Gay Science* (53–5).[17] Both *The Case of Wagner* and *Nietzsche contra Wagner* had been translated in a volume with *The Twilight of the Idols* by Henri Albert published by Mercure de France in 1899,[18] and the rise of Nietzsche's influence in France at the turn of the century can be correlated to the wane in fashion for Wagnerian opera. Ironically, in certain quarters it was Nietzsche himself who became the spear carrier for a sort of 'Latin renaissance.' In an article published in *Mercure de France* in January 1903, for instance, the decadent novelist Édouard Dujardin (who in 1885 had founded the *Revue wagnérienne*) announced the rebirth of a national French music with composers such as Debussy and Saint-Saëns, and, after noting that 'Wagner est à la mode, c'est-à-dire qu'il n'est plus aimé ni compris' [Wagner is fashionable, that is, neither loved nor understood], concluded that 'Les temps changent. L'esprit allemand, par un admirable phénomène, vient de se nier lui-même en produisant le grand homme qui, allemand, représente la pure tradition française classique; je veux parler de Nietzsche' [Times change. By a marvelous phenomenon, the German spirit denies itself in producing the great man who, though German, represents the pure classical French tradition: I mean Nietzsche] (qtd. Le Rider 69).

Marinetti's appropriation of Nietzsche is more ambiguous and reveals his difficulty in articulating an alternative to the decadent poetics already delineated in his article on Pica. For Marinetti, the modernity of Wagner's style lies in precisely those elements that provide the basis for Nietzsche's condemnation, namely Wagner's neglect for the totality of music in favour of the detached elements of phrase, word, and gesture. In *The Case of Wagner* Nietzsche relates the music of his former idol to the question of life that he had already addressed in the second of his *Untimely Meditations.* Referring to literature, he writes: 'What is the sign of every *literary decadence*? That life no longer dwells in the whole. The word becomes sovereign and leaps out of the sentence, the sentence reaches out and obscures the meaning of the page, the page gains life at the expense of the whole – the whole is no longer a whole' (*Case of Wagner* 170). We will return to the question of 'life' later. For now, what is interesting is the fact that Marinetti substantially accepts Nietzsche's diagnosis – he calls it 'une magnifique synthese philosophique' [a magnificent philosophical synthesis] (127) – while at the same time turning it upside down as the basis for his definition of modernity. Implicitly, the metaphor of the mirror is still at work here: the impoverishment of life – of which Wagner's music is, for Marinetti, a symptom – is the reality of modernity that art – as he had already argued in discussing Pica – can only reflect. Thus, Nietzsche is coupled with Bourget, who, in *Essais de psychologie contemporaine* had first articulated the notion of decadence as social pathology – that is, as a sickness not of the individual sensibility, but of society as a whole – and more specifically as a pathology that expressed itself in the fragmentation of unitary structures into constituent elements: thus, the isolated page replaces the book, and the individual replaces social cohesion.[19] While recognizing that Nietzsche points to a cultural crisis that has implications with which the culture of decadentism has not fully dealt, Marinetti sides with the theorists and the practitioners of decadence in terms that recall Baju's celebration of the isolated poem: 'Les meilleurs d'entre nous (les plus vaillants ou les plus chanceux!) ne se contentent-ils pas d'avoir une seule page radieuse dans leur vie?' [do not the best among us (the bravest or most fortunate) content themselves with a single radiant page in their lives?] ('Mascagni contra Wagner' 128). His apology can only conclude with a trenchant answer to his own question of whether the confrontation with Wagner should have been engaged at all: 'Le retour vers le simple et la ligne classique est donc impossible! Non, décidément, la bataille ne pouvait être gagnée!' [The return to simplicity and to the classic line is therefore impossible! No, definitely, the battle cannot be won!] (128). But the question remains of where exactly contemporary culture is going: if a return to the safe haven of tradition is not possible, as Mascagni's failure seems to prove, Marinetti cannot fully dispel the sense of uncertainty that results from his own double fascination with Wagner and Nietzsche, since the latter, too, is advocating not a return to an impossible classicism as a solution to decadence, but rather what he calls in *The Twilight of the Idols* 'saying Yes to life even in its strangest and hardest problems' (562). In other words, Wagner and Nietzsche provide the two poles within which futurism will take its first steps: art and life.

Wagner's artistic practice becomes the correlative of a praxis of life in which the separate domains of experience cannot be recomposed in a meaningful whole, and in which non-quantifiable needs and desires are marginalized into the domain of art, in the 'radiant page' whose brightness cannot illuminate other forms of experience. And yet, within the Mallarmean horizon within which Marinetti's poetry is still located, it is precisely through the isolated fragment that the infinite may open up: 'Nous sommes portés vers les *défauts* de Wagner, l'amour de la nunace, l'indéfini, l'insaissable' [We are drawn towards Wagner's *flaws*, his love for nuances, for the indefinite, for the unseizable] (128). The individual detail or word, released from its function within the scene or syntactical unit – released, in other words, from its function as an instrument of communication – is endowed with the power of suggesting, through an infinite approximation, what cannot be named, as Mallarmé had taught a whole generation of poets with his answer to Huret's 'enquête': '*Nommer* un objet, c'est supprimer les trois faite du bonheur de deviner peu à peu; le *suggérer*, voilà le rêve. C'est le parfait usage de ce mystère qui constitue le symbole: évoquer petit à petit un objet pour montrer un état d'âme, ou, inversement, choisir un objet et en dégager un état d'âme, par une série de déchiffrements' [*Naming* an object means suppressing three quarters of the pleasure of the poem, which is made of the happiness of conjecturing little by little. *Suggesting*, that is the dream. It is the perfect use of this mystery that constitutes the symbol: evoking an object little by little to show a state of consciousness or, conversely, choosing an object to draw from it a state of consciousness through a series of decipherings] (Huret 60).

Nietzsche, on the other hand, points to the need to return to life, although on what terms is precisely what Marinetti will attempt to work out in his way to and in his early theorization of futurism. In any case, the important aspect of this early essay is the sense of impasse that Marinetti clearly perceives, although he defines it as a characteristic of modernity, and identifies it *tout court* with decadence. Decadence, in fact, is not the aftermath of a cultural crisis; rather, it announces the crisis: 'La chevauchée du lucre et de la gloire est harasante. Un élan terrible nous pousse vers la crise, l'istant culminant et le spasme doulaureaux qui epuise, appauvrit, obscurcit toute notre vie de son excès de lumière accumulée' [The path of profit and glory is a wearisome one. A terrible impetus pushes us toward the crisis, the culminating instant, and the painful spasm which exhausts, impoverishes, darkens our life from the excessive light it has accumulated] (128). The question that Futurism will seek to address is precisely how to engage such a crisis.

The First Manifesto: Marinetti's 'Modernolatry' between Decadence and Futurism

The themes of the journey and of 'speed' emerge gradually in Marinetti's poetry. In the collection entitled *Déstruction* (1904), the typical romantic and symbolist motif of the 'invitation au voyage,' – to quote the title of Baudelaire's poem that is certainly its genealogical progenitor – returns insistently, with interesting variations. In the epilogue, 'Invocation à la Mer Vengeresse,' the poet invites his 'heart' to depart on a journey that leaves behind the material world, to voyage, 'sans pilote, sans voile et sans mâts/ [...] vers l'arc profond et fascinant de l'horizon' [without skipper, without sail, without masts / toward the profound and fascinating arc of the horizon] (*Scritti francesi* 259). In 'Le torrent millénaire,'[20] the second poem of the section entitled 'Le démon de la vitesse,' the vehicle is a modern tramway but the goal is the same: the poet, accompanied this time by his 'soul,' embarks on a journey beyond the earthly, physical bounds of existence, and the machine comes to symbolize the power of unbridled imagination, which transfigures the night into a phantasmagoria of light. In both poems, the lyric subject invokes the destruction of reality, by the irrational forces of nature: specifically, by the sea in 'Invocation,' and by technology in 'Le torrent millénaire.' In fact, in the latter poem we can already see the beginning of the identification between nature and technology that Marinetti will later theorize in manifestoes such as 'L'uomo metallizzato e il regno della macchina.' At this point, however, the equation is important because it allows Marinetti to abstract technology from any socio-economic context and to identify it symbolically with power and energy.

This process continues in his third and last volume of pre-futurist poetry, *La ville charnelle* (1908), which closes with the prose poem 'La Mort tient le volant ...,' inspired (according to the epigraph) by the 1907 'Speed Cup' run in Brescia, but also somewhat prescient of the famous accident that Marinetti will repeatedly use in the mythopoetic fashioning of the movement, which we will consider in a moment.[21] In 'La Mort tient le volant ...' Marinetti imagines an automobile race in which a number of fantastical drivers, in their even more fantastical vehicles, defy Death. The poem is a veritable treasure trove of *art nouveau* flourishes and decorative motifs. The vehicles are described as: 'un grand jaguar métallique encore engourdi de sommeil' [a great metallic jaguar still torpid with sleep]; 'chars étranges aux formes agressives [qui o]n eût dit d'énormes revolvers à quatre roues' [strange vehicles of aggressive shape which one would have taken for enormous four-wheeled revolvers]; 'une tourte monstrueuse tiraillée par des forbans coiffés de rouge' [a monstrous turtle pulled by corsairs with red hats] (*Scritti francesi* 368–9). What is interesting, in any case, is the concluding section, which reports the cries of the *chauffeurs*:

> Plus vite que le vent! Plus vite que la foudre!... [...] En vérité... en vétité, on peut bien lancer sa machine sur la cascade de l'averse, en montant vers les nues à grands coup de moteur! [...] Il s'agit de vouloir! Se détache qui veut!... Monte au ciel qui désire!... Triomphe qui croit!... Il faut croire et vouloir!... [...] O mon coeur explosif et détonnant, qui t'empêche de terrasser la Mort?... Qui te défend de commander à l'Impossible?... Et rends-toi immortel, d'un coup de volonté!...
>
> [Faster than the wind! Faster than lightning!... In truth... in truth, we could push our vehicle on the falls of the flood, rising to the clouds by the strength of our engines! It is a matter of willing it! Those who will it, will leave the earth!... Those who wish it, will fly to the sky!...Those who believe will triumph! We must believe and will!... Oh, my explosive and thundering heart, who prevents you from vanquishing Death?... Who forbids you from commanding the Impossible?... And to make yourself immortal by a stroke of will!] (*Scritti francesi* 371)

Several elements make this passage remarkable, aside from its strident rhetoric. First, the machine, although transfigured into a kind of mythical creature,[22] becomes the instrument for overcoming the exhaustion of decadent culture: the struggle with death, which Marinetti stages throughout his early symbolist works is nothing other than a dramatization – almost a literal translation – of the 'culture of crisis' that Marinetti substantially accepted in his essays on Pica and on Mascagni and Wagner. Furthermore, the appeal to the will allows us to determine more clearly the influence of Nietzschean thought on Marinetti. According to Nietzsche, will is the instrument of life, but, as Zarathustra announces in one of the central sections of *Thus Spoke Zarathustra,* such will is not a mere 'will to existence,' a kind of Darwinian struggle for survival,[23] but rather a 'will to power,' understood as a will to self-overcoming. The connection between will and self-creation is explicitly articulated in the final sequence of 'La Mort tient le volant ...' quoted above, in which the overcoming of the material conditions of the subject, its being bound to the earth, is translated into an act of will that allows it to soar into the skies. This is one of the earliest articulations of the myth of flight, the declensions of which run across the history of the movement, from Marinetti's decadent-futurist novel *Mafarka le futuriste* to the theorization of aero-poetry and aero-painting. But there is something else in *Zarathustra* that makes this appropriation interesting. Nietzsche's prophet describes the will as a constant becoming, a recurrent destruction of what has been founded: 'That I must be struggle and a becoming and an end and an opposition to ends – alas, whoever guesses what is my will should also guess on what *crooked* path it must proceed' (227). Becoming is thus both an end and an opposition to ends: in other words, the end, the goal, is not, teleologically, a point of arrival, but rather, the becoming itself, so that any such point is in turn a new point of departure: 'What I create and however much I love it,' Zarathustra continues, '– soon I must oppose it and my love' (227). In 'La Mort tient le volant...,' too, movement is disengaged from any purposefulness. In 'Invocation à la Mer vengeresse' Marinetti could entrust his delivery from 'squalid reality' to a mysterious 'Au-delà' beyond the arc of the horizon, to a destination which can only be dreamed: 'Voici d'ailleurs, tous les vaisseaux étincelants du Rêve/ s'alignent dans le grand large! ... [There, moreover, all the shining vessels of the dream / line up on the open sea] muses the persona of the poet (*Scritti francesi* 259). But this destination, in any case, constitutes the unachievable and yet longed for point of arrival of the poetic journey. In 'La Mort tient le volant...,' on the contrary, it is the journey – or rather, movement, since a journey presupposes a point of arrival – that becomes the aim of the drivers. Space is the enemy that speed destroys, as a mechanic screams to the pilots: 'Voici ton ennemi: l'Espace!... l'Espace devant toi!... Tue-le donc!... Décharges-toi sur lui à brûle-pourpoint!' [There is your enemy: Space!... Space before you!... Kill it, then!... Discharge upon it, at point blank] (370). In the end the metallic jaguar overcomes death itself, biting 'dans son scaphandre vitré de diamants' [into its armor studded with diamonds] (371).

The reappearance of the theme of speed in the manifesto of futurism, and specifically in the eighth of the famous eleven points that constitute the programmatic section of the first manifesto of futurism – 'Il Tempo e lo Spazio morirono ieri. Noi viviamo già nell'assoluto, poiché abbiamo già creata l'eterna velocità onnipresente' [Time and space died yesterday. We already live in the absolute, since we have already created eternal, omnipresent speed] (*TIF* 10–11) – is thus not simply evidence of the sudden appropriation of technological modernity to articulate a new aesthetic project. The theme of speed witnesses to the continuity between Marinetti's pre- and post-futurist poetics. Futurism, in other words, emerges from the interaction of the two very different discourses of late nineteenth-century symbolist poetry and of technological modernity.

In a recent study of Marinetti's practice of *paroliberismo*, Clara Orban has related the language of the manifesto to the growing circulation of Albert Einstein's theory of relativity in the first decade of the century (12: 59–60), which would have provided, at least on the surface, a scientific justification for the futurist interest in the dynamic aspects of reality.[24] A more nuanced account of the relationship between aesthetics and technology has been offered by Gianni Grana, who remarked that Marinetti's 'myth of the machine' – a label that could include the more general characters of the futurist technological imagination – was 'the perception and the pre-figuration [...] of the current and future technological transformations and epistemological modifications, of which the *machine* was only the most suggestive emblem' (5). In other words, technology offers an allegorical structure through which futurism can articulate a poetics that simultaneously provides a kind of resolution to the problematics of late nineteenth-century poetics and a point of departure for the new project of futurism – new not only in the sense that it brings into play new themes and images, but also in the more profound sense that it transforms the very notion of what a poetics is and how it relates to the praxis of life. The theme of speed is the diaphragm, the point of intersection, of these two cultural moments: it looks forward to the anthropological transformations, the new relationship between the individual and the framework of reality, wrought by technological modernity, but it is first appropriated by Marinetti in a way that inserts it squarely within the paradigm of fin-de-siècle poetic theory. It is in this sense that, as suggested above, futurism both provides a closure to the nineteenth century and inaugurates the twentieth: speed is the centre of an allegoric constellation that allows Marinetti to recast and in a sense provide a solution to the two nodes of the dominant poetics of the fin de-siècle: the decadent theme of cultural decline and the symbolist quest for the absolute. Thus, it is in its allegorical dimension, rather than as a reflection on new discoveries of contemporary science, that the theme of speed must be approached. If there is a homology between the two fields, it seems unnecessary to determine a direct influence of, say, Einsteinian physics on Marinetti's poetic theory. Rather, both fields articulate, in ways which are necessarily related, the powerful fracture between the subject and a world that modernity has removed more and more from direct fruition.[25] Symbolism seeks to resolve the fracture between individual and world by attempting to escape the materiality of language and the world in the terms best described by Peter Nicholls in his discussion of Mallarmé: 'Mallarmé [...] cannot extricate himself from language and its attendant difficulties; if he could, we would have pure transcendence – death, the sterile iciness of the Absolute – and not those compromised forms we call art' (39–40). In Marinetti's allegory in 'La Mort tient le volant...,' the machine opens up a realm of experience in which the world, in its material coordinates in space and time, is left behind, and in which the individual is reduced to mere will, to a continuous self-overcoming in a race that casts the new man into a state of endless renewal where death itself is annihilated. More importantly, the Nietzschean overtones of the *poème-en-prose* suggest that Marinetti's continued engagement with the German philosopher should be related to the transformation in his discursive strategy that leads to the foundational manifesto of futurism. The point of this investigation, then, is not to establish whether Marinetti appropriated the terms of Nietzsche's philosophical project correctly, but rather to determine to what extent Marinetti found in it the terms to reorient his own cultural project. Nietzsche offered the ideological apparatus that allowed Marinetti to overcome the impasse of the decadent discourse of cultural decline, while technological modernity provided him with the metaphorical instrumentation to translate it into aesthetic terms.

The Nietzschean influence on futurism, and most specifically on the first manifesto of the movement, is quite evident in several of the symbolic nodes of the text. Consider for instance the violent polemic about the institutional sites of preservation and reproduction of the cultural canon, which closely recalls parts of the section 'On New and Old Tablets' in *Zarathustra*. Marinetti's well-known passage against museums and academies reads:

> È dall'Italia, che noi lanciamo pel mondo questo nostro manifesto di violenza travolgente e incendiaria [...] perché vogliamo liberare questo paese dalla sua fetida cancrena di professori, d'archeologhi, di ciceroni e d'antiquarii.
>
> Già per troppo tempo l'Italia è stata un mercato di rigattieri. Noi

> vogliamo liberarla dagl'innumerevoli musei che la coprono tutta di cimiteri innumerevoli.
>
> [It is from Italy that we launch into the world this manifesto of overwhelming and incendiary violence because we want to free this land from its putrid gangrene of professors, archaeologists, cicerones, and antiquarians.
>
> For too long Italy has been a market of second-hand goods. We mean to free it from the numberless museums that cover it with numberless graveyards.] (*TIF* 11)

The images of the dethroning of the keepers of the established cultural and social norms, and of their funereal effect on the living is clearly derived from Zarathustra's 'new law': 'And I bade them overthrow their old academic chairs and wherever the old conceit had sat; I bade them laugh at their great masters of virtue and saints and poets and world-redeemers. I bade them laugh at their gloomy sages and at whoever had at any time sat on the tree of life like a black scarecrow' (308). Likewise, the rhetoric of the future arising out of the destruction of the past recalls another oracular pronouncement of Zarathustra, in a passage which further delineates the theme of the overcoming of the self which we have seen at work in 'La Mort tient le volant. ...' Zarathustra says: 'O my brothers, I dedicate and direct you to a new nobility: you shall become procreators and cultivators and sowers of the future [...] Not whence you come shall henceforth constitute your honor, but whither you are going! Your will and your foot which has a will to go over and beyond yourselves – that shall constitute your honor' (315). It is therefore in the fundamental opposition that structures the text, namely the opposition between past and present, that we can read the influence of the German philosopher. From the beginning, Marinetti constructs the cultural project of the movement around the question of time: time as history, time as cultural tradition, time, in other words, as an emplotment of past events or as a narrative that not only attempts to provide meaning and coherence to the experiences of the past but also serves as a colonizing project for the future, a blueprint for the ways things should be.

Time thus becomes one of the primary targets of the futurist program. Marinetti's problematization of the question of time and modernity is of course not new, as we have seen in chapter 1. By interpreting modernity as the fall from a lost plenitude, the contradictory discourse of decadence articulated by Anatole Baju both postulates the impossibility of a reconciliation between the now divided realms of art and life, since such a reconciliation can only arise from a return to the social structures of a past that is itself projected into the mythic dimension of a lost utopia, and suggests that the only alternative is the eventual vanishing of the work of art, consumed by the commodity. Historical continuity is preserved at the expense of the present, because the realization that the cultural and social structures of modernity have profoundly changed the relationship between producer, consumer, and cultural product results in turning one's back on the new, and dissolving one's present into the memory of the past. The avant-garde, on the other hand, overturns the terms of the problem. As Guido Guglielmi has put it, 'tradition arrives to the avant-gardes already devalued, and they turn the new into a value' (186). The rejection of tradition and of history is also a Nietzschean theme that finds its most thorough articulation in his second 'Untimely Meditation,' *On the Uses and Disadvantages of History for Life* (1874), the metaphoric and rhetorical structure of which is recalled by Marinetti's manifesto.[26] Nietzsche structures his argument around the distinction between history and life. In particular, he identifies two modes of emplotment of history, two narrative models that constitute the opposite sides of the same coin. In the first – the 'shameless' Hegelian version – the present is the crowning and the fulfillment of the past, and 'the miserable condition' of German man is raised 'to godhood as the true meaning and goal of all previous events' (104). In the second – characterized by 'ironic modesty' – human beings are reduced to the role of epigones, 'pale and stunted late descendants of strong races coldly prolonging their life as antiquarians and gravediggers' (104). While the former narrative can be easily adapted to the necessities of the triumphant bourgeoisie and can even provide a crutch to a fideistic belief in progress as a continuous movement toward perfectibility, the latter offers a more disturbing – but no less stifling – account, one that had already found its most influential model almost a century earlier in Gibbons' *History of the Decline and Fall of the Roman Empire.* Nietzsche, too, refers to the decline of imperial Rome, although with a different perspective: he compares the cosmopolitanism of the imperial era, in which all the world stood before the Roman subject and he lost himself 'in the midst of the cosmopolitan carnival of gods' (83) with modern man who has become sated with the 'world exhibition' prepared by historians and is therefore not able to read any event except as a link in the historical chain.

Nietzsche articulates his critique of history 'for the sake of life and action' (*Untimely Meditations* 59). Subjection to history, the self-assuredness that he represents the peak of history or the weariness of having come at the nadir of the historical process, is what inhibits modern man in his dealings with the world. Thus, forgetting – or, in Nietzsche's words, the ability 'to live unhistorically,' which characterizes the animal – is the means to achieve new health and freedom: '[W]e have observed the animal, which is quite unhistorical, and dwells within a horizon reduced almost to a point, and yet lives in a certain degree of happiness, or at least without boredom and dissimulation; we shall thus have to account the capacity to feel to a certain degree unhistorically as being more vital and more fundamental, inasmuch as it constitutes the foundation upon which alone anything sound, healthy and great, anything human can grow' (*Untimely Meditations* 63). It is at this point that his influence on Marinetti is most evident. The 'rhetoric of sickness,' to use Barbara Spackman's phrase,[27] which allows Nietzsche to align history with illness and 'unhistorical' thought with health is also at work in the first manifesto of futurism, in which the past is described as a force that stifles the present, and that prevents its energies, its vitality, from fully unfolding by directing it within well-worn grooves: 'Per i moribondi, per gl'infermi, pei prigionieri, sia pure: – l'ammirabile passato è forse un balsamo ai loro mali, poiché per essi l'avvenire è sbarrato ... Ma noi non vogliamo più saperne, del passato, noi, giovani e forti *futuristi*!' [We even allow that for the dying, the infirm, the prisoners the admirable past may be a balm for their illness, because the future is barred to them ... But we will have nothing to do with it, with the past, we young and strong *Futurists*] (*TIF* 12).

If Nietzsche formulates a powerful critique of the cultural effects of historicism, it is also clear that his argument, like Marinetti's, is not new to the cultural debate of the second half of the nineteenth century. In particular, the opposition between history and life orients much of the discourse of decadentism, and is clearly articulated by one of Marinetti's (and Nietzsche's) predecessors, Baudelaire himself, who in a note in *Mon cœur mis à nu* (1859–66) outlines a 'theory of true civilization:' 'Peuples nomades, pasteurs, chasseurs, agricoles, et même anthropophages, *tous* peuvent être supérieurs, par l'énergie, par la dignité personelle, à nos races d'Occident. Celles-ci peut-être seront détruites' (*Œuvres complètes* 2: 697) [Nomad peoples, shepherds, hunters, farmers, and even cannibals, may all, by virtue of energy and personal dignity, be the superiors of our races of the West. These will perhaps be destroyed] (*Intimate Journals* 45). Like Verlaine, Baudelaire opposes the vitality and energy of the peoples who have remained outside the narrative of (Western) history with the moral and practical feebleness of a people whose greatness resides in the past, in the shadow of which their present is hopelessly eclipsed. The paradox of this position, which leads to the self-reflexivity of aestheticism, is that art provides a refuge from the utilitarian logic of bourgeois society and from its subordination of history to the triumph of its world-view, but it is this very separation from the social realm that compels art to turn upon itself, to cultivate – and fence off – its own domain, to keep at a distance the conquering barbarians, the bearers of precisely that vitality the enervated 'empire' both longs for and disavows as its other.

'A "fin de siècle" society is, by definition, a society whose historical horizon stops upon itself, a society deprived of any project, and whose becoming seems to be interrupted' (Jouve 9). Futurism clearly understands this impasse, and sees itself not as a continuation of nineteenth-century post-Romantic culture, but as the inaugural move in the construction of a new, sound cultural horizon, neatly severed from the past. And yet, the past resurfaces in the very language of futurism, in the tropes and figures that are deployed to sketch an outline of the program of the movement. Health entails the overcoming of the disease, but the disease leaves its marks upon the body. Thus, Marinetti simply reverses the two symbolic poles of Baudelare's note and Verlaine's 'Langeur' and replaces the twilight of a dying empire with the animal-like vitality of successive waves of futurist barbarians as the metaphor that provides the text with its rhetorical thrust:

> Verranno contro di noi, i nostri successori; verranno di lontano, da ogni parte, danzando su la cadenza alata dei loro primi canti, protendendo dita adunche di predatori, e fiutando caninamente, alle porte delle accademie, il buon odore delle nostre menti in putrefazione, già promesse alle catacombe delle biblioteche.
>
> [They will come against us, our successors; they will come from afar, from every quarter, dancing on the winged cadence of their first songs, stretching out their hooked claws of predators and sniffing like dogs by the door

of the academies the good smell of our putrefying minds, already promised to the catacombs of the libraries.] (*TIF* 13)

In his critical retrieval of the categories that found the discourse of decadence through a Nietzschean perspective, Marinetti takes as the starting point of his project the same opposition between history and life seen at the core of Nietzsche's essay, but he locates this opposition specifically within the realm of art. Thus, Nietzsche's polemic against history is rephrased (and simplified) in terms of art history, a move that allows Marinetti to launch his attack against the institutions that mediate artistic production in bourgeois society. As vehicles of tradition, schools and museums are the practical instruments whereby history stifles life and the dead govern the living:

Musei: cimiteri!... [...]

Che ci si vada in pellegrinaggio, una volta all'anno, come si va al Camposanto nel giorno dei morti... ve lo concedo. Che una volta all'anno sia deposto un omaggio di fiori davanti alla *Gioconda*, ve lo concedo... Ma non ammetto che si conducano quotidianamente a passeggio per i musei le nostre tristezze, il nostro fragile coraggio, la nostra morbosa inquietudine. Perché volersi avvelenare? Perché volere imputridire? [...]

Volete dunque sprecare tutte le vostre forze migliori, in questa eterna ed inutile ammirazione del passato, da cui uscite fatalmente esausti, diminuiti e calpesti?

[Museums: cemeteries! ...

I will even allow that one should go on pilgrimage, once a year, just as we go to the Cemetery on All Souls' Day... I will even allow that once a year flowers should be offered to the *Mona Lisa*... But I will not allow that we should take our sorrows, our fragile courage, our morbid uneasiness on a daily stroll through the museums. Why poison ourselves? Why rot?

Do you then want to waste your best strengths in this eternal and useless admiration for the past, from which you emerge fatally exhausted, diminished and trampled?] (*TIF* 11–12)

This denunciation is not simply an instance of Bloomian 'anxiety of influence' whereby a poet is always already engaged in an agonistic dialogue with his poetic forefathers; rather, it involves a more profound re-conceptualization of the role of the artist. In the fiction that is Marinetti's movement at this early stage, the artist is the herald of modernity; but modernity must be understood not solely in the more obvious and superficial sense of the new technological, industrialized landscape of early twentieth-century Milan – to which, of course, Marinetti does appeal and which he turns into a symbol of modernity *tout court* – but also in the sense outlined by Paul de Man in his re-reading of the second of Nietzsche's *Untimely Meditations* in the essay 'Literary History and Literary Modernity.' There the critic interprets modernity as a synonym of Nietzsche's 'life,' a move that helps to clarify the broader implications of Marinetti's textual strategies. As de Man writes, 'Modernity exists in the form of a desire to wipe out whatever came earlier, in the hope of reaching at last a point that could be called a true present, a point of origin that marks a new departure. This combined interplay of deliberate forgetting with an action that is also a new origin reaches the full power of the idea of modernity' (148). In other words, Marinetti's polemic against the past is not simply functional to asserting the originality of the futurist project in relation to the past literary tradition, since this would simply introduce it within that tradition, as its (critical) continuation. Rather, futurism rejects history as such, levelling its critique not only at one or more specific moments within the literary tradition (though its immediate predecessors, symbolism and decadentism, are especially singled out for censure), but at the past in general. As the name suggests, futurism intended to project itself completely into the future by means of a willful suppression/repression of the past, the 'forgetting' that, as Nietzsche says, is 'essential to action of any kind' (*Untimely Meditations* 62).

However, Nietzsche was also well aware of the ambiguous relationship between decadence and health, between the old order and the new. About the 'good fortune of [his] existence,' he writes in *Ecce Homo*: 'This dual descent, as it were, both from the highest and the lowest rung on the ladder of life, at the same time a *decadent* and a *beginning* – this, if anything, explains that neutrality, that freedom from all partiality in relation to the total problem of life, that perhaps distinguishes me' (222). Decadence/renewal is a hinge that inextricably links, and at the same time separates, the old order and the new, that begins to work itself out from this very moment. Futurism finds itself at such a junction. Its history is an inescapable heritage, which resurfaces in the very language through which it is denied. At the same time, futurism attempts to construct itself as an absolute point of origin, a completely new beginning that comes not *after* but *in place of* the literary and artistic production that chronologically precedes it.

Considered in this light, the heavily symbolist language of the narrative sections of the manifesto – and of the opening paragraphs in particular – is less contradictory than it appears. The story that is being told here is in fact the overcoming of history – and literary history first and foremost – on the part of the futurists, so that a confrontation with tradition constitutes the necessary starting point of this process of renewal. Consider the famous first paragraph:

> Avevamo vegliato tutta la notte – i miei amici ed io – sotto lampade di moschea dalle cupole di ottone traforato, stellate come le nostre anime, perché come queste irradiate dal chiuso fulgòre di un cuore elettrico. Avevamo lungamente calpestato su opulenti tappeti orientali la nostra atavica accidia, discutendo davanti ai confini estremi della logica ed annerendo molta carta di frenetiche scritture.
>
> [We had waked all night, my friends and I, under mosque lamps with domes of embroidered brass, starred like our souls because, like them, irradiated by the closed splendor of an electric heart. We had long trampled our ancient sloth upon opulent oriental carpets, discussing up to the furthest boundary of logic and blackening much paper with our frenzied writing.] (*TIF* 7)

The cultural project, the reflection upon the scope of their movement that opened the manifestoes of Marinetti's predecessors, is here replaced by the event, a distinctive, unique moment that constitutes the point of origin of the movement itself. The space described is ambiguously poised between the real – Marinetti's own sitting-room, as described by, among others, Aldo Palazzeschi ('Marinetti e il futurismo' xv) – and a literary *topos*, the room of the decadent aesthete, with all the orientalist trappings that would have well suited the 'home' of D'Annunzio's Andrea Sperelli.[28] Marinetti follows his literary models in characterizing this environment in terms of artificiality, indolence, and psychological feebleness and languor: like Huysmans's Des Esseintes, that other prototype of the decadent hero, the characters gathered in the room conduct their waking life at night,[29] and they are plagued by a languishing of the soul that makes the effort of poetic production useless. But we also witness other reversals of the decadent stereotypes: the rugs, for instance, are not mere objects of aesthetic enjoyment, but are returned to their function, they are trod upon and become the burial ground of the aesthete's detached *accidia*. Likewise, while Des Esseintes's nocturnal life served to reinforce his distance and isolation from the rest of humanity, for the would-be futurists this loneliness quickly turns into a sense of connection with a teeming life outside the enclosed space of the decadent room, and inspires the first in a series of paeans to modern life.

Pellegrino D'Acierno has rightly observed that in this initial paragraph we have the staging of the first in a series of scenes, namely the 'scene of writing,' which is quickly exchanged for 'the scene of action' (306). What is being rejected here, however, is not writing *tout court*, as D'Acierno has it, but rather, as the carefully described ambiance suggests, a very specific practice of writing, in which the overproduction of texts, of 'frenzied writing' accumulating, like layers of sediment, over reams of paper, is incapable of penetrating the confines of the decadent room. The object of this first futurist polemic, in other words, is the practice of art for art's sake, which links the decadent disdain for the masses with the symbolist disdain for the communicative function of language: in either case, in fact, the work of art folds upon itself to construct a private space (real, like Des Esseintes's house, or metaphorical, like Mallarmé's language of symbols) in which the removal of art from the praxis of life is effected and thematized by turning apartness itself into the content of the work. As Peter Bürger has argued, this constitutes the very ground of possibility of the avant-garde: 'As institution and content coincide, social ineffectuality stands revealed as the essence of art in bourgeois society, and thus provokes the self-criticism of art' (27). Joachim Schulte-Sasse rephrases Bürger's argument in terms of form and content – 'the development leading to Symbolism and Aestheticism can be best described as a transformation of form into content' (xiii) – a reformulation that can lead to further considerations. In fact, one of the characteristics of decadentism is precisely that style becomes the content of the work: Verlaine's 'Empire' indolently pursues a purely formal task, the composition of acrostics, while for Baju, as we have seen, poetic language is severed from social reality. Indeed, writing becomes a metaphor for living, as both involve *style*, the achievement of an effect on the part of the artist or the dandy upon his audience (namely, the reader or the crowd). This effect depends on one's mastery of the art of writing or of living, as in the already quoted maxim that Sperelli's father hands down to his son: 'Bisogna *fare* la propria vita, come si fa un'opera d'arte' [one must *fashion* one's life the way one fashions a work of art] (D'Annunzio 37). But this flattening of style into content can also be read – as Nietzsche does in the second 'Untimely Meditation' – as a loss of the unity of content and form, insofar as one, form, replaces the other. In Nietzsche's characterization, the disease of the modern individual lies in the inability to mediate between the available mass of historical data and the fulfillment of real needs. The content of modern culture is the readily available styles of the past handed down through historical education, and the fracture between interior – what we know – and exterior – what is necessary for life – has been irrevocably consummated. Like post-modern bricoleurs, 'we moderns have nothing whatever of our own; only by replenishing and cramming ourselves with the ages, customs, arts, philosophies, religions, discoveries of others do we become anything worthy of notice, that is to say, walking encyclopedias' (Nietzsche, *On the Uses and Disadvantages* 79). And Nietzsche further adds, by way of a diagnosis: 'He who wants to strive for and promote the culture of a people should strive for and promote this higher unity and join in the destruction of modern bogus cultivatedness for the sake of a true culture; he should venture to reflect how the health of a people undermined by the study of history may again be restored, how it may rediscover its instincts and therewith its honesty' (*On the Uses and Disadvantages* 79–80).

The futurist attack on decadent aestheticism is articulated through a thematization of the problem of content and form: by rejecting autonomy as the category that defines art in bourgeois society, futurism calls for a new relationship between art and the praxis of life, and for a shift back in the direction of content. This in turn entails a new relationship with language. The opening anecdote thus serves to dramatize this double movement. In the first instance, Marinetti counters the inner space of writing, the decadent room, with the outer space of industrial life. Notably, it is not the Futurists who first perform the action that frees them from the 'frenzied' but fruitless activity of the decadent room: rather, it is the intrusion of the outer space of modernity into this inner space that marks the transition toward a different realm of experience. The second paragraph is a profoundly ambiguous passage that insists on the insufficiencies of the imagination to replace a physical, embodied experience of the world.

> Un immenso orgoglio gonfiava i nostri petti, poiché ci sentivamo soli, in quell'ora, ad esser desti e ritti, come fari superbi o come sentinelle avanzate, di fronte all'esercito delle stelle nemiche, occhieggianti dai loro celesti accampamenti. Soli coi fuochisti che s'agitano davanti ai forni infernali delle grandi navi, soli coi neri fantasmi che frugano le pance arroventate delle locomotive lanciate a pazza corsa [...].

> [An immense pride filled our breasts because we felt we were the only ones, at that hour, to be awake and standing, like proud beacons or advanced sentinels before the army of enemy stars, eyeing us from their encampments in the sky. Alone with the stokers who are busy before the hellish furnaces of great ships, alone with the black ghosts who search through the red-hot bellies of locomotives hurled on their mad race.] (*TIF* 7)

On the one hand, we are presented with an identification between the artists and the machinists who control modern technology. On the other, this identification is mediated by means of a purely literary experience, by the appropriation of metaphors that refer intertextually to Marinetti's own *œuvre* – the 'army of hostile stars,' for instance, is a clear nod to Marinetti's French collection *La conquête des étoiles* (1902) – or to the decadent tradition itself. Thus, the sudden shift from this literary-hallucinatory vision to 'il rumore formidabile degli enormi tramvai a due piani' [the formidable noise of the huge double-decker trams] (7) that opens the third paragraph is all the more jarring, its effect duly recorded by the narrator: 'Sussultammo ad un tratto' [Suddenly we jumped] (7). Stylistically, too, this passage introduces a procedure also used to great effect in the eleven points of the 'manifesto' section, namely the use of a paratactical construction to produce 'an extraordinary assembly line' (D'Acierno 308). If the symbolist word loses its communicative, semantic function and tends toward the condition of music, futurism, on the contrary, constructs the page as a collection of objects or images immediately available to the reader.

The complex staging of the conflict – the Oedipal wrestling with the poetic fathers – is only a preliminary step in Marinetti's rhetorical machine. The next section of the text is signalled by an emphatic shift in register, as the tale of the origins of futurism comes to be told in terms of a mythical narrative. The myth is – as might be expected – a myth of origin, a foundation myth through which futurism calls itself out of historical time and locates the originality of its project precisely in the fact that it marks a completely new beginning and introduces a radically new order. Antonio Saccone has rightly observed that Marinetti's intention is 'to transform the mechanical device into an archetypal model, to put technology to the service of mythology' (88).[30] The fascination of futurism with technology is not the result of some sort of fetishistic compulsion. Rather, the movement seizes the possibility of using technology rhetorically against history, as the gateway into a new mode of life in which the individual is returned to a state of plenitude, of strength, of life. Notice the messianic tone of Marinetti's proclamation at this point:

> – Andiamo, diss'io; andiamo, amici! Partiamo! Finalmente, la mitologia e l'ideale mistico sono superati. Noi stiamo per assistere alla nascita del Centauro e presto vedremo volare i primi Angeli!... Bisognerà scuotere le porte della vita per provarne i cardini e i chiavistelli!... Partiamo! Ecco, sulla terra, la primissima aurora! Non v'è cosa che agguagli lo splendore della rossa spada del sole che schermeggia per la prima volta nelle nostre tenebre millenarie!...
>
> ['Let us go,' I said. 'Let us go, friends! Let us leave! Finally, mythology and the mystic ideal are overcome. We are about to witness the birth of the Centaur and we will soon see the flight of the first Angels!... We must shake the gates of life to test their hinges and bolts!... Let us leave! Behold, on earth, the very first dawn! Nothing equals the splendor of the red sword which cuts for the first time through our millennial darkness!...] (*TIF* 8)

Again, we find the opposing images of closure and of shattering boundaries ('We must shake the gates of life'), but we find also the first in a series of figures of rebirth or regeneration – 'the very first dawn' – that culminate with the death and resurrection of the futurist hero.

The rest of Marinetti's narrative is structured by the opposition of life and death imagery. In particular, death is identified as a literary construct, a late romantic and decadent *topos*, anticipating Mario Praz's phenomenology of this motif in his fundamental study *La carne, la morte e il diavolo nella letteratura romantica* (1930). Marinetti writes:

> E noi, come giovani leoni, inseguivamo la Morte [...].
>
> Eppure non avevamo un'Amante ideale che ergesse fino alle nuvole la sua sublime figura, né una Regina crudele cui offrire le nostre salme, contorte a guisa di anelli bisantini! Nulla, per voler morire, se non il desiderio di liberarci finalmente dal nostro coraggio troppo pesante!
>
> [And we, like young lions, hunted Death.
>
> And yet, we had no ideal Lover who would raise her sublime figure to the sky, no cruel Queen to whom we could offer our corpses, twisted like

> Byzantine rings! Nothing for which to die, except for the desire to free ourselves of our too heavy courage.] (*TIF* 8)

Marinetti clearly counters decadent *ennui* with the enthusiastic and almost strident voluntaristic optimism of his manifesto, and death is reduced to a moment of passage, the destructive phase that, by annihilating tradition and the culture it vehicles, opens the way to the futurist renewal of the universe. The 'domestication' of death functions rhetorically to deflect the accusation that the avant-garde is driven by a purely agonistic or even nihilistic impulse[31] because the destructive moment is represented not as an aim in itself (death is neither an 'ideal Lover' nor a 'cruel Queen' to be appeased) but a necessary step toward a radically new approach to artistic activity. In other words, death is the necessary preliminary for the (re)birth of the new.

But Marinetti had already staged another form of death upon entering for the first time his automobile: 'Io mi stesi sulla mia macchina come un cadavere nella bara, ma subito risuscitai sotto il volante.' [I lie in my car like a corpse in a casket, but I was immediately resurrected under its steering wheel] (48). The distance between life and death, birth and dissolution, is short-circuited by means of the machine, which is both grave and maternal womb, and which puts an end to the cultural history that preceded its advent and gives rise to the new order. Nature and technology are conflated in the famous passage that dramatizes a real car accident in which Marinetti was involved.[32] After rolling into a ditch in an effort to avoid two bicyclists, Marinetti breaks into this paean:

> Oh! materno fossato, quasi pieno di un'acqua fangosa! Bel fossato d'officina! Io gustai avidamente la tua melma fortificante, che mi ricordò la santa mammella nera della mia nutrice sudanese... Quando mi sollevai – cencio sozzo e puzzolente – di sotto la macchina capovolta, io mi sentii attraversare il cuore, deliziosamente, dal ferro aroventato della gioia!

> [Oh! Maternal ditch, almost full of muddy water! Beautiful workshop ditch! I tasted avidly your fortifying mud, which reminded me of the holy breast of my Sudanese nurse... When I arose – a dirty and stinky rag – from under the capsized vehicle, I felt my heart pierced deliciously by the red-hot iron of joy.] (*TIF* 9)

The futurist is reborn out of the 'maternal ditch,' suitably anthropomorphized by its association with the Sudanese nurse, and thus rises out of the earth like a new Adam, but at the same time he crawls out of the car, which plays the role of a maternal figure. And, since any hierarchy, any genealogy, threatens to disrupt the relationship between the new futurist being and its mechanical associate, the relationship of filiation that we have just considered is immediately reversed. If after the car accident the machine had 'procreated' the human being, now it is the latter that brings the former back to life by, as it were, the shamanistic gesture of laying hands upon it: 'Credevano che fosse morto, il mio bel pescecane, ma una carezza bastò a rianimarlo' [They thought that it was dead, my beautiful shark, but a caress from me was enough to revive it'] (*TIF* 9).[33]

De Man's remark on the rhetoric of the discourse of modernity is particularly appropriate to the imagery mobilized by Marinetti in this narrative section: 'The human figures that epitomize modernity are defined by experiences such as childhood or convalescence, a freshness of perception that results from a slate wiped clean, from the absence of a past that has not yet had time to tarnish the immediacy of perception' (157). Human and machine generate one another in a closed circuit that preempts the unfolding of a linear genealogy. It is at this point that the new born man-machine can announce its *verbum*, its *future* program in the section entitled specifically 'Manifesto del futurismo,' culminating in the visionary point eleven, in which the symbolic *loci* of modernity stand sharply out against the ambiguous background of the institutions of art.

As the text shifts back to narrative after the manifesto proper, the double bind of the futurist discourse of modernity becomes clearer. The vehement diatribe against the tradition and against the institutions of art (the academy, the museum) is conducted in the terms of Nietzsche's critique of the epigonism implicit in the decadent theory of history. The historically educated bourgeois in Nietzsche's essay turn into 'a race of eunuchs [...] to watch over the great historical world-harem' (*On the Uses and Disadvantages* 84); in Marinetti's text the threat of intellectual castration comes, as might be expected, from the genealogy of the poetic fathers, from their life-in-death in the museums and the libraries:

> In verità io vi dichiaro che la frequentazione quotidiana dei musei, delle biblioteche e delle accademie (cimiteri di sforzi vani, calvarii di sogni crocifissi, registri di slanci troncati!...) è, per gli artisti, altrettanto dannosa

> che la tutela prolungata dei parenti per certi giovani ebbri del loro ingegno e della loro volontà ambiziosa.
>
> [In truth I declare that daily visits to museums, libraries, and academies (cemeteries of fruitless efforts, calvaries of crucified dreams, records of interrupted impulses!...) are for artists as damaging as extended parental tutelage for certain young people drunk with their wit and their ambitious will.] (*TIF* 12)

In either case, liberation lies in a wilful repression of the past, in an active forgetting that again endows the artist with 'his instincts' and returns 'his faith in the "divine animal"' (Nietzsche, *On the Uses and Disadvantages* 84). Marinetti's metaphor points to a common discourse, as it is precisely the wild animal that metaphorizes the futurist artist's relationship with the world. If the futurists were first the incendiaries torching the shrines of culture and the wrecking crew demolishing the citadel of art, they are then replaced by a pack of hunting beasts – which is simply a variation on the metaphor of the young lions used to identify the futurists themselves in the first narrative section. As we have seen in the scene of symbolic rebirth following the accident, with the conjunction of the new-born futurist and his animal-like vehicle, the manifesto again brings together the two great metaphors of the discourse of decadence, articulated by both its proponents and its critics: the futurist is a primitive man, charged, like Baudelaire's cannibals and Verlaine's barbarians, with the task of demolishing a perishing civilization; but the futurist is also a wild animal unencumbered by the weight of history, living in a continuous present because always already in the process of being replaced by the vitalism of the succeeding generations. To a philosophy of history as inevitable decline the futurists oppose the abolition of history itself: there is no teleology, negative or otherwise, in the first manifesto, no movement of history toward either a Hegelian zenith or a decadent nadir, the twin targets of Nietzsche's polemic.[34] The vitality of the present can be preserved only by means of a constant calling into question of one's own project, by the refusal to let one's experience historicize. Thus, the final section continues the narrative interrupted by the manifesto and the polemic against the past to bring the story of the futurist group to its conclusion:

> I più anziani fra noi, hanno trent'anni: ci rimane dunque almeno un decennio, per compier l'opera nostra. Quando avremo quarant'anni, altri

uomini più giovani e più validi di noi, ci gettino pure nel cestino, come manoscritti inutili. – Noi lo desideriamo!

[...] Essi ci troveranno alfine – una notte d'inverno – in aperta campagna, sotto una triste tettoia tamburellata da una pioggia monotona, e ci vedranno accoccolati accanto ai nostri aeroplani trepidanti e nell'atto di scaldarci le mani al fuocherello meschino che daranno i nostri libri d'oggi fiammeggiando sotto il volo delle nostre immagini.

[The oldest among us are thirty. We thus have at least a decade to fulfill our task. When we are forty, let other younger and stronger men throw us into the wastebasket like useless manuscripts. We wish it!

They will finally find us – on a winter night – in the open country, under a bleak shelter drummed by a monotonous rain, and they will see us crouching by our throbbing airplanes, as we warm our hands by the meager fire that our books of today will give off as the flames leap under the flight of our images.] (*TIF* 14)

Toward an Impermanent Work of Art

In its initial phase, then, futurism does not simply reject the cultural tradition, but rather its own historicization through an artistic practice that cultivates dislocation, the ephemeral, and the transitory. The bivouac scene just quoted is emblematic of a notion of art as the impermanent and the transient which is clearly antiphrastically related to the immortal works enshrined in the cemetery of the museum evoked in the manifesto itself. The futurists stage their own destruction on the part of the new generations, following the Nietzschean logic delineated above. However, this moment of assertion of life over history is preceded by an act of self-destruction, the burning of the manuscripts: an act that foregrounds the obsolescent nature of the work of art in modernity, in which its nature of commodity subjects it to the logic of the 'new' and of the fashionable.[35]

The originality of futurism, what further distinguishes the movement from decadentism and inaugurates the experience of the historical avant-garde, is thus the way in which it addresses the question of the loss of the aura of the work of art. One way to understand aestheticism is to read literally the expression 'art for art's sake,' which implies that the function of art is precisely to identify and articulate what differentiates art from other signifying practices: the passing of the aura is thus lived nostalgically, as a trauma or a loss to be made good through a practice of writing which seeks to refine itself of any remnant of materiality, of the communicative function. The understanding of cultural production that informed decadentism was oriented by the opposition between the auratic work of art and the commodity, between the Mallarmean poem and the bourgeois novel *à la* Ohnet. Futurism seeks to break the binary by articulating a third position in which the loss of the aura is the very condition of art in modernity, and therefore must also be the foundation of a practice of art that at the same time does not result in the immediate fruibility characterizing the commodity. It is for this reason that in the manifesto 'Distruzione della sintassi Immaginazione senza fili Parole in libertà' Marinetti reaffirms the distinction between artistic language and the language of everyday communication, which must rely on the conventions that Futurist *paroliberismo* – the practice of 'words in freedom' – rejects. He writes: 'La filosofia, le scienze esatte, la politica, il giornalismo, l'insegnamento, gli affari, pur ricercando forme sintetiche di espressione, dovranno ancora avvalersi della sintassi e della punteggiatura. Sono costretto infatti, a servirmi di tutto ciò per potervi esporre la mia concezione' [Although they will seek synthetic forms of expression, philosophy, the exact sciences, politics, journalism, teaching, business will still have to make use of syntax and punctuation. I am in fact forced to use all that to be able to explain to you my ideas] (*TIF* 65). The echo of Mallarmé's distinction between the 'raw and immediate' state of the word, used for 'telling, teaching, even describing,' and its 'essential' function articulated in 'Crise de vers' (233) is certainly not casual. Nevertheless, the common critique of traditional communicative language leads, as we will see, to two radically divergent theories of poetic language.

A key document in the delineation of a genealogy of futurism is the manifesto in which Marinetti openly distances the movement from symbolism, 'Noi rinneghiamo i nostri maestri simbolisti ultimi amanti della luna' (We Repudiate Our Symbolist Masters, the Last Lovers of the Moon), initially published in 1911 in *Le futurisme,* and translated into Italian for inclusion in *Guerra, sola igiene del mondo*. The text opens with a scene of Oedipal conflict and rebellion similar to the overcoming of the Futurists by their successors in the first manifesto:

> Noi abbiamo sacrificato tutto al trionfo di questa concezione futurista delle vita. Tanto, che oggi odiamo dopo averli immensamente amati i nostri gloriosi padri intellettuali: i grandi genî simbolisti Edgar Poe, Baudelaire, Mallarmé e Verlaine. Noi serbiamo rancore, oggi, di aver nuotato nel

> fiume del tempo, tenendo continuamente rivolta indietro la testa, verso la lontana sorgente azzurra del passato, verso il *'ciel antérieur où fleurit la beauté.'*
>
> [We have sacrificed everything to the triumph of this futurist conception of life – to the extent that, after having loved them immensely, we now hate our glorious intellectual fathers: the great symbolist geniuses Edgar Poe, Baudelaire, Mallarmé, and Verlaine. Today, we bear against them the grudge of having swum in the river of time with our heads constantly turned backwards, towards the distant azure spring of the past, towards the *'ciel antérieur où fleurit la beauté.'*] (*TIF* 302)

For Marinetti, the confrontation with the poetic father is to be carried out at the level of the status of the work of art. He continues:

> I nostri padri simbolisti avevano una passione che noi giudichiamo ridicola: la passione delle cose eterne, il desiderio del capolavoro immortale e imperituro. [...]
>
> Alla concezione dell'imperituro e dell'immortale, noi opponiamo, in arte, quella del divenire, del perituro, del transitorio e dell'effimero.
>
> [Our symbolist fathers had a passion which we consider ridiculous: the passion for eternal things, the desire for the immortal and imperishable masterpiece.
>
> To the conception of the imperishable and the immortal we oppose, in art, that of becoming, of the perishable, the transient and the ephemeral.] (*TIF* 302–3)

The distinction between symbolism and futurism is formulated in terms of their antithetical response to the modernist struggle with the problem of the aura of the work of art. Clearly the source for both positions is Baudelaire, and in particular the theory of modernity delineated in his essay on the artist Constantin Guys, 'The Painter of Modern Life.' According to Baudelaire, the work of art is characterized by a dual nature, as it knots together 'le transitoire, le fugitif, le contingent' [the transient, the fleeting, the contingent] and 'l'éternel et l'immuable' [the eternal and immovable] (*Œuvres complètes* 2: 695; 'The Painter of Modern Life' 403). Because it is transient, modernity is also the element that roots the work of art in a specific moment, as in the case of eighteenth-century paintings in which the 'spirit of the day' can be recognized in the dress of the period that clothes goddesses, nymphs, and sultanas equally. Modernity has body, consistency, a physical dimension resulting from the attempt to capture the presence of the objects and figures of the day: 'Tel nez, telle bouche, tel front remplissent l'intervalle d'une durée que je ne prétends pas de déterminer' [Such and such a nose, mouth, forehead, will be standard for a given interval of time, the length of which I shall not claim to determine here (2: 696; 404). If modernity is material, the eternal is characterized by an inverse process of abstraction and stylization, of distillation, to use Baudelaire's own term: 'Il s'agit, pour lui [Guys], de dégager de la mode ce qu'elle peut contenir de poétique dans l'historique, de tirer l'éternel du transitoire' [The aim for him is to extract from fashion the poetry that resides in its historical envelope, to distill the eternal from the transitory] (2: 694; 402).

The style of Constantin Guys (referred throughout the essay by the initial of his last name) is characterized by this tension between the eternal and the transitory:

> dans l'exécution de M. G. se montrent deux choses: l'une, une contention de mémoire résurrectioniste, évocatrice, une mémoire qui dit a chàque chose: «Lazare, lève-toi!»; l'autre, un feu, une ivresse de crayon, de pinceau, ressemblant presque à une fureur. C'est la peur de n'aller pas assez vite, de laisser échapper le fantôme avant que la synthèse n'en soit extraite et saisie. (2: 698)
>
> [in M. G.'s execution two things stand out: the first is the absorbed intenseness of a resurrecting and evocative memory, a memory that says to every object: 'Lazarus, arise'; the second is a fire, an intoxication of pencil or brush, almost amounting to frenzy. This is the fear of not going fast enough, of letting the spectre escape before the synthesis has been extracted and taken possession of.] (408).

The balance between life and death is a delicate one: the frenzied work of the artist is a result of the impossible task of capturing the fleeting essence of the moment, a modernity pushed to the limit of the presentness of the event.[36] But out of this process of ossification of the fleeting experience into the stasis of form, something 'living' arises, like Lazarus emerging from the tomb: the artistic object as it offers itself to memory – or rather as it evokes in the viewer an experience that is comparable to that of the event itself – so that the memory becomes the spectator's own.

It is not superfluous to recall that Guys was a commercial artist. Baudelaire discusses his pictorial reportages from Bulgaria, Turkey, Crimea, and Spain, stressing the evocative power of the works, 'tableaux vivants et suprenants, décalqués sur la vie elle-même' [scenes throbbing with life and interest, as though moulded on life itself] (2: 701; 410) which, in an anticipation of photography, endow the journalists' written accounts with the documentary power of visual evidence. In a wistful scene that closes the section on 'The Annals of War,' the poet regrets that the illustrations of the Crimean conflict, the lifeline between the theatre of war and the eager crowd of subscribers to the *Illustrated London News* back in the English capital, have been scattered as they were reproduced, day by day, in the newspaper. 'Il est malheureux,' he writes, 'que cet album, disséminé maintenant en plusieurs lieux, [...] n'ait pas passé sur les yeux de l'Empereur. J'imagine qu'il aurait complaisamment, et non sans attendrissement, examiné les faits et gestes de ses soldats' [How sad it is to think that this album, which has now been scattered in a variery of places, [...] should not have been submitted to the Emperor. He, I am sure, would have been glad to see (not without emotion) this record of his soldiers, their day-in, day-out doings] (2: 703; 413). In this contrast, and in the figure of Guys himself, we can see an example of the transition between what Bürger has called courtly and bourgeois art. Guys is the artist who works for the new mass media, and whose product is bought and sold on the marketplace like any other commodity, rather than the artist who produces for a patron. The organic work of art, made possible by a system of production that isolated the artist from the pressure of the marketplace, is already an object of mourning in Baudelaire's essay. Rather, the fragmentation of the 'poème [...] si vaste et si compliqué' [vast and complex poem] (2: 702; 412) of Guys's Crimean drawings into the isolated illustrations printed piecemeal in the newspapers is the cipher of the modern work, created according to the rhythms of industrial production, to the daily requirements of mass-media, not unlike the popular novel whose formal structures came to be adapted to its insertion, in installments, in newspapers and periodicals.

Once again, we can identify in a text by Baudelaire a symptomatology of modernism and a turning point in the articulation of the modern aesthetics: it is with modernity that the ephemeral component of the work of art comes into full view, but this is also a result of a transformation in the institution of art and of the artist for which mass-media have provided a vehicle. In this sense, Bürger's argument that 'in bourgeois art, the portrayal of bourgeois self-understanding occurs in a sphere that lies outside the praxis of life' (48) is only partially true because it does not consider the refunctionalization of a certain type of artistic production, still concerned with the self-representation of bourgeois society and, in the case of Guys, its imperialistic expansion, moved from the empyrean of art to the purgatory of mass communication. For Baudelaire to attribute to Guys the title of artist entails a reorientation of the notion of art itself, as he is forced to wrest it, through the foregrounding of 'modernity,' from the space of the museum, which perpetuates the aura of the work of art, into that of the newspaper, in which the aura is consumed not only by the mass-reproduction of the image, as in the Benjaminian formulation, but also by its identification with the immediate representation of lived events.

The newspaper represents, for better or for worse, the brothel in which art prostitutes itself and becomes information, the ephemeral word whose existence is consumed in the very act of its utterance. Not by chance, '*reportage*' is the term used by Mallarmé to characterize the 'elementary use of speech' that distinguishes writing from *literature*. Poetry, on the contrary, fashions 'un mot total, neuf, étranger à la langue et comme incantatoire' [a total word, new, unknown to the language and as if incantatory]. Thus, it achieves 'cet isolement de la parole: niant, d'un trait souverain, le hasard demeuré aux termes' [that isolation of speech: denying, in a sovereign gesture, the arbitrariness that clings to words] ('Crise de vers,' *Œuvres complètes* 368; *Mallarmé: The Poet and His Circle* 233). Thus, Mallarmé divorces the two elements of the work of art that Baudelaire had declared formed a whole. The poetic word no longer belongs to the order of language because it is no longer a sign but a monad complete in itself, in which the referent is present in its essential nature, like the famous flower that 'musicalement se lève, idée même' [musically arises, the idea itself] (368; 233). Marinetti clarifies his distance from Mallarmé by adapting and inverting the self-understanding of the symbolist theory of language, according to which the poetic word redeems language of its practical function. If for Mallarmé language is like money when it is used for communication, for Marinetti, on the contrary, it is precisely when language is used 'poetically' that it demonstrates its kinship with capital. The work of art in modernity cannot escape its function as commodity by simply attempting to evade the contingent and the ephemeral – that is, modernity itself, in Baudelaire's terms – because the very conception of the immortal masterpiece is an eminently economic one:

> Noi consideriamo invece che nulla sia basso e meschino quanto il pensare all'immortalità nel creare un'opera d'arte, più meschino e più basso della concezione calcolata e usuraia del paradiso cristiano, che dovrebbe ricompensare al milione per cento le nostre virtù terrestri.
>
> [We believe that nothing is as base and petty as the concern for immortality in the creation of a work of art, pettier and more base than the calculated and miserly notion of the Christian paradise, which should recompense at one million percent our earthly virtues.] (*TIF* 302)

A poetics of modernity – that is, a poetics oriented by the contingency, impermanence, and transience that characterizes modernity – would on the contrary reject the fetishization of the poetic word in favor of a practice of continuous becoming that in effect grasps the dynamism and movement of reality itself. Against the Mallarmean investment, Marinetti articulates a poetics of *sperpero*, of waste and dispersal, of scattering of 'mille tesori di forza, di amore, d'audacia, d'astuzia e di rude volontà' [a thousand treasures of strength, love, daring, shrewdness, and rough will] ('Fondazione e manifesto del Futurismo,' *TIF* 14).

However, if Marinetti anticipated in the manifesto of foundation the function of such an anti-institutional poetics, its translation into a theory of language and an actual poetic practice occurred over a remarkably long period of time, and, at least in part, under the stimulus of the technical manifestoes published by the futurist painters between 1910 ('La pittura futurista. Manifesto tecnico,' 11 April 1910) and 1912 ('Prefazione al Catalogo delle Esposizioni di Parigi, Londra, Berlino, Bruxelles, Monaco, Amburgo, Vienna, ecc.' February 1912).[37] Initially, futurist literature is configured in specifically thematic terms; the point of the first manifesto in which Marinetti articulates the propositive part of his program is a particularly good index of the limitations of such an approach:

> 11. Noi canteremo le grandi folle agitate dal lavoro, dal piacere o dalla sommossa: canteremo le maree multicolori e polifoniche delle rivoluzioni nelle capitali moderne; canteremo il vibrante fervore notturno degli arsenali e dei cantieri incendiati da violente lune elettriche; le stazioni

ingorde, divoratrici di serpi che fumano; [...] i piroscafi avventurosi che fiutano l'orizzonte, le locomotive dall'ampio petto, che scalpitano sulle rotaie, come enormi cavalli d'acciaio imbrigliati di tubi, e il volo scivolante degli aereoplani, la cui elica garrisce al vento come una bandiera e sembra applaudire come una folla entusiasta.

[11. We will sing the great crowds excited by work, by pleasure or by revolt; we will sing the multicolored and polyphonic tides of revolutions in the modern capitals; we will sing the vibrant night fervor of shipyards and construction yards ablaze with violent electrical moons; the greedy stations devouring smoking serpents; the daring steamships that sniff the horizon, the broad-chested locomotives that paw at their rails like enormous steel horses bridled with pipes, and the gliding flight of airplanes whose rotors flutter in the wind like a flag and seem to clap like an enthusiastic crowd.] (*TIF* 11)

The sites and devices of modernity become objects of an idealized aesthetic appreciation, and the predominance in this passage of the trope of similitude is a sign, as has been remarked,[38] of the fundamentally traditional poetic horizon within which Marinetti's poetics moves: in order to be dealt with, modernity needs to be translated into images from a pre-modern natural world (the moon, albeit an electrical one, snakes, horses, etc.) declined according to a fundamentally late-decadent decorative sensibility.[39] This, in any case, is an approach that characterizes much of the early poetry of futurism, with the possible exception of the works of Palazzeschi who, by evading a direct engagement with the more overtly fashionable and newfangled aspects of the modern world, was able to begin to articulate, even on a formal level, the new condition of art in modernity. I am thinking for instance of works such as 'E lasciatemi divertire' mentioned above, or 'La passeggiata,' from the second edition of *L'incendiario* (1913), in which the rhythmic scansion of the poem itself is subordinated to the unmediated presentation of advertisements and commercial slogans in what has become a completely commercialized cityscape. On the contrary, for poets such as Corrado Govoni, author of ostensibly futurist poems such as 'A Venezia elettrica' (included in the equally earnestly titled *Poesie elettriche*, 1911), futurism becomes the occasion for the deployment of a series of undisguised decadent *topoi*, from the snapshots of the crumbling city to the figures of Pierrot and Colombina to the images of death and decay. This thematic impulse is also behind Marinetti's earliest statements of poetics, such as the so-called 'Discorso ai Triestini,' first published in 'Rapporto sulla vittoria del Futurismo a Trieste,' the 'introduction' to Palazzeschi's *L'incendiario* (1910). Here the futurist leader calls for 'una grande e forte letteratura scientifica, la quale, libera da qualsiasi classicume, da qualsiasi purismo pedantesco, magnifichi le più recenti scoperte, la nuova ebbrezza della velocità e la vita celeste degli aviatori' [a great and strong scientific literature which, free of any classical remnant, of any pedantic purism, will glorify the most recent discoveries, the new intoxication of speed and the celestial life of aviators] (*TIF* 249), where the very verb *'magnificare'* [glorify] clarifies the celebratory and romanticizing function of art. It is true that the 'Discorso' continues with a passage that already looks forward to the disruption of linear, alphabetical writing in the technical manifestoes of literature:

> La nostra poesia è poesia essenzialmente e totalmente ribelle alle forme usate. Bisogna distruggere i binari del verso, far saltare in aria i ponti delle cose già dette, e lanciare le locomotive della nostra ispirazione, alla ventura, attraverso gli sconfinati campi del Nuovo e del Futuro! Meglio un disastro splendido, che una corsa monotona, quotidianamente ripresa! Già troppo a lungo furono sopportati i capi-stazione della poesia, i controllori di strofe-letto, e la stupida puntualità degli orari prosodici.
>
> [Our poetry is essentially and totally in revolt against traditional forms. It is necessary to destroy the railway track of verse, to blow up the bridges of what has already been said, and hurl the locomotives of our inspiration at random, through the endless fields of the New and of the Future! A splendid disaster is better than a monotonous journey undertaken daily! For too long we have suffered the station-masters of poetry, the controllers of sleeping-stanzas, and the stupid punctuality of prosodic timetables.] (*TIF* 249)

And yet, at this point, this too is nothing more than a extended metaphor that would not become a concrete poetic practice for more than two more years.

We should not forget that in the first manifesto even speed was seen in fundamentally aesthetic terms, as a source of aesthetic pleasure: what makes the racing car superior to the Victory of Samothrace is its higher degree of 'beauty,' not the fact that it transforms the very conception of beauty, that is, the relationship between the work of art and the viewer. In other words, at this point the work of art remains an object of passive and distant contemplation, while the artist too 'preserves' his halo by retaining the function of transforming and aesthetically sublimating the materiality of reality.

The 1910 technical manifesto of the futurist painters is the first text issued by the movement to suggest that a new aesthetics – if the term itself can still be used in this new condition – entails a radical reorientation of the relationship between artist, audience, and work of art.[40] Boccioni and the other signatories had claimed: 'noi vogliamo rientrare nella vita' [we want to enter back into life] (Boccioni et al., 'La pittura futurista' 25), thus calling into question the autonomy of the aesthetic. This overcoming of the fracture between art and life does not go in the direction of the aestheticization of the everyday, but is rather performed 'from below,' as Guido Guglielmi has put it, through the transformation of the work of art from a static object of passive fruition to a communicative practice that 'celebrates the art of life, vital intensity, the values of caducity and surprise, the extemporaneousness of experience' (Guglielmi 172). The futurist painting thus becomes the ground of a constitutive tension: on the one hand, it is an object framed within the institutional context of art exhibitions and therefore aspires to permanence. On the other, in the actual production of the work, the futurist painters seek to articulate a series of strategies that foreground the constructed nature of the work of art, and the fact that it can only find its completion in the necessarily transient moment of reception. Thus, the work of art does not exist in isolation, but postulates the presence of the viewer as a necessary closure of the circuit of communication. Hence, the famous dictum of the technical manifesto: 'La costruzione dei quadri è stupidamente tradizionale. I pittori ci hanno sempre mostrato cose e persone poste davanti a noi. Noi porremo lo spettatore nel centro del quadro' [The construction of paintings is stupidly traditional. Painters have always shown us things and people placed before us. We will place the spectator at the center of the painting] (Boccioni et al., 'La pittura futurista' 24).

In the technical manifesto the painters also outlined the theory of what would become in the 1912 'Prefazione' the key concept of 'simultaneity,' which questions the distinction between subject and object and the possibility for the individual subject to give order and shape to the flux of reality.[41]

> Le sedici persone che avete intorno a voi in un tram che corre sono una, dieci, quattro tre; stanno ferme e si muovono; vanno e vengono; rimbal-

> zano sulla strada, divorate da una zona di sole, indi tornano a sedersi, simboli persistenti della vibrazione universale. E, talvolta sulla guancia della persona con cui parliamo nella via noi vediamo il cavallo che passa lontano. I nostri corpi entrano nei divani su cui ci sediamo, e i divani entrano in noi, così come il tram che passa entra nelle case, le quali alla loro volta si scaraventano sul tram e con esso si amalgano.
>
> [The sixteen people around you on a moving bus are one, ten, four, three; they are still and they move; they come and go, bounce on the street, devoured by a sunny area, then they sit back down again, the persistent symbols of universal vibration. And sometimes on the cheek of the person to whom we speak on the street we see the horse passing in the distance. Our bodies enter the sofas on which we sit, and the sofas enter into us, just like the bus going by enters into the houses, which in turn fling themselves upon the bus and amalgamate with it.] ('La pittura futurista' 24)

This is further clarified in the 'Prefazione,' where the principles of universal dynamism and of the positioning of the viewer at the centre of the painting are brought together:

> Esso [the viewer] non assisterà, ma parteciperà all'azione. Se dipingiamo le fasi di una sommossa, la folla irta di pugni e i rumorosi assalti della cavalleria si traducono sulla tela in fasci di linee che corrispondono a tutte le forze in conflitto secondo la legge di violenza generale del quadro
>
> [He [the viewer] will not witness but will participate in the action. If we paint the stages of a revolution, the crowd bristling with fists and the noisy cavalry charges are translated on the canvas into sheafs of lines which correspond to all the struggling forces according to the law of general violence of the painting.] (Boccioni et al., 'Prefazione' 63–4)

And with an absolutely revolutionary intuition, the painters describe the work of art not as an object but as an '*ambiente* emotivo' [emotional *environment*] (66; emphasis added), a discursive space linking together 'la scena esterna (concreta) e l'emozione interna (astratta)' [the (concrete) external scene and the (abstract) internal scene] (65), that is, world and subject, in a mobile and always renewed configuration, in a dynamic, non-hierarchical, and always contingent relationship.

Marinetti's manifestoes on literature issued between 1912 and 1914 – the 'Manifesto tecnico della letteratura futurista' (11 May 1912); the so-called 'Risposta alle obiezioni' (11 August 1912), issued to clarify the previous manifesto;[42] 'Distruzione della sintassi Immaginazione senza fili Parole in libertà' (11 May 1913); and 'Lo splendore geometrico e meccanico e la sensibilità numerica' (18 March 1914) – attempt to delineate a poetic theory that breaks the frame of referential language. It is significant that in 'Distruzione della sintassi' Marinetti relates the practice of *'parole in libertà'* to a situation which is communicative and non-aesthetic:

> Ora supponete che un vostro amico dotato di questa facoltà lirica si trovi in una zona di vita intensa (rivoluzione, guerra, naufragio, terremoto ecc.) e venga, immediatamente dopo, a narrarvi le impressioni avute. Sapete che cosa farà istintivamente questo vostro amico lirico e commosso?...
>
> Egli comincerà col distruggere brutalmente la sintassi nel parlare. Non perderà tempo a costruire i periodi. S'infischierà della punteggiatura e dell'aggettivazione. Disprezzerà cesellature e sfumature di linguaggio, e in fretta vi getterà affannosamente nei nervi le sue sensazioni visive, auditive, olfattive, secondo la loro corrente incalzante. L'irruenza del vapore-emozione farà saltare il tubo del periodo, le valvole della punteggiatura e i bulloni regolari dell'aggettivazione. Manate di parole essenziali senza alcun ordine convenzionale. Unica preoccupazione del narratore rendere tutte le vibrazioni del suo io.
>
> [Now suppose that a friend of yours endowed with this lyrical faculty finds himself in an area of intense life (revolution, war, shipwreck, earthquake etc.) and that immediately thereafter he comes to tell you his impressions. Do you know what this lyrical and moved friend of yours will do?...
>
> He will start by destroying brutally syntax while he speaks. He won't waste time constructing periods. He won't give a damn for punctuation and the use of adjectives. He will scorn linguistic refinements and nuances, and he will quickly throw at your nerves his visual, auditory and olfactory sensations, following their pressing flow. The impetuousness of the steam-emotion will burst the pipe of the sentence, the valve of punctuation, and the regular bolts of adjectives. Handfuls of essential words without any conventional order. The narrator's only concern, relating all the vibrations of his I.] (*TIF* 70)

Thus even 'normal' communication, at least in the instances when it is provoked by particularly intense sources, requires a collaborative effort on the part of the listeners, who are called upon to re-articulate the magmatic and unstructured material hurled at them. This passage is also notable because it re-introduces into Marinetti's theoretical system that 'I' of which he had proclaimed the end in the climactic eleventh point of the 'Manifesto tecnico:' '**Distruggere nella letteratura l'"io"**, cioè tutta la psicologia. [...] Dunque, dobbiamo abolirlo in letteratura, e sostituirlo finalmente colla materia, di cui si deve afferrare l'essenza a colpi d'intuizione, la qual cosa non potranno mai fare i fisici né i chimici' [**Destroy the I in literature**, that is, all psychology. We must abolish it in literature and replace it finally with matter, of which we must grasp the essence by strokes of intuition – something which neither physicists nor chemists will ever be able to do] (*TIF* 50). As was the case in the manifestoes of the painters, the subject is abolished as ordering principle of the dynamic material of reality, and even in 'Distruzione della sintassi' it reappers as a mere object in the world, rather than as an organizing instance. Against the formal structures of language, the 'old syntax inherited from Homer' or the 'Latin period' which 'ha naturalmente, come ogni imbecille, una testa previdente, un ventre, due gambe e due piedi piatti, ma non avrà mai due ali' [naturally has, like any idiot, a wise head, a stomach, two legs and two flat feet, but will never have two wings] ('Manifesto tecnico,' *TIF* 46), Marinetti proposes a practice of writing that is shifting, unstable, suited to the mobility of the world and the subject's experience of it. Thus, nouns have to be deployed **'a caso, come nascono'** [**at random, as they are born**] (*TIF* 46), all verbal inflections must be eliminated because only the infinitive can express the action in its essential quality,[43] and punctuation must also be abolished because it parses, with rests and pauses, the flow of the action (whereas the mathematical signs advocated by Marinetti should, in the author's intentions, indicate and intensify that movement).

The stage comes to be occupied by 'matter,' whose impulses and movements the futurist work of art is supposed to explore through procedures that range from the introduction of noise, weight and smell (*TIF* 51) to the use of onomatopoeia, which, as Marinetti explains in 'Distruzione della sintassi,' 'serve a vivificare il lirismo con elementi crudi e brutali di realtà' [serves to vivify the lyricism with coarse and brutal elements from reality] (*TIF* 76). The emphasis on procedures that accentuate the mimetic function of language – and in particular onomatopoeia, the various types of which are described in the fourth major technical manifesto of poetry, 'Lo splendore geometrico e meccanico e la sensibilità numerica' – have contributed to an interpretation of *paroliberismo,* the practice of 'words in freedom,' as a form of 'persistent and late naturalism,' as Fausto Curi has written (*Tra mimesi e metafora* 79). In another context, Alberto Asor Rosa has argued that futurist writing 'aspires to consider itself realistic, or better rigorously realistic, or even better ultra-realistic, since it aims at capturing the ultimate essence of things' (59). On the contrary, Marinetti's theory of language is clearly antithetical to any traditional notion of realism or naturalism – that is, to any practice of writing that rhetorically constructs the illusion of an immediate apprehension of reality, without the mediating function of language itself. In fact, the theory of onomatopoeia makes it clear that Marinetti is well aware of the limitations of an aesthetics of mere mimesis. In realism, the mimetic illusion functions because language is not foregrounded; rather, through the use of a style that steers close to linguistic norms and conventions, it is made to appear as a transparent screen behind which things can be perceived in their absolute presence. In 'Lo splendore geometrico e meccanico e la sensibilità numerica,' Marinetti clarifies his theory of onomatopoeia by distinguishing four different types, of which only the first one, '**onomatopea diretta imitativa elementare realistica' [direct imitative elementary realistic onomatopoeia**] (*TIF* 105) is imitative of 'real sounds.' (The function of this kind of onomatopoeia, incidentally, is 'arricchire di realtà brutale il lirismo' [to enrich lyricism of brutal realism] (*TIF* 105)). Consider on the contrary, types two and three (the fourth, 'onomatopoeic psychic accord,' is the result of the combination of several examples of type three):

b) **Onomatopea indiretta complessa e analogica**. Es.: nel mio poema *Dune,* l'onomatopea *dum-dum-dum-dum* esprime il rumore rotativo del sole africano e il peso arancione del cielo, creando un rapporto tra sensazioni di peso, colore, odore e rumore. Altro esempio: l'onomatopea *stridionla stridionla stridionlaire* che si ripete nel primo canto del mio poema epico *La Conquête des étoiles* forma un'analogia fra lo stridore di grandi spade e l'agitarsi rabbioso delle onde, prima di una grande battaglia di acque in tempesta.

c) **Onomatopea astratta**, esperessione rumorosa e incosciente dei moti più complessi e misteriosi della nostra sensibilità. (Es.: nel mio poema *Dune,* l'onomatopea astratta *ran ran ran* non corrisponde a nessun rumore della natura o del macchinismo, ma esprime uno stato d'animo.

> [*b)* **Indirect complex and analogic onomatopoeia**. Ex: in my poem *Dune* the onomatopoeia *dum-dum-dum-dum* expresses the rotary sound of the African sun and the orange weight of the sky, creating a relationship between sensations of weight, colour, odour and sound. Another example: the onomatopoeia *stridionla stridionla stridionlaire* that is repeated in my epic poem *La conquête des étoiles* forms an analogy between the shrieking of great swords and the furious surging of the waves before a great battle of waters in the storm.
>
> *c)* **Abstract onomatopoeia**. The noise and unconscious expression of the most complex and mysterious movements of our sensibility (Ex: in my poem *Dune* the abstract onomatopoeia *ran ran ran* does not correspond to any noise of nature or of machinism, but express a state of mind.] (*TIF* 105–6)

As the label for the third type in particular makes clear, these kinds of onomatopoeia do not simply imitate reality. Rather, they operate by means of the construction of signifiers that relate *conventionally* to the signified – so much so that Marinetti has to explain the expressive function of '*dum-dum-dum-dum*.' Likewise, '*stridionla stridionla stridionlaire*,' far from *reproducing* the sound of the crashing waves, is the result of the deformation of a linguistic sign, the verb *stridere*, which retains its full semantic value. Indeed, it is precisely because the first part of the syntagm *stridionla* retains a certain degree of denotative meaning that the 'onomatopoeia' can be extended connotatively to the roaring waves, thus making the analogy possible. Clearly, this type is even less intuitive; Marinetti himself admits that his 'abstract onomatopoeia' does not correspond to any natural sound.[44]

Analogy is another important compositional procedure that demonstrates the complexity of Marinetti's theory of poetic language. Referred to also in 'Lo splendore geometrico,' analogy was already a central notion in Marinetti's theoretical discourse in the first technical manifesto, where it emerged as the master-trope of futurist writing: 'L'analogia non è altro che l'amore profondo che collega le cose distanti, apparentemente diverse ed ostili. Solo per mezzo di analogie vastissime uno stile orchestrale, ad un tempo policromo, polifonico, e polimorfo, può abbracciare la vita della materia' '[Analogy is nothing other than the profound love that connects distant, apparently different and hostile things. It is only by means of the most extensive analogies that an orchestral style, at once polychromic, polyphonic, and polymorphous will embrace the life of matter] (*TIF* 48). This passage, too, seems to suggest that Marinetti's intention moves in the direction of a theory of immediate correspondence between sign and referent, so that in an analogic relationship two or more linguistic signs point directly to material reality and reveal the connections between disparate objects. However, matter itself appears as something less than solid, which can be grasped only through the recourse to a multiplicity of signifying practices, and in this sense the 'most extensive analogies,' far from referring directly to reality, result in fact in a process of continuous deferral whereby visual and auditory sensations are translated into language.

Futurism thus articulates a theory of language as alienation, as distance between the human subject and the world, which can only be apprehended linguistically – that is, in a meditated way. Sandro Briosi has written that Marinetti 'launches upon the dream of a language which [...] may *coincide* with [the visual perception of the world], making it present even in its reality of a purified datum, fixed in the word: erasing the distance, the tension not – as in the referential use of language – between word and idea, between signifier and signified, but directly between word and thing' (22). Yet, it seems that the situation is more complex, for at least two reasons. First, in the passage quoted above, Marinetti writes that the function of the 'extensive analogies' is to grasp not 'matter,' things in themselves, but rather their 'life.' This conjunction of matter and life may well be the result of a partial misunderstanding of the Bergsonian concepts of *'vie'* and *'matière,'* according to which matter is the passive force that limits and circumscribes life and prevents it from becoming 'pure consciousness.'[45] Nonetheless, the attribution of a sort of *élan vital* to matter itself is not a simple misreading of the French philosopher, but rather the result of a dynamic conception of reality that is already evident in the first manifesto. At best, then, the poet can develop compositional strategies that explode the linearity of language and turn the page into an open space in which are articulated the simultaneous aspects of experience – the textual equivalent of the painting as 'emotional environment' theorized by Boccioni and the futurist painters. Second, and most important, the external world can be grasped, however impermanently, only through language. Marinetti uses the image of the net to illustrate the relationship between language and reality: 'Per avviluppare e cogliere tutto ciò che vi è di più fuggevole e di più inafferrabile nella materia, bisogna formare delle **strette reti d immagini o analogie**, che verranno lanciate nel mare misterioso dei fenomeni' [In order to envelop and catch all that is most fleeting and unseizable in matter, we must form **tight nets of images or analogies**, which will be tossed upon the mysterious sea of phenomena] (*TIF* 49). The metaphor is significant precisely because it indicates the ungraspability of the world of phenomena, its unreconcilable otherness. Like a net, language can at best give momentary form and catch fragments of reality, but cannot capture it in its materiality. One of the limitations of Marinetti's theory of analogy is the tendency to produce lists or catalogues, and indeed, as Perloff has rightly remarked in her discussion of *Zang Tumb Tumb*, the results of this technique can be appallingly obvious (59–60). Yet, this tendency is also the result of a theory of language that lives the fracture between world and language as a kind of competition between two equally unstable orders. In order to pursue phenomena in their mutability and dynamism, language can only generate, through continuous metaphoric displacements, mobile sequences of signs in a process of drift that is, at the limit, endless.

The point of arrival is a textual practice that, by rejecting linearity and conventionality, opens up rather than forecloses interpretative possibilities. For this reason, the moment of reception becomes central in the articulation of a futurist poetics, not simply in the sense that the futurist text is – like any text – a mechanism to generate interpretations, but rather in the sense that the responsibility of meaning production is shifted from the artist to the reader/viewer. In discussing analogy, Marinetti writes that the ultimate goal of 'immaginazione senza fili' [wireless imagination] is an 'essential' art in which the first terms of analogies are abolished and only the second terms are given in an 'uninterrupted sequence.' As a consequence, he adds, 'bisognerà [...] rinunciare ad essere compresi. Esser compresi, non è necessario' [we will have to renounce being understood. Being understood is not necessary] (*TIF* 52). Traditional syntax, compared to 'una specie d'interprete o di cicerone monotono' [a sort of monotonous interpreter or cicerone] (*TIF* 52), had the function of leading the reader to the meaning evoked by the poet. With futurist writing, on the contrary, the active participation of the audience produces meanings that are momentary and ephemeral, that last as long as the communicative situation itself, and are then overcome and replaced by new communicative situations. For this reason, the theatre is identified as the privileged site of futurist experimentation: even in its traditional configurations, the theatrical spectacle replaces the fixed text with an always renewed performance, a communicative action open to infinite variations. But for futurism the theatre is, more importantly, the site where the fragile barrier separating artist and audience, literally represented by the stage, can be crossed most easily, and where the difference between author and spectator can be most effectively overcome. The furthest point of Marinetti's theoretical edifice is thus the manifesto 'Il Teatro del Varietà,' first published in the British newspaper *The Daily Mail* on 21 November 1913 with the title 'The Meaning of the Music Hall.'[46] For Marinetti, both the *pars destruens* and the *pars construens* of variety theatre make it the most appropriate vehicle for the futurist artistic practice. On the one hand, it destroys, through parody or even through a fundamental lack of respect for the integrity and wholeness of the work, the auratic dimension of the work of art. As Marinetti puts it, 'Il teatro del Varietà distrugge il Solenne, il Sacro, il Serio, il Sublime dell'Arte coll'A maiuscolo. Esso collabora alla distruzione futurista dei capolavori immortali, plagiandoli, parodiandoli, presentandoli alla buona, senza apparato e senza compunzione, come un qualsiasi numero *d'attrazione*' [The Variety Theatre destroys the Solemn, the Sacred, the Serious, the Sublime of Art with a capital A. It contributes to the futurist destruction of immortal masterpieces by plagiarizing them, parodying them, presenting them plainly, without apparatus and scruple, like any other *attraction*] (*TIF* 86). On the other hand, however, variety theatre also offers the model for a new form of relationship between artist and audience – a relationship of collaboration rather than passive submission. The variety hall thus turns into a kind of total spectacle, in which 'l'azione si svolge ad un tempo sul palcoscenico, nei palchi e nella platea' [the action takes place at once on the stage, in the boxes, and in the pit] (*TIF* 83–4).[47]

What makes futurism a radical departure from the artistic horizon of fin-de-siècle culture is finally the fact that the loss of the aura of the work of art is not mourned but rather welcomed as the very defining characteristic of the modern work, as Marinetti writes toward the conclusion of the 'Manifesto tecnico':

> Ci gridano: 'La vostra letteratura non sarà bella! Non avremo più la sinfonia verbale, dagli armoniosi dondolii, e dalle cadenza tranquillizzanti!' Ciò è bene inteso! E che fortuna! Noi utiliziamo, invece, tutti i suoni brutali, tutti i gridi espressivi della vita violenta che ci circonda. **Facciamo coraggiosamente il brutto in letteratura, e uccidiamo dovunque la solennit** . Via! non prendete di quest'arie da grandi sacerdoti,

nell'ascoltarmi! Bisogna sputare ogni giorno sull'*Altare dell'Arte*! Noi entriamo nei dominii sconfinati della libera intuizione. Dopo il verso libero, ecco finalmente **le parole in libert !**

[They shout at us: 'Your literature won't be beautiful! We will no longer have verbal symphony, with its graceful singsong, and its reassuring cadences!' This is understood! And what luck! On the contrary, we use all the brutal sounds, all the expressive cries of the violent life which surrounds us. **We bravely make the ugly in literature, and we kill solemnity everywhere**. Cheer up! don't assume those airs of high priests when you listen to me! It is necessary to spit on the *Altar of Art*! We enter the boundless territories of free intuition. After free verse, here are finally **words in freedom!**] (*TIF* 54)

With this final rejection of aesthetics, the high priest or aristocrat of decadentism is replaced by the technician. The best expression of the implications of the de-sacralization of the work of art is the manifesto 'Pesi, misure e prezzi del genio artistico' (1914), an early contribution to the movement by Emilio Settimelli and Bruno Corradini (better known under the pseudonym of Bruno Corra), two of the protagonists of the so-called second Florentine futurism, the futurist group gathered around the journal *L'Italia Futurista*, published in the Tuscan city between 1916 and 1918.[48] In this manifesto, the artist appears perfectly integrated in the marketplace. Outlining the principles of the 'Misurazione' (measurement), the procedure which, with its objective criteria, should replace criticism in assessing the importance of the work and its financial value, the two authors write:

Così, distrutto lo snobismo passatista dell'arte-ideale, dell'arte-sublimità-sacra-inaccessibile, dell'arte-tormento-purezza-voto-solitudine-disprezzo della realtà, anemia malinconica di smidollati che si appartano dalla vita reale perché non sanno affrontarla, l'artista troverà finalmente il suo posto *dentro la vita*: tra il salumaio e il fabbricante di pneumatici, tra il beccamorto e lo speculatore, tra l'ingegnere e l'agricoltore.

[Thus, with the destruction of the *passéiste* snobbishness of the art-ideal, of the art-sublime-sacred-inaccessible, of the art-torment-purity-vow-solitude-scorn of reality, melancholic feebleness of namby-pambies who remove themselves from real life because they are unable to face it, the artist will finally find his place *inside life*: between the pork-butcher and

> the tire-maker, the grave-digger and the speculator, the engineer and the farmer.] (3)

But before we interpret this self-consciously ironic text as the symptom of a quick and early capitulation of futurism to the economic logic of capitalism and to the fundamentally *petit-bourgeois* ideology underlying its revolutionary rhetoric, let us consider some other passages that somewhat complicate the picture.

> [I]l concetto di arte dovrà essere enormemente allargato anche in un altro senso. Infatti non si capisce perché ogni attività debba per forza inscatolarsi nell'una o nell'altra di quelle ridicole limitazioni che si chiamano musica, letteratura, pittura... e non per es. dedicarsi a combinare degli organismi con pezzi di legno, tele carta, piume e chiodi, i quali, lasciati cadere da una torre alta 37 metri e 3 centimetri, descrivano cadendo a terra una certa linea più o meno complessa, più o meno difficile da ottenere, più o meno rara. Quindi **ogni artista potr inventare un arte nuova** la quale sia l'espressione libera delle idiosincrasie particolari della sua costituzione cerebrale modernamente pazza e complicata, e nella quale si trovino mescolati, con nuova misura e modalità, i mezzi d'espressione più diversi: parole, colori, note, indicazioni di forme, di profumi, di fatti, di rumori, di movimenti, di sensazioni fisiche... **cio mescolanza caotica, inestetica e strafottente di tutte le arti gi esistenti e di tutte quelle che sono e che saranno create dalla inesauribile volont di rinnovamento che il futurismo sapr infondere nell umanit** .

> [The concept of art will have to be greatly expanded in another way. In fact, it is not clear why every activity must necessarily be boxed inside one or the other of the absurd limitations that are called music, literature, painting ... and not for instance devote to combining organisms with pieces of wood, canvas, paper, feathers and nails which, dropped from a tower 37 m. and 3 cm. high, will trace in their fall a more or less complex line, more or less easy to delineate, more or less rare. Therefore, **any artist will be able to invent a new art** that will be the free expression of the particular idiosyncrasies of his modernly mad and complicated cerebral constitution, in which will be mixed, in a new measure and with new modalities, the most diverse means of expression: words, colors, notes, indications of forms, of scents, of facts, of noises, of movements, of physical sensations ... **that is, the chaotic, unaesthetic, arrogant mixture of all existing arts and of all those which will be created by the inexhaustible**

> **will of renewal that Futurism will be able to imbue in humanity.**] (Corra and Settimelli 2)

Art is thus configured as a total, creative experience with no other goal than the liberation of the inventiveness and vision of the individual. This might seem to lead in the direction of Benjamin's critique of futurism in the conclusion of his 'The Work of Art in the Age of Mechanical Reproduction.' As is well known, Benjamin argues that fascism domesticates the proletarian masses and thus preserves the social and economic structures of the capitalist state by introducing aesthetics into politics – that is, to use Benjamin's own eloquent expression, by 'giving these masses not their right, but instead a chance to express themselves' (241). But it seems that the original contribution of Settimelli and Corra's manifesto is precisely the fact that they envision 'art' as an individual and non-specialized practice that resists the massification of culture and its subjection to the logic of mass consumption without turning back to an idealized, aristocratic, 'sublime' appreciation of the aesthetic object. In other words, the 'expression' that the two authors call for is an activity that goes against the identification between the 'masses' and their cultural and political models by defending the right of each individual to a creative appropriation and manipulation of material reality. Marshall Berman has written that the constitutive aporia of capitalism is that 'it destroys the human possibilities it creates. It fosters, indeed forces, self-development for everybody; but people can develop only in restricted and distorted ways. Those traits, impulses and talents that the market can use are rushed (often prematurely) into development [...]; everything else within us, everything nonmarketable, gets draconically repressed' (96). Ironically inverting the logic of capitalism, Corra and Settimelli argue that what should be rewarded is precisely what is truly new, that is, what cannot be immediately integrated in and commodified by the market – what has no other function than to be an index of the freedom of its author. They further write:

> Assolutamente certi che le leggi che domandiamo ci saranno date in un tempo prossimo, noi chiediamo sin d'ora che **siano per primi processati sotto l accusa di truffa continuata a danno del pubblico D Annunzio, Puccini e Leoncavallo**: infatti questi signori vendono per migliaia di lire opere il cui valore varia da un minimo di 35 centesimi a un massimo di 40 franchi.

> [Absolutely certain that the laws we demand will be given to us in a near future, we request from this very moment that **D Annunzio, Puccini, and Leoncavallo be tried first with the accusation of repeated fraud against the public**: these gentlemen in fact sell for thousands of liras works whose value varies from a minimum of 35 cents to a maximum of 40 francs.] (3).

The value of art lies in the fact that it has no use value; thus commercially successful artists such as D'Annunzio and the composers Giacomo Puccini and Ruggiero Leoncavallo are precisely those artists who, by not deploying an adequate amount of novelty in their work, fail to meet the criteria of the manifesto. In a paradoxical – and therefore openly contradictory – way, 'Pesi, misure e prezzi del genio artistico' refunctionalizes art by rejecting the aura and its implications, and by turning the work into that object whose very presence in the marketplace serves as a reminder of what the marketplace itself represses: freedom, individuality, originality. Therefore, the purposelessness of the work of art is no longer the ground of a transcendent aesthetic experience, but rather that of a critical reflection on the formation of consensus in modern society through the production and circulation of mass products. This is certainly not a politicization of art – not, in any case, in the Benjaminian sense – but at the very least, it attributes to art an anti-institutional function that allows the articulation of a 'third' critical position alternative to both the impossible auratic work of art of the decadents and the commodity of 'industrial literature.'

It has been said that the study of futurism is the study of its contradictions.[49] Perhaps its most evident contradiction is the general abandonment of the more radical implications of its theory of art after the First World War, when Marinetti *in primis* returned more and more frequently to a practice of writing which both formally and thematically moved closer and closer to the mainstream of the tradition. If the volume *Les mots en liberté futuristes* (1919) constitutes the theoretical and practical *summa* of Marinetti's *paroliberismo* by combining the manifestoes of literature with some of the more revolutionary examples of 'tables of words in freedom' – rightly described by Salaris as the works in which Marinetti's experimentation with the very materiality of the word reaches 'its highest degree of abstraction' (*Dizionario* 90) – the 1921 volume *L'alcova d'acciaio*, a war memoir that recuperates many of Marinetti's previous objects of scorn (from memory and history to traditional syntactical and narrative structures), marks the beginning of the poet's personal 'return to order.' Though interrupted by intermittent bursts of impatience that find expression in the occasional act of provocation or in the momentary return to *paroliberismo,* Marinetti's gradual integration in the institution entailed a redrawing of the boundaries between producer and consumer that his earlier works had pushed to the point of rupture. Nonetheless, the historical importance of futurism lies precisely in the fact that it lived in a non-nostalgic way the twilight of the aura, and it began to theorize an artistic practice in which impermanence is not a deficiency to be resolved but rather the opportunity for an overcoming and a redemption of the isolation of the work of art by dissolving it into the moment of communication. By doing this, futurism opened up a new path in twentieth-century aesthetics that it may not have followed to its furthest end, but that was then pursued by the other avant-gardes, historical and otherwise.

ADVERTISING FUTURISM

There is another aspect of the Futurist cultural strategy that deserves further discussion: its adoption of techniques of communication from the budding advertising industry to publicize its program. This was indeed one of the novelties of the movement that most caught the attention of contemporary audiences, and was usually cited as evidence of the unserious and anti-cultural character of the movement – a sentiment expressed, for instance, by Scipio Slataper who, writing in the Florentine cultural journal *La Voce,* argued that the 'materialità antipatica' [unpleasant materiality] of the propaganda strategies of futurism, such as 'le circolari a getto continuo' [the continuous production of circular letters], was evidence of the movement's lack of 'un vero contenuto spirituale' [a true spiritual content] ('Il futurismo' 204). However, it was precisely this iconoclastic aspect of the movement that led another Florentine intellectual, Giovanni Papini, to a more nuanced and insightful apology of the futurist cultural strategy in a 1913 article for the literary journal *Lacerba,* entitled argumentatively 'Contro il futurismo.' At the age of thirty two, Papini, an indefatigable polemicist and cultural organizer, was already an established figure in the cultural circles that opposed the dominant idealist philosophy represented by Benedetto Croce. Papini had been elaborating a personal interpretation of pragmatism that, by bringing together William James and Henri Bergson, emphasized the vitalistic, transformative, and 'magical' implications of that current of thought. Papini's reaction to futurism was initially critical, but in February1913, in a speech delivered in Rome and significantly entitled (in its published form) 'Contro Roma e contro Benedetto Croce,' he announced the forging of an alliance with the futurists on the basis of a common program of renewal of the nation, the preparation of 'l'avvento [dell'] uomo nuovo il quale non abbia bisogno di grucce e di consolazioni, che non si spaventi del nulla e dei cieli vuoti' [the advent of the new man who will not require crutches and consolations, who will not be afraid of nothingness and of empty skies] (*L'esperienza futurista* 67). This tactical alliance was to be short lived, but it forced the young philosopher, who had heretofore characterized his ultimately political strategy in pointedly elitist terms, to deal with the more populist aspects of the futurist movement.[50] Papini's reflections in 'Contro il futurismo' – where, in spite of the title, he sought in fact to clarify the terms of his own support for Marinetti's project – deserve to be quoted in some detail. They bring into relief the fact that the ruptural quality of futurism was a result not only of its program but also, and perhaps primarily, of its use of techniques of communication mutuated from cultural ambits – advertising in particular – whose position in the field of cultural production was to say the least equivocal in turn of the century Italy, and which even threatened the internal laws of the field itself.

Papini's rhetorical strategy is twofold. On the one hand, he reconnects certain futurist activities with established – 'auratic,' we might say – forms of cultural production. Thus, regarding the famous *'serate futuriste'* – theatrical events in which futurists exhibited themselves in a series of activities (reading of manifestoes, exhibition of paintings, performance of futurist music, etc.) meant to shock or at least challenge the expectations of the audience – Papini reminds his readers that theatres are increasingly employed for non-aesthetic purposes: 'Si presentano alla ribalta il deputato e il ministro per difendere le sue vedute politiche' [The deputy and the minister show up on the stage to defend their political ideas] ('Contro il futurismo' 2). Therefore, by presenting poetry, art, and music, albeit in anti-traditional forms, the futurists are at least returning the theatre to its proper function. On the other hand, Papini also acknowledges that the use of non-canonical forms of communication in the aesthetic debate is the result of the transformed conditions of art in modernity.

Si accusano i futuristi di abusare deliberatamente di cartelloni, manifesti, richiami, esibizioni ecc., che non hanno nulla a che fare con l'arte. E c'è dell'apparenza di vero in questa accusa. Ma siamo di fronte a una diversità di tempi e di temperamenti che bisogna intendere prima di condannare.

La réclame non è arte: d'accordo. Ma è una delle potenze della vita contemporanea, una delle speciali creazioni della nostra civiltà. È uno strumento di cui tutti, più o meno nascostamente, si servono. La réclame non è arte – ma neppure è politica o scienza o industria. Eppure della réclame si servono i partiti politici, gli stessi governi, i ritrovati scientifici, i prodotti industriali. La réclame non è arte ma quando esce un libro ogni buon editore mette cartelloni sulle cantonate e inserzioni sui giornali. [...] Quando D'Annunzio e Benelli, putacaso, stanno per varare una nuova macchina teatrale i giornalisti si presentano compiacentemente a informare la gente, con sapienti interviste e indiscrezioni, che l'opera imminente sarà la più bella fra tutte quelle passate del poeta in discorso, che la concezione è mirabile, la forma nuovissima e altre buggerate dello stesso genere. Se questa non è réclame – sfacciata o subdola che sia – voglio rinchiudermi anch'io nella 'torre d'avorio' dei poeti a un tanto la pagina.

Tutti adoperano e sfruttano la réclame – e un gruppo di artisti novatori, ai quali l'opinione è forzatamente ostile, non debbono servirsi del solo strumento che la civiltà contemporanea offre come difesa contro la cospirazione del silenzio e dell'imbecillità? [...]

Solo il presente esiste; e gli empirei son caduti dal firmamento. Non c'è che una vita e la vogliamo migliore. Noi diamo e vogliamo ricevere. L'artista, come ogni uomo che fa, desidera ormai d'esser subito discusso – coronato di spine o coronato di rose.

[The futurists are accused of deliberately overindulging in posters, manifestoes, advertisements, exhibitions, etc., that have nothing to do with art. And there is a semblance of truth in this accusation. But we are confronted with different times and temperaments that must be understood before they are condemned.

Advertising is not an art, I agree. But it is one of the powers of contemporary life, one of the special creations of our civilization. It is an instrument used by everybody, more or less openly. Advertising is not an art – but it is also not politics or science or industry. And yet, political parties, and even governments, scientific discoveries, industrial products, use advertising. Advertising is not an art, but when a book comes out any good publisher puts posters on street corners and advertisements in newspapers. When D'Annunzio or [Sem] Benelli, let's say, are about to launch another theatrical machine, journalists agreeably inform people, with shrewd interviews and indiscretions, that the forthcoming work will

> be more beautiful than any of the said poet's previous ones, that it was admirably conceived, that the form is truly new, and other stupid things like that. If this is not advertising – whether shameless or surreptitious – I too want to lock myself in the 'ivory tower' of the poets paid a certain amount per page.
>
> Everybody uses and takes advantage of advertising – and a group of innovative artists, to whom public opinion is necessarily hostile, should not employ the only instrument that contemporary civilization offers as a defense against the conspiracy of silence and stupidity?
>
> Only the present exists. The empyreans have fallen down the firmament. There is only one life, and we want it to be better. The artist, like anyone who produces, wants to be discussed immediately – crowned with roses or with thorns.] ('Contro il futurismo' 2–3)

Papini does not evoke the name of D'Annunzio by chance: even the high priest of Beauty as absolute value cannot escape the logic of the marketplace, because at the very moment when his products become public they are inserted in the system of circulation of commodities. Like Baju's fallen aristocrats, artists, whether they like it or not, are already integrated in the economic system that forces them to sell their wares according to its own dynamics, just like politicians sell their images as well as their policies. The distinction between advertising and art remains operative, but only at the expense of the distinction between the work of art and the product of consumption. The loss of the halo is now a reality that transforms the way in which the artist relates to the audience: the artist is a producer, and he writes not for posterity but for the present, to engage his contemporaries.

The most insightful aspect of Papini's vindication of advertising is his representation of contemporary society as fundamentally mediatic. Advertising, as he points out, does not identify with the products that it publicizes, whether these are scientific discoveries (such as the patent medicines that constituted some of its earliest objects), cultural artefacts, or even people (for instance, politicians). Rather, advertising constitutes the 'medium' in which all these products are immersed and which makes their circulation possible; it is the framework that links the text – which, as in the case of politics, can be the producer himself – with its audience. The innovative aspect of futurism lies in this attempt to take control of the discourse generated by its activities, and to play even a key role in its construction.

In his preface to De Maria's anthology of Marinetti's works, *Teoria e invenzione futurista*, the poet Aldo Palazzeschi recalled that Marinetti 'aveva capito fino da allora il potere della pubblicità che doveva raggiungere fatti e persone a tutte le profondità e a tutte le altezze, nessuno escluso della compagine sociale, e riservata allora esclusivamente per le Pillole Pink il cerotto Bertelli e la Chinina Migone' [had already understood the power of advertising in reaching events and people at all depths and heights, with no one excluded in the social body. Up to that point, this power had been reserved only for the Pink Pills, the Bertelli adhesive plaster, and Migone quinine] (xxi).[51] Thus, as we have already suggested, what makes futurism a truly innovative event in the cultural landscape of early-twentieth-century Italian culture is its acceptance of the fallen condition of art and its concerted effort to articulate new ways to foster and control the circulation of its products in the cultural market. Marinetti, in other words, approaches the foundation of futurism as an eminently organizational problem aimed at the broadest possible distribution of the products of the movement.

The history of advertising is tightly bound with the technological innovations that characterize modernity, and it initially followed the evolution of the newspapers, which constituted the earliest vehicle and support.[52] In Italy, as in France, the resistance to the juxtaposition of paid advertisements and news items, a feature which on the contrary had characterized the press of the English-speaking world since the beginning of the nineteenth century, meant that *réclames* were relegated to the final (usually the fourth) page of newspapers and were limited to small announcements that relied mostly on text to deliver their message. A crucial moment of transition occurred with the uncoupling of newspapers and advertising and the transformation of the advertisement itself into an independent text. The invention of lithography in 1773 and of chromolithography in 1836 made it possible to turn the posters and *affiches* used until the end of the eighteenth century mostly for public or official announcements, into the colorful and eye-catching advertisements for theatrical spectacles, art exhibitions, and eventually market products characterizing the modern urban landscape.[53] The advertising poster is thus the exact opposite of the auratic work of art, since, far from closing itself within the institutional space of the museum or the literary magazine, it seeks out its audience, meeting it more than half way, as Benjamin says of the mechanical reproduction, going into the streets with the audience itself as a part of the environment of modernity.

The co-optation of figurative artists by the advertising industry at the turn of the century resulted in the production of posters that reflected and often engaged in a dialogue with the work of non-commercial artists, and shifted the emphasis away from the written and toward the visual code in the articulation of the commercial message. The latter phenomenon is especially important: the lengthy descriptions of the benefits provided by the product that characterizes written advertisements are replaced by images that are meant more to strike than to inform the viewer. In fin-de-siècle advertisements, the written message is thus often reduced to the mere brand name, which is more and more visually integrated into the picture itself, while other necessary information such as the firm's address – if it survives at all – is moved to unobtrusive corners of the poster. Thus, the brand name becomes a crucial element, an overdetermined sign that must perform an array of informative and suasive functions. As Roberto Grandi remarks in his entry on the subject for the *Dizionario della pubblicità*, the brand is considered a category not of the universe of commerce but of communication. In a competitive environment, the brand makes it possible to distinguish a specific product from its rivals. Grandi's observations on this point are important.

> Through a specific brand politics, the producer seeks to realize two objectives. The first objective is a correct positioning on the market, that is, to make it possible for customers to recognize the distinctive qualities of the brand in relation to its most direct competitors. The second objective is a true capitalization: the politics of construction of the brand leads to a sedimentation of the representation of the distinctive qualities of the brand in the public, that is, to the construction of an actual capital, which has also an economic value. (Abruzzese and Colombo 267)

Clearly, along with the potential economic return which is after all the aim of any advertising campaign, what is at stake here is first of all *symbolic* capital. In other words, the advertisement serves not simply to sell a certain type of product, but also to generate, re-enforce, and transform the discourse around the producer, and to position that producer *vis-à-vis* the other players in the field. A successful campaign means that a consumer will remember the brand even after the specific object sold in the campaign is made obsolete by the very logic of the marketplace, which requires a continuous replacement of products.

This strategy on the part of the producer finds its correlative in the effect that brand names have on their audiences. Brand names function as a guarantee, since the consumer can rely on the personal and public history associated with the brand – 'The product commits the producer directly to offer a quality that remains constant over time and space' (Abruzzese and Colombo 267). However they also provide 'a universe of values which allows [the consumer] to orient himself better in contemporary society, especially in his reactions with others' (268). Buying, say, a FIAT or a Ferrari is not only a matter of what one can afford, but also of the cultural and social values that are encoded by such a choice. Thus the purchase of a product entails not only the acquisition of something that has a specific use value and fulfills a certain function, but also the insertion of the individual buyer into a network of symbolic relations that defines him or her in relation to the choices of other consumers.

The truly original move performed by Marinetti lies in his adoption of this logic of advertising in the production and circulation of his movement. During his editorship of *Poesia* Marinetti had already experimented with techniques of self-advertising that would serve him well in the launch of the futurist movement, such as the publication of extensive dossiers in which he reported the reactions of the press to his initiatives. The publication of the manifesto of futurism, then, was interpreted by its earliest critics – who appeared singularly unimpressed by the pretended novelty of Marinetti's gesture – as yet another publicity stunt. As already mentioned, the editorial note of *Le Figaro* read the manifesto against its own discourse, not as an innovative or ruptural move, but rather as the repetition of a gesture already inscribed in an established tradition – that of the foundation of new avant-garde literary movements by means of a public announcement in the newspaper. Likewise, the earliest readers of the manifesto tended to emphasize the canonical nature of Marinetti's gesture. Charles Etienne, in one of the earliest public reactions to the manifesto, wrote: 'Pour ajouter encore à sa renommée l'auteur de la *Ville charnelle* et du *Roi Bombance* [i.e., Marinetti] vient de frapper un grand coup: il a fondé une nouvelle école littéraire à laquelle il a donné le nom de "Futurisme"' [In order to add yet again to his reputation, the author of the *Ville charnelle* and of the *Roi Bombance* has just struck a great blow: he has founded a new literary school that he has named 'futurism'];[54] in other words, business as usual. In *Comoedia* G. De Pawlowski chalked Marinetti's rhetoric up to his age, commenting 'Ah! Jeunesse' (Novelli 212) in his summary of the futurist program. The similarity with other contemporary schools and coteries was also insistently remarked upon. In *Le temps*, Nozière wrote that 'Il va sans dire que ce jeune écrivain [Marinetti] s'applique à présenter sa nouvelle école en déconcertant le public. Ces idées ne sont pas plus folles que d'autres' [it goes without saying that this young writer works hard to introduce his new school by disconcerting the public [...] His ideas are no crazier than those of others] (Novelli 214), and then listed other writers who had already sung the new beauty of speed, thus preempting the futurist claim to this new poetic subject. The lapidary comment of an anonymous writer for *L'intransigeant* sums up the general attitude: futurism is characterized as one of the new schools that 'nous viennent à présent de l'étranger ou de la province. Nous avions hier *le Futurisme* de M.F.T. Marinetti qui dirige *Poesia* à Milan. Mais nous avons en opposition à cette doctrine *Le Primitivisme*, qui date d'aujourd'hui' [we have introduced from abroad or from the provinces. Yesterday we had *the futurism* of M.F.T. Marinetti, who edits *Poesia* in Milan. But in opposition to this doctrine we have *primitivism*, which dates to today] (Novelli 215). Far from announcing the future, Marinetti's movement is already old news, and provincial news to boot.

What was different about Marinetti's launch of the movement, however, was not the gesture itself, but rather the fact that it was only the first move in a complex campaign to bring futurism to the broadest possible audience. The publication of the manifesto in *Le Figaro* was a necessary step in the process of legitimating his cultural project, since the Parisian newspaper had the cultural capital to endow futurism with a degree of authenticity as an avant-garde movement. (Indeed, the editorial note, ironic though it may have been, simply reiterated the canonizing function of getting a manifesto published on *Le Figaro*, since it implicitly brought the new movement into relation with those that had preceded it in *Le Figaro's* august pages.) The importance of such a legitimation was a lesson that Marinetti had learned when the appearance of an earlier version of his text (without the narrative prologue) in several provincial newspapers, including *La Gazzetta dell'Emilia* (5 February 1909), in the two weeks before the French publication, failed to attract any public reaction.[55] What was different was the strategy with which Marinetti operated after the publication of the manifesto: far from being recontained within the institutional sites of the literary debate – the literary magazines and the cultural pages of the newspapers – futurism began to associate itself with several domains both within and without the cultural sphere, and Marinetti and his followers developed a series of strategies aimed at the abolition of the distance between the ambit of aesthetic activity and the domain of everyday life. The techniques developed by the bourgeoning advertising industry were thus gradually and consciously adopted by Marinetti, as is clear from the recollection of the foundation of the movement in *Guerra sola igiene del mondo* (quoted above, p. 97).

Two aspects of that passage are interesting. The first is that Marinetti characterizes futurism in terms of its anti-institutional thrust, as a rejection of the traditional modes of mediation of the work of art, 'gli articoli, le poesie e le polemiche' [articles, poems, and polemics] (*TIF* 235), which have consigned the artist to invisibility. We are dealing once again with the consequences of the loss of the halo, of the fact that in the landscape of modernity nothing distinguishes the artist from the bourgeois. The answer of the decadents had been a complete withdrawal from the stage of daily life for the artificial paradise of art in which – as with the symbolist declension of that theme – the search for a pure poetic word becomes the secret sign through which artists make themselves known not to the world but to their peers. On the contrary, for the futurists – and this theme constitutes the kernel of the narrative section of the first manifesto – the artist must take to the street to make the audience acknowledge his presence, to challenge its attention. The second noteworthy element is implicit in the procedure that led to the foundation of the movement. Clearly, while the futurists did not shy away from actual fists and assaults, the shock that was sought was a symbolic one: the audience must be 'struck,' and advertising provided a storehouse of experiences that could be used for the purpose of selling futurism. Thus, at the origin of the futurist project there is not a theory of poetry or of art, as is the case for poetic movements of the late nineteenth century, but rather the intention of rethinking the relationship between artists and audience: in other words, an organizational rather than a poetic question. The first step in the development of the movement, then, is the invention of a name that functions much like the brand names discussed above. The name serves initially to identify the new formation in relation to other competing movements in the cultural field, and to give the simulacrum of a collective identity to a group that was initially limited to Marinetti himself and some of the Italian poets who were already contributing to *Poesia*.[56] But futurism does not stop at this initial stage: the term itself comes to be associated not only with a certain poetic enterprise, but with a series of cultural values that inflect in new and specific ways the futurist intervention in the most varied domains of activity – just as the brand is meant to evoke in the consumer a series of associations that characterize the product before its specific features and functions are known. In other words, futurism as a brand name serves both to orient the attitude of the audience as the movement colonizes every possible field of cultural activity – from painting to fashion, from music to cuisine – and to suggest that the futurist version will be distinguished by the qualities of anti-traditionalism, dynamism, innovation, and scorn for established conventions. Behind the specific articulations of the principles of futurist poetry, politics, feminism, or economics there lies a set of abstract values that provide the rhetorical connective tissue of the different activities of the movement.[57]

Manifestoes are a crucial instrument for the articulation of such a common discourse that serves not only to coordinate the activities of the various members of the movement by deploying a series of key words and concepts that are adapted to the internal and specific necessities of a particular artistic domain, but also to endow these activities with coherence and consistency within the broader framework of the futurist project. The proliferation of manifestoes between 1909 and Marinetti's death in 1944 – estimates range from over fifty, according to Germano Celant (*Futurismo/Futurismi* 505), to more than 300 according to Salaris (cf. *Bibliografia*), and finally to the more than 400 manifestoes, proclamations, and polemical pieces collected by Caruso in his monumental reprint of futurist texts – is an index of the peculiarity of futurism among the other European avant-gardes. Its expansion in and appropriation of every aspect of everyday life is intrinsic to its radical abolition of the barrier between high and low, between art and lived experience. In this context, where the very distinction between aesthetic and anti-aesthetic is invalidated, new protocols for the evaluation of a certain practice – which can no longer be called 'work of art' or 'work of the artist' since these are precisely the notions that are at stake – need to be elaborated. The manifesto is thus the locus for their articulation, and simultaneously it is the means of reproduction and dispersal of a new normative discourse that serves to tie together the different ambits in which futurism operates.

Furthermore, Marinetti separates the manifesto from the physical support of the newspaper or the literary journal, and turns it into a text free to circulate and encounter its audience outside the traditional institutional environments for artists' proclamations. The poster had freed the advertisement from the formal and stylistic constraints enforced by its insertion in the context of the newspaper, and allowed the product to address directly that same mass audience of consumers produced by modernity – the middle-class crowd among which the Baudelaerian *flâneur* and the artist become invisible. Likewise, manifestoes, printed cheaply in large quantities in the form of leaflets, gave the movement an unprecedented freedom and directness of publicity. A result of the new independence of the manifesto was the experimentation with new means of distribution. Manifestoes could be brought to the public by pasting them on the street, like advertising posters, by distributing them during the *serate futuriste*; they could even become the instrument for bigger publicity stunts, such as the famous shower of copies ('800,000,' boasted Marinetti hyperbolically) of the 'Discorso futurista di Marinetti ai Veneziani' from the newly rebuilt Torre dell'Orologio in Venice on the unsuspecting passers-by on 8 July 1910 (cf. *TIF* 34).[58]

The launch of the movement was accompanied by a carefully orchestrated campaign that made use of techniques that even anticipated the advertising industry itself, such as the use of the mail to reach a selected target audience of intellectuals, who were invited to join the movement in a personal letter that also included the text of the first manifesto. Another mailing, including the French text of the manifesto and a translation in the relevant language, was sent to major international newspapers, thus buying some early international publicity. The responses to this invitation – whether negative or positive – in turn became further fuel for the futurist advertising machine, as Marinetti published in the next-to-last issue of *Poesia* two dossiers, one with a copious selection of answers to his letter, and the other with complete reprints of the articles in the foreign press elicited by the manifesto.

Pierre Loti's reaction is indicative of the dislocating effect of Marinetti's move. The aesthetic sensibility of the famous author of exotic travel narratives was as far from futurism as possible, as he did not fail to remark in his letter: 'J'ai le culte passionné du passé, l'horreur et le dégoût du modernisme. Si vous avez lu une seule ligne de mes livres, comment ne le savez-vous pas et comment pouvez-vous, sans rire, me demander une adhésion, même partielle, à votre manifeste?' [I have a passionate cult for the past, and a horror and disgust for modernism. If you have read a single line of my books, how could you not know that, and how could you ask me in all seriousness to support, even partially, your manifesto?] ('Adhésions et objections' 11) Naturally, the point of

Marinetti's move was not to garner the affiliation of authors such as Loti, but rather to force the interpellated intellectuals –whether their reaction was hostility, support, or simply amusement – to acknowledge and validate the presence of futurism, to contribute to the discursive economy on the basis of which futurism constructed quickly and efficiently its symbolic capital.

The publication of manifestoes as independent leaflets also allowed for a greater degree of typographical experimentation than was possible within the limitated specifications of a newspaper or journal article. The two- or four-page leaflets soon assumed a fairly standard format: the first page bore the title of the manifesto in large block capitals with the the name/brand futurism prominently displayed ('MANIFESTE INITIAL DU **FUTURISME**'; '**Manifesto dei Drammaturghi futuristi**'; **Manifesto futurista della Lussuria**'),[59] while the text closed with the signature of the issuer(s), followed by the date[60] and the address of the '*direzione*' of the movement – namely Marinetti's own Milan residence at Corso Venezia 61 (or after Marinetti's move to Rome in 1925, his new address, 30 Piazza Adriana). On numerous occasions the final page was partially or entirely dedicated to listing the cadres of the movement, with the various artists listed by 'discipline.' Capital letters and bold were used in the body of the text to highlight key points or to bring the programmatic section into relief. Even the structure of the manifestoes often followed a similar scansion, with a long preamble in which the author or authors address their audience and articulate the position of their adversaries, followed by a series of numbered conclusions or programmatic points.[61] This suggests that, while Marinetti used it in a truly innovative way, the manifesto still performed a fundamentally theoretical function that differentiated it from the properly creative texts – poems, paintings, or even clothes and dishes – of the movement. The repetition of the same formal solutions thus served to emphasize the continuity of the different cultural proposals of the movement: whether written by Marinetti or by one of his followers, the manifesto was immediately recognizable as futurist, and that recognition was functional to the evocation of a certain horizon of expectations on the part of the readers depending on their attitude toward the brand presenting the 'product' that it aimed to sell. Thus, even the limited graphic devices – the different type sizes and fonts noted above – are not a result of the application of the 'typographic revolution' theorized in the manifesto 'Distruzione della sintassi Immaginazione senza fili Parole in libertà' (which in any case was published only in

1913), as has been suggested (cf. Salaris, *Dizionario* 74). More simply, they are the adaptation of an advertising technique from the newspaper industry – the use of large headlines to catch the attention of the buyer.

Finally, it is remarkable that the issuing of leaflet manifestoes quickly dwindled after the First World War and almost vanished after the mid-twenties: of the manifestoes collected by Caruso, the last one published as a leaflet by the 'Direzione del movimento futurista' is Fedele Azari's 'La flora futurista ed equivalenti plastici di odori artificiali' (1924; cf. Caruso 168); the last circular signed by Marinetti, 'Il tattilismo,' dates back to 1921. The futurists did not stop writing manifestoes after the early 1920s: instead they now published them mostly in the many small futurist magazines and journals that sprang up in several parts of Italy. While I have no interest in rehashing the arguments for and against the division of the futurist experience into two almost opposite phases – a so-called first futurism, which would constitute the truly innovative moment and which ended with the deaths of Boccioni and of Sant'Elia during the First World War; and a second futurism, which gathered secondary figures and repeated uninspiredly the gestures of a sterile rebellion – I believe that this involution in the use of the manifesto is another symptom of the more general 'return to order' to which futurism also answered after the war, and above all, after the fascist regime curtailed any manoeuvring space for a properly political movement. The renunciation of the use of manifestoes to bring futurism to the people did not mean the end of the movement as such, but certainly signaled its return to more traditional, and institutional, forms of literary communication – to a practice that no longer sought out its audience with the tenacity of an advertising campaign, but rather returned to the safe harbour of the museum and the book. In this sense, the vanishing of the futurist leaflet manifesto is as significant a sign of the transformation of futurism and its normalization as Marinetti's admission into the newly established Accademia d'Italia in 1929.

Chapter Three

Anarchists and Scientists: Futurism in England and the Formation of Imagism

One of the features that distinguishes futurism from *fin-de-siècle* avant-garde movements such as symbolism and *décadisme* is its totalizing hubris. This is exemplified not only by its attempt to construct a movement that would simultaneously unify the different domains of cultural production and imbricate in a complex network of relations the disparate experiences of artists in Italy, but, above all, by the missionary zeal with which Marinetti and his associates propagandized futurism throughout the continent – an enthusiasm which earned the futurist leader the nickname 'Caffeine of Europe.' The new media are objects of fascination – symbols of a technological modernity that promises a radical transformation of the relationship between the subject and the world – but they are also, and perhaps most importantly, the tools through which this revolution is carried out. While the problem of the *qualitative* difference between the work of art and the serialized products of technology is never fully resolved by an artistic practice that is finally unwilling to reject completely the validity of aesthetic judgement, there is no question that Marinetti quickly adapted the techniques of distribution of mass products to the works elaborated by himself and by his fellow futurists. In particular, the careful management of the image of the group became the signature strategy of the impresario of futurism, who sought to coordinate and supervise all aspects of the public reception of the movement. It was not simply a question of ensuring that there was a solid and coherent theoretical foundation underlying the different activities of the movement. In fact, Marinetti left other members of the movement significantly free to elaborate their own programs and, as we have seen, was even influenced in turn by questions raised and techniques proposed by some of these members. His often firm interventions in the drafting of a manifesto or a public document had usually to do not with issues of poetics, but rather with controlling the potential effect of the text on the public image of the group. Among these managerial activities, the *'arte di far manifesti'* [art of making manifestoes], which Marinetti, in a famous letter of September 1913 to Gino Severini, claimed to 'possess,' was of capital importance (Drudi Gambillo 1: 294). Thus, for instance, Severini found himself repeatedly admonished in 1913 over a manifesto (possibly 'Le analogie plastiche nel dinamismo,' [plastic analogies in dynamism] which he was to publish only in 1957) that, according to the futurist leader, failed, both in form and timing, to integrate with the other propaganda efforts of the movement. In the 1913 letter mentioned above, Marinetti first remarked on the stylistic failings of Severini's text, pointing out that 'il titolo non va assolutamente, perché troppo generico, troppo già contenuto nei titoli di altri manifesti' [the title does not work at all, too generic, already too much comprised in the title of other manifestoes] (Drudi Gambillo 1: 294), while in later correspondence he questioned the opportunity of the publication of the text, since 'tutta la stampa è piena (più di 100 couppures) di un annuncio di un piccolo concerto di *bruiteurs* fatto in casa mia,' [...] 'I manifesti, accumulandosi, si distruggono a vicenda' [the press is now full (over 100 coupures) of announcements of a small concert of *bruiteurs* that was held in my house. When they accumulate, manifestoes destroy one another] (Drudi Gambillo 1: 295). On the other hand, Marinetti had nothing to except regarding the content of the manifesto, which he found 'molto bello e molto importante, ma pubblicarlo così sarebbe pubblicare un bellissimo articolo, non già un manifesto' [very beautiful and very important, although publishing it the way it is would mean publishing a wonderful article, not a manifesto] (Drudi Gambillo 1: 294).

While Paris remained inevitably the city to which the futurists looked for both inspiration and consecration, it was also fairly impermeable to their penetration, and the exchange between the Italian and the French figurative avant-garde never went much further than a reciprocally fecund process of influence.[1] In fact, the French capital constituted a sort of promised land rather than a land of conquest; for the major figures of futurism, from Boccioni to Palazzeschi to Soffici, a pilgrimage to Paris represented a rite of passage from the provincialism of Italian cultural life to the cosmopolitanism of the *ville de la lumière*. In other words, Paris could not be conquered because, as the embodiment of the avant-garde city, it inspired respect rather than the contempt reserved for the other European capitals, from Venice to Rome to London. This attitude is evident in a letter dated 1 March 1912 written by Boccioni to Vico Baer, a young Jewish intellectual with whom the futurist painter entertained a frequent correspondence: 'Del resto il pubblico è imbecille in tutti i paesi e come non capisce in Italia non capisce qui [London], non capisce in Francia. Solo che in Francia ad esempio, essendovi più cultura moderna, più centri artistici, l'ambizione d'essere un innovatore, un capo scuola è più compresa al di fuori del successo immediato' [After all, the public is stupid, and it does not understand in Italy or here [London] or in France. The only difference is that in France, for instance, there is a more modern culture, more artistic centres, the ambition of being an innovator, a *capo-scuola* is understood more, beyond immediate success] (*Scritti* 348). Two weeks later, in a further letter to Baer, the painter confided his uncertainty on whether to return to Milan or to remain in 'a more favorable environment' such as Paris. Of course Severini, who was from the beginning the member of the Futurist movement most receptive to the lesson of Cubism, spent most of his artistic life in Paris, and Marinetti himself, well into the early years of the futurist enterprise, remained an Italian poet writing in French, the language in which he first published his major works until the First World War.[2]

Thus, if the train was one of the symbolic *loci* of futurism, it was not only for the obvious reason that it stood for modern technology, velocity and dynamism, but also because it quite literally provided a vehicle for the circulation of the movement itself. Futurism was the first artistic movement to take advantage of the innovations in communication technology to take control of its own public image: the telegraph allowed futurist organizers to be in close contact with gallery owners in the major capitals of the continent, and to supervise the public display of futurist works; the railroad made it possible for both the artists and their works to move from one city to the next, using the echo of the popular press to build momentum and expectation over the futurist spectacle. The year 1912 is the *annus mirabilis* in which futurism exploded on the European scene, with exhibitions in Paris, London, Bruxelles, and Berlin, in a tour that was reprised, with new stops, in the next two years, but was abruptly halted by the First World War.[3] The correspondence among the protagonists of this Futurist tour emphasizes the managerial role of Marinetti, who was not only a source of financial capital for the artists in need,[4] but also the one who most clearly understood how to carry out an effective publicity campaign. Indeed, his physical presence played a significant role in the success of the futurist campaigns, as we will see below. In April 1912 Boccioni reported to Carrà on the comparatively low interest concerning the exhibition in Berlin at the Sturm Gallery, owned by the writer and composer Herwath Walden, whose journal (entitled *Der Sturm*) had published several futurist manifestoes in German. Boccioni wrote, 'Ma temo che non ci sia il rumore tremendo di Parigi e di Londra, causa la *réclame* male organizzata. Marinetti dovrebbe essere qui, sarebbe necessario. Io non sono né giornalista né letterato, né ho il suo nome, la pratica di stampa...' [I am afraid there won't be the exceptional noise of Paris and London, because of the badly organized *réclame*. Marinetti should be here, he would be needed. I'm not a journalist or a writer, nor do I have his name or his practice with the press.] (*Scritti* 353).

The newspapers and the popular press were especially suited to sustaining a constant presence on the public scene, both in Italy and abroad. The manifesto, as we have seen, has close links with the newspaper. Thus, even in countries where there was not an active futurist artistic practice, the publication of manifestoes in the popular press became a way to establish a presence, to get the public interested and involved in the futurist project. This is something that Marinetti realized early on. His manifestoes, and then those of his followers, were immediately circulated outside of France and Italy (as mentioned above, the manifesto of foundation, or sections thereof, had been quickly translated into Spanish, English, German, and Russian), and in some cases were followed by *ad hoc* manifestoes addressed to the audience in a specific country. (For instance, 'Contro la Spagna passatista' [Against past-loving Spain] was published in 1911 by the journal *Prometeo* of Madrid). An index of the performative efficacy of this strategy is the appearance of 'futurist' groups in places quite outside Marinetti's sphere of influence. While the foundation of a futurist movement in Japan after the publication of a Japanese translation of the manifesto may constitute the most remote example, a more important example is the role played by futurism in the literature of late-imperial Russia and the early Soviet Union, where the name came to provide a unifying label for a series of avant-garde manifestations which found in it the ground for a common identity and intent.[5] In this chapter I will discuss the reactions to futurism in England and the role of futurist activities in the formation of the imagist movement. In particular I will consider how the imagist elaboration of a theoretical apparatus was affected by the avant-garde horizon established in great part by the activities of the futurists. The manifesto becomes in this case the site where this 'anxiety of influence' is most clearly felt, and where a series of antidotes against it are experimented.

'CRAZY EXPLODING PICTURES': THE RECEPTION OF FUTURISM IN ENGLAND, 1910–1914

Futurism in the British Press

Marinetti's ability to publicize the movement and his skill at taking advantage of the 'noise' provoked by the press was especially useful to penetrate those countries in which the movement did not have an already established network of connections with local intellectuals and, most importantly, with the publishing world. The reaction of the international press to the foundation of futurism, duly presented by Marinetti in a dossier published in the April–July issue of *Poesia*, is in this sense instructive. While the French press, directly provoked by Marinetti, had the lion's share of responses, it is notable that three German and three Spanish-language periodicals (two from Buenos Aires) intervened in the debate. In particular the Argentinian *La nacion* published a long article by Rubén Darío, in which the leader of the Latin American *modernismo* introduced Marinetti ('un buen poeta, un notable poeta') and then outlined a point by point critique of the programmatic section of the manifesto, not neglecting to remind his readers, in passing, that a *'futurismo'* had already been founded by the Catalan poet Gabriel Alomar. The British press, on the other hand, seems to have paid scant attention to the new movement. According to the dossier, only two English-language newspapers reported on the birth of futurism: the British *Daily Telegraph* and the American *Sun* of New York. The article in the *Sun* was mainly devoted to excerpts from the manifesto and to the reaction of Edmond Haraucourt in the French periodical *Le Gaulois*. The *Daily Telegraph*, however, anticipated two of the most recurrent objections characterizing the English reception of the movement: the distinction between poetry and poetics – or between the production of works of art and the articulation of programmatic statements[6] – and the futurist fascination with technology, which, for the newspaper, was a result of the relative industrial underdevelopment of Italy in comparison to other European nations.[7]

This was perhaps understandable in light of Marinetti's cultural politics in the years preceding the foundation of futurism since the author of *Mafarka le futuriste*, was, as we have seen, inserted in the cultural circuit of the *fin-de-siècle* French avant-garde. On the other hand, Marinetti had had limited contacts with the English literary and artistic world, not only because the cultural epicentre of Europe was the French capital, but also, more pragmatically, because he himself did not speak English (all his lectures and performances in England were held in French). On a few occasions *Poesia* had published contributions by important figures of British symbolism, including W.B. Yeats (October 1906–January 1907), Arthur Symons (April–June 1906), and T. Sturge Moore (June–July 1905), but only the minor poet Fred G. Bowles collaborated on a regular basis, faithfully publishing in the journal from the first issue to its brief rebirth under the editorship of Mario Dessy in 1920–1921. Finally, the last issue of the first series of *Poesia* included 'The Singer's Journey,' a poem by Douglas Goldring, who was Ford Madox Ford's editorial assistant on the prestigious *English Review* and was himself the editor of *The Tramp*, a small review dedicated, as the title suggests, to travel literature. An unlikely venue for futurism, *The Tramp* nonetheless published, in August 1910, excerpts of 'Contro Venezia passatista' and of the manifesto of foundation of the movement, introduced by Goldring himself. This was the first appearance of a futurist text in a British literary publication; in an interesting coincidence, that same issue of *The Tramp* included Wyndham Lewis's second published story, 'A Breton Innkeeper,' which suggests that the future leader of the vorticist movement must have been aware of the program and of the propaganda tactics of futurism from their early days.

Needless to say, *The Tramp* did not offer the kind of exposure that *Le Figaro* had afforded Marinetti in France. In the years between 1910 and 1914, up to the eve of the First World War (Marinetti's last lecture in London in 1914 was on 15 June) a series of initiatives established the presence of the Italian movement not only in the art world but even in the popular imagination of England, thanks in great part to the attention paid by the popular press to the extravagant and grandiloquent leader of the movement. Futurism played a catalyst role, as Giovanni Cianci has rightly put it,[8] in the formation of the English avant-garde, whose programs, articulated in a rhetoric that consciously either rejected or adopted the strategies of futurism, represented a reaction to the occasionally useful but overall cumbersome and stifling presence of these Italian interlopers.

Marinetti made his first visit to England to proselytize the futurist *verbum* in December 1910. The exact details of this visit, including the actual dates, remain for the most part unknown. The only contemporary evidence that allows us to date the lecture with some approximation is a short article in *The Vote*, the official journal of the Women's Freedom League, usually attributed to Margaret Wynne Nevinson, the mother of the soon-to-be futurist painter C.R.W. Nevinson.[9] Since this article, published in the 31 December 1910 issue of the weekly magazine, states that Marinetti's 'address' was held 'the other day at the Lyceum Club,' it appears fairly conclusive that Marinetti's own later recollections, which led a number of scholars to place the trip in the spring of 1910, are in fact incorrect, and that the correct date is sometime toward the end of 1910.[10] The fact that Marinetti's first lecture in England was reported by a suffrage magazine can be explained in light of the venue for the event, although again how and why Marinetti was invited to speak to this particular institution remains unclear. Founded in late 1903 or in 1904[11] under the guidance of its honorary secretary, Constance Smedley, the Lyceum Club was one of the most successful and active women's clubs in London, and the first 'to brave the male clubland of Piccadilly' (Crawford 124), where it had its headquarters. Membership was open to women 'who have published any original work in Literature, Journalism, Science, Art, or Music,' 'who have University qualifications,' and/or 'who are wives and daughters of distinguished men' (*The Lyceum Club*). It promoted numerous cultural activities, and was international in scope. According to Constance Smedley's autobiography, *Crusaders*, it had branches all across the Commonwealth, the Americas, and Europe, including Florence, Rome, Milan, and Genoa. It seems therefore possible that Marinetti's contacts with the English club might have been established through one of its Italian chapters. In any case, what must finally be emphasized is the fact that Marinetti's first intervention in the English cultural milieu was almost universally unnoticed (to my knowledge, it was not even advertised in the press).

The reception of the movement in 1912, when the Sackville Gallery hosted the travelling futurist exhibition on its first stop after Paris, was significantly different, as it benefited from a new art market that was looking to the Continent for novelties and investments. The 1910 exhibition 'Manet and Post-Impressionism,' organized by the artist and critic Roger Fry at the Grafton Galleries, had opened up the otherwise insular British art market to more recent developments in France.

Although Fry's exhibit cautiously relied on the canonical representatives of post-impressionism (Cézanne, Van Gogh and Gauguin were the central figures of the show), it also put forward artists like Odilon Redon, Maurice de Vlaminck, Georges Rouault, and, most importantly, Henri Matisse and Pablo Picasso, thus bringing onto the British scene the first signs of both fauvism and cubism. The extraordinary debate that ensued, which involved critics and artists alike in the columns of major newspapers and periodicals ranging from *The Times* to *The Pall Mall Gazette* to the *Morning Post*, thrust modern art very much to the centre of public attention. Setting aside the terms of the critical debate itself, the *Daily Graphic* reported, only four days after the opening, that 'every day the exhibition of the Post-Impressionists is crowded.' The *Art Journal* was forced to admit the success of the show, at the same time declaring what it considered its failure on aesthetic grounds: 'Cordial dislike for the efforts of this band of artists has been expressed by many people who have visited the Grafton Galleries, and not a few have used words of absolute condemnation. Nightmare art, as it has been called, is good as a sensation, however, and the show has been well attended' (qtd. Wees 27).

The popular success of Fry's exhibition paved the way for the futurist show two years later. In fact, the formation of a market open to novelties from the Continent made it possible not only for the futurists to find an audience that recognized, if not necessarily accepted, the revolutionary aesthetics of the avant-garde, but also for their works to find potential buyers willing to invest in it. Thus, if in an early letter[12] from London Severini could write to Boccioni that in spite of a certain success from the point of view of propaganda, sales had been non-existent ('nemmeno un ghello di vendita'), in the end several works were sold (including Boccioni's *The City Rises*, acquired by the famous conductor and composer Ferruccio Busoni for a total of 11,500 francs), as Marinetti boasted in a press release distributed to the major Italian newspapers.[13] But the already established debate on the validity of non-representational art also meant that the futurists were unable to engage fully their audience on their terms, as their operation was inevitably compared by critics and reviewers with that of the French pictorial avant-garde that had already found its champion in London in the influential figure of Roger Fry. In particular, this meant that futurism could be comfortably engaged on purely aesthetic terms, and brought back safely within the confines of the museum, since the battle over the disruptive social and political implications of the avant-garde and its potential threat to the order of British society had already been fought over post-impressionism.

Some critical receptions of Fry's exhibition had in fact initially played out the theme of contemporary art as a symptom of modern social decadence, comparing – as Wake Cook did in the *Pall Mall Gazette* – its assaults on 'the innocence of the public' to the anarchist rebellion 'against freedom' (qtd. Wees 26). A similar parallel between the artistic avant-garde and political anarchism was drawn in 1912 by *The Illustrated London News* in its report of the futurist exhibition at the Bernheim Gallery in Paris, one of several such articles published in major newspapers, such as *The Daily Mirror*, and the specialized press (for instance, *The Art Chronicle*), that prepared the London public for the arrival of the Italian artists. The title of the article, 'The New Crazy Exploding Pictures by "Art Anarchists,"' easily captured the imagination of a public made receptive by the wave of anarchist exploits across Europe in the previous two decades, and, most importantly, by the resurgence of anarchist activities, particularly the strikes directed by syndicalist-anarchist union leaders that reached their culmination during the period in which the futurists arrived in London. Furthermore, the nationality of the perpetrators of many of these exploits – the 1894 attempted bombing of the Greenwich Observatory by French anarchist Martial Boudin (from which Joseph Conrad drew the subject for his 1907 novel *The Secret Agent*); Sante Caserio's deadly stabbing of French President Marie-François Sadi Carnot in the same year; Michele Angiolillo's murder of Spanish Prime Minister Antonio Canovas del Castillo in 1897; and Gaetano Bresci's assassination of the Italian King Umberto I in 1900 (to avenge the victims of the 1898 riots in Milan), to name only the most spectacular – had established a close association between anarchism and foreigners, particularly Italians, although recent events such as the strikes demonstrated the threatening revolutionary force of the movement and its rootedness in Great Britain.[14] Lawrence Rainey has suggested that the juxtaposition of the futurist exhibition and the concomitant intensification of the protest activities on the part of miners and suffragettes turned the artistic movement into a 'cipher' of the contemporary crisis, of which the post-impressionist exhibition had also been held up as evidence (cf. Rainey 14). On the contrary, it can also be suggested that the equation between anarchists and artists served rhetorically to minimize the threat of both to their respective institutional sites, parliament and the museum. The tongue-in-cheek report of the *Illustrated London News*, for instance, served precisely to undercut the politically revolutionary potential of the works on display. Quite significantly, the anonymous reporter for the British periodical did not mention any of the overtly political works in the exhibition, such as Carlo Carrà's *Funeral of the Anarchist Galli,* the very title of which invites a political reading, or Luigi Russolo's *Rebellion,* which portrays a bright red rising crowd, fists lifted, in 'lines of force' that form a stylized wedge shattering an urban landscape.[15] What did interest the reporter were the works that portrayed the non-threatening aspects of modern life, with a marked preference for the paintings of Gino Severini, who often took as his subject the Parisian nightlife (*The 'Pan Pan' Dance at the Monico, The Haunting Dancer, Yellow Dancers*) or aspects of French everyday life (*The Milliner, The Boulevard*). The exoticism of Severini's works thus made it possible to deflect in the direction of amusing and harmless entertainment the more threatening implications of this artistic anarchism. Here is the opening of the article:

> What do you think of the picture at the top of the page [Severini's *'Pan Pan' Dance*]? It looks, you will say, like an 'explosion:' like, in fact, an artistic bomb. Who throw [sic] bombs? Why, anarchists, of course. But the idea of anarchy is too tame for the painters of the school to which this painting belongs. They call themselves 'The Post-Anarchists of Art,' meaning that they are everything any anarchist is and some more. ('The New Crazy "Exploding" Pictures')

In order to domesticate the anti-aesthetic project of futurism, the reporter even renamed the movement, taking a cue, most likely, from point 9 in Marinetti's manifesto of foundation in which, sandwiched between the often-quoted 'we will glorify war – the world's only hygiene' and 'the scorn of women,' one can also find the glorification of 'il militarismo, il patriottismo, il gesto distruttore dei libertarî, le belle idee per cui si muore' [militarism, patriotism, the destructive gesture of libertarians, the beautiful ideas for which one dies] (*TIF* 11).[16] But this is also one of the points that best illustrate the ambiguous and unresolved tension between politics and aesthetics in the futurist program: on the one hand, Marinetti envisions the movement as the instrument for a project of social transformation, a cleansing operation preliminary to the 'futurist reconstruction of the universe,' to quote the title of the 1915 manifesto by Balla and Depero; on the other, by appealing to the category of beauty, Marinetti combines oppositional ideologies (for instance, patriotism and anarchism) in an unreconcilable tangle, holding them precariously together by considering them as objects of aesthetic contemplation rather than as political programs with real and potentially revolutionary effects in the practice of life. In other words, in Marinetti's manifesto aesthetics and politics size each other up, in a constant jockeying for supremacy: the wishful intention of an art that will transform the world is never divorced from the equally wishful intention of turning the world into art. This tension is indeed resolved in the *Illustrated London News* article, which cuts the Gordian knot by re-encoding the futurist programs in terms of a purely artistic enterprise. The futurists may go beyond anarchy, but their explosions are safely contained within the gallery, the equivalent of the museum as the locus in which the new works of art vie for consecration. They are blasts of light and colour, whose aim is no more dangerous than that of capturing the excitement of the world of popular entertainment and the normality of everyday life. Severini's own explanation of the *'Pan Pan' Dance* could not have been more disarming: 'I give you all my impressions as I receive them in the great café at Monte Carlo while this exciting dance is going on around me. This is the sensation I have painted. It is a picture of my mind.'

The *Daily Chronicle* of 9 March 1912 also made an explicit connection between futurism and social protest in an article by William Maas entitled 'Pictures on Strike. Art and Anarchy in Sackville Street,' which opens: 'The passion that prevails for breaking rules, windows, agreements, conventions, and anything else that may happen to be lying about has seized very furiously a small band of Italian artists.' The article goes on to define the 'Manifesto of Futurism' as a 'Strike Manifesto.' However, far from developing the relationship (if any) between 'breaking windows' and breaking aesthetic rules, Maas finally turns to a mocking account of the difficulties involved in making sense out of a futurist painting, and the connections between the artistic movement and workers and suffragette demonstrations – indeed, rather archly hinted at to begin with – are dropped altogether. However, the threat posed by contemporary art to the structures of bourgeois society never seems too far from the author's mind if, after declaring himself unable to even 'venture' to provide a description, he concludes that in any case, were he to succeed, 'as a citizen it would imperil my privilege at the ballot-box' – a privilege denied, of course, to the mad and to women.

From the beginning, then, the English press engaged futurism in a struggle for definition. While in Italy the press had served to further the aims of the movement, and had functioned as a sort of resonance box for its iconoclastic gestures, in England the futurists found themselves the object of a normalizing operation that both curtailed their freedom of operation and brought their project back firmly into the ambit of art. As will be seen, the one occasion on which Marinetti sought to take the initiative had disastrous results for his objective of linking the Italian and the English avant-garde. Furthermore, the reception of futurism by the popular press played an important role in shaping the reaction of the figures of English arts and letters who would prove to be most receptive to its presence. Finally, then, if in Italy Futurism had from the beginning sought to close the gap between the aesthetic and the political, and to interpret ideologically the relationship between artist and audience, in this new cultural context Marinetti and his companions found themselves hard pressed to capture the initiative in the process of self-definition that had allowed them to reorient the artistic discourse in Italy. In particular, the political dimension of futurism was almost completely erased from the reports in the British press. For instance, Marinetti's forceful support of the Italian war against the Ottoman Empire for the conquest of Lybia (for which he had even issued the manifesto 'Tripoli italiana,' dated 11 October 1911), and his volume *La bataille de Tripoli*, which was based on his experiences as a war reporter, were not mentioned in spite of the fact that the Italian colonial enterprise, begun a little more than six months before the opening of the futurist exhibition and still in progress, had encountered a strong hostile reaction in the British press and in general public opinion.[17] Only F.S. Flint, writing in the *Poetry Review* in August 1912, well after the end of the first burst of the futurist craze, mentioned Marinetti's activities on the Lybian front, going so far as to state that 'the responsibility for the war in Tripoli has been attributed to him' ('Contemporary French Poetry' 142).

And yet, it would be difficult to deny that the futurists themselves contributed to the 'institutionalization' of the movement – a process that began precisely with the international tour of 1912, in which futurist artists presented themselves before their audiences as nothing more than producers of works of art. Severini's comment on the *'Pan Pan' Dance* seems quite significant as it signals an important shift in the rhetoric of the public discourse of futurism: now the site of the aesthetic experience is no longer the viewer but the artist, so that the distance between the two poles of aesthetic communication, which, as we have seen, futurism had sought to overcome, was re-established. If viewers are indeed placed 'at the center of the painting,' what they encounters there is not the 'atmosphere' of the figure, the dynamic relations that connect discrete objects, but rather an articulation of the subjective experience of perception of the artist. Severini speaks of 'impressions,' a remark significantly consistent with the formula through which the English avant-garde would later seek to identify the regressive character of futurism, namely 'accelerated impressionism.' It is to the futurists' implication in the domestication of their project that I now want to turn.

From Propaganda to Pedagogy: 'The Exhibitors to the Public'

Press reports were not the only means available to British viewers to become acquainted with the new movement. The Sackville Gallery published a catalogue that included, in addition to a number of reproductions, an abridged version of the manifesto of foundation ('Initial Manifesto of Futurism'), the technical manifesto of Futurist painting, here titled 'Manifesto of the Futurist Painters,' and the English version of a text entitled 'The Exhibitors to the Public,' which had already appeared in French in the catalogue of the Bernheim gallery. This latter text, pointedly *not* a manifesto – it was called a 'preface' in a closing note to the text, which further specified that it was based on 'the *lecture* on Futurist Painting, delivered by the painter, Boccioni, at the Circolo Internazionale Artistico, at Rome, on May 29th, 1911' (19; emphasis added) – can help us understand how the consolidation of the movement and the translation of its project into a series of works facilitated its assimilation into the artistic milieu of the British capital. In other words, if the futurists sought to articulate a new model of aesthetic communication, the adoption of a form of discourse that eschewed the overtly confrontational and future-inflected rhetoric of the manifesto seemed to run counter to that very model, and to return the viewer to a traditional position of passive reception.

In their study of the manifesto, Jeanne Demers and Line McMurray have proposed a three-fold scansion of the production of manifestoes, a sequence of 'gestures' that traverses the space from the moment of the rejection of the institutional sites and practices of (cultural) power to the consolidation of new forms of validation of the performance of the avant-garde producer. 'The first, *declarative,* [phase] will play the function of self-nomination and of position-taking [...]. A second, *explicative*, phase, already locked by this intention of being/doing [*vouloir être/faire*] then begins [...]. This action will usually find its object, its complement in a third, *demonstrative*, phase' (80). Their analysis of the manifesto in terms of J.L. Austin's speech act theory is an important step in the direction of defining it as a *pragmatic* genre, that is, of describing the manifesto not so much in terms of formal features, but rather in terms of the performative effects elicited by the text. As we move from the first to the third category identified by Demers and McMurray, we can also see the predominance of certain specific speech acts over others. Let us briefly consider the two initial manifestos of painting, 'Manifesto dei pittori futuristi' and 'La pittura futurista. Manifesto tecnico' in comparison with 'The Exhibitors to the Public.' Of the five classes of illocutionary acts described by Austin, the first two manifestoes show a prevalence of what he called 'commissives' and 'exercitives.' The former are defined as speech acts that 'commit the speaker to a certain course of action' (157). The 'primary performative' of this class is 'shall' (158), and the ambiguity of that modal verb nicely captures the ambiguity of the commissive itself: on the one hand, it expresses an obligation; on the other, it projects it into the future. It is the mark of a work in progress, just as a manifesto announces not what has been done, but what its issuers are committed to accomplishing. Furthermore, note that the verb 'oppose' is one of the examples of the commissive: the declaration of what the issuer(s) of the manifesto aim to do and what they are against are two sides of the same coin. This declaration of intentions can assume different forms. In the 'Manifesto dei pittori futuristi' it is expressed, for instance, by the eight conclusive points in which the signatories declare what they intend to do: 'noi vogliamo: 1. Distruggere il culto del passato [...] 2. Disprezzare profondamente ogni forma di imitazione,' etc. [We want to: 1. Destroy the cult of the past 2. Scorn profoundly any form of imitation] (22). In the technical manifesto we have the declaration of war against the subjection to the most superficial aspects of the artistic tradition, such as **'il patinume e la velatura dei falsi antichi' [the dirty patinas glazing of fake antiques]**, etc. (26).

'Exercitives,' on the other hand, are distinguished by the fact that they advocate a certain course of action. Unlike the 'commissives,' which primarily bind the utterer, 'exercitives' are directed at the audience, and exercise their effect upon it. While the class is quite broad, and includes acts that require authority on the part of the issuer (for instance, 'declare closed' or 'declare open'), the ones that recur in the manifestoes are those whose felicitous performance depends on whether or not the addressee chooses to follow the advice. The 'proclamation' is an example of such a speech act, as it invites the reader to agree with and accept the suggestion of the issuer. The examples again abound. One example is the 'proclamations' closing the 'Manifesto tecnico' that delineate the program of the movement: **'NOI PROCLAMIAMO: 1. Che il complementarismo congenito una necessit assoluta nella pittura, come il verso libero nella poesia e come la polifonia nella musica; 2. Che il dinamismo universale deve essere reso come sensazione dinamica' [We proclaim: 1. That congenital complementarism is an absolute necessity in painting, like free verse in poetry and polyphony in music; 2. That universal dynamism must be rendered as a dynamic sensation]** (26). Thus, these texts are configured as programmatic statements binding their signatories, but they also position receivers as potential issuers if they accept and follow the principles proposed by the futurists. Jean-Marie Gleize has written that 'the manifesto addresses itself mostly to a creator, possibly from above and possibly against the reader' (14). It seems, however, that the situation is more complex, for reasons that the following analysis should help to clarify. The manifesto performs its work of seduction on the reader, who, as such, is positioned in the no-man's-land between participation and antagonism. Thus the encounter between the manifesto and the reader pushes the latter into one of the two camps: in other words, the oppositional moment of the manifesto is successive to the act of reception, because it is only by not accepting the exhortations of the text that the reader becomes the enemy. As the discourse of a marginal(ized) group, the only authority that the manifesto can invoke – aside from a generic modernity that requires, *ipso facto*, a break with the past in order to emerge in its proper configuration – is precisely the authority that ensues from its ability to transform its receivers into potential new issuers.

The situation in 'The Exhibitors to the Public' is significantly different: it marks not only an abandonment of the manifesto genre on the part of the painters (it is, to my knowledge, the last major text signed *collectively* by the five 'founders' of pictorial futurism; Boccioni, Severini, Carrà, Russolo, and Balla),[18] but also a retreat into the territory of exposition rather than a new foray into the projectual dimension of the movement. In other words, the manifestoes proclaimed what the futurists were bound to do, and the terms of the enterprise on which they invited their audience to follow them, but the introduction to the catalogue has the more sober task of describing what the movement has already accomplished. The very title serves to differentiate clearly and hierarchically the addressers from the addressees. Most importantly, however, the text displays a significant shift away from the prescriptive tone of the manifestoes and toward the descriptive – or, to put it differently, from the performative to the constative.[19] This shift entails a parallel transformation in the rhetoric of the manifesto. The appeal to the reader, in the form of declarations, prohibitions, or recommendations, is almost non-existent, while the descriptive function of the text is stressed by the repetition of verbs such as 'illustrate' or 'explain': "A few examples will illustrate our theory' (11); 'Let us explain again by examples' (12); 'we may further explain our idea by a comparison drawn from the evolution of music' (15). While the manifestoes inflected their project in the future through the use of modal verbs and the future tense, the text in the catalogue consistently uses the past tense to describe what has been done in the works on display. The opening of the third paragraph is unequivocal: 'What we have attempted and accomplished, while attracting around us a large number of skillful imitators and as many plagiarists without talent, has placed us at the head of the European movement in painting' (9). The exhibition is thus already a retrospective through which the movement can determine both what it has achieved and its position in the history of Western art. Instead of destroying its achievements to make room for the new generations, as Marinetti had promised in the first manifesto, futurism in its turn develops and institutionalizes a series of rules of composition and of reception of the works that it deploys, for the benefit of the viewer, in a text that seems aimed more at preserving the status quo of the futurist orthodoxy than at exalting 'ogni forma di originalità, anche se temeraria, anche se violentissima' [any form of originality, even if daring, even if extremely violent] (Boccioni et al., 'Manifesto dei pittori futuristi' 22). Ultimately, then, this catalogue text witnesses to the constitutive aporia of the avant-garde, the impossibility of dwelling on the threshold of the event without either taking form – and therefore leaving behind tangible and immutable traces of its presence – or dissolving itself in the moment of the performance. (It is an aporia that could not be evaded even by Dada, which from the beginning understood its anti-institutional thrust in ways that Futurism, still too much involved in the discourse of aestheticism from which it had originated, could not theorize.)[20]

And yet, 'The Exhibitors to the Public' does not position itself monologically on the side of the *ars poetica*. The necessity to place the viewer at the centre of the picture is still emphasized, with the difference that here, unlike in the 'Technical Manifesto,' the viewer is told what he or she should see. 'The Exhibitors to the Public' was not, finally, a work of futurist propaganda, but rather a work of futurist pedagogy. It was the attempt to control the interpretation that amused the critics and drew their sharpest reaction. The anonymous reviewer for *The Times* (1 March 1912) was the first to make this point, reporting that 'the manifesto is not very clearly reasoned,' that 'the artists are very anxious to explain that they are not academic,' and finally adding: 'but what can be more academic than the employment of a method, no matter what that method may be, as a means of escaping from the commonplace?' ('The Futurists'). A week later, on 9 March, C.H. Collins Baker picked up on the same theme, accusing the futurists of using manifestoes as a rather ineffective educational tool: '[W]e instantly suspect exhibitions whose catalogues are prefaced with introductions and concluded with manifestoes. For experience teaches that painters who are so tremendously impressed by their rebelliousness that they think the public and the silly critics must be educated and initiated by lengthy explanations, metaphorically speaking do not wash' (300). Nor was this critique limited to the popular press. Writing for the *The English Review*, Walter Sickert remarked: 'The Futurist movement confesses to a literary origin; and the alliance of the pen with the brush has its dangers for both. No amount of explanatory doctrine and militant defence will make a bad draughtsman into a good one. Painting that requires literary explanation stands self-condemned' (149).

The image of futurism that emerges from the catalogue, then, is that of a school with its formulaic norms and its preferred subject matters. The descriptions of the paintings (added at the request of the owner of the Sackville Gallery to be of use for 'queste *bestie di Inghilesi*' [these *beastly English*], as Boccioni wryly wrote quoting Benvenuto Cellini)[21] further contributed to this perception of the futurist movement, as they characterized the works in the familiar terms of the discourse of the cubist representation of multiple planes on the surface of the canvas,[22] or of the impressionist rendition of the subjective perception of external reality.[23] Rossella Caruso echoes Boccioni in suggesting that the catalogue notes served to 'translate a system of lines and colour pre-sumably new to the London public' (580), but I suggest that the reverse was more likely the case: since the terms used by the futurists to decode their pictures would have been familiar to art critics as a result of the recent debate over modern French art, the futurists might easily be interpreted not as the halcyons of a new artistic era but rather as the provincial epigons of French modernism. The apparently obsessive attempt to control the interpretation of the works via manifestoes and descriptions seems to belie futurism's most original contribution, namely the supposed centrality of the spectator in the interpretative process.

Thus, while the 1910 post-impressionist exhibition had been received by the press as a threat to society, an attack on 'young artists' virility,' a 'pornographic' affair, a 'plague' or 'pestilence' (cf. Wees 24), the futurist show provoked remarkably little alarm.[24] Among the almost one hundred articles on futurism published in 1912 – over half of which were dedicated to the Sackville exhibition – one would be hard pressed to find inspiring tirades against the degeneration of modern mores and the menace of futurism to the fabric of British society. Rather, the generally negative responses to the Italian movement took the form either of the often amused and sceptically ironic (and at times even parodic) journalistic report, or of the critical investigation of the formal aspects of futurist painting. For journalists, the futurists were at worst nothing more than a further example of the divarication between the world of art and the tastes of the public; P.G. Konody's report from Paris in *The Illustrated London News* of 17 February 1912 makes this clear, by placing Futurism at the end of 'the worst excesses that we have seen of late years on painted canvas,' namely the 'revolutionary Post-Impressionists of two years ago and the unintelligible Cubists of last year.' By far the most violent critique of the show came from Konody himself in the *Pall Mall Gazette*, where he referred to the show as a 'nightmare exhibition.' In this case, too, the nightmarish quality of the works results from their formal characteristics, rather than from the fact that they could be interpreted as the symptoms of a more general social malaise: they were simply unreadable, like 'a Kodak film on which three or four different views have been exposed.' Konody's further comments demonstrate the inoculative effect[25] of the recent exhibitions on the British public: 'Fortunately, the exponents of Post-Impressionism and Cubism have trained our faculties to accept the new and the revolutionary without going into hysterics of indignation, and it is not likely that the visitors to the gallery will be roused to anything but mild amusement, or that Sir W.B. Richmond will throw vitriol at the offending canvases although he may in future substitute a new joke on "Futilism" for the somewhat stale reiteration of his "Post-prandial Impressionism"' ('The Italian Futurists'). Other reviewers amused themselves at imitating the futurists' effort at self-explanation.

Thus E.S.G., the reviewer for *The Graphic*, described Severini's *'Pan Pan' Dance* (the largest and probably most cited canvas in the exhibition) in terms that intentionally echoed the artist's description: 'if the spectator will blink his eyes rapidly in front of the picture he will imagine that it is quite right, and that he is looking at a more or less correct representation of a crowded café, brilliantly lit, and flickering with movement. That, we imagine, was the intention of the artist in this picture – to give the impression of a riotous Montmartre café'

The popular press thus turned futurism into a spectacle, an unwitting parody of contemporary artistic tendencies. If the word 'futurism' was to become a synonym for modern art in the years just before the First World War, as Wees has remarked, it could also easily be used as a shorthand for its foibles and exaggerations. Thus the notice for the Practical Correspondence College published in *The Art Chronicle* of 5 April 1912 used the term 'Futurism' to attract the reader's attention, and to sell a very different brand of artistic production: 'FUTURISM may be all very well for "Young Italy," the Picture Gallery people, and those who like it. There is always a little vogue for crazy work and sensationalism. The trouble is that vogue doesn't last, neither does it affect those who buy drawings.' Thankfully a quick correspondence course with the college would ensure that the student would emerge able 'to do saleable work – and sell it' ('Futurism'). And Severini complained that the exhibit had not earned him any money ...

Some critics were less quick to dismiss the futurists' self-assured proclamations of ground-breaking originality, but ultimately were firm in rejecting such claims, generally interpreting the Italian movement as a declension of the post-impressionist revolution in the relationship between the viewer and the work of art. The critic for *The Daily Graphic* argued: 'The idea at the root of post-impressionistic painting was that of conveying to the beholder the sense of things rather than their outward and visible form. [...] The Italian Futurists carry this principle a stage further' (Phillips). But the Post-Impressionist exhibition cast a long shadow over futurism for other reasons. The success of Fry's show was not limited to a widening of the aesthetic horizon of the British public, but it also resulted in a reorientation of the critical discourse in the direction of what would be later known as formalist criticism – that is, a critical model concerned with the relationship among the structural components of a work rather than with its possible referents.[26] Fry's reasoned and not altogether negative account of the futurist exhibition thus ultimately failed the works on the ground that their 'result is much more of a psychological or scientific curiosity than a work of art' (945).[27] While suggesting that 'Boccioni (in his later works) and Severini do manage to give a vivid pictorial echo of the vague complex of mental visions,' the critic – who a few months later excluded the futurists from his second post-impressionist exhibition held in December 1912 arguing that they 'have succeeded in developing a whole system of aesthetics out of a misapprehension of some of Picasso's recondite and difficult works' (qtd. Hulten 471) – simply inverted the terms of the futurist polemic, levelling against them the critique of being – at least from the point of view of technique – passéiste: '[W]hat strikes one is the prevalence in their work of a somewhat tired convention, one that never had much value and which lost with the freshness of novelty almost all its charms, the convention of Chéret, Besnard, and Boldini. It is quite true that the Futurist arranges his forms upon peculiar and original principles [...] but the forms retain, even in this fragmentary condition, their well-worn familiarity' (945). Such a critique of the futurist emphasis on movement and dynamism, rather than on the formal structures of the work of art was by no means limited to Fry. His evaluation was echoed by other reviewers for the popular press, including Collins Baker who, in his review for *The Saturday Review,* failed futurist art on the ground that, in spite of the artists' protestations to the contrary, it was ultimately mimetic rather than analytical, and therefore the product of a backward rather than revolutionary approach: 'Art as a manifestation of developed mentality is not chaotic, kaleidoscopic, watery; it is concentrated and selective' (301).

Flux and Form: Futurism and Vorticism

Chaos versus order, fluidity versus solidity – Collins Baker's metaphors also anticipated, *in nuce,* the terms of the discussion over futurism and, more in general, over the shape and structure of artistic modernity that would take place between 1912 and the beginning of the war. But as formal issues come to the foreground of the critical debate, we witness also the beginning of a process of progressive divergence between the Italian and the English avant-garde. Put in terms of the simplest model of communication, the futurists are particularly concerned with the transaction between the addresser (the artist) and the message (the text), and between the message and the addressee (the audience). In spite of the rhetorical ambiguities examined above, this concern is re-stated in 'The Exhibitors to the Public' by the reiteration of the declaration from the technical manifesto that the spectator *'must in the future be placed in the centre of the picture'* (14), and also by the insistence on the role of the artist as the translator of the dynamism that governs 'nature,' here understood as the fabric of the world that inextricably links subject and object: 'these force-lines,' the painters write, 'must encircle and involve the spectator so that he will in a manner be forced to struggle himself with the persons in the picture' (14). In 'Fondamento Plastico della scultura e pittura futurista' (1913), Boccioni clarifies the Bergsonian roots of the futurist concept of dynamism:

> L'accusa di cinematografia ci fa ridere come una volgare imbecillità. Noi non suddividiamo le immagini visuali, noi ricerchiamo un segno, o meglio, una forma unica che sostituisca al vecchio concetto di divisione, il nuovo concetto di continuità.
>
> Ogni suddivisione di moto è un fatto completamente arbitrario, come è completamente arbitraria ogni suddivisione di materia. Henri Bergson dice: 'Toute divisions de la matière en corps indépendents aux contours absolutement determinés est une division artificielle.'
>
> The accusation of cinematography makes us laugh as a vulgar imbecility. We do not break down visual images, we seek a sign, or rather a unique form that may replace the old concept of division with the new concept of continuity.
>
> Any subdivision of movement is a completely arbitrary fact. Any subdivision of matter is likewise arbitrary. Henry Bergson says: 'Any division of matter in independent bodies with absolutely determined shape is an artificial division.'] (*Scritti* 42)[28]

The notion of continuity, which finds one of its most impressive realizations in Boccioni's own 1913 sculpture *Unique Forms of Continuity in Space*, governs not only the poetic research of the group but also its underlying model of communication. The work exists not in isolation, but rather in a continuum that links the artist to the audience, so that the process of semiosis reproduces, on the metacommunicative level, the general structure of the futurist universe. The distinction between artist, work, and audience is, if not arbitrary, at the very least a forceful disruption of the lines of force linking the three moments of the communicative process.[29]

A further consequence of this reorientation of the relationship between artist and audience is, as seen in chapter 2, that the work itself is constructed as always already requiring the mediating presence of the spectator in order to close the semiotic process. It is by definition an open text, in Eco's terminology, insofar as it actively promotes 'textual cooperation' (*Lector* 58), rather than seeking, as in the case of the English modernists, the splendid isolation of the organic work of art, even if that organicity is a kind of Holy Grail, the object of an impossible quest to overcome the fragmentation of the modern condition. The confrontation between the Italian and the English avant-garde is one of the points of disjunction of the two currents through which we can recapitulate the experience of literary modernity. The stake – and the element of disjunction – is again the relationship between art and the praxis of life, or put otherwise, the question of the autonomy of the aesthetic. For futurism, art and life are organically linked. Marinetti's definition of futurism as 'un *continuo sforzo per sorpassare tutte le leggi dell'arte e l'arte stessa* mediante qualcosa d'imprevisto che si può chiamare *vita-arte-effimero*' [a *continuous effort to overcome the laws of art and art itself* through something unexpected which can be called *life-art-ephemeral*] (*Collaudi* 129) is perhaps its best emblem: art, like life, must live in and for the moment, in the present of its reception, to be overcome by new formations that reflect the continuous flux of reality. G. Battista Nazzaro has pointed out that for futurism 'form must be adherent to the reality of things, and if that reality locates itself in the continual becoming of technology, its form also must change in order to survive, eternally recreating itself in contradiction with the very premises of its birth' (85). But if form must adhere to reality, then the formal dimension of the futurist text signals the distance between the project of the movement and that of nineteenth century realism or naturalism. In the latter, syntactical structures are functional to the construction of a hierarchically organized linguistic space that clearly orients the relationship between the reader and the textual environment. As objects are evoked in their dense and mute presence, the reader is pushed to the margins of the space of representation, a likewise mute witness of the unfolding of the 'possible world' activated by the text. In the futurist work, however, the destruction of traditional syntactical or representational structures serves to insert readers or viewers in the process of construction of the textual world, as they are required to recreate the spatial and temporal coordinates that the text refuses to posit. Lautréamont's dictum that 'poetry must be made by all. Not by one' is realized by an artistic practice that seeks to annul the distance between artist and audience, in a theatricalization of the experience of art seen by Guido Guglielmi as the true cipher of the avant-garde: 'The ambition of the avant-garde will be that of overcoming art by realizing it in the domain of communication, that is, in a pragmatic domain. It is not by chance that their *medium* is not the book but the theatre, and the theatre as spectacle' (175).

On the contrary the second tendency, within which we can situate English modernism, is the critical heir of aestheticism, insofar as it seeks new means to legitimize the autonomy of the aesthetic. While, like the avant-garde, English modernism takes as its point of departure the critique of art as an institution – and in this sense the futurists could revendicate their initial kinship with the project of other formations such as the post-impressionists and the cubists, 'who have displayed a laudable contempt for artistic commercialism and a powerful hatred for academism' (Boccioni et al., 'The Exhibitors' 8) – it does so not to reject altogether the institution itself, but rather with the intention of carrying out its restructuring from within, through a renewal of the protocols that grant aesthetic validity to the work of art rather than through a wholesale re-articulation of the aesthetic experience resulting in its dissolution in the ephemeral gesture of the act of communication.[30] In this case, form makes it possible to redefine the distinction that the futurist avant-garde seeks to abolish, namely, the distinction between art and life. Form is the means through which the multiplicity and fluidity of life can be resolved into the unity of the work of art. Bürger's description of the organic and the non-organic work of art is useful to clarify this distinction. He writes: 'In the organic [...] work of art, the unity of the universal and the particular is posited without mediation; in the nonorganic [...] work to which the works of the avant-garde belong, the unity is a mediated one. Here, the element of unity is withdrawn to an infinite distance, as it were. In the extreme case, it is the recipient who creates it' (56). In the work of art of the English modernists, the moment of mediation is sought not at the level of reception but rather at the level of the work itself through formal procedures. In other words, form resolves the multiplicity, particularity, and contingency of experience into the unicity, universality, and permanence of the work of art. As mentioned above, in the modernist work this formal resolution is lived problematically, insofar as the experience of modernity is itself one of disconnection and alienation, of 'a multitude of fragments, speaking incommensurable private languages' (Berman 17). And yet, the dialectic of fragment and whole, and the quest for an adequate formal structure in which this dialectic may find a resolution, orient a great number of the canonical works of modernism, whether their end result is success or failure; this dialectic also underlies the return to myth or to certain foundational works of the Western tradition (consider, for instance, the structuring function played in this sense by the *Odyssey* or the *Divine Comedy*) as ordering principles through which to counter the fragmentation of modernity. Daniel Schwarz has remarked on this difficult balancing act as a characteristic of modernism: 'Isn't Modernism a search for informing principles that transcend cultures *as well as* a recognition of both the diversity and continuity of culture? Modernism sought to find an aesthetic order or historic pattern to substitute for the crumbling certainties of the past' (4). Having rejected both aesthetics and history, the futurist avant-garde, on the other hand, implicitly rejects the very possibility of any transcendental principle. The flow of reality can be recomposed only in the immanent event of the act of communication.

In this context vorticism, the only English movement to have experimented with avant-garde strategies such as the issuing of manifestoes, is symptomatic of the different articulations of this modernist project. The history of the difficult relationship between futurism and vorticism, and in particular between Marinetti and the leader of the English group, Wyndham Lewis, is well known.[31] Born in 1882, Lewis studied at the Slade School of Art until 1901, then spent much of the period between 1902 and 1908 on the Continent, travelling through Spain and studying and painting in Munich and Paris.[32] When he returned to England, he brought a first hand knowledge of the latest developments of the European avant-garde that few of his contemporaries could match. Indeed his large canvas *Kermesse*, exhibited in July 1912 at the Allied Artists' Association exhibition in London has been described as 'the first English painting to show the influence of Cubism' (Meyers 35). In addition to painting, Lewis had also shown a considerable talent as a writer, with a series of sketches based on his Spanish travels published in Goldring's *The Tramp* and in Ford's *English Review*. Furthermore, while his taste for written polemic would fully unfold only in later years, by 1913 he had already emerged as the *enfant terrible* of the English artistic milieu. This reputation derived in great part from a very public quarrel with Roger Fry over a commission for his Omega Workshop, a kind of artists' cooperative that produced post-impressionist designs for household objects for its select clientele. (Lewis believed that the commission in question had in fact been meant specifically for himself and fellow painter Spencer Gore, and that it had been appropriated by Fry.) As a result, Lewis led a secession of the more radical wing of Fry's collaborators – including Frederick Etchells, Cuthbert Hamilton, and Edward Wadsworth – and turned this internal quarrel into a public spectacle with a 'Round-Robin Letter' sent to the press and supporters of the workshop, in which he and his companions denounced Fry and his artistic and administrative practices.[33] In recalling the years of the English avant-garde, painter William Roberts wrote: 'It was the impact of the manifestoes of the Italian Futurist poet Marinetti upon him, that made Lewis realise how valuable a manifesto of his own would be to himself. Fry was the first to feel the force of this new weapon; it was inevitable that sooner or later he would be served with a manifesto; as an ally he was too powerful for the comfort of someone aiming at a leading role in the English revolutionary art movement' (qtd. Cork 1: 98). The letter can hardly be called a manifesto; rather, it outlines in great detail the reasons for Lewis's grievance and the events behind it. Roberts's recollections, however, demonstrate that even at this stage Lewis's public interventions appropriated the rhetoric of revolution that characterized the Continental avant-garde in order to distinguish himself among the various competitors in the English intellectual milieu, and to carve a recognizable public identity.

When Marinetti came to England for a series of conferences in the fall of 1913, Lewis was thus an already well-known figure among what Ford called with ironic affection *les jeunes*. Lewis and the painter C.R.W. Nevinson organized a dinner in honour of the Italian poet at the Florence Restaurant in London on 18 November, and according to an anecdote told by fellow artist David Bomberg, the two almost came to blows when Nevinson claimed that he and not Lewis had first kissed Marinetti's hand when the Futurist leader stepped off his train at Victoria Station. Such idyllic relations, however, were not to last. In 1914, during Marinetti's fourth and last expedition to England before the war, the equivocal association between the Italian poet and the English avant-garde came to a head. Accompanied as always by an extensive press coverage of his activities, Marinetti returned to London in May and June to present an exhibition of futurist art works at the Doré Gallery and to give a series of 'lectures,' that included recitations from his poem 'The Siege of Adrianople' and, at the Coliseum, a musical presentation performed on Luigi Russolo and Enrico Piatti's *intonarumori* (or 'noise-tuners,' as they were called in England). Among other activities, he also performed at the Rebel Art Centre, a workshop and art school founded by Wyndham Lewis that served as meeting place for many of the artists who would later be associated with vorticism.[34] As late as the end of May, Lewis published a somewhat critical but not altogether negative profile of Marinetti in *The New Weekly*. In it he argued that, in spite of his many reservations regarding the cultural implications of the program of the futurist leader, Marinetti's very presence had the beneficial effect of calling into question the dominant assumptions of the artistic milieu, and concluded: 'England has needed these foreign auxiliaries to put her energies to rights and restore order. Marinetti's services, in this home of aestheticism, crass snobbery or languorous of distinguished phlegm, are great' (*Creatures of Habit* 32).

The event that precipitated the final rupture between the Italian movement and its sometime allies was a manifesto, 'Vital English Art,' issued by Marinetti and Nevinson on Rebel Art Centre stationery but without the permission of the Centre itself, and published in *The Observer* on 7 June 1914 as well as in other papers. The manifesto, divided into a section of eleven points against as many aspects of English culture and a section of six programmatic points, concluded with a call to arms that did not refrain from naming names: 'So we call upon the English public to support, defend and glorify the genius of the great Futurist painters or pioneers and advance-forces of vital English Art – ATKINSON, BOMBERG, EPSTEIN, ETCHELLS, HAMILTON, NEVISON, ROBERTS, WADSWORTH, WYNDHAM LEWIS.' The ambiguity of this sentence is obvious, as it gives the impression that the artists listed are indeed futurists. Lewis was not amused, and was quick to arrange his response. First, repeating a well-worn futurist strategy, he and other fellow artists, including Jacob Epstein, Frederick Etchells, Edward Wadsworth, the sculptor Henri Gaudier-Brzeska, and the philosopher T. E. Hulme, organized a punitive expedition against Marinetti and Nevinson, and on 12 June disrupted the evening of lecturing and noise-tuner performances at the Doré Gallery.[35] More importantly, Lewis and the other artists called upon in 'Vital English Art' (with the significant addition of Ezra Pound) signed a joint letter to *The Observer* in which they dissociated themselves from the manifesto. During the ensuing brief exchange in the press with Nevinson, Marinetti, who in the meantime had returned to Italy, remained outside the fray.[36]

The very public divorce between the two groups had other repercussions, and resulted in important changes in a publication that had already been in the works for some time, the journal *Blast*. When on 1 April the magazine *The Egoist* advertised the forthcoming publication of the first issue of the new publication, no such a thing as 'Vorticism' seemed to exist; the subject of the journal, according to the notice, was to be 'Cubism, Futurism, Imagisme and all Vital Forms of Modern Art.' The eclecticism of *Blast* was contradicted by the final product, which appeared on 1 July 1914 with the proud subtitle 'Review of the Great English Vortex,' and with the last-minute addition of a ligature in which the terms 'Vorticism' and 'Vortex' appeared prominently as a means of solidifying the identity of the group.[37]

That there was more at stake in this debate than the mere protection of the autochthonous identity and the independence of the British artists is, however, clear from Lewis's own reflections on art before the 'Vital English Art' debacle. From the beginning Lewis had emphasized the distance between his conception of the function of art and that of the futurists, in terms that are perfectly coherent with the more pointedly polemical pieces published in *Blast*. In November 1913 Lewis participated in the 'Exhibition of English Post-Impressionists, Cubists and Others' in Brighton, where he had exhibited his works in a 'Cubist Room' with, among others, Nevinson, David Bomberg, and the Omega Workshop secessionists. In a separate foreword to the exhibition catalogue Lewis distanced the artists of the 'Cubist Room' from both futurism and cubism and explained the aesthetic principles of the group: 'Beneath the Past and the Future the most sanguine would hardly expect a more different skeleton to exist than that respectively of ape and man. [...] The work of this group of artists for the most part underlines such geometric bases and structure of life and they would spend their energies rather in showing a different skeleton and abstraction than formerly could exist, than a different degree of hairiness or dress. All revolutionary painting today has in common the rigid reflections of steel and stone in the spirit of the artist' ('The Cubist Room' 57). For Lewis, futurism is a superficial movement on two accounts: first, it understands modernity in terms of its most exterior aspects, such as technology and the machine, rather than in terms of the transformative effects that these have on the way in which human beings relate to their environment. The practical results of the introduction of this or that invention are not what is significant for art, since 'Man with an aeroplane is still merely a bad bird.' Rather, art should reflect upon modernity as a condition of existence that transforms the way in which the individual conceives the world. 'But,' Lewis continues, 'a man who passes his days amid the rigid lines of houses, a plague of cheap ornamentation, noisy street locomotion, the Bedlam of the press, will evidently posses a different habit of vision to a man living amongst the lines of a landscape' ('The Cubist Room' 57). Second, Lewis repeats the by now familiar critique that the futurist theory of art is substantially mimetic because it limits itself to the reproduction of the surface of reality, a surface that now includes the new dimension of speed. The futurist polemic against tradition and its projection toward the future through its infatuation with technology is then a symptom of its literal superficiality: by taking life as its object, it falls into the trap of mimesis, that is, of the subordination of art to the reproduction of the surface of reality. On the contrary, the function of art is to endow life with order and meaning by giving form to its underlying structures, which are not time-bound and therefore are not subjected to the superficial transitoriness of cultural customs, practices, and innovations.[38] In this sense, Lewis's modernism can be configured as paradoxically anti-modern if we understand modernity in the Baudelairian sense delineated in chapter 2 – that is as the transient and fleeting, that which reflects the manners and habits of a certain historical moment, of which dress is precisely an example. Like Marinetti, Lewis breaks apart the 'duality of art,' but in this case the aspect that comes to constitute the foundation of his theoretical edifice is the element that, in Baudelaire's description, 'is eternal and invariable' ('The Painter of Modern Art' 393) and does not depend on the contingencies of the historical situation.[39]

Lewis's indictment has also a strategic function, as it serves to deny the futurist claim to a revolutionary aesthetic. The mimetic thrust of futurist art is in fact the symptom of its unredeemable *passéisme,* as it makes futurism a sort of 'Impressionism up=to=date' ('Melodrama' 143) – that is, a representation of reality as immediately perceived by the individual subject rather than the articulation of a universal truth about the structure of reality itself.[40] For this reason, Lewis singles out for praise Giacomo Balla's more abstract works, which he sees as purified of the persistence of debris and fragments of life: 'His paintings are purely abstract: he does not give you bits of automobiles, or complete naturalistic fragments of noses and ears, or any of the Automobilist [i.e., futurist] bag of tricks in short' ('Melodrama' 144). Elsewhere, Lewis turns upside down the rhetoric of futurism and inserts the movement into the continuity of Italian art history, from the Renaissance onward, since it is merely a contemporary permutation of the concern of Western art with the representation of life. But if art must return to life, for Lewis the question then becomes why art should be of any interest at all when life is itself more readily available. With the sarcasm that characterizes his best polemical salvoes, he writes: 'The Futurist statue will move : then it will live : but any idiot can do better than that with his good wife, round the corner. Nature is definitely ahead of us in contrivances of that sort' ('Futurism, Magic and Life' 135).

On this basis, Lewis postulates the irreconcilable opposition between art and life. The terms of this opposition and of the implications of his theory of art are voiced in his 1918 novel *Tarr*.[41] In a conversation with his lover Anastasya the eponymous protagonist (who is, not surprisingly, a painter) defines two conditions for art. The first, *deadness*, is opposed to the 'naked pulsing and moving of the soft inside of life' and is represented by 'A hippopotamus' armoured hide, a turtle's shell, feathers or machinery' (299); the second condition is 'absence of *soul*,' that is, of interiority and psychological depth. Art is therefore structure abstracted from its incidental functions, form withdrawn from purpose. Art is 'dead' – that is inert, still, removed from the realm of action – but, paradoxically, it cannot die, because it lives a peculiar sort of life that has nothing to do with the breathing and pulsating existence of things in the world. '*Life*,' Tarr philosophizes further, 'is anything that could live and die. *Art* is peculiar; it is anything that lives and that yet you cannot imagine as dying' (298). And if death, the threat and fear of extinction, is what characterizes the life of impermanent objects and beings, art, by being already dead, 'disentangled from death and accident' (299), returns to assume the autonomy that the futurists had challenged.

THE INVENTION OF IMAGISM: EZRA POUND AND THE RHETORIC OF THE AVANT-GARDE

The Artist as Scientist: A Model of Literary Communication

Another interesting, and, I believe, more complex example of how the introduction of futurism into England and its critical reception intersected with and affected the terms of the already existing local debate on the function of the artist in modernity is that of its influence on the aesthetic theory of Ezra Pound and on the formation of imagism.[42]

While the canonical accounts of the history of imagism have tended to construct the movement launched by Pound in 1912 as the foundational moment of Anglo-American modernism, more recent historians of the period – in particular Lawrence Rainey in his important essay on Pound and Marinetti in *Institutions of Modernism* – have reconstructed the broader context of internal and external conditions that influenced its birth. Rainey has articulated eloquently the ways in which the arrival of futurism on the British scene transformed the discourse on aesthetics:

> Futurism in London in 1912 to 1914 mounted a sustained interrogation of the concept of aesthetic autonomy, blurring the boundaries of a category formerly deemed self-evident, precipitating a species of legitimation crisis in the concept of art itself. Yet the crisis was not purely or solely conceptual: it derived its special power from the ways in which Marinetti's activities elided and confused the distinction separating different spheres of cultural production – most important, those associated with art and those linked with the production of entertainment as a commodity. (12)

The point to be emphasized is that futurism arrived on the British cultural scene at a crucial moment in Pound's own reflection on the question of the function of artist and the autonomy of art, and that it affected the poet's cultural strategy in increasingly visible ways. Futurism seemed to provide a challenge to the theoretical apparatus that Pound was developing and on the basis of which he was constructing his own public persona, and the American poet found himself shifting rhetorical gears in response to the challenge. In both form and content imagism is thus a critique of futurism that simultaneously takes advantage of certain procedures inaugurated by futurism.

In 1911 Pound had begun to contribute to British and American periodicals with increasing frequency. His articles reflected the varied nature of his interests, and ranged from scholarly studies of the troubadours to critical considerations on the state of American culture, and to bibliographical notes and reviews. The unifying element of this essayistic production is the attempt to define the proper function of the artist, which, as Pound argues in 'The Wisdom of Poetry' (1912), becomes visible in modernity precisely as a consequence of the formation of the aesthetic as an autonomous field. 'Poets in former ages were of certain uses to the community; i.e., as historians, genealogists, religious functionaries. [...] The troubadour and jongleur were author, dramatist, composer, actor and popular tenor. In Tuscany the canzone and the sonnet held somewhat the place of the essay and the short story. [...] Has the poet, apart from these obsolete and accidental uses, any permanent function in society? (*EPPP* 74).[43] This passage offers several motives for reflection. The closing question suggests that for Pound the issue of the autonomy of the aesthetic had become a theoretical problem before the futurists precipitated the 'crisis of legitimation' described by Rainey. What Pound is suggesting here is the necessity of defining the terms upon which the activity of the poet grounds its legitimacy, since these terms can no longer be derived from the ancillary and incidental practical functions that poets were called upon to perform in pre-modern social communities. Pound thus finds himself in an interstitial space between aestheticism and the avant-garde. On the one hand, he does not reject autonomy as a characteristic of art, and in this sense he does not see his poetic project in conflict with the institution of art. On the other hand, however, the question of the *social function* of poetry places him in a critical relationship with the cultural horizon of aestheticism, since it entails a closure of the gap between art and life that constitutes the very foundation of aestheticism. In other words, if with aestheticism the autonomy of art, its 'apartness from the praxis of life,' had become the content of the work of art (Bürger 48), for Pound the issue that the modern artist must address is how to protect this autonomy while allowing art to play a social role, since autonomy is what ensures the freedom of the work of art from the laws of the marketplace and distinguishes it from the commodity. (It is thus not by chance that certain of the incidental functions performed by 'poets in former ages' are compared to forms of popular entertainment such as theatre, opera, and story-telling.) Furthermore, tradition becomes an even more crucial point of reference because it is through the exploration and mastery of tradition that the modern artist can distinguish between what is essential and what is incidental to the practice of art. The function of art that Pound seeks to isolate is 'permanent': it does not belong specifically to modernity – although it becomes visible in modernity, because the other functions have withered – and it links the modern poet with a specific tradition that can be traced back to the origins of modern European literatures. Thus, the study and the practice of poetry are sides of the same coin, since it is only by learning from what the masters of the tradition have accomplished that the modern poet can 'make it new,' that is, articulate new ways to return poetry to its proper function.

It is therefore not surprising that we find the earliest formulation of the 'permanent function' of poetry in a scholarly essay. The month before the futurist exhibition opened at the Sackville Gallery, the weekly *New Age* published the sixth installment of a series of articles on and translations of medieval poetry collectively entitled 'I Gather the Limbs of Osiris,' and dedicated, as the editorial note to the first few sections read, to 'expositions and translations in illustration of the "New Method in Scholarship"' (*EPPP* 43). Far from being merely the afterglow of an academic career cut short by the gossips surrounding his brief tenure at and dismissal from Wabash College in 1907–8 and his ensuing move to Europe, Pound's contribution to A.R. Orage's journal *The New Age: A Weekly Review of Politics, Literature and Art* (which was to publish many of the leading figures of English modernism) was the result of a theoretical reflection on the language of poetry that was to have important repercussions on his own poetic practice. In this particular section, subtitled 'On Virtue,' Pound offers what he calls a metaphor of the creative process centered on the notion of *virtù* – that is, the individual and distinctive procedure through which thought is given form. Pound identifies different forms of *virtù* that distinguish the poet from the painter or the musician: 'some think, or construct, in rhythm, or by rhythm and sound; others, the unfortunate, move by words disconnected from the objects to which they might correspond, or more unfortunate still in blocks and *clichés* of words; some, favoured of Apollo, in words that hover above and cling close to the things they mean' (*EPPP* 53). In the description of the use of language on the part of the 'unfortunate' we can identify a declension of the symbolist censure of the instrumental use of the word, which was formulated most cogently in Mallarmé's 'Crise de Vers.' This theme, however, also links Pound to the linguistic research of his contemporaries Charles Sanders Peirce and Ferdinand de Saussure on the conventional relationship between symbol and referent (Peirce) or signifier and signified (Saussure). Everyday language functions by means of conventional relations between words and what they signify. Poetry, on the contrary, denies 'le hasard demeuré aux termes' [the arbitrariness that clings to words] (Mallarmé, 'Crise de vers' 368/233), and brings forth the object it names in its essentiality. For Pound, then, the poetic word establishes a necessary and integral relationship between the order of language and the order of things. To be more precise, it is through its articulation through poetic form that a specific experience becomes 'visible' in its true nature, below the layers of language sedimented by habit and usage.

Pound's adoption of the forms and the voices – the personae – of the troubadours and the early Italian poets in his earliest volumes of poetry was the result of a careful operation of appropriation aimed at recovering the freshness and precision of the poetry of origins and overcoming the poetic 'fustian,' the *clichés* and commonplaces, of nineteenth-century poetic diction. In this sense, Arnault Daniel and Guido Cavalcanti were interpreted by Pound as the founders of a tradition of poetry of precision with which he sought to reconnect. Arnaut Daniel was, for Pound, 'the best artist among the Provençals, trying the speech in new fashions, and bringing new words into writing, and making new blendings of words, so that he taught much to Messire Dante Alighieri' ('Arnaut Daniel,' *Literary Essays* 111). As for the Florentine poet, Pound clarified the terms of his fascination with him in a well-known passage of the essay 'Cavalcanti.'

> When the late T.E. Hulme was trying to be a philosopher in that milieu, and fussing about Sorel and Bergson and getting them translated into English, I spoke to him one day of the difference between Guido's precise interpretive metaphor, and the Petrarchan fustian and ornament, pointing out that Guido thought in accurate terms; that phrases correspond to definite sensations undergone; in fact very much what I had said in my early preface to the Sonnets and Ballate.
>
> Hulme took some time over it in silence, and then finally said: 'That is very interesting'; and after a pause: 'That is more interesting than anything I have ever seen in a book.' (*Literary Essays* 162)

Cavalcanti was capable of forging a precise and accurate language, which, like the 'virtue' of those 'favored by Apollo,' could perform the elusive task of bridging the gap between words and things. Cavalcanti's language translates the conceptual content of the poem into a figurative language that is clear and precise, and that has a primarily epistemological rather than aesthetic value. As Pound further writes in 'Cavalcanti,' 'In Guido the "figure," the strong metamorphic or "picturesque" expression is there with the purpose to convey or to interpret a definite meaning' (*Literary Essays* 154). In other words, in Cavalcanti's poetry there is a necessary and inseparable relationship between form and content: precision belongs to individual words and to the metaphoric structures into which those words are inserted; thus, it is through words that an abstract emotion or intellectual notion finds a shape in which it can be made visible and communicated. Content does not pre-exist form, but rather becomes a recognizable and identifiable problematic precisely when it finds an adequate formal expression. Pound's counter-examples, of course, include Petrarch – whose figurative language, according to Pound is mere ornament, 'the prettiest ornament he could find, but not an irreplaceable ornament' ('Cavalcanti,' *Literary Essays* 154)[44] – and, more recently, the decorative poetic diction of Victorian verse.[45]

Pound's understanding of the mechanisms governing poetic language allowed him to recast in new terms the question of the function of the poet in modernity. In *Ezra Pound: Purpose/Form/Meaning*, Marianne Korn has traced the origins of Pound's model of the oppositional relationship between artist and public to late nineteenth-century aestheticism; indeed as early as 1908 Pound's correspondence reveals an antagonistic attitude recalling that on which hinges the rhetoric of the French decadents. For instance, in a letter to his friend the poet William Carlos Williams dated 21 October 1908, he wrote: 'As for the 'eyes of too ruthless public': damn their eyes. No art ever grew by looking into the eyes of the public, ruthless or otherwise. You can obliterate yourself and mirror God, Nature, or Humanity but if you try to mirror yourself in the eyes of the public, woe be unto your art' (*Selected Letters* 6). However, this sense of alienation was coupled with a revendication of the *professional* status of the artist that was more in tune with the division of knowledge in specialized disciplinary realms characterizing modernity. In his first major statement of poetics, 'Prologomena' [*sic*] (*Poetry Review*, February 1912), Pound follows his articulation of four poetic principles with a distinction between the 'amateur' and the 'expert' that serves to emphasize the specialized nature of the work of the artist – work which is not merely the result of inspiration, but rather requires as a foundational element the study of tradition as a storehouse of 'discoveries' made by predecessors that the new poet can appropriate as tools of the trade: 'The experimental demonstrations of one man may save the time of many – hence my furore over Arnaut Daniel – if a man's experiments try out one new rime, or dispense conclusively with one iota of currently accepted non-sense, he is merely playing fair with colleagues when he chalks up his results' (*EPPP* 61). The expert is thus the poet who has 'knowledge of technique of surface and technique of content' (*EPPP* 61). The major target of Pound's criticism, however, is not the 'amateur,' but rather the artist integrated in the capitalist marketplace, whose works are circulated like commodities. The distinction between the commercial writer and the 'serious artist' is articulated in the essay 'Patria mia' (1913).[46] Pound's comparison occurs in the context of a broader critique of literary periodicals, a medium for which Pound had little love, believing it to be one of the sources of the decline in American letters. His analysis of the function of periodicals articulates the conflict between the two modes of validation that find their battle ground in the turn-of-the-century field of cultural production: the accumulation of economic versus symbolic capital.

The opposition between the artist and the magazine editor is interesting for the metaphorical fields that it mobilizes. In 'Patria mia' Pound superimposes the distinction between artist and editor on that between scientist and tradesman. The passage deserves to be quoted at length.

> Throughout, it is a question not of popular ignorance or of popular indifference, but of pseudo-artists and of a system of publishing control. The arts can thrive in the midst of densest popular ignorance. They can thrive, I suppose, despite any number of false priests and producers of commercial imitations, but in this latter case the nation will not know that the arts stay alive, and the sham will grow.
>
> The serious artist does not play upon the law of supply and demand. He is like the chemist experimenting, forty results are useless, his time is spent without payment, the forty-first or the four hundredth and first combination of elements produces the marvel, for posterity as likely as not. The tradesman must either cease from experiment, from discovery and confine himself to producing that for which there is a demand, or else he must sell his botches, and either of these courses is as fatal to the artist as it would be to the man of science.
>
> All editors that are not by nature and inclination essentially base, do, by any continuing practice of their trade become so. That is to say the system of magazine publication is at bottom opposed to the serious man in letters. (*Selected Prose* 110)

Against the commodification of the product of the artist and its integration in the capitalist circuit of exchange, Pound forcefully reasserts the autonomy of the aesthetic. What is significant, however, is not so much Pound's argument, which follows coherently from the premises of aestheticism, but rather the metaphoric field that is invoked to legitimate the autonomous status of the artist. Against the model of art as a lay religion, which oriented the discourse of the decadents and which led Baju to define it as 'un sacerdoce réservé à quelques initiés' [a priesthood reserved for a few initiates] ('Eux' 1), Pound adopts scientific research as the paradigm through which to re-articulate the function of poetry. While Pound ultimately derives from romanticism the notion of the spiritual superiority and the guiding role of the artist, and on occasion utilizes religious metaphors that look back to the previous model of self-understanding of the poet's role,[47] the identification of the work of the artist with that of the scientist allows the American poet to articulate a re-legitimization of poetry that does not set it in opposition to the positivist foundations of modern science, but rather draws from those foundations the very justification of poetry. Pound's discursive strategy is significant, especially when compared to those of the other figures considered in this study. In Baju's rhetoric of decadence, the loss of the halo cannot be compensated, and the only space left to the artist is that of turning his alienation, his functionlessness, into a new kind of negative function, thus defining art as that which withdraws from life. Consequently, the organizing metaphor of his project, the aristocrat, entailed a retreat from the present into an imagined past. Futurism, on the contrary, eventually renounced the halo altogether; the theorization of the ephemeral and impermanent work of art continuously replaced by newer and newer products resulted in the representation of the artist as the incendiary, perpetually overcoming, in a cycle of creation and destruction, his own achievements.[48] Pound recuperates the halo, the function through which the difference between the artist and his audience can be articulated, by isolating within modernity the domain that is endowed with the sacrality and authority that once belonged to the sacred work of art: positive science. Furthermore, such a fascination with science, which might have constituted a point of contact with futurism, in fact implicitly places Pound in an antinomic relationship with the Italian movement. For Marinetti in particular, science resolves itself in its technological applications, resulting in a radical revolution in the way in which human subjects live their relationship with themselves and the world. Science in other words is not a neutral category that only performs a hermeneutical function, bringing to visibility and translating into its objective language the mechanisms that regulate the operations of the world; rather, science is first and foremost a transformative practice that through its technological implementations, affects the way in which reality not only is experienced but also is encoded through semiotic systems such as language. If the futurists isolate speed as the object of their reflection it is not simply because of what the English avant-garde disparagingly branded, in Lewis's term, 'automobilism'[49] (that is, the fetishization of the superficial aspects of modernity), but rather because velocity provides the metaphoric field through which the futurists can come to grips with modernity itself. 'Speed' – the cipher of the global marketplace that begins to unfold in the nineteenth century – is characterized by the multifold increase in the circulation of goods, information, and people, and symbolically summarizes the fracture between modernity and pre-modern modes of social organization. For Pound, on the contrary, science offers an ahistorical model through which the work of the artist can be represented, and through which the distance between artist and audience can be asserted and justified.[50]

In a recent study of contemporary American poetry, Vernon Shetley begins his enquiry into the 'death of poetry' in contemporary culture by focusing on the issue of 'difficulty' as an index of the divorce between artist and audience that characterizes modernity. He argues:

> What the outcry over modernist difficulty indicates [...] is that a gulf opened between poets and readers: difficulty was an effect, and not a cause, of the disappearance of the common reader. Earlier instances of extreme poetic obscurity occurred within interpretative communities sufficiently close-knit to transmit, along with the poems, ways of reading adequate to them. In an earlier age Eliot might have circulated his poems, as Donne did, in manuscript, with the far greater opportunity to control and shape the terms of reading that such a means of distribution entails. (9)

Perhaps in tune with the funereal tone set by the title of his study, *After the Death of Poetry*, Shetley concludes his argument in terms of a lack, a 'disappearance' that characterizes modernity – the vanishing of the common reader. But perhaps such a vanishing is the result of not so much a disappearance as a proliferation of interpretative communities – each characterized by different degrees of cultural competence – that came with the emergence of mass media and mass audiences after the mid nineteenth century. The 'close-knit' communities evoked by Shetley were possible in specific historical circumstances in which access to cultural production and reception operated on the basis of exclusion, and the fruition of art was a social act that characterized the hegemonic class. In modernity, on the contrary, readership becomes segmented in the 'different groups of readers [that] have different skills and expectations' (9) described by Shetley, and access to cultural products occurs along multiple and parallel lines, through the multiplication of audiences, from the 'intellectual' to the 'bourgeois' to the 'mass,'[51] and of media, from the popular newspaper to the middle-brow opera to the poetry chapbook. Within such an articulate field of cultural production, 'obscurity' becomes not a problem to be overcome but rather an index that distinguishes the work of art from the readily enjoyable commodity.[52]

In this context, it is remarkable that Pound uses precisely the category of obscurity as the grounding for his identification of the work of the artist with that of the scientist. His essay 'Psychology and the Troubadours,' first published in *Quest* in October 1912 (and signed, quite unusually for the poet, as Ezra Pound, M.A., almost as if to emphasize its 'scientificity'), begins with the question of obscurity, with which *trobar clus* has been charged, not only by its modern critics but also by the critical discourse contemporaneous with it. According to Pound, the opposition between two schools of medieval poetry, one that had 'the popular ear' and one that was on the contrary 'obscure,' is in fact a characteristic not only of early poetry but of poetry *tout court*: 'At this early date we find poetry divided into two schools; the first school complained about the obscurities of the second – we have them always with us. They claimed, or rather jeered in Provence, remonstrated in Tuscany, wrangle to-day, and will wrangle to-morrow – and not without some show of reason – that poetry, especially lyric poetry, must be simple, that you must get the meaning while the man sings it' (*EPPP* 85). Whatever its merits, the poetry of the first school is tiring precisely because its accessibility finally results in repetitiveness: 'the first songs [...] are especially tiresome if one tries to read them *after* one has read fifty others of more or less the same sort' (*EPPP* 86). The poetry of the second school, on the contrary, reveals something new, and in that lies its force. Its obscurity is a function of its power of innovation that Pound describes as a 'revelation': 'The second sort of canzoni is a ritual. It must be conceived and approached as a ritual. It has its purpose and its effect. These are different from those of simple song. They are perhaps subtler. They make their revelations to those who are already expert' (*EPPP* 86).

In the same essay, Pound defines the artist as someone who 'perceives at greater intensity and more intimately than his public' and as 'the seeing one among the sightless' (*EPPP* 83), but this almost sacral notion of the artist's role is quickly re-articulated through a pseudo-scientific metaphor: 'The interpretative function is the highest honour of the arts, and because it is so we find a sort of hyper-scientific precision is the touch-stone and assay of the artist's power and of his honour, of his authenticity' (*EPPP* 84). Precision – a key notion in the poetics of imagism, but clearly also a definition for the power of the poetic word to 'cling close' to the thing described in the section 'On Virtue'of 'I Gather the Limbs of Osiris' – is the linchpin between the interpretative function played by art and that played by science. Poetic language, then, has a cognitive function that makes it complementary to the language of science: 'Now that mechanical science has realized his [the poet's] ancient dreams of flight and sejunct communication, he is the advance guard of the psychologist on the watch for new emotions' ('The Wisdom of Poetry,' *EPPP* 75).

The scientific paradigm allows Pound to legitimize further the antagonistic relationship between audience and artist. In an article published in October 1914 in *Poetry* (the American journal founded in 1912 by Harriet Monroe of which Pound had become the self-appointed foreign correspondent) Pound took to task the Whitman quote that served as the journal's motto – 'To have great poets there must be great audiences too' – asking rhetorically: 'Can we have no great inventors without a great audience of inventors?' (*EPPP* 286). Coherently with the argument that the artist brings to light the inner life of human beings, while the scientist describes their material conditions,[53] Pound states that the audience cannot provide the ground of validation for the artist, because it constitutes his very material: 'The artist is not dependent upon the multitude of his listeners. Humanity is the rich effluvium, it is the waste and the manure and the soil, and from it grows the tree of the arts. As the plant germ seizes upon the noble particles of the earth [...] so does the artist seize upon those souls which do not fear transmutation, which dare become the body of the god' (286).[54]

The deployment of what Julia Kristeva has called a rhetoric of abjection is functional to articulating an antinomic relationship between the artist and the audience. In Pound's essay the artist emerges as a sort of superego who arrogates to himself the role of 'moral conscience, of self-observation, and of the formation of ideas' (Laplanche and Pontalis 621), while the audience is represented as his unclean other whose presence threatens his very existence because it calls into question the means of his legitimation.[55] Thus, in 'Audience' Pound emphatically places solely upon the artist the function of validating his activity by identifying him with the ideal audience in a closure of the circuit of communication within the self that recalls that put forward by the decadents: 'It is true that the great artist has always a great audience, even in his lifetime; but it is not the *vulgo* but the spirit of irony and of destiny and of humor, sitting within him' (*EPPP* 286).[56]

By October 1914, when 'Audience' appeared in *Poetry,* Pound had already gone through the experience of imagism and had recently embarked in vorticism, the two crucial phases of his attempt to appropriate the strategies of the Continental avant-garde to generate interest around his own activities and those of what he later described as 'a certain group of advancing poets' for the purpose of 'set[ting] the arts in their rightful place as the acknowledged guide and lamp of civilization' (*Selected Letters* 48).[57] In an article entitled 'Vorticism' published in September in the *Fortnightly Review,* he attempted to explain the terms of the transformation of his imagist poetics into those of vorticism. With remarkable consistency, Pound returned to the question of the cognitive function of poetry in the terms first used in 'The Wisdom of Poetry,' which was published in April 1912 and thus preceded the foundation of Imagism, and was contemporaneous with the first wave of futurist activities in England. In both essays, Pound uses the example of the formula of the circle as a correlative to the work of the poem: '[W]e learn that the equation $(x - a)^2 + (y - b)^2 = r^2$ governs the circle. It is the circle. It is not a particular circle. It is the circle free of space and time limits. It is the universal, existing in perfection, in freedom from space and time. Mathematics is dull as ditchwater until one reaches analytics. But in analytics we come upon a new way of dealing with form. It is this way that art handles life. The difference between art and analytical geometry is the difference of subject-matter only' ('Vorticism,' *EPPP* 283). Analytical geometry defines the eternal structures that underlie the contingency and finitude of phenomena, their being in the world; likewise the poem provides a formulation that translates human experiences into their universal and necessary formal expression. And as with science, the results of the artist's work must be evaluated according to principles inherent to the field itself. Thus, the metaphor of the artist as scientist allows Pound to provide a theoretical ground on which to justify the exclusion of the general public from the process of consecration of the artist. 'The rules of the game of science,' Lyotard has written, 'are immanent in that game,' and 'there is no other proof that the rules are good than the consensus extended to them by the experts' (29). It is precisely to this form of consensus that Pound appeals in 'Vorticism,' and this further allows him to articulate his distance from the futurists. While futurism resolves its 'anxiety of influence' by refusing altogether to engage with the tradition, Poundian imagism/vorticism welcomes such an engagement, but only if is made 'by some intelligent person whose idea of "the tradition" is not limited by the conventional taste of four or five centuries and one continent' (*EPPP* 282). The relationship between poet and audience is thus articulated in Pound's early aesthetics through a pyramidal structure with the poet located at the apex. Between him and the general audience, which constitutes the base, there is an intermediate layer that bridges the gap between the two outer levels. In Pound's pseudo-scientific discourse this intermediate tier is comparable to the engineer who translates into practical terms the theoretical knowledge produced by the scientists, who on the contrary work 'for no cause save their own pleasure in the work' (*EPPP* 75). The engineer is a liminal figure who understands the abstract language of the scientist, but who can also turn it to practical purposes, to the construction of 'bridges and devices' (*EPPP* 76) because he also speaks the language of the many. It is through this translation of the 'obscurity' of poetry – which is a necessary condition because through poetry is given form precisely what did not have form before – that the poet attains 'universality,' which in 'I Gather the Limbs of Osiris' Pound defines as being 'understood of the "many" and lauded of "the few"' (*EPPP* 57).

This complex dialectic between 'the many' and 'the few' also explains some of the more peculiar aspects of Pound's cultural strategy. Michael Levenson has remarked on the ambiguity between the 'essentially elitist nature' of modernism and Pound's 'relentless propagandizing' (*Genealogy* 148). I would suggest that the terms of this ambiguity are implicit in the very scientific model that provides the metaphoric structure for Pound's aesthetics, and explain his persistent pedagogism. In discussing the mechanisms that guide the pragmatics of scientific knowledge, Lyotard points out that teaching is a necessary complement to the activity of research for no other than fundamentally institutional reasons. In research the 'competence required concerns the post of sender alone' (25), because the specific competences of the addressee – of the audience – do not affect the validity of the results; however, that competence is not inherent to the researcher himself, but must rather be legitimated by a community who can verify that the necessary criteria of scientificity have been met. In other words, as Lyotard writes, 'one's competence is never an accomplished fact. [...] The truth of the statement and the competence of its sender are thus subject to the collective approval of a group of persons who are competent on an equal basis. Equals must be created' (24). Pound is confronted by precisely this aporia: in the very moment that he argues that the autonomy of art is founded on the fact that, like science, art reveals eternal and non-contingent truths, he then must postulate the existence of a community whose consensus can indeed validate the 'truth' of the work and distinguish it from the fake and the stereotyped. Lacking such a community, the competence of the artist – and therefore his results – is also suspect. Thus, the artist must take on the role of disseminator of knowledge in order to form, within the broader audience, a restricted public that can potentially move into the ranks of the experts and validate the artist's competence. The production of critical essays, pedagogic works, and statements of poetics that runs parallel to Pound's poetic production is therefore functional to such a necessity of forming a cohesive interpretative community. Pound's strategy however is significantly different from that of futurism: whereas Marinetti made use of popular vehicles for the circulation of his aesthetic theories – the newspaper, the variety theatre, the freely distributed leaflet – Pound, following his 'scientific' model, limited his intervention to sites highly endowed with cultural capital that promised an already select audience. For this reason his engagement with the public genre of the manifesto happened along non-canonical lines, and served to position his imagist project in a critical relationship with the avant-garde.

The Art of Not Making Manifestoes: F.S. Flint's 'Imagisme' and Pound's 'A Few Don'ts by an Imagiste'

As we have already noted, the arrival of futurism in 1912 and Marinetti's 'performances' offered Pound an alternative model of communication between artist and audience, and a blurring of the boundaries between art and commodity that influenced if not the aesthetics at least the cultural strategies of the American poet. In 'Prologomena' he had referred to the existence of a 'movement' (*EPPP* 62) in English poetry, but the term was clearly being used in the broadest sense to indicate the direction in which Pound envisioned the art to be moving – 'it [poetry] will, I think, move against poppy-cock, it will be harder and saner' (63) – rather than in the sense of an organized and coordinated collaborative project. The four point 'Credo' included in the same essay, which recalls the programmatic section of technical manifestoes, was emphatically presented as a series of personal beliefs (indeed, the first three principles are introduced by an anaphoric 'I believe,' and the fourth by a more tentative 'I think') rather than as a general and collective program.

Pound initially appeared to have little interest in futurism, although this may also be due to a question of competences, since the Italian movement was introduced to the British public mainly as a movement in the figurative arts.[58] Even after Marinetti's arrival in England the literary dimension of futurism received scant attention, and its founder was portrayed rather as an eccentric theorizer than as a practitioner, in poetry, of the same aesthetics that oriented the works of Boccioni, Severini, and the other painters. While the press published several of Marinetti's manifestoes between 1912 and 1914, the same cannot be said for his poetry or for futurist poetry in general. With the exception of a small anthology of poems by Marinetti, Buzzi, and Palazzeschi published in the September 1913 special issue of the journal *Poetry and Drama* (whose editor, Harold Monro, had been one of Marinetti's earliest contacts in England)[59] the literary works of the movement did not find a space in any way comparable to that conquered by the artists. Since, the more spectacularly ludicrous and propagandistic activities of Marinetti were not balanced by a rounded portrayal of the futurist leader as a poet, it was easy to dismiss him as a kind of clownesque figure. Consider for instance the report of Marinetti's Bechstein Hall performance in *The Times*, which concluded with the following account of the performance of three futurist poems: 'Two were in Italian and dealt with a suicide and his watch, and with a lunatic asylum; the third, a French one of his own composition, glorified the automobile in work of destruction. He ended with a passionate defence of war. Whatever element of truth may underlie doctrines deprecating an excessive veneration of the past, the anarchical extravagances of the Futurists must deprive the movement of the sympathy of all reasonable men' ('The Aims of Futurism' 2).

If Pound might have been fascinated by the power of seduction of Marinetti's brand mixture of art and entertainment, it is also clear that he could not appropriate such a model for his own poetic project precisely because, turning the discourse on art into a public spectacle and the artist into a performer, it shifted control of that discourse away from the producer and to the mass media. If Marinetti could reach an audience of millions through newspaper reports of his and his companions' activities, what in fact reached such a broad audience was not so much the poetic and artistic program of the movement, but rather the ironic or dismissive portrayal of the anarchists of the arts. This was not necessarily a problem for Marinetti, who, having chosen to conduct his futurist propaganda according to the rules of advertising was well aware of the fact that any kind of publicity – and in particular, publicity that in turn would generate further discussion around the movement – served to circulate more effectively the 'brand name' of futurism. Such a commercial approach, however, was antithetical to the Poundian model of aesthetic communication examined above, which postulated a fundamentally passive role for the audience and a legitimation of the artist derived not from the media but from his own peers – which certainly did not include the members of the commercial press. If futurism showed Pound the uses of a public persona, it also, and perhaps most importantly, showed him its potential abuses and the necessity of controlling its production.

It is in this context that the rhetorical artifices of the so-called manifestoes of imagism become especially significant in understanding Pound's cultural strategy. The foundation of the movement was recalled, almost half a century after the fact, by one of its protagonists, the poet and Pound's fellow American expatriate H.D. in her memoir *End to Torment*:

> 'But Dryad' (in the Museum tea room), 'this is poetry.' He [Pound] slashed with a pencil. 'Cut this out, shorten this line. "Hermes of the Ways" is a good title. I'll send it this to Harriet Monroe of *Poetry*. Have you a copy? Yes? Then we can send this, or I'll type it when I get back. Will this do?' And he scrawled 'H.D. Imagiste' at the bottom of the page. (18)

Indeed, years after the fact, Pound himself admitted that 'The name [imagism] was invented to launch H.D. and Aldington before either had enough stuff for a volume.'[60] Like futurism, then, imagism is initially a virtual poetic movement that begins life through the act of a signature which, to quote Derrida's discussion of the 'Declaration of Independence,' 'invents its signers' (8). Significantly, however, the signature is not that of the subject who names himself or herself through this gesture; rather it serves to impose an avant-garde identity on a third party, and thus to give substance to a spectral presence that was already haunting certain narrow circles of Anglo-American modernism. Even as he names the movement with which he will be identified, Pound seems to perform a critical operation, assuming the role of the expert who can guarantee the validity of the work of one of his peers, and legitimate the appearance – indeed, the significance – of the movement before the public. And it is precisely as the expert that Pound would construct his public imagist persona, in an operation of 'cultural ventriloquism' that transposes into a new context the poetic strategy underlying the use of masks in his early poetry: speaking *en imagiste* in the few public documents on the group which bear his signature – in particular, the famous 'A Few Don'ts by an Imagiste' – Pound puts on the facade of the *caposcuola* and plays with it so as to position himself and his poetics in a critical stance in relation to the contemporary cultural milieu.

The existence of imagism had been announced in passing in Pound's first letter to Harriet Monroe (18 August 1912), in which he responded to her request for a contribution to her journal by writing: 'I send you all that I have on my desk – an over-elaborate post-Browning "Imagiste" affair and a note on the Whistler exhibit' (*Selected Letters* 10). The poem in question, published in the October issue of *Poetry*, was 'Middle-Aged. A Study in an Emotion,' which indulges in some of the archaicizing flourishes characteristic of Pound's early poetry – consider the opening: "Tis but a vague, invarious delight / As gold that rains about some buried king' (*EPPP* 81) – and does not quite display the 'lachonic speech' which Pound would describe as one of the characteristics of imagism in another letter to Monroe in October. Obviously Pound, having coined the term, was beginning to circulate it before it had clearly come to be identified with a specific poetics. By October, imagism, in the guise of H.D.'s poems, had become 'the sort of American stuff that I can show here and in Paris without its being ridiculed. Objective – no slither; direct – no excessive use of adjectives, no metaphors that won't permit examination. It's straight talk, straight as the Greek!' (*Selected Letters* 11). In defining H.D.'s poetry, Pound was also re-articulating the principles already expressed in 'Prologomena.' The metaphor that 'permit[s] examination' is anticipated by the notion of 'symbol' developed in the 'Credo': 'I believe that [...] if a man use "symbols" he must use them that their symbolic function does not obtrude' (*EPPP* 60). Above all, in the closing paragraph, Pound envisions the following characteristics for twentieth-century poetry: 'We will have fewer painted adjectives impeding the shock and stroke of it.

At least for myself, I want it so, austere, direct, free from emotional slither' (*EPPP* 63).

In October 1912, the existence of the 'Imagistes' was also communicated officially to the poetry-reading public in Pound's preface to 'The Poetical Works of T.E. Hulme,' an appendix to his fourth volume of poetry, *Ripostes*. After introducing Hulme and recalling the time of the poems' composition some two years earlier, Pound wrote:

> As for the 'School of Images,' which may or may not have existed, its principles were not so interesting as those of the 'inherent dynamists' or of *Les Unanimistes*, yet they were probably sounder than those of a certain French school which attempted to dispense with verbs altogether; or of the Impressionists who brought forth:
>
> 'Pink pigs blossoming upon hillside';
>
> or the Post-Impressionists who beseech their ladies to let down slate-blue hair over raspberry-coloured flanks. [...]
>
> As for the future, *Les Imagistes*, the descendants of the forgotten school of 1909, have that in their keeping. (*Ripostes* 59)

The composition history of *Ripostes*[61] suggests that the preface to the appendix could have been inserted in the volume at any time between March 1912, when Pound sent the completed volume to his publisher, and 18 August 1912, when he received a second set of proofs. (This later date is in fact quite convincing, since the letter to Monroe in which the proofs are mentioned is the same one in which he also promises to send her the 'over-elaborate post-Browning "Imagiste" affair' quoted above.) The influence of futurism on Pound's announcement of the latest 'ism' (or *isme*, to use his Frenchified flourish) has been rightly remarked,[62] although the earlier part of the note on the 'School of Images' makes the reference paradoxically more specific and more vague. The French school that sought to do away with verbs is most likely futurism, whose technical manifesto of literature had recently been issued (11 May 1912).[63] However, the reference to Jules Romains's unanimism and to impressionism expands the network of references well beyond the Italian movement to the whole of the French avant-garde milieu to which English readers were being exposed by the critical writings of young poets such as F.S. Flint.[64] Pound's note is finally a backhanded acknowledgment of the existence of an institutional context that conditions the way in which cultural legitimation is produced: the proliferation of imported 'isms' in England demonstrated the performative power of systems of classification in a cultural context more and more dominated by the much vituperated journalistic discourse that mediates the reception of the work of art in modernity. The question for Pound then was that of launching something resembling an avant-garde movement while retaining firm control over its definition and dissemination.

What is striking about the origins of imagism is how much it appears to be a sort of private affair, quite removed from the kind of engagement with a mass audience that had characterized futurism. There were no public announcements, no self-avowed manifestoes, not even the kind of pseudo-avant-garde shock antics that Pound would try out less than two years later during his vorticist phase (his contribution to the activities of Lewis's Rebel Arts Centre, for instance, was apparently a banner that read, bombastically, 'End of the Christian Era'). If imagism was an avant-garde at all, it was a 'moderate avant-garde,' to use Luigi Baldacci's rather appropriate oxymoron coined to describe Massimo Bontempelli's *Novecentismo*: an avant-garde, that is, which 'has given up from the start its aggressive role' (65). The arena within which imagism moved was carefully delimited: the pages of *Poetry* and the 1914 anthology *Des Imagistes*, which marked, at least for Pound, the end rather than the beginning of the imagist moment. By the summer of 1914, the requests of Amy Lowell, who had become the financial backer of the group, for new and regular public initiatives (in particular, the publication of further anthologies) threatened both Pound's control of the operation and his sense of the 'integrity' of the poetics it named, and he cut his relations with it.

Indeed, while the principles of imagism – directness of presentation, spareness, clarity – would remain keywords in Pound's critical vocabulary, the actual documents on the group in which these principles are outlined are only a handful, and can be quickly summarized. In 'Status Rerum,' a report of the condition of poetry in London as of the end of 1912 for the readers of *Poetry* (January 1913), Pound inserted yet another elliptical reference to'the youngest school that has the nerve to call itself a school,' that is, the *Imagistes*. Here Pound added an important caveat meant to deflect the accusation of academicism that, as we have seen, had been levelled at the futurists: 'To belong to a school does not in the least mean that one writes poetry to a theory. One writes poetry when, where, because, and as one feels like writing it. A school exists when two or three young men agree, more or less, to call certain things good; when they prefer such of their verses as have certain qualities to such of their verses as do not have them' (*EPPP* 112).

Pound does not name names (Richard Aldington is referred to immediately after this paragraph, but whether he is in fact one of the mysterious imagists remains ambiguous), nor, for the moment, does he lay out a program. This latter function was reserved for the central pieces of imagist propaganda – F.S. Flint's 'Imagisme' and Pound's 'A Few Don'ts' – which appeared in the following issue of *Poetry.* Afterward, references became scant until the attempted merger with vorticism.[65]

The central concern for Pound, then, was to retain the tightest control over the definition of imagism, to construct an image of the group that would not entail a rejection of the essentially elitist view of the social function of the artist delineated above. In other words, by insisting on the serious, professional nature of the group's activities, Pound carried out a complex and ultimately unsuccessful operation of mediation between high and low culture, utilizing select techniques of publicity of mass culture to carve a position and an audience for his poetic project without simultaneously redrawing the boundary between high and low culture or questioning the autonomous status of the aesthetic. Thus, Pound was able to play with the avant-garde horizon of expectations fostered by the activities of the various post-impressionist groups to reassert the validity of the institution of literature, within which imagism – with a gesture that, by overturning the revolutionary rhetoric of the avant-garde, becomes in turn paradoxically iconoclastic – firmly roots itself. Flint's article begins precisely by violating such expectations: 'The *imagistes* admitted that they were contemporaries of the Post Impressionists and the Futurists; but they had nothing in common with these schools. They had not published a manifesto. They were not a revolutionary school; their only endeavor was to write in accordance with the best tradition, as they found it in the best writers of all time – in Sappho, Catullus, Villon' (*EPPP* 119). Clearly, the most immediate 'father' that needs to be metaphorically killed, or whose presence must at least be exorcised, is Marinetti himself. Against the hegemonic temptation of the Italian movement, Pound (via Flint) invokes the specificity of the group's program. Flint contrasts the methods of the two movements very carefully; the reference to the practice of writing manifestoes is significant because it serves as a denial of the horizon of expectations upon which the text acts. Imagists do not write manifestoes because they are concerned with Art, with the practice of writing poetry, which in itself is complete and should not require interventions outside its own domain in the public space of newspapers and theatre performances.

In any case, it would have been unlikely that the astute reader of the chronicles of modern art would have mistaken 'Imagisme' for a manifesto, since from the very beginning the rhetoric of the text seems designed to undermine the phatic, direct relationship between artist and audience that characterizes the genre. The first person pronoun that opens the text emphatically does *not* designate an imagist (inspite of the fact that by the time that the first anthology was published Flint was represented in it with five poems): donning the guise of the roving reporter, Flint admits to being as much in the dark about imagism as his audience, thus identifying with the public rather than with the artists whose poetics he is about to illustrate. The text was even accompanied by an editorial note in which Flint's article was described as the response to 'the many requests for information regarding *Imagism* and the *Imagistes*' (*EPPP* 119), suggesting that the public itself was clamouring for more information about the elusive school. We are then confronted with an overturning of the typical manifesto situation of the avant-garde artist hectoring his audience in order to provoke a reaction. Here the artist condescends to address the audience via its demotic representative, the journalist, only to re-iterate the essentially autonomous status of his work and the radical difference of art from the production of commodities for mass consumption. Like an esoteric creed, the 'Doctrine of the Image' has not been committed to the materiality of form, to writing, and in any case it is of interest only to the initiate and not to the general public, among which it 'would provoke useless discussion' (*EPPP* 119).

Flint here functions as a framing device between the reader and the poet; quite literally, he provides a voice for the artists who, at this stage, remain removed in their isolation.[66] The possibility of an exchange of roles, of a breakdown of the frame that divides the producer and the consumer, is thus curtailed. This text shows that, to answer the rhetorical question that closes Foucault's essay 'What Is an Author?' it matters very much who is speaking because the significant new questions that Foucault proposes take this issue as their starting point. In other words, in order to ask certain crucial questions – 'Where does [discourse] come from; how is it circulated; who controls it' (138) – we must begin by considering how the homodiegetic narrator, the author(ity) who validates the discourse, is textually constructed. While they give body to the elusive spectre of imagism, Flint and Pound are careful to retain for the producer the authorial function that allows him to maintain control over the public discourse on the poetics of the school. In avant-garde manifesto writing, the 'I' that speaks, and speaks on behalf of the 'we' of the group, is always constructed as, potentially, the 'I' of the reader, because it asks the reader to place himself in the position of emitter, to claim authorship of the principles delineated in the manifesto. Claude Leroy has argued that the maker of the manifesto, 'presents himself as the first reader, and not the creator, of a transcendental truth, carefully handed down, without loss or transformation, to his own reader. Through the emulation specific to the system, the latter metamorphoses in his turn into an always first reader of a truth that he will then reveal to his own receiver, so as to place him in the position of a new first reader, and so on' (126). If the 'I' of the author stands for the collective authority of the movement, then the reader, who is explicitly called upon as potential member of the avant-garde elite, can participate in that collective authority and thereby claim to be a persona of the 'I' of the author. The reader is thus positioned between these two poles of revelation and creation, discovery and manipulation. The injunctive tone, the recurrence of the hortatory and imperative modes of address that dominate manifesto writing are the epiphenomena of this strategy to involve the reader, so that the reader becomes a producer, places himself in the position of the emitter of the manifesto, and takes for himself active responsibility for its theses. Not so in Flint's text, which seeks to control, rather than destabilize, the demarcation between public and private space, between artist and audience, thus reaffirming the traditional institutional roles of poet, reader, and, in a mediating function, critic – reaffirming, in other words, the auratic distance between the audience and the work of art.

The well-known history of the essay 'Imagisme' confirms this reading. The text was first drafted by Pound, who then asked Flint to publish it under his own name. (In addition to being a friend of Pound's, Flint also brought to the text the not inconsiderable legitimating power of his established reputation as an expert on the 'isms' of the symbolist and post-symbolist French milieu.)[67] Finding that the 'interview' was too idiosyncratically Poundian, Flint rewrote it in a form that was then further edited by Pound himself.[68] The corrected typescript shows that, along with Flint's flights into decorativism, the dialogic structure of the original text, all contextual elements of the interview – such as the use of reported speech for Flint's questions and Pound's answers and the interviewer's description of his subject's irritated reactions – and direct references to the group – such as its membership, which in Flint's draft is specified to consist of 'three poets, one or two affiliated writers, and a ... penumbra!' (Middleton 38) – were carefully excised by

Pound. The resulting text reads throughout not as an interview but as a cold and impersonal report that opens no space of intervention for the reader. The text ends by emphasizing the closure of the group – 'They are stricter with themselves than with any outsider' (*EPPP* 119) – and even the 'few rules' revealed to the audience are couched not in the imperative of the manifesto, which entails a call to the reader to perform a certain action, but in the constative, as norms regulating the activities of those who already belong to the group: 'They had a few rules, drawn up for their own satisfaction only, and they had not published them' (*EPPP* 119).[69]

But after being confronted with the chill stare of the Imagists, who delighted in taking apart the work of 'approaching poetasters' by rewriting it 'using about ten words to his fifty'[70] (*EPPP* 119), the reader would have turned to the companion piece of this imagist primer, Pound's 'A Few Don'ts by an Imagiste,' the pedagogical thrust of which is unmistakable. Divided into two sections – 'Language' and 'Rhythm and Rhyme' – the text offers a series of prescriptions that reverse the situation encountered in the previous text. And indeed, 'Imagisme' and 'A Few Don'ts' work in conjunction to construct and differentiate two audiences, which must exist simultaneously in order for the imagist project to be pulled off. These two audiences are nothing other than 'the many' and 'the few' of 'I Gather the Limbs of Osiris,' the general audience and the experts that fill out the lower strata of the pyramid that we have discussed above. Within an already restricted section of the field of cultural production, delimited by the choice of site for the publicization of the new poetic group, Pound further circumscribes portions of his audience differentiated in terms of competence and function. The many are addressed by Flint and are kept at arm's length: their task is to 'understand,' that is, to have the necessary – but passive – knowledge to decipher the work of art and to distinguish between good and bad poetry in the Poundian sense. The rules through which they are required to approach the aesthetic artifact are quite literally not up for discussion, because, as Pound explains in 'A Few Don'ts,' only the producers can legitimately intervene in the cultural debate: 'Pay no attention to the criticism of men who have never written a notable work' (*EPPP* 120). But the question then becomes: who can legitimately determine the 'notable' character of a work of art?

This is where 'A Few Don'ts' comes into play: this text serves to form the second, restricted audience of potential producers and members of the school. Here the receiver is addressed directly either through the pronoun 'you,' (notably absent from Flint's article) or through the imperative (usually put, as Pound says, 'in Mosaic negative'), in a communicative situation characteristic of the pedagogical model. In other words, Pound imparts on his addressee the linguistic and rhythmic rules that the would-be poet must learn in order to produce the kind of poetry that will have the potential to be recognized as 'notable' by the strict and demanding imagist arbiters. Once again, Pound's game is played on both sides of the poetic discourse. On the one hand, there is no question that the poet is inherently and essentially different from the members of his audience, that he possesses a unique and innate *virtù*; he thus closes the essay on a distinctly romantic note by quoting Duhamel and Vildrac's conclusion to their *Notes sur la technique poetique*: *'Mais d'abord il faut etre un poete'* [sic] ['But first one must be a poet'] (*EPPP* 122). On the other, Pound also emphasizes the professional dimension of the work of the poet, the fact that it is the result not merely of inspiration but, most importantly, of an extensive preparatory work to acquire the expertise necessary to perform the role effectively. The figure of the 'expert' is repeatedly invoked to ground Pound's argument: 'What the expert is tired of today the public will be tired of tomorrow'; 'Don't imagine that ... you can please the expert before you have spent at least as much effort on the art of verse as the average piano teacher spends on the art of music' (*EPPP* 120). Finally, and almost inevitably, the scientist appears as validating metaphor: 'The scientist does not expect to be acclaimed as a great scientist until he has *discovered* something. He begins by learning what has been discovered already. He goes from that point onward. ... He does not expect his friends to applaud the results of his freshman class work. Freshmen in poetry are unfortunately not confined to a definite and recognizable classroom. They are "all over the shop." Is it any wonder "the public is indifferent to poetry?"' (121)

We may recall the apocalyptic ending of Marinetti's manifesto of foundation of futurism, with its annihilation of each generation of poets by the next. Pound's text, on the contrary, serves to ensure the continuation and reproduction of a certain institutional structure of validation through the affirmation of a series of cultural values, of poetic norms whose observance will make it possible for the would-be poet, the 'candidate' or 'neophyte' (*EPPP* 127), to eventually join the ranks of the experts. If we consider again Lyotard's argument that the institutional logic of the 'scientific game' entails that equals must be created in order to establish the validity of the scientist's own work, the splendid circularity of Pound's strategy becomes evident. 'A Few Don'ts' imparts the apodictic rules through which, according to the experts (that is, the imagists), a notable work can be created, its worth established by the imagists themselves; once the candidate has accomplished this task, he is no longer a 'neophyte,' but becomes one of the experts who can in turn validate the work of the other authorities, including his former teachers. The literary values handed down by the current experts to those who will come after them ensure that the new generation will enter without shock or rupture the institution of the poetic canon, and in turn, by accepting and redeploying the lessons of its elders, validate the canonization of the previous generation. The often remarked link between modernist writing and New Criticism[71] is nothing other than the successful application of this logic, the reproduction and canonization through critical discourse of those very criteria of objectivity and impersonality proposed both in their works and in their militant criticism by the high modernist poets themselves (Pound and, most influentially, T.S. Eliot).

The paradigm of scientific research also allows for a re-articulation of the relationship between the present and the literary tradition that avoids the shallows of both decadent epigonism and futurist denial. In 'A Few Don'ts,' Pound offers a view of tradition reduced to a mere series of forms or techniques, the formal expression of the 'discoveries' with which the neophyte must become acquainted. 'Let the candidate fill his mind with the finest cadence he can discover, preferably in a foreign language so that the meaning of the words may be less likely to divert his attention from the movement; e.g., Saxon charms, Hebridean Folk Songs, the verse of Dante, and the lyrics of Shakespeare – if he can dissociate the vocabulary from the cadence. Let him dissect the lyrics of Goethe coldly into their component sound values, syllables long and short, stressed and unstressed, into vowels and consonants' (*EPPP* 121). The analytic gaze of the scientist/poet looks past such issues as the material production and the cultural functions of poetry – all, as we have seen, rather incidental matters – to penetrate the innermost secrets of form, broken down into its most minute components, like laboratory specimens under the microscope.

The laboratory thus replaces the ivory tower as the justification of the hermetic separation between art and life. While the futurists revoked any normative power to tradition and looked to 'life,' understood as an ultimately unseizable flow, to find new formal solutions that could articulate materially their notion of the ephemeral nature of the work of art, Pound's imagism invokes tradition precisely to insulate the work of art from transitoriness and impermanence. Once the artist produces something new, it takes its place along with the other discoveries and thus ensures its immortality.

Lyotard has written that 'the game of science [...] implies a diachronic temporality, that is, a memory and a project. The current sender of a scientific statement is supposed to be acquainted with previous statements concerning its referent (bibliography) and only proposes a new statement on the subject if it differs from previous ones. [...] This diachrony, which assumes memory and the search for the new, represents in principle a cumulative process' (26). Pound could have hardly put it differently, providing the aspiring poet, as he does in 'A Few Don'ts,' with both a list of references (a bibliography) and a project for the future, the discovery of something new. Note, however, that the diachrony described by Lyotard does not amount to a history: it is merely a 'cumulative process,' a sequence of results recorded for posterity and open to infinite additions. The tradition – scientific or literary – is a closed circuit, and in a curious way the affirmation of its centrality becomes a way to sidestep any engagement with the historical conditions of literature, and to reassert its autonomy. It is in this sense that Pound's dictum 'make it new' is radically different from Marinetti's search for a 'nuova bellezza' (*TIF* 98). For the futurists, the new aesthetics can be articulated only by crossing over the boundaries traced by tradition, while for Pound the new is such only because its novelty is made visible by a confrontation that takes place within those same boundaries.

The culmination of this line of enquiry is Eliot's grand style rehabilitation of tradition in his 1919 essay 'Tradition and the Individual Talent' (called by some a 'manifesto of modernism').[72] Guido Guglielmi has written that in Eliot's essay the 'perceptive, synchronic, communicative' word of the avant-garde is implicitly countered by a notion of the poetic word as 'interpretative, diachronic, temporal' (183). If that is the case, however, the limitation of that temporality lies in the fact that it is firmly framed within the structure of the canon – of the institution, if you will – whose presence is hypostatized and de-historicized. To be sure, the tradition is not simply inherited, but must be obtained 'by great labour,' as Eliot himself writes (49). And yet, that labour, like the preparatory work of the would-be imagist poet, does not allow for a move that would call the institution in question and interrogate – as the avant-garde does – its origins, its foundations, and finally its legitimacy. Indeed, the tradition exists outside history, structurally predisposed to accept changes from within through the insertion of the new work of art, but also and simultaneously always already complete. Eliot's description of the tradition as 'the mind of Europe' thus lines up together Shakespeare, Homer, and 'the rock drawings of the Magdalenian draughtsmen' (51) as if they all shared an a-historical essence that allowed them to exist side by side in its great unfolding. If anything, Eliot anticipates a vision of the institution that can assimilate even that which questions its foundations precisely by placing it in relation to other works and therefore bringing it into its own normalizing confines.[73]

To conclude, then, does it matter whether we can identify either 'Imagisme' or 'A Few Don'ts' as manifestoes?[74] The very fact that Pound, via Flint, felt the need to deny any generic relationship between the programmatic texts of imagism and the manifesto, of course, suggests that even for the American poet the point was not moot, and that something was at stake in playing the new poetic school against the propaganda tactics associated with the avant-garde. Such a denial of influence was motivated by the fact that Pound understood that his project of aesthetic renewal went in the opposite direction of that of the avant-garde, even while realizing, with the suspicions that we have discussed above, the usefulness of its strategies. However, in terms of the pragmatic functions that the genre is called to perform, as seen in previous chapters, we can certainly remark on the affinity of these texts and the manifesto, and speak in this case, with Abastado, of a 'manifesto effect.' Like Baju's or Marinetti's manifestoes, Pound's two texts (always keeping in mind the peculiar conditions of composition of 'Imagisme') serve the function of delineating both a narrative of legitimation for the artist, and a model of the relationship between artist and audience. This is naturally the result of the fact that decadentism, futurism, and imagism, for all their local differences, belong to the same historical horizon and both register and address in their peculiar ways the crisis of legitimation that constitutes the engine driving the process of self-reflection of European modernism.

Conclusion

In opening his important genealogical study of English modernist literature, Michael Levenson remarked on the simultaneous vagueness and inevitability of the term 'modernism,' which is firmly entrenched in the critical tradition, but the boundaries of which are at best loosely sketched on the cultural landscape of the period that extends from the last two decades of the nineteenth century to the Second World War (and possibly beyond). Indeed, as a period term, modernism is particularly elusive. Post-modernism, from its beginnings in architectural criticism, has been represented as a fundamentally international and cross-cultural phenomenon, and its features seemed so intimately bound up with broader shifts in cultural and social paradigms as to describe a general 'condition' rather than a specific cultural formation. Modernism, however, has operated in a kind of twilight zone between the narrow confines of Anglo-American literary history and a more general usage that is especially characteristic of art criticism, but that also inspired wide-ranging and articulate analyses of the period, such as the pioneering volume by Malcolm Bradbury and James McFarlane, and theoretical and historiographic studies such as Eysteinsson's *The Concept of Modernism* or Berman's comparative investigation of the development of the modernist ideological and cultural horizon. And yet, in literary studies the acknowledgement of the international and interdisciplinary dimension of the phenomenon, its general use to label the complex series of cultural reactions to modernity and the process of modernization, is often followed by the definition of a specifically Anglo-American canon stretching from Henry James and Joseph Conrad to the Auden generation.[1] The recent *Cambridge Companion to Modernism* presents an instance of this ambiguity, as it juxtaposes a fundamentally Anglo-American literary modernism with a much more inclusive canon in the visual arts, where it includes the Continental avant-garde tradition stretching from Cézanne's post-impressionism to cubism to Dada and surrealism, and in cinema, where figures such as Charles Chaplin and Orson Welles are juxtaposed to Robert Wiene and Sergei Eisenstein. Nor do other critical traditions offer better options. In Italy, for instance, the alternative between a broadly conceived decadentism and a narrowly defined avant-garde has meant that on the one hand the label most often used to describe the period between the turn of the century and the Second World War has inevitably cast onto it a shadow of moral and ethical suspicion, and that on the other hand the notion of avant-garde has come to designate a kind of anti-institutional practice of art that does not easily accommodate figures such as Italo Svevo or Luigi Pirandello, who on the contrary sought a less antagonistic and more dialectical relationship with tradition and the institution.

What I have attempted to do in selecting the texts, figures, and movements discussed in this study was to cut cross boundaries of national traditions and period labels in order to show a series of continuities traversing European literature at the turn of the century. In this context, the *fil rouge* linking late-nineteenth-century aestheticism, the historical avant-garde, and Anglo-American modernism was the crisis of legitimation of the artist and of the practice of art that entailed a complex process of self-examination and re-evaluation of the validity and uses of the models of literary communication inherited from tradition. Indeed, what distinguishes modernist art is precisely what we could describe as its self-reflective moment – that is, the fact that it thematizes the very conditions of possibility of art itself. This self-reflective moment can be expressed in a number of ways, from the attention to the formal and structural dimension of the work, which in certain instances such as suprematism or abstract art may lead to the suspension of representation and the foregrounding of form, to the proliferation of narratives focusing on the artist, from *À rebours* to *Death in Venice* to *Portrait of the Artist as a Young Man* to the late memorialistic works of Marinetti, and to – as in the texts that we have examined – the articulation of new narratives of legitimation that redefine the relationship between artist and audience, and therefore reconstitute a kind of manufactured halo to replace the one lost by the artist to the new social and economic conditions of modernity. In the three moments here considered, we have seen the repetition of the same gesture: the production of manifestoes as the textual site where such a process of renegotiation is carried out, in a space that lies ambiguously on the threshold between the modern mass media and the traditional venues of literary production. The supplemental function of the manifesto is to be understood also in this sense: it constituted the ground on which to articulate what up until the crucial juncture of literary modernity had been taken for granted, namely, the justification for the very existence of the artist.

The responses, as we have seen, vary radically from the moment in which the question emerges with aestheticism to the high point of the avant-garde. Futurism has played a central role in this investigation because its roots in *fin-de-siècle* aestheticism and its influence on the formal and rhetorical strategies of the avant-garde and modernist movements that followed make it the *trait-d'union* among the different articulations of the modernist crisis of legitimation. The decadent/symbolist origins of Marinetti's poetics are especially important since, as already suggested, the avant-garde/modernist phase cannot be fully understood unless it is considered in its critical relation with aestheticism. Baju's decadentism, which constituted the point of departure for our enquiry into the crisis, is the movement in which the problem of the function of the aesthetic in modernity emerges with greatest clarity, not in small part because of the obsessive production of manifestoes and other forms of textuality that foreground questions of the relationship between artist and audience, and the function of art. Decadentism thus marks the moment when the eclipse of the Kantian model of the aesthetic experience begins. Confronted with the 'bad' consensus elicited by industrial literature, by a form of artistic production that takes the commodity as its model, the decadent artist constructs the difference of his activity in purely oppositional terms, inverting the logic of the marketplace. Thus, the opposite of the immediately consumable work of art is the work that resists appropriation by using language not as a means of linking the artist to the audience, but rather as a means of widening that space to the point of incommunicability. In this sense, then, the halo, understood as a manifest difference from the public, is continually and compulsively produced through a practice of writing that puts on display its difference from everyday communication, in the name of the absolute and transcendental values of 'Beauty' and 'Art,' still understood with capital letters.

The foundation of futurism and the issuing of its first manifesto is the material sign of the transition from the fundamentally aestheticist poetics that underlies Marinetti's early literary and critical production to an aesthetics of modernity that moves from the appropriation of a series of new thematics to the articulation of a new form of literary communication. Futurism arrives at the point of overturning the logic of aestheticism: what characterizes the work of art in modernity is precisely its transience, its ephemeral and always precarious coming into existence in the moment of its reception. This in turn raises a series of formal issues that Marinetti attempts to resolve through the theorization of 'words in freedom' and more in general, through a practice of writing that foregrounds the function of the audience in the production of signification. The legitimating narrative of futurism thus presents the loss of the halo in a utopian rather than a nostalgic manner, as an opportunity for the abolition of the institutional boundaries between art and other domains of social activity by means of the identification of a series of values – dynamism, simultaneity, innovation, technology – that allow for a compenetration between art and life in which both are simultaneously re-articulated.

The problem of the distance between artist and audience is also the ground on which the difference between futurism and the English modernist movements is played out. In this sense, the reception of futurism in England and the confrontation between Marinetti and the futurist painters on the one hand and the imagists and the vorticists on the other allows us to identify the dialectic between an anti-institutional avant-garde and a modernist aesthetics whose revolutionary thrust is discharged within the space of the institution itself. In both instances we witness an oppositional relationship between artists and audience, but in futurism this initial antagonism is directed against a specifically *bourgeois* audience, and can be overcome by the acceptance, on the part of the reader/viewer, of the new aesthetic and social principles advanced by the movement. Readers are therefore always appellated as potential producers, even if they do not engage in a traditional artistic practice, since futurism considers itself a revolution of the spirit that changes not simply art but more in general the way in which human beings live their relationship with their natural and social environment. For the English movements, on the contrary, the antagonistic relationship between artist and audience is fundamental and constitutive to a theory of art that is engaged in a crucial process of redefinition of its own specificity and difference *vis-à-vis* all other domains of social activity, and that must therefore construct the reader/viewer not as a collaborator but as passive receiver. English modernism, at least in its Poundian configuration, constitutes a theoretically sophisticated attempt to appropriate a discourse characteristic of modernity – in this case, that of science – in order to re-establish the rights and privileges of the artist. And yet, the exchanges between the two formations are as interesting as their much remarked points of conflic. If, on the one hand, Pound finds himself forced to enter the public arena in order to defend the right and even the necessity of the artist to remain outside that arena as a result of the new strategies of communication and the changed horizon of expectations fostered by the avant-garde, on the other hand, it is precisely at the moment in which the critical thrust of futurism becomes tempered by its attempt to penetrate within the advanced posts of the institution of art – the art galleries of the European capitals – that the underlying ambiguities of its program emerge. Finally, then, in spite of and behind its anti-institutional rhetoric and the 'artificial optimism' of its celebration of the fluidity of life in opposition to the static immobility of museum art, futurism never completely overcomes the nostalgia for the lost halo. As the movement began to build a canon and a tradition – or, in a word, to historicize – the poet and the artist often assumed the role of pedagogue to impart lessons of futurist aesthetics to their audience, thus re-establishing the distance that their artistic practice had intended to abolish.

In a recent essay on the modernism/post-modernism debate Sanford Schwartz has observed that one of the effects of the theorization of a specifically post-modern culture has been the parallel construction, almost as a foil to the post-modern celebration of difference, multiplicity, and heterogeneity, of a monolithic and one-dimensional image of modernism 'associated with identity, unity, and homogeneity' (11).[2] The obsessive production of manifestoes might seem to confirm this received idea of an oppositional relationship between the two moments: do not manifestoes, after all, witness to the desire of endowing a cultural project with order and coherence, to find a series of positive values – a centre that does hold – in the face of the maelstrom of modernity? But if we take modernism as a phenomenon of (at the very least) European dimensions, in all its contradictory and conflictual articulations, we can see, I believe, that modernism and post-modernism are in fact the two faces of the same experience of alienation on the part of the intellectual: in both cases, the point of departure is the loss of the halo, of an organic and integral relationship between the artist and his social environment. Whether that distance becomes an obstacle to be overcome through the definition of a coherent and wide-ranging program or a space of freedom that opens up the possibility of a cultural practice that rejects the 'grand narratives' in favour of contingent local games is, it seems to me, less important than the fact that the historical problem confronting both approaches is the same. As I have tried to suggest in my analysis of futurism, the Italian movement even anticipates certain thematics and strategies of the post-modern cultural discourse, while it frames its project in terms of 'strong' ideological categories. In any case, to return to the point of departure, Baudelaire at the dawn of modernism had already envisioned both options, coupling modernist nostalgia (the poet who recovers the halo from the street) with post-modern anti-identitarianism (the poet who, halo-less, is free to assume any identity, and thus travels incognito). The one thing in which he could no longer believe was that of a transcendental sanction of the poetic activity: the halo, picked up or trampled by the traffic, was in any case lost, and modern/post-modern literature is still coming to terms with that loss.

Notes

Introduction

1 Pope is quoted in Poggioli 216.

2 The literature on these issues is of course very extensive. The following works have been especially influential for my own elaboration: Astradur Eysteinsson, *The Concept of Modernism*; Marshall Berman, *All That Is Solid Melts into Air*; Stephen Kern, *The Culture of Time and Space*; Frederick R. Karl, *Modern and Modernism*; Matei Calinescu, *The Five Faces of Modernity*.

3 We should not forget that the two founders of structural linguistics and semiotics, Ferdinand de Saussure and Charles Sanders Peirce, belong to the horizon of modernism. Although Saussure's *Cours de linguistique générale* was only published posthumously in 1916, his theory of the sign was developed in his university courses between the end of the nineteenth century and the first decade of the twentieth. Peirce was widely read in Europe at the turn of the century, and his pragmatism influenced, among others, the young Giovanni Papini and his peculiar interpretation of futurism in the years preceding the First World War.

4 The converse of this double-jointed characterization of art is to be found in Baudelaire's own *œuvre* in a passage quoted by Benjamin, which recalls closely Benjamin's own description of the Angel of History in his 'Theses on the Philosophy of History' (cf. *Illuminations* 257). Baudelaire writes: 'Jostled in this mean world, jostled by the crowd, I am like a weary man whose eyes, looking backwards, into the depth of the years, sees nothing but disillusion and bitterness, and before him nothing but a tempest which contains nothing new, neither instruction nor pain' (qtd. Benjamin, *Charles Baudelaire* 154). The disillusion regarding the eternal values of art is thus not redeemed by

the false novelty of modernity, in which the new becomes fashion, and is subject to the capitalist principle of consumption.

5 Cf. Berman 159.

6 Unless otherwise indicated, all translations are mine.

7 Here and throughout the book I will refer to the figure of the poet with masculine pronouns and adjectives even in the cases where, unlike Baudelaire's parable, such figures may not appear to be specifically gendered. The sense of a crisis, of a sudden and epoch-making shift in the social function of the artist is in fact an experience that characterizes specifically the production of male artists, who see their privileged role threatened by the rise of mass media, popular literature, and so on. Needless to say, the argument cannot be generalized to women writers and artists, whose work found new legitimation at exactly the same time, in many instances thanks to the new venues that their male counterparts decried. (Popular fiction, for instance, was often associated with a female authorship and readership.)

8 The statement in *Fusées* is preceded by another aphorism on prostitution: 'L'amour, c'est le goût de la prostitution. Il n'est même pas de plaisir noble qui ne puisse être ramené à la Prostitution' [Love is the desire to prostitute oneself. There is, indeed, no exalted pleasure which cannot be related to prostitution]. In this context, Baudelaire seems to reject the possibility of a pure art, that is of an artistic practice completely removed from exchange with an audience and, therefore, from its transformation into a commodity.

9 On this theme, see also Luperini, *L'allegoria del moderno* 91–3.

10 The similarity was first observed by Berman; cf. especially 155–7.

11 In an Italian context, of course the very term *'vate'* calls to mind the figure of Gabriele D'Annunzio.

12 Foucault writes: '[Discourse] was a gesture charged with risks long before it became a possession caught in a circuit of property values. But it was at the moment when a system of ownership and strict copyright rules were established (toward the end of the 18th and the beginning of the 19th century) that the transgressive properties always intrinsic to the act of writing became the forceful imperative of literature' (125). It is in this transition from the regulation and definition of the authority of the author on moral or religious grounds to its insertion into the system of the circulation of commodities that I am interested in here.

13 On the rise of the bourgeoisie and literary production, see for instance Ian Watt's *The Rise of the Novel*, especially chapter 2. As Watt notes, the middle-class writer is in the historically unique situation of writing for his own class: 'This is probably the supremely important effect of the changed composition of the reading public and the new dominance of the booksellers

upon the rise of the novel; not so much that Defoe and Richardson responded to the new needs of their audience, but that they were able to express those needs from the inside much more freely than would previously have been possible' (59).

14 On the relationship between technology and the transformation in the subject's relation to space and time, see Kern.

15 Cf. Bürger 49.

16 Cf. Berman on the twentieth-century city, which the transformations in nineteenth-century Paris anticipate: 'Modernist architecture and planning created a modernized version of pastoral: a spatially and socially segmented world – people here, traffic there; work here, homes there; rich here, poor there; barriers of grass and concrete in between, where haloes could begin to grow around people's heads once again' (168).

17 Another note from *Fusées*: 'Le plaisir d'être dans les foules est une expression mysterieuse de la jouissance de la multiplication du nombre. / *Tout* est nombre. Le nombre est dans *tout*. Le nombre est dans l'individu. L'ivresse est un nombre' [The pleasure of being in crowds is a mysterious expression of sensual joy in the multiplication of Number. / *All* is Number. Number is in all. Number is in the individual. Ecstasy is a Number (*Œuvres complètes* 1: 649; *Intimate Journals* 3)]. For a classic analysis of the dialectic of crowd and individual, see the section on the '*flâneur*' in Benjamin's 'The Paris of the Second Empire' (*Charles Baudelaire* 35–66).

18 On the ambiguous relationship between 'futurism and the crowd,' see Christine Poggi's essay of that title.

19 Cf. sections X–XII of 'On Some Motifs in Baudelaire,' in *Charles Baudelaire: A Lyric Poet in the Era of High Capitalism.*

20 Cf. note 6 in 'The Work of Art in the Age of Its Mechanical Reproduction': 'with the secularization of art, authenticity displaces the cult value of the work' (244).

21 Bürger has pointed out the limitations of Benjamin's belief in the revolutionary potential of the withering of the aura. Cf. for instance p. 30 of *Theory of the Avant-Garde*, where Bürger writes: 'That, since the invention of film, distribution techniques have affected production in turn cannot be doubted. The quasi-industrial techniques whose dominance in certain areas is the result of this fact have proved anything but "shattering," however. What has occurred is the total subordinating of work contents to profit motives, and a fading of the critical potencies of works in favor of a training in consumer attitudes' (30).

22 On the rise of the *feuilletons*, see for instance Schwarz 26–44, and Pinkney 122–7.

23 On the conjunction of newspapers, advertising revenues, and *feuilletons*, see also Benjamin, *Charles Baudelaire* 27–31.

24 Cf. Hans Robert Jauss: 'The distance between the horizon of expectations and the work, between the familiarity of previous aesthetic experience and the "horizontal change" demanded by the reception of the new work, determines the artistic character of a literary work, according to an aesthetics of reception: to the degree that this distance decreases, and no turn toward the horizon of the yet-unknown is demanded of the receiving consciousness, the closer the work comes to the sphere of the 'culinary' or entertainment art' (25). Jauss's description seems to me to be especially applicable to the experience of the aesthetic that begins with modernity. The 'aura' – the distance between the work of art and the audience – is not simply a function of the work itself but rather a function of its institutional mediation in the moment of fruition. Thus, when the work of art no longer fulfills a sacral or social function, and instead faces its audience as individuals in the 'half-way' fashion that we have seen above, the distance has to be re-created by the work itself. This is one reason, I suggest, for the centrality of the category of the new – that is, of the wilful violation of the audience's horizon of expectation – in modernism.

25 On this duality, see Richard Klein's comparison of 'Perte d'auréole' with the poem 'Bénédiction.'

26 On this complex problem, see Hewitt's *Fascist Modernism*.

27 Cf. 'Modernismo/Modernismi' 15.

28 On the greater radicalism of the avant-garde *vis-à-vis* modernism (or, to use the term that he prefers, 'modernity'), see Calinescu (95–7). For Calinescu, the avant-garde is more dogmatic and less tolerant than modernism, whose elements it borrows and exaggerates. 'It is quite clear that the avant-garde would have been hardly conceivable in the absence of a distinct and fully developed consciousness of modernity; however, such an acknowledgment does not warrant the confusion of modernity or modernism with the avant-garde, a confusion that frequently occurs in Anglo-American criticism' (96–7). For an important articulation of the distinction between the two notions in terms of their respective relationship to tradition (and therefore to the institution of art), see also Guido Guglielmi's essay 'Memoria e oblio della storia' in his *La parola del testo*.

29 An even more interesting and revealing example of the resistance of the manifesto to any absolute definition is Larry Peer's anthology *The Romantic Manifesto*. In his introduction, Peer provides an articulate and well-informed definition of the genre: 'The outer form of the manifesto is characterized by that brevity and concision of expression that suits a public decla-

ration. Its inner form is characterized by an attitude of assertion, a tone of declamation and explanation, and a purpose of conversion, drawing battle lines or, rarely, persuasion by conciliation' (2). While the general description accounts for both 'inner' and 'outer' form, for both the structure and rhetorical thrust and the content, it quickly becomes evident that the selection of 'manifestoes' in Peer's anthology is guided for the most part by content. The common denominator of these texts, which range from a choice of Schlegel's *Athenäum Fragments* to Madame De Staël's *On Germany* to John Keats's famous letter on imagination to Coleridge's *Biographia Literaria* (which can be described in many ways, but certainly not as brief or concise), seems in fact to be simply a shared programmatic or even didactic attitude and, to a lesser extent, a critique of specific cultural and political institutions. But if this is the case, how is a manifesto different from, say, a statement of poetics (an *Ars poetica à la* Boileau), an essay, a critical study, or a philosophical treatise? Significantly, the word 'manifesto' appears in Peer's volume only as a label applied in the editorial commentaries of the anthologized works, and in the introduction, where he offers as examples texts quite unlike those in the rest of his book: Thomas Jefferson's *Declaration of Independence*, Marx and Engels's *Communist Manifesto*, and two products of the avant-garde, Wyndham Lewis's journal *Blast* and André Breton's *Manifesto of Surrealism*. On the contrary, several of the texts in the volume fall so obviously outside the generic parameters Peer himself has delineated as to beg the question of how the two aspects of the book, the theoretical articulation and its practical exemplifications, can possibly be reconciled.

Such a retrospective use of the term is not limited to the field of literary studies. Don Wolfe's anthology of documents from the English Civil War entitled *Leveller Manifestoes of the Puritan Revolution* extends the label to a collection of texts none of which were thus called by their authors. The closest term actually found in these documents is 'manifestation' (cf. 'A Manifestation from Lieutenant Col. John Lilburn etc.,' 387). However, in this case the editorial operation can be justified on the basis of the structural homogeneity of the texts selected and of the fact that, as we will see in chapter 1, it is in the seventeenth century that the term 'manifesto' begins to acquire its current meaning, and therefore its use was then less systematic.

30 This, it seems to me, is the main difference between such acts and a kidnapping or any other violent act in which money is the ultimate aim. In the latter case, the relationship between sign and referent is univocal, the victim stands for his or her money and is in fact immediately replaceable by it: the substitution of the sign for the referent is in fact the purpose of the action,

and once the 'thing itself,' the ransom, is achieved, the sign, the victim, no longer has any value for his or her captors. In a politically motived terrorist action, there must be a surplus of signification, and the financial rewards of the operation, if any, are incidental to the symbolic value of the victim.

I should note at this point that much of this book – and this section in particular – was written before 11 September 2001. It now seems to me impossible to write about terrorist actions without making reference to the destruction of the World Trade Center and the attack on the Pentagon. I do not think that the horror of those actions is in any way diminished by the suggestion that in that case too – or perhaps, especially – it was precisely the symbolic value of the targets that was the foremost consideration.

31 Cf. Moréas's open letter to France published in the first issue of *Le Symboliste* (7 October 1886) and republished in *Les premières armés du symbolisme* (56–8).

32 On the events surrounding the publication of Moréas's manifesto, see Pakenham's introduction to Moréas.

33 I am here following the distinction articulated by Jean-Marie Gleize between texts that seek to seduce the reader in order to gain agreement (for Gleize, this is what distinguishes prefaces) and texts that aim at the subjection of the reader (manifestoes). 'To seduce / to enlist [*enjôler-enrôler*] are the two poles which characterize the two practices' (14). Again, the point is precisely to note the weakness of such distinctions as categories on which to base a classification.

34 See also Abastado: 'A manifesto is produced and received (the two perspectives are connected) as a speech act, as a text of rupture and foundation' ('Introduction' 6).

In this context, an important and useful example of how the category can be used to interpret a certain historical moment in light of the concerns that have emerged to visibility as a result of the subsequent evolution of the field of literary production is Fernand Desonay's essay on sixteenth-century manifestoes. Although Desonay does not thematize the historiographic implications of the retrospective application of the term, his theoretical understanding of the genre offers some useful elements for our own investigation. The author accepts the established critical tradition, begun with Sainte-Beuve's *Tableau historique et critique de la poésie et du théatre français au XVIe siècle* (1828), which considers Joachim du Bellay's *Deffence et illustration de la langue françoyse* (1550) as, in the words of Verdun L. Saulnier, 'the first modern manifesto in our language' (Saulnier 49). This, however, follows an account of the fundamental differences between it and other coeval texts (Desonay cites Pierre de Ronsard's preface to his

Quatre premiers livres des 'Odes' as a further example) and the late medieval *artes poeticae* and treatises of rhetoric that came before. As Desonay argues, 'what [the Middle Ages] lack – in other words, what characterizes the Renaissance – is an evolved form of the consciousness [*sens*] of and taste for the art of writing in relation to a broader conception of the dignity and role of the writer' (251). In other words, what the Renaissance man of letters discovers is the value of originality, and in this epochal caesura lies the space in which the manifesto can develop. 'To say "manifesto" means to say "a feverish climate,"' Desonay continues: 'the people of the Renaissance joyously, powerfully, bravely affirmed their own originality. That is what counts. In history, a rupture is much less the result of events than of the resolutions of human beings' (251). The discontinuity that marks the boundary between the Middle Ages and the Renaissance, at the level of literary history, is the result of a reorientation of the discourse on and around the role and function of the man of letters, no longer subjected to the rules handed down by tradition, but capable of projecting his poetic enterprise into the future, as a gift to be spent by later generations. Of course, Desonay does not claim that the *querelles littéraires* were invented by the Renaissance: rather, he points to a transformation in the discursive strategies that differentiate them from earlier debates. Du Bellay's essay is a manifesto because it looks towards the future, it entrusts to it the generations to come, it calls for what is to be done rather than taking stock of what has been (and should continue to be) done. Hence, the author's comment that the 'true formula' of the manifesto is du Bellay's invocation: 'May France, made pregnant by Apollo, soon beget a great poet' (qtd. 258). And Desonay further comments: 'Joachim du Bellay defends above all an ideal which he does not yet display except than in the prospect of his own hope' (259).

Desonay's classificatory gesture, his critical appropriation of the term 'manifesto' to define a body of works that pre-dates the usage of the word here invoked, allows us to isolate the series of features which, according to the author, should characterize the genre, and whose presence in the writings of du Bellay, Ronsand, and their contemporaries legitimizes his anachronistic operation. On the level of content, the manifesto proclaims the advent of the new – a new poetic program, a new order – and implicitly the passing of the order that came before. In this re-orientation of the field of cultural production, the role of the intellectual also changes; one of the functions of the manifesto is precisely that of defining new terms that govern access to the category (hence, in this case, the new emphasis on individual originality and the ensuing re-evaluation of the prestige of the writer).

But this is also an announcement before the fact, a preparatory step, which, while waiting for 'the great poet' to be born, at least creates a 'myth' of a revolution (263). On the formal level, the manifesto is characterized by a violent, combative tone, a rhetoric of aggressivity 'which seems to be inseparable from the debates which incite and stir up the irritable race of poets' (255).

The usefulness of Desonay's article – from the point of view of the present work – does not rest so much on whether it accurately represents the terms of the literary debate in mid sixteenth-century France. Rather, it is the mechanism whereby the author has been able to construct a model of the period founded upon the conventions of a later literary genre that is of interest: as we will see in chapter 1, the manifesto becomes a text of rupture within the established institutional structures of the field of cultural production and a site in which artists are engaged in a project of legitimation of their own function at a very specific historical moment, namely in the transitional period between aestheticism and the avant-garde. Desonay's use of the category, however, allows one to identify a line of continuity between the epochal shift between the Middle Ages and the Renaissance on the one hand and modernism on the other – a continuity of which one symptom, on a textual level, is the recurrence of a rhetorical strategy that foregrounds the voice of the artist and his subjectivity at the expense of the normative role of tradition, and of the reader's mastery of the rules of decodification. The shift in the dominant discourse governing the relationship between the artist and tradition is located by Desonay at this juncture in the sixteenth century, and is signaled by the publication of the *Deffence et illustration de la langue françoyse*. Therefore, the text is both model and specimen of manifesto writing: on the one hand, the affirmation of the new and the antagonistic relationship with tradition is precisely what marks the text, *a posteriori*, as a manifesto; on the other, because of the transformation which the text signals, originality becomes one of the central evaluative parameters in determining the relative position of the artist in the field of cultural production, and the activity of manifesto writing becomes increasingly important and codified.

35 This normative function was already remarked by Tristan Tzara in his caustic 'Manifeste dada 1918,' which begins by laying out precisely the conventions of manifesto writing:

> Pour lancer un manifeste il faut vouloir: A.B.C., foudroyer contre 1, 2, 3, s'énerver et aiguiser les ailes pour conquérir et répandre de petits et de grands a, b, c, signer, crier, jurer, arranger la prose sous forme d'évidence, absolue, irréfutable, prouver son non-plus-ultra et soutenir que la nou-

veauté ressemble à la vie comme la dernière apparition d'une cocotte prouve l'essentiel de Dieu. (*Sept manifestes dada* 203)
[To put out a manifesto you must want: ABC
to fulminate against 1, 2, 3,
to fly into a rage and sharpen your wings to conquer and disseminate little abcs and big abcs, to sign, shout, swear, to organize prose into a form of absolute and irrefutable evidence, to prove your non plus ultra and maintain that novelty resembles life just as the latest appearance of some whore proves the essence of God. (*Seven Dada Manifestoes* 76)]

A manifesto, Tzara suggests, functions by offering a Manichean and totalizing picture of the field in which it operates: to want ABC entails the countermove of fulminating against 1, 2, 3. Furthermore, the act through which the dissemination of the positive values is represented is an inherently colonizing one: it involves conquest, the subjection of the audience to the values and ideals – the little abcs and the big abcs – expressed by the issuer. It is finally an instrument to impose consensus, if nothing else by means of a strategy of exclusion that contemplates only two alternatives: either one accepts the program of the group that issues the manifesto, or one is placed in the position of the enemy – the bourgeois, the philistine, the passeist. The manifesto is thus a binary mechanism: *tertium non datur.* And yet, even Tzara's text does not wholly renounce a manifesto function, as it articulates the narrative of legitimation of dada at the same time as it denounces the strategies of the other avant-garde movements: it is precisely its 'distrust of unity' (77), formulated in the splendidly paradoxical statement 'I am against systems, the most acceptable system is on principle to have none' (79), and more in general its cultivation of contradiction, that constitutes the paradigm regulating the activities of the movement. In this sense, Tzara's text is not so much an anti-manifesto, as has been argued (cf. Abastado, 'Manifeste Dada'), but rather a 'meta-manifesto' – that is, a manifesto that simultaneously deploys and reveals the conventions of manifesto writing.

Chapter 1

1 This is the etymology proposed by, among others, the *Oxford English Dictionary* (ad loc.), and Cortelazzo and Zolli (ad loc.). Picoche remarks that both the formation of the word and the second element are obscure. Battisti and Alessio, in their *Dizionario etimologico italiano*, also do not venture a hypothesis, and describe the Latin word as 'of unclear origin.'

2 Frédéric Godefroy's *Dictionnaire de l'ancienne langue française et de tous ses*

dialectes du IXe au XVe siècle gives 1365 as the earliest attestation of this meaning, although the *Trésor de la langue française* considers it an isolated instance. In Italian, this meaning is obsolete, according to Battaglia. A further obsolete meaning in Italian, possibly related to the former, is that of a nautical logbook.

3 An even more interesting, albeit unusual, early nominal use of the word (it is attested only in Randle Cotgrave's 1611 French–English lexicon, which offers 'the shameful part' [*la partie honteuse*] as a synonym) is found in the *Satyre Ménippée*, where, as E. Huguet reports in his *Dictionnaire de la langue française du XVIe siècle*, the word is used with the meaning of 'private parts': 'celuy [le figuier] dont Adam et Eve couvrirent leur manifeste estoit le figuier de Paradis' [it [the fig tree] with which Adam and Eve covered their private parts was the fig tree of Paradise] (qtd. Chouinard, 23). What makes this use especially curious is the almost complete reversal in the meaning of the term, which comes to signify that which must be hidden (probably precisely because suddenly seen as shamefully manifest, 'on display'). Chouinard calls this usage, quite rightly, a hapax legomenon.

4 Rod Heimpel has recently argued for a specifically French origin of the manifesto as a political genre (cf. especially 11–13).

5 The quote in the *Grande dizionario della lingua italiana* is from the 1559 edition, published in Venice.

6 In addition to the meanings discussed hereafter, which are common to the three linguistic areas with which this book is concerned (Italy, England, and France), there are also local meanings that, though clearly related to the etymology of the word and to its other acceptations, are of secondary interest for our purpose. In particular, the term 'manifesto' in Italian has perhaps the broadest semantic field, as it still indicates the actual written documents posted to notify the public or some event, and its meaning has extended to include advertisement posters (a '*manifesto elettorale*' in Italian may well indicate a party platform, but more likely refers to the propaganda posters of a given party or candidate). In English the now obsolete meaning of 'a proof, a piece of evidence' was common throughout at least the second half of the seventeenth century, as attested by the examples provided in the *Oxford English Dictionary* ranging from 1644 to 1686. The nineteenth century sees both a normalization of the use of the term 'manifesto' and an increasingly greater application to domains other than that of political discourse.

7 Interestingly, the slightly later *Thresor de la langve francoise tant ancienne que moderne*, compiled by Jean Nicot and published in 1621, reports only the adjectival form, defined in Latin as 'apertus, manifestus, planus.'

8 On the relationship between social revolution and manifesto production,

see Alain Meyer, for whom 'the first manifestoes arise in a period of rupture: they are contemporaneous to the great political and mental upheavals at the end of the 18th century' (29). See also Demers, 'Le manifeste, crise – ou caution? – du système,' esp. p. 9.

9 The increased visibility of the rising middle class is evidenced by other forms of pamphlets and broadsheets that although not necessarily called manifestoes, perform a similar function of self-definition and affirmation, and outline alternative programs to those of the sovereign and the ruling feudal class. Don Wolfe's anthology *Leveller Manifestoes* provides several good examples of the conflation of the discourse of religious and class difference during the English Civil War. See for instance *The Mournfull Cries of Many Thousand Poore Tradesmen* on 'the intensified class appeal of Leveller propaganda' (273).

10 Needless to say, other kinds of texts document this transformation in the process of legitimation of political authority. Manifestoes co-exist, and are often almost or completely synonymous with several other pragmatic genres, and any attempt to make clear cut-distinctions among them will result in an inevitably prescriptive discourse that is contradicted by the fluidity of the continuum linking these different genres. The American Declaration of Independence, for instance, is perhaps the most obvious example of a text that foregrounds the crisis of the feudal model of power and shifts authority from the sovereign to the people, as Jacques Derrida has well argued in his analysis of its rhetorical structure (cf. 'Declarations of Independence').

11 On the aporia of the male-gendering of the 'people' in Marechal's manifesto, see Lyon 45.

12 On the political use of the metaphor of the avant-garde, which becomes widespread only after the French Revolution, cf. Calinescu 100–2, which also corrects Poggioli's earlier argument on the convergence of the two avant-gardes on the eve of the 'bourgeois revolution' of 1848 with Gabriel Désiré Laverdant's Fourierist tract *De la mission de l'art et du rôle des artistes* (1845) (cf. especially 113–16).

13 Cf. Bourdieu's *The Field of Cultural Production*, especially the essay of the same title.

14 On anarchism and the avant-garde, see Sonn, chapters 7 and 8; Charle, *Naissance des 'intellectuels'* 99–137; and Weir.

15 Unless otherwise noted, all quotes from Marinetti's manifestoes are found in *Teoria e invenzione futurista*, abbreviated as *TIF*.

16 On this topic, see also Verita Datta's important monograph *Birth of a National Icon*.

17 Indeed, for Charle the legislation of primary education is in great part 'the

governmental sanction of an expectation and a need which had appeared before it' (*La crise littéraire* 17). For these and other statistics, see Charle, *La crise littéraire à l'époque du naturalisme.*

18 On the press laws of 1881, see Sonn 13–14. Useful information on the technological innovations can be found in Schulz 55.

19 The survey and an analysis of its result appear in Charle, *Naissance des 'intellectuels'* 119–26. For a good study of the positions that emerge in this *enquête*, see also Datta 54–8.

20 Cf. Schulz 63.

21 The political opinions of the signatories of the petition for Descaves verged from Goncourt's reactionary positions to the radicalism of Clovis Huguet, a socialist member of Parliament, further emphasizing the fact that what was at issue was a general principle. Indeed, as Datta has remarked, the emphatic defence of the moral superiority of the intellectual elite as such, regardless of the individual political sympathies of its members, is one of the recurrent themes of the cultural debate of the period up to and including the Dreyfus affair (cf. in particular 65–7). On the contrary, more clearly politicized gestures divided the field. Charle cites as a particularly telling example the petition in defence of Jean Grave, who had been imprisoned and condemned for the publication of his book *La societé mourante et l'anarchie.* On the surface, the situation resembles that of Descaves's work, but the petition was initiated by a militant journalist, Henri Leyre. In discussing Zola's refusal to sign the document, Charle points out that in the case of Descaves 'all the men of letters had felt affected, whereas for Jean Grave only the sympathizers of his political sensibility mobilized. One can draw the lesson that Zola himself was to draw for *J'accuse* four years later: the mobilization of "intellectuals" can be realized only when what is at stake are Truth (whereas here one is fully immersed in politics) and Justice (while in this [Grave's] case, society observed the rules of law)' (135).

22 See also Beret Strong (6–7), who remarks that the formation of avant-garde groups was fostered by the end of the patronage system and the necessity for the artist to enter the economic arena and become subject to its rules of exchange.

23 Charle defines a literary group as 'a structure for the accumulation of symbolic and social capital and [...] an essential instrument in the struggle for the conquest of symbolic power and for consecration in the literary field' (*La crise littéraire* 18).

24 The figure is given in the list of works by Descaves in his pamphlet on the trial, *Sous-offs en cour d'assises* (n.p.).

25 On early Parisian poetic circles, see Marquèze-Pouey, especially 50–7.

26 The criticism that a narrow reading would give undue pre-eminence to minor figures is an established one. Already in Huret's *enquête*, Emile Zola thundered against the publicity surrounding Moréas: 'Pour faire contrepoids à l'immense labeur positiviste des ces cinquante dernières années, on nous montre une vague étiquette "symboliste" recouvrant quelques vers de pacotille. [...] Car enfin, qu'ont-ils fait, ceux qui prétendent nous tuer si vite, ceux qui vont bouleverser demain toute la littérature? [...] A présent on parle de Moréas. De temps en temps, comme cela, la presse, qui est bonne fille, se paie le luxe d'en lancer un pour se distraire et pour embêter des gens. Qu'est-ce que c'est que Moréas? Qu'est-ce qu'il a donc fait, mon Dieu!' [They show us, as a counterweight to the immense positivist labour of the last fifty years, a vague 'symbolist' label, which conceals some shoddy verse. ... And in the end what have they done, these people who mean to kill us so quickly, who tomorrow will overthrow all literature? ... Now there's talk of Moréas. Once in a while, the press, which is a good sort, treats itself to the luxury of pushing someone in order to distract and to dull people. Who is this Moréas? My God, what has he done to have such impudence?] (190–1). More recently, Bertrand Marchal has remarked that 'this *stricto sensu* symbolism is a minuscule symbolism, which hardly lasted some ten years' (5). The opposite of such a reading would identify in symbolism the very essence of poetry, and would thus see the poetic movement as a return of poetry to its fundamental roots. This is for instance the thesis at the core of Guy Michaud's monumental *Message poétique du symbolisme*: 'Thus, in the end the symbolist movement did not invent anything. Like its detractors argued, believing that they would thus besmirch it, symbolism has always existed. The symbol is the very foundation of art, because art is the reconstruction of the real according to the secret correspondences and the sovereign harmony of creation. [...] Symbolism, the poetic movement, rediscovers *poetic truth*' (419).

27 See for instance Binni's contrastive description of the classical, romantic and decadent paradigms: 'For the classics, the poet was the expert of the human heart, for the Romantics he was that heart itself, for the decadents he is the musical conscience of an inner life so profound that it becomes confused with mystery. Postkantian idealism greatly contributed to this new vision of reality. Deformed by the poetics, it became incredulity toward the outer world, unless it derives from the root from which blossoms the I of the poet' (21). On the historiography of decadentism in Italy, see Scrivano, the first chapter of Gioanola's *Il decadentismo*, Giovannetti's *Il decadentismo*, and Moroni's essay 'Sensuous Maladies: The Construction of Italian Decadentism.'

28 On this, see Bürger 47.

29 Indeed, as Raymond Williams has pointed out, the lowest common denominator of the different cultural projects grouped under the label of 'modernism' – including even the avant-garde as a more radical form of negation aiming at a revolutionary program of liberation of humanity – lies precisely in the articulation of an innovative, experimental artistic program (see the chapter 'The Politics of the Avant-Garde' in *The Politics of Modernism*, esp. 49–50).

30 See Eagleton, especially ch. 14.

31 One could even read the phenomenon of the avant-garde as the result of the formation of this kind of market of symbolic goods. The accumulation of symbolic capital, initially disjuncted from an immediate economic return, is in fact a future investment as it translates into economic capital as the artist becomes canonized within the artistic field. This argument is convincingly developed by Rainey in *The Institutions of Modernism*, a study of the role of patronage and investments in the formation of the canon of English modernism. See also Bourdieu 39–40.

32 As Géraldi Leroy and Julie Bertrand-Sabiani have recently remarked, 'the avant-garde benefits [...] in its own eyes and often in the eyes of public opinion of a valorizing image. Its constant strategy is in fact that of turning its handicaps into marks of excellence. Its lack of money is presented as the sign of its disinterestedness and of its moral intransigence' (194).

33 In his satirical ballad 'Moréas chante,' published in November 1891 in *La plume*, Frédéric-Auguste Cazals thus pokes fun at the leader of the newly founded 'École roman':

Je sais fort bien que la roture
Ne lira point ce livre-ci,
Mais que m'importe leur censure
Si je suis lu par ... Duplessi! (qtd. Richard 71)

34 On the role of the press in the consecration of symbolism, see for instance Michaud 393–9. The interest in artists' opinions, if not in their works, is also witnessed by the fashion for the '*enquête*' in the last two decades of the nineteenth century and into the twentieth century. Schultz cites at least ten, ranging in topic from 'the influence of Scandinavian letters' to 'the artistic education of the contemporary public' (239–40), and admits that the list is not exhaustive (one could, for instance, add F.T. Marinetti's frequent uses of the genre in his journal *Poesia*, which promoted surveys on 'the honours tributed to Carducci' (February 1905), 'the beauty of Italian women' (April to September 1905), and free verse (October 1905 to May 1908)).

35 Genette writes: 'The epitext is any paratextual element not materially

appended to the text within the same volume but circulating, as it were, freely, in a virtually limitless physical and social space. The location of the epitext is therefore anywhere outside the book – but of course nothing precludes its later admission to the peritext' (344).

36 Baju was actually born Adrien Joseph Bajut. It is not clear why he dropped the last consonant from his surname, or why he exchanged his first name with his younger brother Anatole Albert, who took up the name of Adrien. (Raynaud has suggested that the trick might have been an attempt on the part of Baju to avoid reprisals for his literary activities from his superiors in Saint-Denis.) The most thorough biographical source on Baju remains Noel Richard's *Le mouvement décadent*, which carefully documents Baju's youth and the period of *Le Décadent*.

37 Tailhade's scorn, however, did not keep him from collaborating with the second series of *Le Décadent*, to which he contributed thirty poems and seven prose pieces. Tailhade further vituperates Baju in a short profile in his volume of memoirs *Quelques fantômes de jadis* (95–104).

38 The publication of the short-lived *Le Symboliste* (only four issues appeared between October and November 1886) followed a direct polemic between Baju and Kahn and his associates. Baju had opened the pages of *Le Décadent* to Kahn, who directed *La Vogue*, and to the symbolist group connected with Kahn's review. As a result, issue 25 of *Le Décadent* (25 September 1886), which included pieces by Moréas, Paul Adam, Jules Laforgue, and Kahn himself, seemed to mark a new direction for the journal, so much so that the issue was introduced by an editorial note in which Baju announced triumphantly:

> A partir de ce numéro, le *Décadent* cesse d'être l'organe exclusif des «Jeunes». Il devient le journal militant des écrivains de la nouvelle école littéraire.
>
> Chaque numéro contiendra une chronique don't les signatoires seront successivement: *MM. Paul Adam, Jean Ajalbert, Edouard Dujardin, Gaston Dubreuilh, Félix Fénéon, Charles Henry, Gustave Kahn, Jules Laforgue, Jean Moréas, Charles Vignier, Téodor de Wyzewa.*
>
> [Starting with this issue, *Le Décadent* ceases to be the exclusive organ of the *Youth*. It becomes the militant paper of the writers of the new literary school.
>
> Each following issue will include a chronicle whose authors will be successively *MM. Paul Adam, Jean Ajalbert, Edouard Dujardin, Gaston Dubreuilh, Félix Fénéon, Charles Henry, Gustave Kahn, Jules Laforgue, Jean Moréas, Charles Vignier, Téodor de Wyzewa.*]

Contrasts between the newcomers and the old editorial board of *Le Déca-*

dent led to a quick annulment of the hasty marriage. Issue 25 thus remained the only result of this attempt at a collaboration between the two groups. The first issue of *Le Symboliste*, which appeared less than two weeks later, carried a notice by Jacques Plowert (i.e., Paul Adam) that laid the responsibility of the debacle on Baju, guilty, according to the writer, of not accepting Kahn's demand that certain members of the editorial board of *Le Décadent* be excluded. On the episode and on the contrasting interpretations of its protagonists, see Richard 85–92.

39 The proliferation of military metaphors in the debate on *fin-de-siècle* literature, a phenomenon that also characterizes the avant-garde, is, among other things, a reflection of the increasing competition of the different players within the field for a restricted audience.

40 Cf. Meltzer 752.

41 For a discussion of this question, see also Jonard 219.

42 A comprehensive list of Baju's 'avatars,' as the critic calls them, is provided by Richard, 41–6.

43 The bibliography on decadence is extensive. On the history of the notion itself, see in particular Calinescu, esp. 157–71; Jonard; Décaudin, 'Définir la décadence'; Le Goff; and the more recent monograph by Giovannetti. Jean Pierrot's *The Decadent Imagination* provides a useful historical introduction to the period and a survey of the major themes of French literary decadentism. On decadentism as a European cultural and artistic phenomenon, see also Mario Praz's volume *The Romantic Agony* and his essay 'Decadentismo.' More importantly for this study, David Weir argues for an interpretation of 'decadence' within the framework of modernism in his *Decadence and the Making of Modernism*.

44 There are no indications that Bourget had in fact read Nisard, although he might have heard about him through the decadent novelist Barbey d'Aurevilly. On the question, see Calinescu 338, n. 32.

45 Louis Marquèze-Pouey has noted that 'the military defeat, the tragedy of the Commune, and the misery of a Republic badly established and already undermined by scandals' haunted the imagination of even that generation of poets who had not themselves lived through these events (22). The question is extensively examined by Digeon (see especially 353–63).

46 'Aux lecteurs!' was simply signed 'La rédaction,' obviously with the intention of suggesting the existence of a collective project behind the journal. Its authorship has been traditionally attributed to Baju, although Richard, never particularly generous in regards to Baju's intellectual capabilities, has suggested that the 'polished and burnished' style of the piece shows the influence of Baju's friend and collaborator Maurice du Plessys (24).

47 Baju, however, does dub the programmatic texts of the decadent school 'manifestoes' on certain occasions. See for instance 'Chronique' in issue 27 (1886).

48 On this dialectic, cf. Demers and McMurray 68.

49 The term 'déliquescence,' semantically linked to 'decadence' by virtue of the common implication of dissolution and fragmentation, is, like its relation 'liquescence,' typical of the lexicon of decadentism and symbolism. The already mentioned parody of decadentism, for instance, was entitled precisely *Le déliquescences d'Adoré Floupette, poèmes décadents*. The term is recorded, in its un-prefixed form, in Paul Adam's *Petit glossaire pour servir à l'intelligence des auteurs décadents et symbolistes*, with the definition 'État de ce qui se fond' [The state of what dissolves] and Floupette's title as an example (57).

50 Baju's most scathing critique of popular literature is to be found in the article entitled 'Littérature industrielle,' published early on in the run of *Le Décadent* (n. 5, 6 May 1886). In this piece, Ohnet is attacked for being unable to stay within the boundaries of either 'official art' or 'industrial art,' thus producing an unclassifiable hybrid. In fact, what makes this particular essay especially interesting is not so much Baju's gleeful ridicule of Ohnet's style and penchant for mixed metaphors, but rather the author's concern with the fact that this blurring of generic boundaries affects negatively both high and popular art by reducing the multiplicity of art to an undifferentiated morass, 'un produit incestueux sorti du coït monstrueux' [an incestuous product of a monstruous coitus], and a 'mixture innomée de style montépinois et richebourgiaque' [unnameable mixture of *montépinois* and well-to-do-ish] (*montépinois* refers to Xavier de Montépin, a popular novelist and collaborator of Alexandre Dumas père). This literary production threatens not only the distinction between high and low literature (and in this sense, Baju's diatribe is an obvious example of the formation of the 'great divide' of high and popular culture discussed above), but the very individuality and identity of the text. Baju thus reasserts at the level of literary form the opposition between the distinctive individual (the artist or, in this case, his product) and the undifferentiated members of the mass audience.

51 The question of legitimation and of the different procedures that govern it in different models of knowledge production is also discussed by Lyotard (6–9). Indeed, the question of legitimation constitutes one of the most important links between modernism and post-modernism.

52 Cf. on this Gianni Vattimo's observation in 'The Death or Decline of Art' that in the *Critique of Judgement* 'aesthetic pleasure is not defined as that

which the subject experiences in relation to the object, but is rather the pleasure which derives from the recognition of belonging to a group – which, for Kant, is humanity itself – that shares the same capacity for appreciating the beautiful' (56).

53 Cf. Eagleton: 'To dissolve the law to custom, to sheer unthinking habit, is to identify it with the human subject's own pleasurable well-being, so that to transgress that law would signify a deep self-violation' (20).

54 Bourdieu notes this phenomenon in his essay 'The Market of Symbolic Goods,' where he writes: 'The emergence of the work of art as a commodity, and the appearance of a distinct category of producers of symbolic goods specifically destined for the market, to some extent prepared the ground for a pure theory of art, that is, of art as art' (*The Field of Cultural Production* 114).

55 Cf. Spackman, 'Interversions.' In this important essay, Spackman discusses the 'inversion' of bourgeois moral and ethical values in decadent literature, but the procedure – which first and foremost serves to resist the totalizing hubris of bourgeois society – applies well also to the domain of cultural legitimation.

56 See for instance Baudelaire's 'Les yeux des pauvres' [The Eyes of the Poor], in which the persona of the poet witnesses to the emptying out of the experience of the aesthetic in the eyes of a starving man and his children, for whom it becomes literally – to use Eagleton's expression – 'a discourse of the body' (*Ideology of the Aesthetic* 13), the beautiful coming to be identified with what fulfills the primal need for food.

57 Cf. Calinescu 105–6.

58 This theme links the different articulations of decadentism and symbolism across Europe. For instance, in 'A People's Theatre' W.B. Yeats wrote, 'I want to create for myself an unpopular theatre and an audience like a secret society where admission is by favour and never to many' (*Plays and Controversies* 212). The early D'Annunzio – himself certainly not blind to the lures of a mass audience – also plays with this theme. The protagonist of *Il piacere*, the genial amateur etcher Sperelli, answering his lover Elena Muti's question of why he keeps his work so far away from 'il grande pubblico' [a mass audience] argues:

> Anzi, il mio sogno e l''Esemplare Unico' da offerire alla 'Donna Unica.' In una società democratica com'è la nostra, l'artefice di prosa o di verso deve rinunziare ad ogni benefizio che non sia di amore. Il lettor vero non è già chi mi compra ma chi mi ama.
>
> [Indeed, my dream is 'the Unique Exemplar' to be offered to the 'Unique Woman.' In a democratic society like ours, the prose- or verse-wright

must renounce any profit that does not come from love. The true reader is not the one who buys me, but the one who loves me.] (55)

59 See the article 'Quintessence' (*Le Décadent* n. 23, 11 September 1886), in which Baju proposes the name 'Quintessents' as a positive alternative to name the school of *affineurs de la pensée* [refiners of thought] otherwise known as decadents.

60 The question of the evolution of Baju's political thought warrants a more thorough study than is possible here, because in its inconsistent unfolding it seems to me symptomatic of a more complex attempt to negotiate the new relationship between intellectuals and political life. The proud disdain for the commodification of cultural products – the industrial literature discussed above – leads Baju to profoundly anti-democratic positions in his decadent phase. Such disdain finds expression in statements such as the following:

> Leurs [the decadents'] personnages toujours pris dans la bonne société, ont généralement parcouru tout le cercle des jouissances ordinaires et sont en quête de sensations nouvelles. Leurs valets, leurs ouvriers sont regardés comme des accessoires automatiques de la vie bourgeoise, considérés inaptes à jouir des raffinements indispensables aux classes supérieures. [Their characters are always taken from high society, they have generally traversed the whole compass of ordinary pleasure and are seeking for novel sensations. Their valets, their workmen are regarded as automatic accessories of bourgeois life, and considered unfit to enjoy the refinements necessary to the superior classes.] ('Esthétique décadente' 1)

Likewise, the French Republic comes repeatedly under attack for its implicit materialism (see for instance 'L'Esprit des jeunes,' n. 16, 24 July 1886). But with only a minimal shift in his rhetoric and in the targets of his critique, Baju can declare himself a socialist in the manifesto 'La littérature de demain' [The Literature of Tomorrow], published in 1891 in *L'Evénement*, after the second series of *Le Décadent* had ceased publication. The enemy is now no longer the Republic as such, but a more shifting mark, the '*argyrocratie*,' that is, 'the government of money' (Mitchell 38), but this is certainly contiguous with the previous polemic against the commercialization of art. And while the masses are not ostracized in 'La littérature de demain,' and are even indicated as the final beneficiary of the work of the intellectual, the relationship remains strictly monologic. Again, the 'people,' the workers and, more in general, the proletariat, are not the subject of the Revolution, but rather their quite passive recipients: they remain a faceless crowd upon which the intellectual does his progressive work: 'Ce sont les foules que nous voulons élever aux conceptions artistiques les plus nobles, car, pour nous, il n'y a pas d'homme supérieurs: il n'y a que les hommes inférieurs' [We want to elevate the crowds to the noblest artistic concepts because, for us, there are no superior men; there are only inferior ones] (Mitchell 39). Ultimately, Baju's socialism seems to look forward to a kind of collective intellectual production closer to the unanimism of Jules Romains than to the collaborative projects of the avant-garde. See for instance Baju's paragraph on 'les déclassés' in his 1892 pamphlet *L'anarchie littérarie*, where he writes that 'la littérature sera de moins en moins individualiste; les idées nouvelles tendent à se manifester par des groupements particuliers' [literature will be less and less individualist. New ideas tend to manifest themselves by means of specific groups] (28).

61 It is, however, important to remember in this context that the very definition of the genres shifts significantly in the second half of the nineteenth century, as witnessed by the rise of an apparently oxymoric genre like the 'prose-poem' (see for instance Giusti, esp. 42–7). The very definition of poetry and prose is no longer based on formal and structural features, but rather depends on the degree of referentiality of the text, so that poetry is any linguistic production that foregrounds what Roman Jakobson has called the 'poetic function'of language. As Bertrand Marchal remarks in his lucid exposition of this radical reorientation of the system of genres, 'Symbolism consecrates the imperialism of poetry over literature, a poetry which henceforth rejects the referential logic of narrative and of description and which finds in music a model of development which is no longer controlled by an extrinsic tempo, that of the events, but by an inner rhythm' (25).

62 Cf. Hustvedt: 'The decadents despised liberal, capitalist democracy because it purported to make all individuals equal, and to make everything – objects and even ideas – commensurable with money. [...] Consequently, the anti-bourgeois position of the decadents took the form of a nostalgia for a past system of positive distinction (they affected to be monarchists, to long for the old regime).' (15).

63 On the figure of the clown in decadent/symbolist and avant-garde poetry, see Tamburri 72–6.

Chapter 2

1 Marinetti published his early manifestoes (as well as his works) either first in French or simultaneously in French and Italian. Unless I need to refer specifically to the French versions, I will use the Italian titles and texts throughout.

2 The text published in *Le Figaro* was a shorter version of the final text. The manifesto received different titles as it was republished in pamphlets and leaflets, either in full or limited to the central section, which is specifically entitled 'manifesto.' The Italian text was first published in *Poesia* 5.1–2 (1909). Two examples of the French leaflets and one of the Italian version are included in Caruso (items 1–3). On the history of the composition of the manifesto of foundation, see the critical edition by De Villers and, specifically on its dating, his subsequent note 'Ancora sul manifesto,' as well as Lista's *F.T. Marinetti*, 77–82.

3 De Maria repeats this claim in many of his writings on Futurism. See also 'Marinetti poeta e ideologo' xxix–xxx and 'Una panoramica del futurismo italiano' viii–ix. Furthermore, the thesis that futurism represents the movement that established the conditions of possibilities for later, more successful avant-gardes was articulated as early as 1948 by J. Michel in his *Histoire du surréalisme*, and was followed throughout the 1960s (that is, before futurism enjoyed a critical revival in Italy) in French historiography (cf. Jannini, 'Note e documenti' 93–6).

4 Cf. Asor Rosa, 'Il futurismo nel dibattito intellettuale italiano dalle origini al 1920.'

5 The 'transitional' status of Futurism has been argued most cogently by Giovanni Lista, who in his monograph on Marinetti calls it 'the glory and the limitation' of the Italian movement. He writes: 'Located between two cultures, Marinetti's *œuvre* can be studied in two opposite ways: as an overcoming of late symbolism and as a direct anticipation of dada and surrealism, and can thus appear as revolutionary or rather limited and ineffectual, the culmination of the nineteenth century or the first dimension of the twentieth' (*F.T. Marinetti* 10). If the acknowledgment of this liminality helps to explain, to a certain extent, some of the contradictions of the movement, especially in its earliest phase, it does not, however, invalidate the historical role played by futurism in initiating the process of critique of the institutions of cultural production and mediation that characterizes in general the historical avant-garde. I fundamentally concur with Lista that the insistence on the ruptural quality of the movement, and in particular of the issuing of the first manifesto – considered, as we have seen, a veritable ground zero of the avant-garde – has resulted in an underestimation of the continuity between its earliest poetics and late symbolism. However, my own conclusions are quite different from Lista's, although our differences are more a matter of emphasis than of substance. While he proposes to retro-date the appearance of 'Futurism as a doctrine' (41) to 1905, and more specifically to the introduction of speed as the privileged symbolic node in Marinetti's

poetics, I believe that this new element does not radically change the Italian writer's conception of poetic language and of the work of art. It is only with the articulation of a specifically futurist theory of language in the manifestoes of 1912–14 that Marinetti makes the transition from a purely thematic expansion of his polemic and poetic apparatus still belonging to a substantially decadent/symbolist horizon to the wholesale critique and reinvention of the institution of literature that characterizes the avant-garde proper. On this issue, see also Renato Barilli's essay 'D'Annunzio e Marinetti.'

6 The bibliography on the relationship between futurism and fascism is extensive. See in particular Nazzaro, *Futurismo e politica*, and specifically on the early years of both movements, Gentile's essay 'Il futurismo e la politica. Dal nazionalismo modernista al fascismo (1909–1920).'

7 On the diminished political ambitions of the futurist movements in the second half of the 1920s – that is, during the period in which the regime consolidates its power after the murder of the socialist deputy Giacomo Matteotti (June 1924) and the promulgation of the first restrictive *'leggi fascistissime'* in 1925 – Claudia Salaris writes: 'Marinetti's position within Fascism was certainly not easy, and for a long time the Futurist fringes bore the mark of impurity. [...] What in the end guaranteed Marinetti from a real marginalization was his old friendship with Mussolini, who, in any case, never considered the possibility of making Futurism a state art, and never offered special consideration to the movement. But politically the leader of the group [...] saw himself merely as a "precursor," [... and] therefore could easily be appointed to the Accademia d'Italia' (*Filippo Tommaso Marinetti* 185–6). In spite of his rhetoric, then, Marinetti let the regime inscribe and confine him back into tradition: politically, as a precursor of fascism, and literarily, as a member of the very institution entrusted with the continuation, rather than the disruption, of the Italian cultural tradition.

8 Many of Marinetti's volumes of futurist political and aesthetic theory were the result of an assemblage of previously published manifestoes and articles, often variously manipulated from one reprinting to the next. As De Maria remarks in his editorial note, in spite of the claim printed on the cover and the title-page of the book, that the text had been 'published in French five years ago in Paris' (*TIF cxxxiv*), the contents of *Guerra sola igiene del mondo* only partially coincide with the 1911 volume *Le futurisme*, to which the assertion clearly refers. A comparison between the rhetorical structure of the two redactions of the introductory section is instructive. In the French version, 'Les premières batailles,' Marinetti constructs a communicative situation that closely recalls that of the manifestoes: the addressee is appealed to through a series of phatic gestures, such as the call to the

reader that opens the text – 'Je tiens à vous déclarer que nous aimons trop passionnément nos idées futuristes, pour qu'il nous soit possible de les revêtir de formes diplomatiques et de masques élégants' [I am proud to declare to you that we love our futurist ideas too passionately to be able to dress them in diplomatic forms and elegant masks] (*Futurisme* 77) – and recurs throughout the early sections (cf. p. 78: 'Vous êtes au courant, sans doute, du déchaînement de polémiques et de la rafale d'injures et d'enthousiastes applaudissements qui ont accueilli ce manifeste' [Doubtless, you are aware of the series of polemics and of the storm of abuse and of enthusiastic accolades that welcomed this manifesto]). Deictic references serve to locate the reading in space and time, as if it were a public performance: 'Je serai donc forcément agressif dans *ce* livre' [Thus, I will be forcibly aggressive in *this* book]; 'j'ai l'orgueil de déclarer *ici* que tous les étudiants d'Italie sont aujourd'hui avec nous' [I am proud to declare *here* that all Italian students are with us] (77–8, emphasis added). Finally the recourse to the present tense emphasizes the nature of work in progress of the futurist program: 'Les circonstances nous commandent des gestes brutaux' [Circumstances impose on us brutal actions]; 'Notre mouvement s'élargit chaque jour, gagnant les milieux littéraires et artistiques du monde entier' [Our movement expands every day, conquering the literary and artistic milieux of the whole world] (77–8)).

The text thus translates on a textual level the theatrical dimension of the communicative strategies of futurism, as the addresser engages his audience directly as in a futurist evening. In the Italian text, on the other hand, the experience of futurism appears already historicized and displaced into a past that distances it from the reader, for whom it no longer presents itself as a vital and accessible experience. For example, the text begins with a reconstruction of the birth of futurism, precisely located in the past, and the dominant tense is also the past: futurism '*era* una bandiera rinnovatrice, antitradizionale, ottimistica, eroica e dinamica, che si *doveva* inalberare sulle rovine del passatismo' [*was* a young renewing, anti-traditional, optimistic, heroic and dynamic flag that *had* to be raised over the ruins of passeism] (235, emphasis added); 'il nostro movimento *andò* allargandosi ogni giorno di più' [Our movement *expanded* every day more and more] (235, emphasis added).

9 To date, there is not a critical biography of Marinetti. Lista's *F.T. Marinetti* is by far the best biographical study of the futurist leader, but it focuses mostly on his early career (on which, see also Günter Berghaus's informative and detailed short volume *The Genesis of Futurism*). Claudia Salaris's two biographical volumes, the copiously illustrated *Filippo Tommaso Mari-*

netti and the more thorough *Marinetti. Arte e vita futurista* are based to a great extent on Marinetti's own auto-biographical writings, which are not always paragons of reliability. Gino Agnese's *Marinetti: una vita esplosiva*, a work that straddles between biography and 'faction,' is rather short on documentation. On Marinetti's pre-futurist poetry, see especially Gaetano Mariani's *Il primo Marinetti* and chapter 2 of Baldissone's *Filippo Tommaso Marinetti*.

10 For a detailed discussion of the Latin Renaissance, see Angela Ida Villa's *Neoidealismo e rinascenza latina* (in particular part 1, chapter 2, which reconstructs with the aid of much first-hand documentation the terms of the debate in Italy).

11 On the cultural tyranny of foreign intellectuals – and in particular Wagner, Nietzsche, and Ibsen – in France, de Bouhélier writes: 'Toutes nos déroutes militaires ne me paraissent pas aussi effrayantes que cette conquête intellectuelle où sont parvenus récemment, malgré Zola, malgré Barrès, malgré Bruneau et Gustave Charpentier, les dramaturges norvégiens et allemands' [All our military routs do not seem to me as frightful as this intellectual conquest which Norwegian and German playwrights have recently achieved, in spite of Zola, in spite of Barrès, in spite of Bruneau and Gustave Charpentier] (Mitchell 57).

12 On the French 'provincial renaissance,' see Décaudin 128–4. The history of *naturisme* is detailed in Patrick Day's study of the movement.

13 Marinetti explicitly compares the two artists in his response to an *enquête* in which *L'Ermitage* had invited about two hundred poets to indicate their favourite modern non-living poet (results published in January 1902):

J'aime entre tous, le poète
STÉPHANE MALLARMÉ
parce que, méprisant tout ce qu'il se prouva facile en des poèmes tels que '*Les Fenêtres*' et '*Apparition*,' il rêva de créer une symphonie poètique aussi définitive et magique que celle exécutèe par Richard Wagner.

[I love among all, the poet
STÉPHANE MALLARMÉ
because, despising all that appears simple in poems such as 'Les Fenêtres' and 'Apparition,' he dreamed of creating a poetic symphony as definitive and magical as that executed by Richard Wagner in music.] (121).

14 As Brunella Eruli remarks (377), *La Plume*, in spite of its claim after 1900 of being the '*Organe de l'école romane*' had not relinquished its previous ties with symbolism. Marinetti's article is, if anything, exemplary of the review's openness.

15 The event was in fact supposed to be held in seven cities, but the performance in Naples had to be postponed to the 19 January because the tenor Ravazzolo was indisposed.

16 The three conferences from which I quote are all reprinted in Morini's *Pietro Mascagni*. The specific titles and dates are: 'L'evoluzione della musica,' held at the Teatro Goldoni in Venice, and published in *La cronaca musicale*, 15 March 1900, under the title 'Il testamento musicale del secolo XIX'; 'Nicola Piccinni,' held at the teatro Piccinni in Bari on 27 May 1900, and published in *La cronaca musicale* on 15 June 1900; 'Il melodramma dell'avvenire,' held at the Popular University of Milan on 22 Novembre 1903, and published in *Il Corriere della Sera* on 23 Novembre 1903. The correspondence between Mascagni and Illica on *Le maschere* is also in Morini. For further authorial comments on *Le maschere*, see also Mascagni's own *Mascagni parla* (1945), and ch. 20 of Stivender's *Mascagni*, which collects (at times with questionable editorial methods) the texts of various articles by and interviews with the composer.

17 *Destruction* was already completed by the winter of 1902 (cf. Eruli 380).

18 *The Case of Wagner* had already been translated by Daniel Halévy and Robert Dreyfus in 1892–3. For a more detailed account of Nietzsche's early translations into French, see Jacques Le Rider's *Nietzsche en France*.

19 On the influence of Bourget's *Essais* on Nietzsche's theory of decadence, see the notes to *Il caso Wagner*, and Calinescu (186–7).

20 The poem was reprinted in *La rénovation esthétique*, July 1906, with a significantly different title: 'La folie des tramways.' It was later recuperated for futurism and published for a third time, with the subtitle 'Futurist Song,' as '...Hors du possible noir en plein azur absurde!' in the penultimate issue of *Poesia* (April–July 1909).

21 Like 'La folie de tramways,' this prose-poem was recuperated for futurism. It appeared in Italian as 'La morte prese il volante (visione futurista d'una corsa di automobili)' in *Poesia* of April–July 1909.

22 One of Marinetti's most famous early works on the automobile, titled 'À l'automobile' when it was first published in *Poesia* (1905), and, in the final version, 'À l'automobile de course,' appeared in *La ville charnelle* as 'Dythirambes à mon Pégase.'

23 Nietzsche distances himself from Darwin, and mocks Darwinian interpretations of his thought in a number of places – for instance, the first section of 'Why I Write Such Good Books' in *Ecce Homo* (261).

24 On the echoes of the contemporary anti-positivist scientific debate in the aesthetic theory of Marinetti and other futurists, see, in addition to Grana, quoted below, La Monica's 'Il tempo e lo spazio morirono ieri.'

25 See on this point Grana, who writes: 'The imaginative "liberation" of art corresponds, with a broad correlation of images, to the cognitive "liberation" of natural science, which concurred in reforming general culture, in modifying radically the models and images of the world, and the inherited blueprints of natural order' (8).

26 The question of Nietzsche's influence on Marinetti has been variously examined, although usually focusing on the doctrine of the *Übermensch*. See in particular De Maria, 'Marinetti poeta e ideologo' xxxvi–xxxviii, cxxvi; Berghaus 12–16; Blum viii, 180, n. 36; Nicholls 89–93; Fazio 141–2. As Manuela Angela Stefani has pointed out (8), before the First World War the reception of Nietzsche's thought in Italy was limited to the most superficial aspects of his theories of the 'superman' and the will to power. Although the first Italian translation of the second 'Untimely Meditation' appeared only in 1926, Pasquale Villari had discussed Nietzsche's theory of history as early as 1891 in an article published in *Nuova antologia* entitled 'La storia è una scienza?' (cf. Fazio 13). Furthermore, it is likely that Marinetti would have read Nietzsche in the French translation, as happened with other German philosophers (cf. the list of authors that Marinetti planned to read around 1895–6 in De Villers, *Le premier manifeste* 146–9). The first French translation of the *Untimely Meditations* was published in 1907, but references to the second 'Meditation' appeared as early as 1874 (cf. Bianquis, 119, 4). Marinetti himself of course denied any Nietzschean influence, most notably in 'Contro i professori' (1910), in which he characterized the 'grande filosofo tedesco' [great German philosopher] as 'passatista che cammina sulle cime dei monti tessalici, coi piedi disgraziatamente impacciati da lunghi testi greci' [a passeist who walks on the tops of the Thessalian mountains, with his feet unfortunately tangled in long Greek texts] (*TIF* 306).

27 The link between decadence and physical and moral dis-ease is a central theme in Nietzsche; see for instance *Ecce Homo*, passim (but esp. section 1, 'Why I Am So Wise').

28 See for instance the description of Sperelli's house, *Il piacere* 16–18.

29 Cf. *A rebours*:

> Ce qu'il [Des Esseintes] voulait, c'étaient des couleurs dont l'expression s'affirmât aux lumières factices des lampes; peu lui importait même qu'elles fussent aux lueurs du jour, insipides ou rêches, car il ne vivait guère que la nuit, pensant qu'on était mieux chez soi, plus seul, et que l'esprit ne s'excitait et ne crépitait réellement qu'au contact voisin de l'ombre. (20)
>
> [What he [Des Esseintes] wanted was colours the effect of which was

confirmed and strengthened under artificial light; little he cared even if by daylight they should appear insipid or crude, for he lived practically his whole life at night, holding that a man was more truly at home, more himself and his own master, and that the mind found its only real excitant and effective stimulation in contact with the shades of evening.] (*Against the Grain* 12)

30 The association of technology with mythological figures, in any case, was also fairly common in fin-de-siècle iconography. See for instance the poster for the 'Mostra del ciclo e dell'automobile' (Bicycle and Automobile Expo), held in Milan in May–June 1907, and that for the fifth 'Esposizione internazionale di autombili' (International Automobile Expo), held in Turin in January–February 1908. In the former (reproduced in Ceserani 21), the automobile seems to compete with a winged, angelic figure that recalls the 'last flight of angels' of Marinetti's first manifesto, while in the latter (Abruzzese and Colombo 463) the automobile is driven by an angel. Alberto Abruzzese's observation regarding what he calls the 'amphibious role' of tradition in early advertising also reflects the ambiguous position of futurism between the celebration of technological modernity and the necessity of articulating a symbolic order through which to give shape to modernity itself: 'The ambivalent relationship [of advertisement] with tradition is documented for instance by the posters for automobiles, in which the message emphasized the disruptive value of speed as a revolution in the traditional relations of space and time, but also balanced the effect of estrangement through strong images from the rural, anti-metropolitan landscape, or the classical iconology of the ancient world and its pre-mechanical mythologies' (Abruzzese and Colombo 462–3).

31 This critical tradition is best represented by Poggioli; see especially 68–74. For Poggioli, 'followers of the avant-garde in the arts act as if they were disposed to make dung heaps of themselves for the fertilizing of conquered lands, or mountains of corpses over which a new generation may in its turn scale the besieged fortress. A proper *course au flambeau*, agonism then transforms into *futurism*' (68). Thus, the Italian critic comes to argue that, while of little interest in itself, the Italian movement has provided the name for a fundamental aspect of the experience of the avant-garde, arguing that 'the futurist moment belongs to all the avant-gardes' (68).

32 Cf. De Villers, 'Ancora sul manifesto.'

33 This scene was first read as a metaphor of rebirth by Calvesi (cf. 17–18). On this passage, see also Blum 49 and Poggi 25. While I agree with the gist of Poggi's argument, I would suggest that the 'deliberate confusion of identities [which] serves both to feminize and eroticize technology' does not

leave the futurist subject untouched since, coming at the end of a series of metaphors of maternity and birth, Marinetti's life-giving touch is not completely free of the feminine that the narrative attributes to the other mother figures, the ditch, the nurse, and the car itself. In other words, if the machine is constructed as both phallic and feminine, so is its futurist companion and counterpart. Incidentally, this passage also demonstrates the impossibility of escaping history, which here creeps back into Marinetti's discourse in the form of personal memories.

34 Cf. *On the Uses and Disadvantages of History for Life*: 'The belief that one is a latecomer of the ages is, in any case, paralysing and depressing: but it must appear dreadful and devastating when such a belief one day by a bold inversion raises this latecomer to godhood as the true meaning and goal of previous events, when his miserable condition is equated with a completion of world history' (104).

35 See Saccone's pointed comment: 'Here Marinetti, among other things, specifies his theory of artistic practice as an incessant act of procreation, which is to be reduced to ashes and regenerated continually in order to deny repetition' (*'La trincea avanzata' e 'la città dei conquistatori'* 18). For a critique of the category of the new, see Carla Benedetti's *Il tradimento dei critici*, especially pp. 48–59 and 83–96.

36 Baudelaire does note that Guys 'dessine de mémoire, et non d'après le modèle, sauf dans le cas (la guerre de Crimèe, par example) où il y a nécessité urgente de prendre des notes immédiates, précipitées, et d'arrêter les lignes principales d'un sujet' [draws from memory, and not from a model, except in those cases (the Crimean war, for example) where there is an urgent need to take immediate, hurried notes and to establish the broad outlines of a subject] (2:698; 407). Drawing from memory is here thus opposed not to the immediate drafting of the object, but rather to the recreation of the scene through a model, which would add an intermediate mimetic layer to the process of reproduction of the event: in other words, the event is first reproduced by the model so that it can be reproduced, in the second degree, by the painter. The distinction is important: memory offers a direct link to the event, a link that the formalizing, intermediate stage of the model would sever.

37 This was the title under which the text was published in Italian in the catalogue to the exhibition held in Florence from November 1913 to January 1914. As the title suggests, the text served as preface to catalogues for the exhibitions held throughout Europe in 1912 (see chapter 3). While the content remained fundamentally the same throughout, slight modifications were made to tailor the preface to the specific context. The first publication

was in the catalogue for the exhibition in Paris at the Bernheim gallery (1912), where it appeared under the title 'Les Exposants au Public.'

38 Cf. Ballerini 21–2.

39 The critique of Futurism as an 'aesthetic of "content"' had already been advanced by Giuseppe Prezzolini in his article 'Alcune idee chiare intorno al futurismo' published in *La Voce* on 10 April 1913 (now in De Maria, *Marinetti e i futuristi* 271–2).

40 On the influence of futurist painting on Marinetti, see also Calvesi.

41 Cf. Boccioni et al., 'Prefazione,' 62. On the concept of simultaneity and its introduction in the futurist vocabulary in the 'Prefazione,' see also Bergman, especially 170–9.

42 'Risposta alle obiezioni' was also published on other occasions as 'Supplemento al Manifesto tecnico della letteratura futurista' and 'Polemiche intorno al Manifesto tecnico della letteratura futurista' (cf. *TIF* cxxxiv and 55).

43 Cf. point 2 of the 'Manifesto tecnico': '**Si deve usare il verbo all infinito,** perché si adatti elasticamente al sostantivo e non lo sottoponga all'*io* dello scrittore che osserva o immagina' [**The verb must be used in the infinitive**, so that it will adapt elastically to the noun and will not submit it to the *I* of the writer who observes or imagines] (*TIF* 46). This is perhaps the point where Marinetti's critique of the ordering function of the subject is most evident.

44 For a detailed discussion of futurist onomatopoeia, see also White, especially 28–35.

45 On the influence of Bergson on Marinetti's, see Curi's 'Nota su Marinetti e Bergson' in his *Tra mimesi e metafora* 115–123.

46 On the history of the music-hall and Marinetti's exposure to its French, English, and Italian varieties, see Berghaus, *Italian Futurist Theatre* 161–72. The Italian version of the manifesto, 'Il Teatro del Varietà,' from which I quote, is a substantially longer expansion of the English text.

47 In an essay on Marinetti's major work of *paroliberismo*, *Zang Tumb Tumb* (1914), Jeffrey Schnapp has argued that the apparent openness of the futurist text is in fact recontained precisely in the moment of its public performance, which 'supplement[s] the mediacy of the literary word with the physical immediacy of its transmitter and transmission' (91). While I do not necessarily disagree with some of Schnapp's conclusions, and in particular with his argument that performance is instrumental in the project of 'the translation of art into action, poetry into politics' (78), I do not think that this is achieved simply by short-circuiting the distance between text and audience, the mediating function of language, in order to effect a col-

lapse of 'the space of analysis, of interpretation and of reading' (78). Indeed, the 1916 manifesto 'La declamazione dinamica e sinottica' (Dynamic and Synoptic Declamation), Marinetti's major statement on the performance of futurist works, begins by rejecting the model of the declaimer as seducer (used by Marinetti himself, as he freely admits). Instead, the manifesto details a number of anti-mimetic techniques of enstrangement and distancing such as the dehumanization of the face and the voice, the geometrization of physical movements, and the use of sound-producing tools. The viewer is thus surrounded and confronted by a series of linguistic, visual, auditory, and physical signs producing an 'environment,' to use again Boccioni's term, in which meaning is produced actively by the audience rather than imposed by either the performer or the text.

48 On futurism in Florence, see in particular Walter Adamson's *Avant-Garde Florence*, the proceedings of the conference *Futurismo a Firenze 1910–1920*, edited by Gloria Manghetti, and Laura Dondi's essay 'Dal "secondo futurismo fiorentino" del periodo eroico al "secondo futurismo."' Specifically on *L'Italia Futurista*, see the volume edited by Maria Carla Papini.

49 Cf. De Maria, 'Marinetti poeta e ideologo' xlvii.

50 See for instance his article in *Leonardo* 'Campagna per il forzato risveglio' (1906), written under the pseudonym Gian Falco: 'La mia propaganda non si perde tra le nebbie dell'universalità. Mi bastano pochi uomini che sappiano e sentano ciò ch'io voglio' [My propaganda will not be lost in the fogs of universalism. All I need are a few men who know and feel what I want] (313).

51 The 'Pink Pill' was a well-known medicinal supposed to have restorative properties; Marinetti himself was dubbed 'Poeta Pink.' A famous satirical cartoon by Giovanni Manca, published in the periodical *Il Pasquino* and reprinted in the last issue of *Poesia*, represented Marinetti, crowned with laurel, striding down a street festooned with signs with the word futurism, at the head of a parade of circus musicians and clowns, and some well-dressed men bearing placards which read 'Pink.'

52 For a thorough and detailed history of advertising, see Raúl Eguizábal Maza's *Historia de la publicidad*.

53 In Italy advertising posters were introduced by the *Impresa di Affissioni* founded by Antonio Montorfano, who had previously specialized in the production of theatre posters. On the origins of advertising in Italy, see in particular Ceserani's *Storia della pubblicità in Italia* and the relevant entries in Abruzzese and Colombo's *Dizionario della pubblicità*.

54 For a copious selection of contemporary reactions to futurism in France, see

Novelli's extensive bibliography, from which I take this and other quotations.

55 Even the existence of this earlier version was all but forgotten until it was noticed by Jean-Pierre de Villers (see his *Le premier manifeste* 15). Salaris reports that after its publication on *La Gazzetta d'Emilia*, the manifesto appeared on *Il Pungolo* (6 February) and *La Tavola Rotonda* (14 February), while *Il Mattino* announced the receipt of the manifesto and the foundation of the new literary school of futurism on 8–9 February (*Marinetti. Arte e vita* 61). Lista has insisted on the importance of the earlier appearances of the manifesto, even suggesting that 'the foundation of futurism took place in Italy, and not in Paris,' and that the publication of 'Le futurisme' on the front page of *Le Figaro* was 'almost an act of commemoration of what had already taken place' (*F.T. Marinetti* 80). Clearly, I disagree with Lista on this point, since I believe that in order for the movement to be legitimated it had to find a forum with the appropriate cultural capital and mediating role. What had been virtually buried in the back pages of Italian provincial newspapers gained immediate visibility and notoriety once it appeared in *Le Figaro*.

56 The first roster of futurists appeared in the second manifesto of the movement, 'Tuons le Claire de Lune!,' first published in the last issue of *Poesia* (August–October 1909) and, in Italian, as 'Proclama futurista,' the introduction to Paolo Buzzi's volume of poetry *Aeroplani*. It includes Paolo Buzzi, Federico De Maria, Enrico Cavacchioli, Corrado Govoni, and Libero Altomare.

57 On the use of futurism as a brand name, and more in general, on the adoption of advertising strategies on the part of the movement, see also Fael. On futurism and advertising, see also the introduction to Salaris's volume *Il futurismo e la pubblicità*.

58 The story of the Venice blitz, however, may well be apocryphal, since there seems to be no independent confirmation in the newspapers of the time that it actually took place. I thank Giovanni Lista for bringing this to my attention.

59 See the anastatic reproduction of these manifestoes in Caruso (items 1; 11; 29).

60 The dates are not completely reliable. The recurrence of the number 11 in this and in other contexts (for instance, many manifestoes have eleven points) was due to Marinetti's superstitious belief in the lucky nature of that number.

61 The standardization of the form of the manifesto occurs mostly in the years between the foundation of the movement and the First World War. Mari-

netti's own manifestoes are often characterized by a freer use of the discursive and programmatic sections of the text.

Chapter 3

1 Although not free of a totalizing rhetoric that would have certainly pleased Marinetti, the 1986 exhibition 'Futurismo & Futurismi' held at Palazzo Grassi in Venice provided a useful opportunity for an in-depth analysis of the reciprocal influences between the two artistic milieux by juxtaposing works by, among others, Pablo Picasso, Georges Braque, Robert and Sonia Delauney, and Marcel Duchamp to those of the major futurists of the 1910s. On futurism in France, see Jannini's essay 'Note e documenti sulla fortuna del Futurismo in Francia.'

2 Even *Zang Tumb Tumb*, the incunabulum of '*paroliberismo*' was first drafted in French. (This the draft in now held by the Beinecke Library at Yale University.)

3 On the 1912 futurist exhibitions, see Cohen. The author also discusses the difficulties in sketching the precise route of the exhibit after its major stop in Berlin.

4 'Prega Marinetti di mandarmi 150 lire pel ritorno a Parigi [...] *Senza Marinetti non posso partire*. Pensa se sono allegro' [Kindly ask Marinetti to send me 150 lire to come back to Paris ... *Without Marinetti I can't leave*. Imagine how happy I am], a dejected Severini wrote Boccioni from London on 1 March 1912 (Drudi Gambillo 1: 235).

5 See Lawton, Introduction. The section entitled 'Futurism in the World' provides a useful summary of the capillary dispersion of the movement throughout Europe, China, Japan, and the Americas.

6 'M. Marinetti writes like Walt Whitman gone mad. But Whitman sang, instead of telling us what he was going to sing. Why do not the futurists write their poems about railway trains and aeroplanes, their sermons in steam-engines, and books in racing motor-cars, instead of telling us they mean to write them?' ('Le Futurisme et la presse' 23–4)

7 'The burning of museums, recommended in the manifesto, reminds one of go-ahead young Romans today, whom nothing irritates so much as to be asked about the Arch of Constantine or the Borghese Palace, and who in reply point out the beauties of their tramway service' ('Le Futurisme et la presse' 24).

8 'La catalizzazione futurista' is the title of his study of the influence of the Italian movement on the English cultural milieu. See *Modernismo/Modernismi* 156–74.

9 My doubts about the authorship of the article stem from the fact that, of the two articles published on page 112 of the 31 December 1910 issue of *The Vote*, Nevinson seems to be only the author of the first one, 'Woman the Spoilt Child of the Law.' The report on Marinetti's lecture, which occupies three quarters of the second column, is clearly separated from the previous article, which is on a very different subject. Many of the more informational pieces in *The Vote* were in fact published anonymously, although the editorial note opening each issue asserts that 'The Editor is responsible for unsigned articles only' (I quote from the same issue). To complicate matters further, in this period *The Vote* did not indicate an editor, although it listed five people as directors (cf. p. 116 in the 31 December 1910 issue), among whom Charlotte Despard, the president and honorary treasurer of the League, was likely to have had primary editorial responsibilities. On the Women's Freedom League, see Crawford 720–4.

10 A number of sources report that Marinetti was in London and held a lecture at the Lyceum Club in the spring of 1910. Baronti Marchiò places this visit in June (16); Gioè reports that it took place in April, but also lists a second visit – and a second lecture at the Lyceum Club – in December. However, the doubts already expressed by Cianci as to the actual occurrence of this event ('Futurism and the English Avant-Garde' 28, note 5) seem quite warranted, as there is no contemporary documentary evidence to witness to it. Significantly, references to this lecture (all from futurist sources) date from several years after the event supposedly took place. On this occasion, Marinetti is said to have read his 'Discorso futurista agli inglesi' [Futurist speech to the English], which, however, was published only in 1915 in *Guerra sola igiene del mondo*, a miscellaneous collection of various manifestoes and other programmatic and propaganda pieces. In this volume, it bears the simple subtitle 'pronounced at the Lyceum Club in London'; it was only when the piece was reissued in the miscellany *Futurismo e fascismo* (1924), that it was dated 'June 1910.' The other influential source for the early visit to England is Balilla Pratella's 'Il futurismo e la guerra,' a chronology of futurist interventionist activities dating from 1908 (just before the foundation of the movement) to 1915, dated 11 December 1915 and first published as a flyer with both the manifesto 'L'orgoglio italiano,' signed by Marinetti, Boccioni, Russolo, Sant'Elia, Sironi and Piatti (Caruso, item 76) and the piece 'L'unica soluzione del problema finanziario,' by Marinetti (Caruso, item 77). According to Pratella, Marinetti was in London in March and April of 1910. On the basis of this testimony Caruso attributes the 'Discorso futurista agli inglesi' to April 1910, although he himself reprints the version from *I manifesti del futurismo* (1919). It is possible that Pratella either

simply misdated Marinetti's first visit, or perhaps willingly shifted it from the fall/winter to the spring so that it would precede the famous exhibition 'Monet and the Post-Impressionists' organized by Roger Fry at the Grafton Galleries, an event that marked the introduction of avant-garde art into England.

Goldring, who is sometimes referred to as a source confirming Marinetti's visit in April (Wees 92 and Gioè 173), does not mention a month and in any case his account of the futurist leader's descent on London – 'a flamboyant personage adorned with diamond rings, gold chains and hundreds of flashing teeth' (64) – in his 1943 memoir *South Lodge* is less than reliable, as he also conflates the 1912 futurist exhibition with the 1914 performances that included noisetuner 'concerts': 'In addition to readings of his works accompanied by the banging of drums and loud noises from a band of "cacophonists" and "gluglutineurs," he organized a show of Futurist Painting' (64). Notably, Goldring makes no mention of Marinetti's visit in his giddy editorial notes to 'Futurist Venice' and 'Declaration of Futurism' – the selections from 'Contro Venezia passatista' and 'Fondazione e manifesto del Futurismo' that he published in *The Tramp*. In fact, the one-time contributor to *Poesia* implies that the texts had been received, in translation, by mail, as part of Marinetti's wide-ranging publicity campaign: 'Signor Marinetti's manifesto is so courageously worded, in its quaint English, that it deserves a wide publicity. It is such fun! ... We quote the Franco-Italian poet's letter in its entirety' ('Futurism' 487). Finally, since there were, to my knowledge, no accounts of Marinetti's lectures in the press, if he did travel to London in the spring of 1910, this first outing on British soil must have been a dismal failure indeed.

11 Crawford gives 1904 as date of foundation, but the pamphlet outlining the constitution of the Club is dated 21 November 1903 (cf. *The Lyceum Club*).

12 Early, that is, if one accepts the date proposed by the editors of *Archivi del futurismo*: 1 March 1912. The problem with this date is that on that same day Boccioni was already in London, as witnessed by the above mentioned letter to Baer dated 1 March by its author (cf. *Scritti* 347). Furthermore, since the *vernissage* of the exhibition was on 1 March, as Boccioni's letter states unequivocally, it is to say the least odd that Severini would have already complained about poor sales. Since Severini's letter only bears the place and day of the week ('London Saturday'), it is possible that the letter was in fact written after March 15 on which date Boccioni was back in Paris (cf. letter to Baer of 15 March 1912; *Scritti* 349); it may even date from the following year, when Severini had a personal show at the Marlborough Gallery.

13 The text, with annotations by Busoni scholar Laureto Rodoni, is available at www.rodoni.ch/pitturafuturista/aapitturafuturista.html.
14 On the presence of foreign anarchists in Victorian England, see Oliver. On anarchism between the end of the century and the First World War, see also Quail.
15 On the relationship between Futurism and the anarchist movement, see especially Lista, 'Marinetti et les anarcho-syndacalistes,' and Ciampi.
16 The Italian version of the manifesto uses the word 'libertarî,' but the French version used 'anarchistes,' as did both the English translation published in *Poesia* 3–6 (April–July 1909) and the one published in the 1912 exhibition catalogue.
17 On the British reaction to the Italo-Turkish war, see Bosworth, especially 171–3. See also Mack Smith 243–9. The links between Futurist nationalism and Italian colonialism did not escape political journalists, however. The journalist Francis McCullagh, who in 1912 published a volume on the Lybian war, *Italy's War for a Desert*, was challenged to a duel by Marinetti, as the journalist ironically recounted in his introduction to the book. See also Peppis 77–83.
18 The travelling exhibition of 1912 had been the first to bring together – at least in its original intentions – works by all five signatories of the manifestoes on painting. In the end, Balla did not participate, in spite of the fact that one of his works, *Lumière électrique*, had been announced in the French catalogue. This painting most likely was never exhibited, and it was not listed in the English catalogue or in those of the subsequent sites of the exhibition. However, his signature at the end of 'The Exhibitors to the Public' was retained in all the catalogues.
19 In *How to Do Things with Words*, Austin points out that 'stating' is also a form of illocutionary act, since it finds its validation in the assessment of the truth or falsity of a statement, and assessing is itself an illocutionary act that requires the felicitous performance of certain rules (148–9). Yet, the distinction remains operatively useful since it allows for differentiation between speech acts with distinct rules of satisfaction.
20 Not surprisingly, the early stage of the movement's historicization also saw its commodification. The 1913 review of the 'Post-Impressionist and Futurist Exhibition: From Pissarro to Severini' in the *Daily Sketch* opened with the bemused observation: 'Funny folks, these post-impressionists and futurists. Their latest proud announcement is that their works are now being collected by "hard-headed business men." Even a Mayor – his worship of Scarborough – has taken to buying their canvases, and, what is more, keeping them by him.' And after doubting the aesthetic sense of such patrons,

the 'irreverent critic' went on to note: 'Still, the futurists must know their market, or they wouldn't trouble to have shows' ('The Confetti School of Painting' 6).

21 Letter to Vico Baer, 1 March 1912 (*Scritti* 348). Apparently, however, the notes were found to be a useful tool since they were added to the catalogue of the Berlin exhibition .

22 Consider for instance the description of Boccioni's *Laughter* ('The personages are studied from all sides and both the objects in front and those at the back are to be seen, all these being present in the painter's memory') or *The Street Enters the House* ('The painter does not limit himself to what he sees in the square frame of the window as would a simple photographer, but he also reproduces what he would see by looking out on every side from the balcony') (21).

23 The words 'impression' and 'sensation' occur several times, and are used by all four exhibitors. Much rarer is the term 'synthesis' (used especially by Carrà), which in the critical vocabulary of futurism indicates an elaboration on the part of the artist of the interaction between subject and object.

24 Valerio Gioè's bibliographies of futurism in England, which cover the period from 1910 to 1915, can be integrated with Caruso's at times imprecise but useful article on the critical reception of the 1912 exhibition.

25 I use the notion of 'inoculation' in the sense defined by Barthes in *Mythologies*: 'one immunizes the contents of the collective imagination by means of a small inoculation of acknowledged evil; one thus protects it against the risk of a generalized subversion ... [T]he bourgeosie no longer hesitates to acknowledge some localized subversions: the avant-garde, the irrational in childhood, etc.' (150–1)

26 See for instance Falkenheim, especially 29–32 and 87–110, and Drucker 71–4.

27 Compare Fry's review with Apollinaire's, published on 9 February 1912 in *Le Petit Bleu*. The French poet identifies the originality of the futurists specifically in their willingness to move from an analytical dissection of the subject characteristic of the French avant-garde, in which the subject itself becomes a mere object of study and not of interest as such, and toward 'une peinture plus synthétique' [a more synthetic kind of painting] that allows the artist to engage in a new representation of reality. The superior technique of the French artists – which Apollinaire does not call into question – results in rather timid painting: 'l'art nouveau qui s'élabore en France,' he writes, 'semble ne s'en être guère tenu jusqu'ici qu'à la mélodie et les futuristes viennent nous apprendre – par leurs titres et non par leurs œuvres – qu'il pourrait s'élever jusqu'à la symphonie' ('Chroniques d'art' 232) [the

new art that is being fashioned in France seems until now to have limited itself to melody, and the futurists have taught us – by their titles, not their works – that it can attain the fulness of a symphony] ('Art News' 204). It should be noted that the idea of 'synthesis' was taken directly from the futurist vocabulary, as the futurists themselves spoke of their works as 'the synthesis of *what one remembers* and of *what one sees*' in 'The Exhibitors to the Public' (12; the sentence appears on p. 6 of the French version of the catalogue).

28 On the influence of Bergson on Boccioni (who here quotes from *Matière et mémoire*), see Maurizio Calvesi's entry on the painter in Hulten's *Futurism & Futurisms* (427–9).

29 Severini reiterated this point in an article that appeared in the *Daily Express* on 11 April 1913, on the occasion of his solo exhibition at the Marlborough Gallery:

> We want to put ourselves intuitively in the midst of the objects, to form with them one single unity.
>
> We want to represent the heart of things.
>
> The technical manifesto of Futurist painting said: –
>
> 'The spectator must be placed in the centre of the picture.'
>
> In looking at a Futurist picture you must not try to find out what it is about. You must let yourself be gripped by the emotion, entirely plastic or creative, that emanates from the work.
>
> You must put away your knowledge of the exterior appearance of things, for that knowledge is very far from the ideal and complex truths towards which our efforts tend.

30 Here I am also thinking of the distinction proposed by Raymond Williams between 'groupings [...] seeking to provide their own facilities of production, distribution and publicity; and [...] fully oppositional formations, determined not only to promote their own work but to attack its enemies in the cultural establishments and, beyond these, the whole social order' (50–1). Williams considers these as subsequent phases in the development of the avant-garde, but this is not to be understood simply in chronological terms. Rather, the phases can function to distinguish the boundaries within which moved contemporaneous cultural projects.

31 In addition to the works quoted elsewhere in this section, see Cianci's essays 'Un futurismo in panni neoclassici' and 'Wyndham Lewis vorticofuturista'; Lyon ch. 3, especially 94–113. The most comprehensive and sophisticated overview of the English movement remains Dasenbrock's *The Literary Vorticisim of Ezra Pound and Wyndham Lewis*.

32 On Lewis's life, see O'Keeffe's recent biography *Some Sort of Genius*.

33 The 'Round-Robin' letter is reprinted in Lewis, *Letters* 47–50. As the editor of the volume, W.K. Rose, notes 'The stir created by this document, composed by Lewis, focused public attention on the group of rebellious young artists of whom Lewis was the leader' (47).

34 On the Rebel Art Centre and its origins, see Wees 68–72.

35 It was on this occasion that the term 'Vorticists' was first applied to the group. See Cork's discussion of the press accounts of the evening (1: 232). The *Manchester Guardian* reported that 'the new Seceders from the Marinetti group, Messrs Wyndham Lewis, and Co., [...] now call themselves the Vorticists' (qtd. 1: 232). Cf. also the report in *The Times* of 13 June: 'The little group of English painters, about a score in number [in fact a lot fewer], who have hitherto associated themselves with the advanced art movement founded and led by Signor Marinetti, are now disavowing allegiance to the Italian school. They purpose inventing a more characteristically English form of expression in line and cube and colour. "Vorticist" art, as the new form is to be called, will symbolize the vortex of present-day life, the whirlpool into which all hustle and bustle of everyday movement converges. It will blend, it is stated, the basic motives of Impressionism and Futurism' ('"Vorticist Art"'). It is perhaps noteworthy that in both articles Lewis is clearly indicated as the leader of the group.

According to Cork, Lewis had considered founding a movement called 'Blasticism,' of which *Blast* would have been the organ, but had been deterred from going forward with it because of his allies' resistance to the idea (1: 234). On the notion of 'vortex' in Pound, see Materer's 'Pound's Vortex' and chapter 1 of his *Vortex*. For a discussion of futurist precedents of the term 'vortex,' see Cianci, 'Futurism and the English Avant-Garde' 15.

36 In a letter of 17 July 1914 to Monro, Marinetti expressed his regret for the break with the English avant-garde. Cf. Lawton, 'Marinetti in Inghilterra' 148.

37 On these changes, see Wees 163 and Cork 1: 235–6. It is also interesting to note that in the advertisement in *The Egoist*, the foregrounded contribution was neither the 'story by Wyndham Lewis' nor the 'poems by Ezra Pound,' but an unspecified (in both content and signatories) manifesto, as if that were necessary to establish *Blast* as a *bona fide* avant-garde journal. Lewis wrote most of the editorial and critical pieces for both issues of the journal.

On the influence of futurism on the textual practices of vorticism, and in particular of Apollinaire's 'Anti-tradition futuriste' on the manifesto that opens *Blast*, see Cork 1: 249–50, and Windsor.

38 For Lewis's long standing polemic with what he called 'time art,' see in particular his *Time and Western Man*.

39 A crucial role on Lewis's reflection was played by T.E. Hulme's aesthetic theory based on a reinterpretation of the categories of 'abstraction' and 'empathy' articulated by Wilhelm Wörringer in his *Abstraktion und Einfühlung* (1908) in terms of the opposition between classicism and romanticism. On Hulme's influence on English modernism, see Levenson, chs. 3 and 6.
40 Pound also repeatedly defined futurism as 'accelerated Impressionism' in his vorticist propaganda. Cf. 'Vortex Pound' (154), and *Gaudier-Brzeska* (90).
41 The novel was completed in 1915 and serialized in *The Egoist* between 1916 and 1917. Its composition is therefore contemporaneous with Lewis's engagement with vorticism. On its composition and publication history, see Paul O'Keeffe's afterword to his edition of the novel.
42 The bibliography of the influence of futurism on Pound is extensive. In addition to the works cited elsewhere in this chapter, see also Cianci, 'Pound and Futurism'; Wees, 'Futurismo, vorticismo'; and Weisstein.
43 Unless otherwise noted, all quotes from Pound's essays are from *Ezra Pound's Poetry and Prose*, abbreviated *EPPP*.
44 On the influence of Daniel and Cavalcanti on Pound, see respectively Stuart Y. McDougal's *Ezra Pound and the Troubadour Tradition* and David Anderson's *Pound's Cavalcanti*.
45 Cf. for instance 'Prologomena': 'As for the nineteenth century, with all respect to its achievements, I think we shall look upon it as a rather blurry, messy sort of a period, a rather sentimentalistic, mannerish sort of a period' (*EPPP* 62).
46 The 1913 version of 'Patria mia' revised and collected, with some additional material, articles published in two series in *The New Age*: 'Patria Mia' (11 installments, 5 September to 14 November 1912), and 'America: Chances and Remedies' (6 installments, 1 May to 5 June 1913). The passage quoted below was added to the 1913 version, but some of its points – most specifically the comparison of the artist's 'experiments' with those of the scientist – had already been made in the final section of 'America: Chances and Remedies' (cf. *EPPP* 146).
47 Not by chance, as Mark Kyburz has observed (57, note 1), religious metaphors became more frequent after 1914 under the influence of Yeats, whose poetics had formed within a symbolist horizon.
48 On the figure of the incendiary in futurism, see Antonio Saccone's essay 'Figurazioni del personaggio incendiario: Marinetti e Palazzeschi' in his *'La trincea avanzata' e 'La città dei conquistatori,'* 63–86.
49 Cf. Lewis's 'The Melodrama of Modernity.'
50 Clearly, here I am interested in determining not the extent of Pound's

knowledge of contemporary scientific theories but rather the rhetorical and pragmatic function of the appeal to scientific discourse as a legitimating instance. The specific influences of scientific theories on Pound's poetics are discussed in great detail by Ian Bell in *Critic as Scientist*, and by Martin Kayman (especially ch. 3 of his *The Modernism of Ezra Pound*). Maria Luisa Ardizzone's introduction to *Pound e la scienza* is also a useful contribution to this debate.

51 I use the terms developed by Bourdieu in his essay 'The Field of Cultural Production' in the volume of the same title.

52 In this context, it is important to keep in mind what Vittorio Spinazzola has written about the expansion of the literary public; his argument is equally applicable to both the Italian cultural milieu and those of France and England, where the process of mass acculturation occurred earlier:

> As a whole, the old and new audiences no longer appear as an organic community, confident of its privileged access to written texts and unified by the cult of a shared system of aesthetic values. [...] Instead of appreciating the push towards the dynamization and the strengthening of a traditionally elitist literary life, the attention was rather focused on the undoubted imbalances and contradictions opened by the entry into the field of social groups which had previously been excluded from literary fruition and which had different concerns from those of the refined humanists.
>
> From this perspective, this was not an evolution but a degeneration. The liberalization of access to the world of books was considered as the fatal cause of a lowering of their quality, in obeyance to the logic driving the publishing market, the quest for profit. Hence the prevalence of a drably mediocre production, elaborated by writers in tune with the lazy expectations of a massified audience, with little or no competence in the field of letters. [...]
>
> The truth is more complex, articulated, and stratified. As with all other areas of relational activities, even in the literary field modernity resulted in both certain instances of homologation on a mediocre level, and, at the same time, a series of drives towards differentiation answering to the emergence of new interests and desires in the imaginary of a very composite collectivity.
>
> Certainly, the new categories of readers of more recent acculturation prefer works which are at their level of competence and evaluation. This however does not mean that in the past they had been able to access works of greater quality, and that they have then let themselves be lured by inferior products. The truth is that today like yesterday very intellec-

> tualized literature is unapproachable for them: a fact that should be acknowledged and meditated, but not interpreted as a symptom of decay in comparison to pre-modern times. [...]
>
> A fundamental datum emerges from such a complex situation: the fragmentation of the unity of the traditional audience, which mirrors the decline of a univocal and absolute idea of literature, which was expected to be universally shareable since it was founded on the axiological principles legislated by the guardians of the literary institution: that particular kind of specialized writers and readers that are the critics. (180–2)

Pound's intervention in the debate is functional to a re-articulation of the legislating function of the critic that draws its legitimation from the discourse of modernity.

53 Cf. the conclusion of 'The Wisdom of Poetry': 'As the abstract mathematician is to science so is the poet to the world's consciousness' (*EPPP* 76); and part 1 of 'The Serious Artist,' first published in *The New Freewoman* on 15 October 1913: 'The arts, literature, poesy, are a science, just as chemistry is a science. Their subject is man, mankind and the individual. The subject of chemistry is matter considered as to its composition' (*EPPP* 186)

54 Pound's rhetoric was certainly influenced by his close collaboration with Lewis in this period. Cf. the passage quoted above with Lewis's manifesto 'Long Live the Vortex!,' where he writes: 'The only way Humanity can help artists is to remain independent and work unconsciously. WE NEED THE UNCONSCIOUS OF HUMANITY – their stupidity, animalism and dreams' (7).

55 Cf. also Pound's December 1913 letter to Monroe where he writes: 'It is the function of the public to prevent the artist's expression by hook or by crook. Ancora e ancora' (*Selected Letters* 13).

56 Harriet Monroe's rebuttal to Pound's polemic, published in the same issue of *Poetry*, is interesting for several reasons. First, she points to the competing discourses of legitimation that orient the field of cultural production, noting that a rejection of the 'great audience' entails the retreat into the confines of the coterie, and to a marginal position within the field of culture: 'No small audience today can suffice for the poet's immediate audience, as such groups did in the stay-at-home aristocratic ages; and the greatest danger which besets modern art is that of slighting the "great audience" whose response alone can give it authority and volume, and of magnifying the importance of a coterie' (31). Second, she argues that such marginality is not a necessary but a historical condition for the poet – Dante is her example of a poet whose epic 'like all greatest art, was based upon the whole life of his time' (31). Finally, she uses a scientific image that complicates

Pound's positivist notion of science: 'Science is explaining more and more the reactions and relations of matter and life. It becomes increasingly clear that nothing can stand alone, genius least of all' (32). Her model of scientific knowledge, which instead of dividing reality into individually knowable entities reveals the interconnections that link them is interestingly in tune with the futurist model of a dynamic universe.

57 The letter, dated January 1915 and addressed to Harriet Monroe, explained Pound's 'disassociation' from Amy Lowell's imagist collection *Some Imagist Poets*, which marked his withdrawal from the group he had himself created. Commenting on this letter, Levenson has pointed out that the expression anticipates Pound's famous dictum that artists are the 'antennae' of the race (Levenson 148). It is also interesting to notice that here Pound is appropriating the terms of Shelley's equally renowned definition of the poets as 'unacknowledged legislators of the World,' but with a significant inversion of the adjective. For Shelley it is the poets themselves who in the first instance cannot grasp rationally their guiding role when the *Zeitgeist* speaks through them: poets 'measure the circumference and sound the depths of human nature with a comprehensive and all-penetrating spirit, and they are themselves perhaps the most sincerely astonished at its manifestations, for it is less their spirit than the spirit of the age' (140). For Pound such a guiding role comes not only to consciousness, but must translate also into social recognition – hence, the problem of who is endowed with the necessary expertise to legitimize, or in Poundian terms, to acknowledge, true poetry from sham. (See also Pound's polemic against both imitation and against the critics in the same letter to Monroe.) Finally, the metaphor of the 'antennae' translates the Shelleyan metaphor into the language of mdern technology, thus bringing this metaphor into the same broad semantic field that orients Pound's critical discourse.

58 Pound began to write about the figurative arts only in 1914 (his first essay on the subject was the article 'The New Sculpture,' in *The Egoist*, 16 February 1914), with the intensification of his friendship with Wyndham Lewis and Henri Gaudier-Brzeska that would ultimately lead to the foundation of the vorticist movement.

59 On Marinetti and Monro, see Lawton, 'Marinetti in Inghilterra.'

60 From an unpublished letter to Glenn Hughes dated 26 September 1927 (qtd. Rainey 31). The anecdote in the tea-shop was also recalled by Richard Aldington in his memoir *Life for Life's Sake* (135). On the role of H.D.'s poetry in shaping the poetics of imagism see Pondrom, 'H.D. and the Origins of Imagism' (which also articulates an important critique of Pound's 'altruism' in initiating the movement), and Benstock 321–30. On the origins of

imagism as 'a publicity stunt,' see Coffman, ch. 1; this book provides also a thorough historical account of the evolution of the school.

61 Cf. Rainey (note 43, 182–4).

62 Cf. Rainey 29.

63 Pound is clearly thinking of point 2: **'Verbs must be used in the infinitive'** (*TIF* 46). The date of the manifesto, incidentally, would constitutes the *terminus post quem* for dating the appendix; according to Salaris ('Manifesto tecnico' 177), the text was not distributed until June 1912.

64 Flint began reviewing contemporary French poetry as early as 1908. His extensive survey of the French symbolist landscape, which concludes with a discussion of futurism, appeared in the August 1912 issue of *The Poetry Review*. See in particular Cyrena Pondrom's *The Road to Paris*, which anthologizes several major contributions to the debate on French poetry in England in the first two decades of the twentieth century. Pound himself began publishing a series of articles on the Parisian cultural scene, 'The Approach to Paris,' in September 1913 in *New Age*.

65 In reviewing Yeats's *Responsibilities* for *Poetry* (May 1914), for instance, Pound distinguishes the poetics of the Irish poet from those of imagism: '"Is Mr. Yeats an Imagiste?" No, Mr. Yeats is a symbolist, but he has written *des images* as have many good poets before him' (*EPPP* 242). According to Longenbach, Pound considered Yeats a 'seminal' part of the Imagist movement (31).

66 Within the fiction of Flint's text the identity of the '*Imagiste*' who has condescended to speak with him remains hidden, although the editorial note makes it clear that it is Pound. This is incidentally the first time that Pound is publicly identified unambiguously as an imagist, since in the other previous instances (the Hulme preface and 'Status Rerum') he had himself assumed the role of the reporter.

67 Cf. Middleton: 'At the time, Flint knew more about the new French poetry than anyone else in England or America. He corresponded with numerous young French poets and had a quite extraordinary grasp of their ideas and practice' (35).

68 Cf. Martin's account, based on an interview with Flint (36).

69 Cf. Lyon: 'Pound's eschewal of "we" in *imagisme* suggests a self-marginalizing group to which *no one* is offered access or the chance of self-alignment' (134).

70 But does this scene not reproduce the act of foundation of imagism, that is, Pound's editorial intervention on H.D.'s poems? Was H.D. a poetaster, then, until Pound remade her as an imagist? Was the slip unconscious?

71 For a concise discussion of this question, see Kyburz 10–18.

72 Cf. David Richter's introduction to the text in his anthology *The Critical Tradition* (465), and Guglielmi (183).
73 Cf. Bürger's discussion of the incorporation of Duchamp's ready-mades into the museum (53).
74 'Imagisme' has been traditionally assigned the role of manifesto of the movement – cf. Perloff, Coffman, Zach, and Bianchi, who extend the label to 'A Few Don'ts' (113) – but more recent studies which have thematized the implications and the limitations of such a gesture of classification have emphasized the distance of Pound's texts from the genre. Rainey describes 'A Few Don'ts' as 'implicitly in opposition to the genre of the manifesto' in its very title (31), while Lyon reads the two texts as a critical reaction to manifesto writing (129–35).

Conclusion

1 Among the most recent examples of this tendency, see for instance Peter Childs's *Modernism*.
2 The first, almost exemplary document of this *querelle* of the moderns and the post-moderns, is Ihab Hassan's influential 'POSTmodernISM.'

References

Abastado, Claude. 'Introduction à l'analyse des manifestes.' *Littérature* 39 (1980): 3–11.

– 'Le "Manifeste Dada 1918": Un tourniquet.' *Littérature* 39 (1980): 39–46.

Abruzzese, Alberto, and Fausto Colombo, eds. *Dizionario della pubblicità: storia, tecniche, personaggi*. Bologna: Zanichelli, 1994.

Adam, Paul [as Jacques Plowert]. *Petit glossaire pour servire à l'intelligence des auteurs décadents et symbolistes*. 1888. Ed. Patrick McGuinness. Exeter: University of Exeter Press, 1998.

Adamson, Walter L. *Avant-Garde Florence: From Modernism to Fascism*. Cambridge: Harvard University Press, 1993.

'Adhésions et Objections.' *Poesia* 3–6 (1909): 5–11.

Agnese, Gino. *Marinetti: una vita esplosiva*. Milano: Camunia, 1990.

'The Aims of Futurism.' *The Times* 21 March 1912: 2.

Aldington, Richard. *Life for Life's Sake: A Book of Reminiscences*. New York: Viking Press, 1941.

Althusser, Louis. 'Ideology and Ideological State Apparatus.' *Lenin and Philosophy and Other Essays*. Trans. Ben Brewster. London: New Left Books, 1971.

Anderson, David. *Pound's Cavalcanti: An Edition of the Translations, Notes, and Essays*. Princeton: Princeton University Press, 1983.

Anderson, Perry. 'Modernity and Revolution.' *Marxism and the Interpretation of Culture*. Ed. Cary Nelson and Lawrence Greenberg. Urbana: University of Illinois Press, 1988. 317–38.

Apollinaire, Guillaume. 'Art News: The Futurists.' *Apollinaire on Art: Essays and Reviews 1902–1918*. Ed. Leroy C. Breunig. Trans. Susan Suleiman. New York: Viking, 1972. 200–205.

– 'Chroniques d'art. Les futuristes.' *Œuvres complètes de Guillaume Apollinaire*. Ed. Michel Décaudin. Paris: André Ballard et Jacques Lecat, 1966. 4: 228–32.

Ardizzone, Maria Luisa. 'Alle radici del «Paradiso» dei *Cantos*.' Preface. *Ezra Pound e la scienza. Scritti inediti o rari*. By Ezra Pound. Ed. Ardizzone. Milan: Scheiwiller, 1987. 11–48.
Asor Rosa, Alberto. 'Il futurismo nel dibattito intellettuale italiano dalle origini al 1920.' De Felice: *Futurismo, cultura e politica*, 49–66.
Austin, J. L. *How to Do Things with Words*. Ed. J. O. Urmson and Marina Sbisà. Cambridge: Harvard University Press, 1975.
Bagni, Paolo. *Genere*. Scandicci: La Nuova Italia, 1997.
Baju, Anatole. *L'anarchie litterarie*. 1892. Paris: Vanier, 1904.
– 'Aux lecteurs!' *Le Décadent littéraire & artistique* 1.1 (1886): 1.
– 'Chronique.' *Le Décadent littéraire & artistique* 1.5 (1886): 1.
– 'Chronique.' *Le Décadent littéraire* 1.27 (1886): 1–2.
– 'Deux littératures.' *Le Décadent littéraire* 1.30 (1886): 1.
– 'Esthétique décadente.' *Le Décadent littéraire & artistique* 1.10 (1886): 1.
– 'Eux.' *Le Décadent littéraire* 1.21 (1886): 1.
– 'Le fumisme.' *Le Décadent littéraire* 1.22 (1886): 1.
– [?]. 'Litterature industrielle.' *Le Décadent littéraire & artistique* 1.5 (1886): 3.
– 'Quintessence.' *Le Décadent littéraire* 1.23 (1886): 1.
– 'Zim-Boum!' *Le Décadent littéraire* 1.9 (1886): 1.
Baju, Anatole [as Louis Villatte]. 'Chronique littéraire.' *Le Décadent littéraire & artistique* 1.1 (1886): 3.
Baju, Anatole [as Pierre Vareilles]. 'Le progrès.' *Le Décadent littéraire & artistique* 1.1 (1886): 2.
– 'Décadence.' *Le décadent littéraire & artistique* 1.3 (1886): 1.
– 'Le poète décadent. Fantasie' *Le Décadent littéraire & artistique* 1.4 (1886): 2.
Baldacci, Luigi. *Massimo Bontempelli*. Turin: Borla, 1967.
Baldissone, Giusi. *Filippo Tommaso Marinetti*. Milan: Mursia, 1986.
Ballerini, Luigi. *La piramide rovesciata*. Venice: Marsilio, 1975.
Barilli, Renato. 'D'Annunzio e Marinetti: un "cambio della staffetta."' *L'Italia contemporanea. Studi in onore di Paolo Alatri*. Ed. by C. Carini and P. Melograni. Naples: Edizioni Scientifiche Italiane, 1991. 2: 133–49.
Baronti Marchiò, Roberto. *Il futurismo in Inghilterra: tra avanguardia e classicismo*. Rome: Bulzoni, 1990.
Barthes, Roland. *Mythologies*. Trans. Annette Laveers. New York: Farrar, Straus & Giroux, 1972.
– 'The Reality Effect.' *The Rustle of Language*. Trans. Richard Howard. New York: Hill & Wang, 1986. 141–8.
Battaglia, Salvatore. *Grande dizionario della lingua italiana*. Turin: UTET, 1960–
Battisti, Carlo, and Giovanni Alessio. *Dizionario etimologico italiano*. 5 vols. Florence: Barbèra, 1952.

Baudelaire, Charles. *The Flowers of Evil*. Trans. James McGowan. Oxford: Oxford University Press, 1993.
– *Intimate Journals*. Trans. Christopher Isherwood. London: Black Spring Press, 1989.
– *Œuvres complètes*. Ed. Claude Pichois. 2 vols. Paris: Gallimard, 1975–6.
– 'The Painter of Modern Life.' *Selected Writings on Art and Literature*. Trans. P. E. Charvet. London: Penguin, 1992. 390–435.
– *The Parisian Prowler. Le spleen de Paris. Petits poèmes en prose*. Trans. Edward K. Kaplan. Athens: University of Georgia Press, 1989.
Bell, Ian. *Critic as Scientist: The Modernist Poetics of Ezra Pound*. London: Methuen, 1981.
Benedetti, Carla. *Il tradimento dei critici*. Turin: Bollati Boringhieri, 2002.
Benjamin, Walter. *Charles Baudelaire: A Lyric Poet in the Era of High Capitalism*. Trans. Harry Zohn. London, NLB, 1973.
– *The Origin of German Tragic Drama*. Trans. John Osborne. London: NLB, 1977.
– 'The Work of Art in the Age of Its Mechanical Reproduction.' *Illuminations*. Trans. Harry Zohn. New York: Shocken Books, 1968. 217–52.
Benstock, Shari. *Women of the Left Bank: Paris, 1900–1940*. Austin: University of Texas Press, 1986.
Berghaus, Günter. *The Genesis of Futurism: Marinetti's Early Career and Writings 1899–1909*. Leeds: Society for Italian Studies, 1995.
– *Italian Futurist Theatre, 1909–1944*. Oxford and New York: Clarendon Press, 1997.
Bergman, Pär. *'Modernolatria' et 'simultaneità': recherches sur deux tendances dans l'avant-garde littéraire en Italie et en France à la veille de al première guerre mondiale*. Stockholm: Bonnie, 1962.
Berman, Marshall. *All That Is Solid Melts into Air: The Experience of Modernity*. New York: Viking Penguin, 1988.
Bianchi, Ruggero. 'Imagismo.' Cianci: *Modernismo/Modernismi*, 113–26.
Bianquis, Geneviève. *Nietzsche en France. L'influence de Nietzsche sur la pensée française*. Paris: Librairie Félix Alcan, 1929.
Binni, Walter. *La poetica del decadentismo*. 1936. Florence: Sansoni, 1988.
Blum, Cinzia Sartini. *The Other Modernism: F. T. Marinetti's Futurist Fiction of Power*. Los Angeles: University of California Press, 1996.
Boccioni, Umberto. *Gli scritti editi e inediti*. Edited Zeno Birolli. Milan: Feltrinelli, 1971.
Boccioni, Umberto, Carlo Carrà, Luigi Russolo, Giacomo Balla, and Gino Severini. 'The Exhibitors to the Public.' *Exhibition of Works by the Italian Futurist Painters*. London: The Sackville Gallery, 1912. 9–19.
– 'La pittura futurista. Manifesto tecnico.' *Marinetti e i futuristi*. Ed. Luciano De Maria. Milan: Garzanti, 1994. 23–6

– 'Prefazione al Catalogo delle Esposizioni di Parigi, Londra, Berlino, Bruxelles, Monaco, Amburgo, Vienna, ecc.' *Marinetti e i futuristi*. Ed. Luciano De Maria. Milan: Garzanti, 1994. 59–66.

Bosworth, R.J.B. *Italy, the Least of the Great Powers: Italian Foreign Policy before the First World War*. Cambridge and NewYork: Cambridge University Press, 1979.

Bourdieu, Pierre. *The Field of Cultural Production*. Ed. Randal Johnson. New York: Columbia University Press, 1993.

Bourget, Paul. *Essais de psychologie contemporaine: études littéraires*. Ed. André Guyaux. Paris: Gallimard, 1993.

Bradbury, Malcolm, and James McFarlane, eds. *Modernism*. Harmondsworth: Penguin, 1976.

Briosi, Sandro. *Marinetti e il futurismo*. Lecce: Milella, 1986.

Bürger, Peter. *Theory of the Avant-Garde*. Trans. Michael Shaw. Minneapolis: University of Minnesota Press, 1984.

Calinescu, Matei. *Five Faces of Modernity: Modernism, Avant-Garde, Decadence, Kitsch, Postmodernism*. Durham: Duke University Press, 1987.

Calvesi, Maurizio. 'Il manifesto del futurismo e i pittori futuristi.' *L'arte moderna* 5: 37 (1967): 1–32.

Caruso, Luciano. *Manifesti, proclami, interventi, e documenti teorici del futurismo, 1909–1944*. 4 vols. Florence: Coedizioni SPES-Salimbeni, 1980.

Caruso, Rossella. 'La mostra dei futuristi a Londra nel 1912: recensioni e commenti.' *Ricerche di storia dell'arte* 45 (1991): 57–64.

Caws, Mary Ann. 'The Poetics of the Manifesto. Nowness and Newness.' Introduction. *Manifesto: A Century of Isms*. Ed. Caws. Lincoln: University of Nebraska Press, 2001. xix–xxxi.

Ceserani, Gian Paolo. *Storia della pubblicità in Italia*. Roma: Laterza, 1988.

Charle, Christophe. *La crise littéraire à l'époque du naturalisme: roman, théâtre et politique: essai d'histoire sociale des groupes et des genres littéraires*. Paris: Presses de l'École normale supérieure, 1979.

– *Naissance des 'intellectuels' 1880–1900*. Paris: Minuit, 1990.

– *Social History of France in the Nineteenth Century*. Trans. Miriam Kochan. Oxford and Providence, RI: Berg, 1994.

Childs, Peter. *Modernism*. London and New York: Routledge, 2000.

Chouinard, Daniel. 'Sur la préhistorie du manifeste littéraire (1550–1828).' *Études Françaises* 16.3–4 (1980): 21–29.

Ciampi, Alberto. *Futuristi e anarchici – quali rapporti? Dal primo manifesto alla prima guerra mondiale e dintorni (1909–1917)*. Pistoia: Archivio Famiglia Bernieri, 1989.

Cianci, Giovanni. 'La catalizzazione futurista: la poetica del vorticismo.' Cianci: *Modernismo/Modernismi*, 156–74.

– 'Futurism and the English Avant-Garde: The Early Pound between Imagism and Vorticism.' *AAA. Arbeiten aus Anglistik und Amerikanistik* 6.1 (1981): 3–39.
– 'Modernismo/Modernismi.' Cianci: *Modernismo/Modernismi*, 15–45.
Cianci, Giovanni, ed. *Modernismo/Modernismi: dall'avanguardia storica agli anni trenta e oltre*. Milan: Principato, 1991.
Cohen, Milton A. 'The Futurist Exhibition of 1912: A Model of Prewar Modernism.' *European Studies Journal* 12.2 (1995): 1–32.
Collins Baker, C.H. 'Futurist Academics.' *The Saturday Review* 9 March 1912: 300–1.
Coffman, Stanley K. *Imagism: A Chapter for the History of Modern Poetry*. New York: Octagon Books, 1972.
'The Confetti School of Painting.' *The Daily Sketch* 17 October 1913: 6.
Cork, Richard. *Vorticism and Abstract Art in the First Machine Age*. 2 vols. Berkeley and Los Angeles: University of California Press, 1976.
Corra, Bruno, and Emilio Settimelli. *Pesi, misure e prezzi del genio artistico. Manifesto futurista*. Milano: Direzione del movimento futurista, 1914. Rpt. Caruso: *Manifesti, proclami, interventi*, I: item 60.
Cortelazzo, Manlio, and Paolo Zolli. *Dizionario etimologico della lingua italiana*. 5 vols. Bologna: Zanichelli, 1979–1988.
Cotgrave, Randle. *A Dictionarie of the French and English Tongues*.1611. Menston: Scholar Press, 1968.
Crawford, Elizabeth. *The Women's Suffrage Movement: A Reference Guide 1866–1928*. London: UCL Press, 1999.
Curi, Fausto. *Perdita d'aureola*. Torino: Einaudi, 1977.
– *Tra mimesi e metafora. Studi su Marinetti e il futurismo*. Bologna: Pendragon, 1995.
D'Acierno, Pellegrino. 'The Manifesto as Text.' *Comparative Literary History as Discourse: In Honor of Anna Balakian*. Ed. Mario J. Valdés, Daniel Javitch, and A. Owen Aldridge. Bern: Peter Lang, 1992. 305–16.
D'Annunzio, Gabriele. *Il piacere*. 1889. *Prose di romanzi*. Ed. Annamaria Andreoli. Milan: Mondadori, 1988. 1: 3–358.
Dasenbrock, Reed Way. *The Literary Vorticism of Ezra Pound and Wyndham Lewis: Towards the Condition of Painting*. Baltimore: Johns Hopkins University Press, 1985.
Datta, Venita. *Birth of a National Icon: The Literary Avant-Garde and the Origins of the Intellectual in France*. Albany: State University of New York Press, 1999.
Day, Patrick L. *Saint-Georges de Bouhélier's* Naturisme: *An Anti-Symbolist Movement in Late-Nineteenth-Century French Poetry*. New York: Peter Lang, 2001.
Décaudin, Michel. *La crise des valeurs symbolistes*. Toulouse: Privat, 1960.
– 'Définir la décadence.' *L'esprit de décadence*. Paris: Minard, 1980. 5–12.
A Declaration Sent to the King of France and Spayne from the Catholiques or Rebells

in Ireland: With a Manifesto of the Covenant or Oath [...]. Paris, 24 April 1642. Trans. R. C. Gene. London, 1642.

De Felice, Renzo, ed. *Futurismo, cultura e politica*. Turin: Fondazione Giovanni Agnelli, 1988.

De Maria, Luciano. 'Marinetti poeta e ideologo.' Introduction. Marinetti: *Teoria e invenzione futurista*, xxix–c.

– 'Una panoramica del futurismo italiano.' Introduction. *Marinetti e i futuristi*. Ed. De Maria. 2nd ed. Milan: Garzanti, 1994. vii–xlii.

– 'Il ruolo di Marinetti nella costruzione del futurismo.' De Felice: *Futurismo, cultura e politica*. 33–47

De Maria, Luciano, ed. *Marinetti e i futuristi*. Milan: Garzanti, 1994.

Demers, Jeanne. 'Entre l'art poétique et le poème: le manifeste poétique ou la mort du père.' *Études Françaises* 16.3–4 (1980): 3–20.

Demers, Jeanne, and Line McMurray. *L'enjeu du manifeste/Le manifeste en jeu*. Québec: Préambule, 1986.

Derrida, Jacques. 'Declarations of Independence.' Trans. Tom Keenan and Tom Pepper. *New Political Science* 15 (1986): 7–15.

– *Of Grammatology*. Trans. Gayatri Chakravorty Spivak. Baltimore: Johns Hopkins University Press, 1974.

Descaves, Lucien. *Sous-offs en cour d'assises*. Paris: Tresse & Stock, 1890.

Desonay, Fernand. 'Les manifestes littéraires du XVIe siècle, en France.' *Bibliothèque d'humanisme et renaissance* 14 (1952): 250–65.

De Villers, Jean-Pierre. *Le premier manifeste du futurisme. Édition critique avec, en fac-similé, le manuscript original de F. T. Marinetti*. Ottawa: Éditions de l'Université d'Ottawa, 1986.

– 'Ancora sul manifesto.' *Futurismo oggi* 20.1–4 (1998): 3–5.

Digeon, Claude. *La crise allemande de la pensée française (1870–1914)*. Paris: Presses universitaires de France, 1959.

Dondi, Laura. 'Dal «secondo futurismo fiorentino» del periodo eroico al «secondo futurismo».' De Maria: *Marinetti e i futuristi*, xliii–liv.

Drucker, Johanna. *Theorizing Modernism: Visual Art and the Critical Tradition*. New York: Columbia University Press, 1994.

Drudi Gambillo, Maria, and Teresa Fiori, eds. *Archivi del futurismo*. 2 vols. Roma: De Luca, 1958.

Eagleton, Terry. *The Ideology of the Aesthetic*. Cambridge, MA: Basil Blackwell, 1990.

Eco, Umberto. *Lector in fabula: La cooperazione interpretativa nei testi narrativi*. 1979. Milan: Bompiani, 1985.

– *The Limits of Interpretation*. Bloomington: Indiana University Press, 1990.

Eguizábal Maza, Raúl. *Historia de la publicidad*. Madrid: Editorial Ersema & Celeste Ediciones, 1998.

Eliot, T.S. 'Tradition and the Individual Talent.' *The Sacred Wood: Essays on Poetry and Criticism*. 1920. London: Methuen, 1950. 47–59.
Encyclopedie ou dictionnaire raisonné des sciences, des arts et des mestiers. Paris: Briasson et al., 1757.
Eruli, Brunella. 'Bibliografia delle opere di F.T. Marinetti (1898–1909).' *La rassegna della letteratura italiana* 72 (1968): 368–88.
E.S.G. 'Is It Art? – the Foibles of Futurism.' *The Graphic* 9 March 1912: 339.
Eysteinsson, Astradur. *The Concept of Modernism*. Ithaca: Cornell University Press, 1990.
Fael, Ariella. 'Pubblicità e manifesti del futurismo: aspetti tecnici nuovi e problemi politici.' *Il futurismo: aspetti e problemi*. Ed. Romain H. Rainero. Milan Cisalpino, 1993. 147–73.
Falkenheim, Jacqueline V. *Roger Fry and the Beginnings of Formalist Art Criticism*. Ann Arbor: UMI Research Press, 1980.
Fazio, Domenico M. *Il caso Nietzsche: La cultura italiana di fronte a Nietzsche 1872–1940*. Settimo Milanese: Marzorati, 1988.
Ferdinand III. *A Declaration or Manifesto Wherein the Roman Imperiall Majesty makes known to the States and Peers of Hungarie, what reasons and motives have compelled him to proceed in open Warre against the Prince of Transylvania*. N.p: Blackmore, 1644.
Flint, F.S. 'Contemporary French Poetry.' 1912. *The Road from Paris: French Influence on English Poetry 1900–1920*. Cambridge: Cambridge University Press, 1974. 86–145.
Foucault, Michel. 'What Is an Author?' *Language, Counter-Memory, Practice: Selected Essays and Interviews*. Trans. Donald F. Bouchard and Sherry Simon. Ithaca: Cornell University Press, 1977. 113–38.
Fournier, Vincent. 'Manifestes littéraires.' *La grande encyclopedie*. Paris: Librairie Larousse, 1974. 12: 7570.
France, Anatole. 'Examen du Manifeste.' Moréas. *Les premières armés du symbolisme*, 45–55.
Fry, Roger. 'The Futurists.' *The Nation* 2 March 1912: 945–6.
Furetière, Antoine. *Le dictionaire universel*. 1690. Paris: SNL – Le Robert, 1978.
'Futurism.' *The Art Chronicle* 5 April 1912: 242.
'Le Futurisme et la presse internationale.' *Poesia* 3–6 (1909): 12–34.
'The Futurists.' *The Times* 1 March 1912: 11.
Genette, Gerard. *Paratexts: Thresholds of Interpretation*. Trans. Jane E. Lewin. Cambridge: Cambridge University Press, 1997.
Gentile, Emilio. 'Il futurismo e la politica. Dal nazionalismo modernista al fascismo (1909–1920).' De Felice: *Futurismo, cultura e politica* 105–59.
Gioanola, Elio. *Il decadentismo*. Rome: Studium 1972.

Gioè, Valerio. 'Futurism in England: A Bibliography (1910–1915).' *Bulletin of Bibliography* 44.3 (1987): 172–188.

– 'Il futurismo in Inghilterra: bibliografia (1910–1915) – supplemento.' *Quaderno* 16 (1982): 76–83.

Giovannetti, Paolo. *Decadentismo*. Milan: Editrice Bibliografica, 1994.

Girtin, Tom. *The Abominable Clubman*. London: Hutchinson, 1964.

Giusti, Simone. *L'instaurazione del poemetto in prosa (1879–1898)*. Lecce: Pensa MultiMedia, 1999.

Gleize, Jean-Marie. 'Manifestes, préfaces: sur quelques aspects du prescriptif.' *Littérature* 39 (1980): 12–16.

Goldring, Douglas. 'Futurism.' *The Tramp* (August 1910): 487–8.

– *South Lodge. Reminiscences of Violet Hunt, Ford Madox Ford and the English Review Circle*. London: Constable , 1943.

Grana, Gianni. 'Scienza e letteratura di avanguardia: il futurismo.' *Rivista di studi italiani* 8.1–2 (1989): 1–14.

Grand dictionnaire de l'Académie françoise. 1694. Geneve: Slatkine, 1968.

Guglielmi, Guido. *La parola del testo. Letteratura come storia*. Bologna: Il Mulino, 1993.

Hassan, Ihab. 'POSTmodernISM. A Paracritical Bibliography.' *New Literary History* 3.1 (1971): 5–30.

H.D. *End to Torment: A Memoir of Ezra Pound*. Ed. Norman Holmes Pearson and Michael King. New York: New Directions, 1979.

Heimpel, Rod S. *Généalogie du manifeste littéraire*. New Orleans: University Press of the South, 2001.

Hewitt, Andrew. *Fascist Modernism: Aesthetics, Politics, and the Avant-Garde*. Stanford: Stanford University Press, 1993.

Horkheimer, Max, and Theodor W. Adorno. *Dialectic of Enlightenment*. Trans. John Cumming. New York: Continuum, 1988.

Hulten, Pontus, ed. *Futurism & Futurisms*. London: Thames and Hudson, 1986.

Huret, Jules. *Enquête sur l'évolution littéraire*. 1891. Ed. Daniel Grojnowski. Paris: J. Corti, 1999.

Hustvedt, Asti. 'The Art of Death: French Fiction at the Fin de Siècle.' *The Decadent Reader: Fiction, Fantasy, and Perversion from Fin-de-siècle France*. Ed. Hustvedt. New York: Zone, 1998. 10–29.

Huysmans, J.-K. *À rebours*. Vol. 7 of *Œuvres complètes de J.-K. Huysmans*. Paris: Crès, 1929.

– *Against the Grain*. New York: Dover, 1969.

Huyssen, Andreas. *After the Great Divide: Modernism, Mass Culture, Postmodernism*. Bloomington: Indiana University Press, 1986.

Jakobson, Roman. 'The Speech Event and the Functions of Language.' *On Lan-*

guage. Ed. Linda R. Waugh and Monique Monville-Burston. Cambridge: Harvard University Press, 1990. 69–79.

Jameson, Fredric. Foreword. Lyotard: *The Post-Modern Condition*. vii–xxi.

Jannini, Pasquale. 'Note e documenti sulla fortuna del Futurismo in Francia.' *La fortuna del futurismo in Francia*. Rome: Bulzoni, 1979. 1–104.

Jauss, Hans Robert. 'Literary History as a Challenge to Literary Theory.' *Towards an Aesthetic of Reception*. Trans. Timothy Bahti. Minneapolis: University of Minnesota Press, 1982. 3–45.

Jonard, Norbert. 'Alle origini del Decadentismo. Il termine e il significato.' *Problemi* 59 (1980): 196–220.

Jouve, Séverine. *Les décadents: bréviaire fin de siècle*. Paris: Plon, 1989.

Karl, Frederick Robert. *Modern and Modernism: The Sovereignty of the Artist, 1885–1925*. New York: Atheneum, 1985.

Kayman, Martin. *The Modernism of Ezra Pound: The Science of Poetry*. London: Macmillan, 1986.

Kern, Stephen. *The Culture of Time and Space 1880–1918*. Cambridge: Harvard University Press, 1983.

Klein, Richard. '"Benediction"/"Perte d'aureole": Parables of Interpretation.' *MLN* 85 (1970): 515–28.

Konody, P.G. 'Futurism the Latest Art Sensation.' *The Illustrated London News* 17 February 1912: 225.

– 'The Italian Futurists.' *Pall Mall Gazette* 1 March 1912: 5.

Korn, Marianne. *Ezra Pound: Purpose / Form / Meaning*. London: Pembridge Press, 1983.

Krysinski, Wladimir. 'Une automobile, une mitraillette, un gifle et un singe crevé: Marinetti et ses avatars slaves.' *Études françaises* 16.3–4 (1980): 79–103.

Kyburz, Mark. *'Voi altri pochi': Ezra Pound and His Audience, 1908–1925*. Basel, Boston, and Berlin: Birkhäuser, 1996.

Laplanche, Jean, and Jean-Bertrand Pontalis. *Enciclopedia della psicoanalisi*. 2 vols. Trans. Luciano Mecacci and Cynthia Puca. Roma and Bari: Laterza, 1993.

La Monica, Giuseppe. '«Il tempo e lo spazio morirono ieri».' *Il futurismo*. Ed. Maurizio Calvesi. Milan: Fabbri, 1976. 48–9.

The Late King James's Manifesto Answer'd. London: Richard Baldwin, 1697.

The Late King James's Second Manifesto, Directed to the Protestant Princes, Answered Paragraph by Paragraph. London: Richard Baldwin, 1697.

Lawton, Anna. Introduction. *Russian Futurism through Its Manifestoes, 1912–1928*. Ed. Lawton. Ithaca and London: Cornell University Press, 1988. 1–48.

Lawton, Anna Maltese. 'Marinetti in Inghilterra: scritti inediti.' *Il verri* 5th series; v. 10 (1975): 138–49.

Le Cardonnel, Georges, and Charles Vellay. *La littérature contemporaine, 1905. Opinions des écrivains de ce temps, accompagnées d'un index des noms cités*. Paris: Société du Mercure de France, 1905.

Le Goff, Jacques. 'Decadenza.' *Enciclopedia*. Turin: Einaudi, 1978. 4: 389–420.

Le Rider, Jacques. *Nietzsche en France: de la fin du XIXe siecle au temps present*. Paris: Presses Universitaires de France, 1999.

Leroy, Géraldi, and Julie Bertrand-Sabiani. *La vie littéraire à la Belle Epoque*. Paris: Presses universitaires de France, 1998.

Levenson, Michael H. *A Genealogy of Modernism: A Study of English Literary Doctrine 1908–1922*. Cambridge: Cambridge University Press, 1984.

Levenson, Michael, ed. *The Cambridge Companion to Modernism*. Cambridge and New York: Cambridge University Press, 1999.

Lewis, Wyndham. 'The Cubist Room.' *Wyndham Lewis on Art: Collected Writings 1913–1956*. Ed. Walter Michel and C. J. Fox. New York: Funk & Wagnalls, 1969. 56–7.

– 'Futurism, Magic and Life.' *Blast* 1 (1914): 132–5.

– 'Long Live the Vortex!' *Blast* 1 (1914): 7–8.

– 'A Man of the Week. Marinetti.' *Creatures of Habit and Creatures of Change: Essays on Art, Literature and Society 1914–1956*. Ed. Paul Edwards. Santa Rosa, CA: Black Sparrow Press, 1989. 29–32.

– 'The Melodrama of Modernity.' *Blast* 1 (1914): 143–4.

– 'Our Vortex.' *Blast* 1 (1914): 147–9.

– *Tarr: The 1918 Version*. Ed. Paul O'Keeffe. Santa Rosa, CA: Black Sparrow Press, 1990.

– *Time and Western Man*. Ed. Paul Edwards. Santa Rosa, CA: Black Sparrow Press, 1993.

Lista, Giovanni. 'Marinetti et les anarcho-syndacalistes.' *Présence de F.T. Marinetti*. Ed. Jean-Claude Marcadé. Lausanne: L'Age d'homme, 1982. 67–85.

– *F.T. Marinetti: l'anarchiste du futurisme*. Paris: Séguier, 1995.

Lista, Giovanni, ed. *Futurisme: manifestes – proclamations – documents*. Lausanne: L'Age d'Homme, 1973.

Longenbach, James. *Stone Cottage. Pound, Yeats, and Modernism*. New York: Oxford University Press, 1988.

Louis XVIII. *Grande Declaration du Roi, adressée a tous les Français, ou, Réponse de Sà Majeste au Manifeste des Princes*. Limodin: Imprimeur de la section de Lombards, [1791?].

Luperini, Romano. *L'allegoria del moderno: saggi sull'allegorismo come forma artistica del moderno e come metodo di conoscenza*. Roma: Editori Riuniti, 1990.

The Lyceum Club, London. A Social and Residential Club for Women. N.p. [Westminster?]: n.p, 1903.

Lyon, Janet. *Manifestoes: Provocations of the Modern*. Ithaca: Cornell University Press, 1999.

Lyotard, Jean-François. *The Postmodern Condition: A Report on Knowledge*. Trans. Geoff Bennington and Brian Massumi. Oxford: Manchester University Press, 1984.

Maas, William. 'Pictures on Strike. Art and Anarchy in Sackville Street.' *Daily Chronicle* 9 March 1912: 6.

Mack Smith, Denis. *Modern Italy: A Political History*. Ann Arbor: University of Michigan Press, 1997.

Mallarmé, Stephane. 'Crise de verse.' *Œuvres complètes*. Ed. Henri Mondor and G. Jean-Aubry, Paris: Gallimard, 1945. 360–8. Trans. by Rosemary Lloyd. *Mallarmé: The Poet and His Circle*. Ithaca: Cornell University Press, 1999. 227–33.

Manghetti, Gloria, ed. *Futurismo a Firenze 1910–1920*. Verona: Bi & Gi editori, 1984.

'The Manifesto of Near 150 Knights, and Eminent Merchants and Citizens of London, Against the Jews now in England.' London [?]: n.p., 1689.

A Manifesto or Declaration Set Forth by the Undertakers of the New Church. Boston: n.p., 1699.

Marchal, Bertrand. *Lire le symbolisme*. Paris: Dunod, 1993.

Marechal, Sylvain. 'Manifeste des égaux.' *Histoire de Gracchus Babeuf et du Babouvisme*. Ed. Victor Advielle. Genève: Slatkine Reprints, 1978. 1: 197–201. Ed. and trans. John Anthony Scott. *The Defense of Gracchus Babeuf Before the High Court of Vendome*. [Amherst]: University of Massachusetts Press, 1967. 91–5.

Mariani, Gaetano. *Il primo Marinetti*. Florence: Le Monnier, 1970.

Marinetti, Filippo Tommaso. *Collaudi futuristi*. Ed. Glauco Viazzi. Naples: Guida, 1977.

– *Le Futurisme*. 1911. Ed. Giovanni Lista. Lausanne: Âge d'homme, 1980.

– 'Mascagni contre Wagner.' *La plume* 283 (1901): 127–128.

– *La grande Milano tradizionale e futurista. Una sensibilità italiana nata in Egitto*. Ed. Luciano De Maria. Milan: Mondadori, 1969.

– 'Vittorio Pica.' *Anthologie-Revue de France et d'Italie* 2.7 (1898): 129–32.

– *Scritti francesi*. Ed. Pasquale A. Jannini. Milan: Mondadori, 1983.

– *Teoria e invenzione futurista*. Ed. Luciano De Maria. Milan: Mondadori, 1968.

Marino, Adrian. 'Le manifeste.' *Les avant-gardes littèraires au XXe siècle*. Ed. Jean Weisberger. Budapest: Akadémiai Kiadó, 1984. 825–34.

Marquèze-Pouey, Louis. *Le mouvement décadent en France*. Paris: Presses universitaires de France, 1986.

Martin, Wallace. '"The Forgotten School of 1909" and the Origins of Imagism.' *A Catalogue of the Imagist Poets*. New York: J. Howard Woolmer, 1966. 7–38.

Marx, Karl and Friedrich Engels. *Manifesto of the Communist Party*. 1848. *The Marx-Engels Reader*. Ed. Robert C. Tucker. 2nd ed. New York: Norton, 1978. 469–500.

Mascagni, Pietro. *Mascagni parla: appunti per le memorie di un grande musicista*. Ed. Salvatore de Carlo. Milan: De Carlo, 1945.

– *Mascagni: An Autobiography*. Ed. David Stivender. White Plains: Pro/Am Music Resources; London: Kahn & Averill, 1988.

Materer, Timothy. 'Pound's Vortex.' *Paideuma* 6.2 (1977) 175–6.

– *Vortex: Pound, Eliot, and Lewis*. Ithaca: Cornell University Press, 1979.

McDougal, Stuart Y. *Ezra Pound and the Troubadour Tradition*. Princeton: Princeton University Press, 1972.

Meltzer, Françoise. '*Fatal Attraction* Redux: "La Faënza."' *The Decadent Reader: Fiction, Fantasy, and Perversion from Fin-de-siècle France*. Ed. Asti Hustvedt. New York: Zone, 1998. 752–64.

Meyer, Alain. 'Le manifeste politique: modèle pur ou pratique impure?' *Littérature* 39 (1980): 29–38.

Meyers, Jeffrey. *The Enemy: A Biography of Wyndham Lewis*. London: Routledge & Kegan Paul, 1980.

Mézeray, François-Eudes de. *Abregé chronologique de l'histoire de France*. Vol. 3. Amsterdam: D. Mortier, 1740.

Michaud, Guy. *Message poétique du symbolisme*. Paris: Nizet, 1947.

Middleton, Christopher. 'Documents on Imagism from the Papers of F. S. Flint.' *The Review* 15 (1965): 31–51.

Mitchell, Bonner. *Les manifestes littéraires de la Belle Époque, 1886–1914: Anthologie critique*. Paris: Seghers, 1966.

Monroe, Harriet. '[The Audience] II.' *Poetry* (October 1914): 31–2.

Moréas, Jean. *Les premières armes du symbolisme*. Ed. Michael Pakenham. Exeter: University of Exeter, 1973.

Morini, Mario, ed. *Pietro Mascagni*. 2 vols. Milan: Casa Editrice Musicale Sonzogno, 1964.

Moroni, Mario. 'Sensuous Maladies: The Construction of Italian Decadentism.' *Italian Modernism*. Ed. Luca Somigli and Mario Moroni. Toronto: University of Toronto Press, forthcoming.

Nazzaro, Gian Battista. *Futurismo e politica*. Napoli: JN Editore, 1987.

– *Introduzione al futurismo*. Naples: Guida, 1984.

Nevinson, Margaret Wynne [?]. 'Futurism and Woman.' *The Vote* 31 December 1910. 112.

'The New Crazy "Exploding" Pictures by "Art Anarchists."' March 1912. Hulten: *Futurism & Futurisms*, 572.

Nietzsche, Friedrich. *The Case of Wagner.* Trans. Walter Kaufmann. *The Birth of Tragedy and The Case of Wagner.* New York: Vintage, 1967. 145–92.

– *Il Caso Wagner.* Italian trans. Ferruccio Masini. *Opere di Friedrich Nietzsche.* Ed. Giorgio Colli and Mazzino Montinari. Vol. 6, tome 3. Milan: Adelphi, 1970. 3–50; 472–87.

– *Ecce Homo.* Trans. Walter Kaufmann. *On the Genealogy of Morals and Ecce Homo.* New York: Vintage, 1967. 199–335.

– *Thus Spoke Zarathustra.* Trans. Walter Kaufmann. *The Portable Nietzsche.* Harmondsworth: Penguin, 1954. 112–439.

– *On the Uses and Disadvantages of History for Life.* 1874. *Untimely Meditations.* Trans. R.J. Hollingdale. Cambridge: Cambridge University Press, 1983. 57–123.

Nicot, Jean. *Thresor de la langve francoise tant ancienne que moderne.* 1606. Paris: Picard, 1960.

Novelli, Novella. 'Contributo a una bibliografia della fortuna del Futurismo in Francia (1909–1920).' *La fortuna del futurismo in Francia.* Rome: Bulzoni, 1979. 205–69.

O'Keeffe, Paul. *Some Sort of Genius: A Life of Wyndham Lewis.* London: Jonathan Cape, 2000.

Oliver, Hermia. *The International Anarchist Movement in Late Victorian England.* London: Croom Helm, 1983.

Orban, Clara Elizabeth. *The Culture of Fragments: Word and Images in Futurism and Surrealism.* Amsterdam and Atlanta: Rodopi, 1997.

Palazzeschi, Aldo. *L'incendiario.* 1910. Ed. Giuseppe Nicoletti. Milan: Mondadori, 2001.

– 'Marinetti e il futurismo.' Marinetti: *Teoria e invenzione futurista*, xv–xxvi.

Palmer, Roger. *The Earl of Castlemain's Manifesto.* N.p.: n.p., 1681.

Pakenham, Michael. Presentation. Moréas: *Les prèmieres armés du symbolisme*, v–xxviii.

Papini, Giovanni. 'Contro il futurismo.' *Lacerba* 1.6 (1913): 1–4.

– *L'esperienza futurista, 1913–1914.* 1919. Florence: Vallecchi, 1981.

Papini, Giovanni [as Gian Falco]. 'Campagna per il forzato risveglio.' 1906. *La cultura italiana del '900 attraverso le riviste. 'Leonardo' 'Hermes' 'Il Regno.'* Ed. Delia Castelnuovo Frigessi. Turin: Einaudi, 1960. 1: 312–316.

Papini, Maria Carla, ed. *L'Italia futurista (1916–1918).* Rome: Edizioni dell'Ateneo & Bizzarri, 1977.

Peer, Larry, ed. *The Romantic Manifesto: An Anthology.* New York: Peter Lang, 1988.

Pelletier, Anne-Marie. 'Le paradoxe institutionnel du manifeste.' *Littérature* 39 (1980): 17–22.

Peppis, Paul. *Literature, Politics, and the English Avant-Garde: Nation and Empire, 1901–1918*. Cambridge and New York: Cambridge University Press, 2000.

Perloff, Marjorie. *The Futurist Moment: Avant-Garde, Avant Guerre, and the Language of Rupture*. Chicago and London: University of Chicago Press, 1986.

Phillips, Claude. 'Italian Futurist Painters.' *The Daily Telegraph* 2 March 1912: 9

Picoche, Jacqueline. *Dictionnaire etymologique du Français*. Paris: Robert, 1979.

Pierrot, Jean. *The Decadent Imagination, 1880–1900*. Trans. Derek Coltman. Chicago: University of Chicago Press, 1981.

Pinkney, David H. *Decisive Years in France, 1840–1847*. Princeton: Princeton University Press, 1986.

Poggi, Christine. 'Dreams of Metallized Flesh: Futurism and the Masculine Body.' *Modernism / Modernity* 4:3 (1997): 19–43.

– 'Futurism and the Crowd.' *Critical Inquiry*, 28.3 (2002): 709–48.

Poggioli, Renato. *The Theory of the Avant-Garde*. Trans. Gerald Fitzgerald. Cambridge: Harvard University Press, 1968.

Pondrom, Cyrena N. 'H.D. and the Origins of Imagism.' *Sagetrieb* 4.1 (1985): 73–97.

Porter, Laurence M. *The Crisis of French Symbolism*. Ithaca: Cornell University Press, 1990.

Pound, Ezra. *Ezra Pound's Poetry and Prose: Contributions to Periodicals. Volume I, 1902–1914*. Ed. Lea Baechler, A. Walton Litz, and James Longenbach. New York and London: Garland, 1991.

– *Gaudier-Brzeska: A Memoir*. London: Marvell Press, 1960.

– *Literary Essays*. Ed. T.S. Eliot. New York: New Directions,1954.

– *Ripostes of Ezra Pound: Whereto Are Appended the Complete Poetical Works of T.E. Hulme*. 1912. London: Elkin Matthews, 1915.

– *Selected Letters of Ezra Pound. 1907–1941*. Ed. D.D. Paige. New York: New Directions, 1972.

– 'Vortex Pound.' *Blast* 1 (1914): 153–4.

Praz, Mario. 'Decadentismo.' *Enciclopedia del novecento*. Milan: Istituto dell'Enciclopedia Italiana, 1977. 2: 10–23.

– *The Romantic Agony*. Trans. Angus Davidson. London: Oxford University Press, 1970.

Quail, John. *The Slow Burning Fuse*. London: Paladin, 1978.

Racokzkie, George, Prince of Transylvania. *The Declaration or Manifesto of George Racokzkie, Prince of Transylvania, to the States and Peeres of Hvngarie*. London: Edward Blackmore, 1644.

Rainey, Lawrence S. *Institutions of Modernism: Literary Elites and Public Culture.* New Haven: Yale University Press, 1998.

Raynaud, Ernest. *La mêlée symboliste (1870–1890): portraits et souvenirs.* Paris: La Renaissance du livre, 1918.

– *La mêlée symboliste (1890–1900): portraits et souvenirs.* Paris: La Renaissance du livre, 1920.

Richard, Noël. *Le mouvement décadent: dandys, esthètes et quintessentes.* Paris: Nizet, 1968.

Richelet, Pierre. *Dictionnaire françois, tiré de l'usage et des meilleurs auteurs de la langue.* 1679. Geneva: Slatkine, 1970.

Romani, Bruno. *Dal simbolismo al futurismo.* Florence: Sandron, 1969.

Russell, Charles. *Poets, Prophets and Revolutionaries: The Literary Avant-Garde from Rimbaud to Postmodernism.* New York: Oxford University Press, 1985.

Saccone, Antonio. *'La trincea avanzata' e 'La città dei conquistatori.' Futurismo e modernità.* Naples: Liguori, 2000.

Salaris, Claudia. *Dizionario del futurismo. Idee provocazioni e parole d'ordine di una grande avanguardia.* Rome: Riuniti, 1996.

– *Filippo Tommaso Marinetti.* Scandicci: La Nuova Italia, 1988.

– *Il Futurismo e la pubblicità. Dalla pubblicità dell' arte all'arte della pubblicità.* Milan: Lupetti, 1986.

– 'Manifesto tecnico della letteratura futurista.' *Il Novecento. I. L'età della crisi.* Turin: Einaudi, 1995. Vol. 4, tome 1 of *Letteratura italiana. Le opere.* Ed. Alberto Asor Rosa. 177–209.

– *Marinetti. Arte e vita futurista.* Rome: Editori Riuniti, 1997.

Saulnier, Verdun L. *Du Bellay.* Paris: Hatier, 1968.

Savinio, Alberto. *Dico a te, Clio.* Milan: Adelphi, 1992.

Schnapp, Jeffrey. 'Politics and Poetics in Marinetti's *Zang Tumb Tuuum.*' *Stanford Italian Review* 5.1 (1985): 75–92.

Schultz, Joachim. *Literarisch Manifeste der 'Belle Epoque' Frankreich 1886–1909.* Frankfurt am Main and Bern: Peter Lang, 1981.

Schwartz, Sanford. 'The Postmodernity of Modernism.' *The Future of Modernism.* Ed. Hugh Witemeyer. Ann Arbor: University of Michigan Press, 1997. 9–31.

Schwarz, Daniel R. *Reconfiguring Modernism: Explorations in the Relationship between Modern Art and Modern Literature.* New York: St Martin's Press, 1997.

Scrivano, Riccardo. *Il decadentismo e la critica.* Florence: La Nuova Italia, 1963.

Severini, Gino. 'Get Inside the Picture. Futurism as the Artist Sees It.' *Daily Express* 11 April 1913: 4.

Shelley, Percy Bysshe. 'A Defence of Poetry.' 1821. *The Complete Works of Percy*

Bysshe Shelley. Ed. Roger Igpen and Walter E. Peck. New York: Gordian Press, 1965. 7: 109–140.

Shetley, Vernon. *After the Death of Poetry: Poet and Audience in Contemporary America.* Durham: Duke University Press, 1993.

Shulte-Sasse, Jochen. 'Foreword: Theory of Modernism versus Theory of the Avant-Garde.' Bürger, *Theory of the Avant-Garde.* vii–xlvii.

Sickert, Walter. 'The Futurist "Devil-among-the-Tailors."' *The English Review* 10 (1912): 147–54.

Slataper, Scipio. 'Il futurismo.' *La cultura italiana del '900 attraverso le riviste: La Voce (1908–1914).* Turin: Einaudi, 1960. 203–5.

Smedley, Constance. *Crusaders: The Reminiscences of Constance Smedley.* N.p.: Duckworth, 1929.

Sonn, Richard D. *Anarchism and Cultural Politics in Fin de Siècle France.* Lincoln: University of Nebraska Press, 1989.

Spackman, Barbara. *Decadent Genealogies: The Rhetoric of Sickness from Baudelaire to D'Annunzio.* Ithaca: Cornell University Press, 1989.

– 'Interversions.' *Perennial Decay: The Aesthetics and Politics of Decadence.* Ed. Liz Constable, Dennis Dennisoff, and Matthew Potolsky. Philadelphia: University of Pennsylvania Press, 1999. 35–49.

Spinazzola, Vittorio. 'Le articolazioni del pubblico.' *Letteratura italiana del Novecento: Bilancio di un secolo.* Ed. Alberto Asor Rosa. Turin: Einaudi, 2000. 180–202.

Stefani, Manuela Angela. *Nietzsche in Italia: rassegna bibliografica 1893–1970.* Assisi-Rome: Carucci, 1975.

Sternhell, Zeev. *The Birth of Fascist Ideology: From Cultural Rebellion to Political Revolution.* Trans. David Maisel. Princeton: Princeton University Press, 1994.

Strong, Beret E. *The Poetic Avant-Garde: The Groups of Borges, Auden, and Breton.* Evanston: Northwestern University Press, 1997.

Tailhade, Laurent. *Quelques fantômes de jadis.* Paris: L'Édition française illustrée, 1920.

Tamburri, Anthony. *Of* Saltimbanchi *and* Incendiari: *Aldo Palazzeschi and Avant-Gardism in Italy.* Rutherford: Fairleigh Dickinson University Press; London and Toronto: Associated University Presses, 1990.

Traversetti, Bruno. *Le parole e la critica: guida terminologica alla letteratura.* Roma: Cooperativa scrittori, 1978.

Tzara, Tristan. *Sept manifestes dada.* In *Dada est tatou. Tout est dada.* Ed. Hanri Béhar. Paris: Flammarion, 1996. 199–238.

– *Seven Dada Manifestoes.* In *The Dada Painters and Poets. An Anthology.* Ed. Robert Motherwell. Cambridge: Harvard University Press, 1981. 76–82.

Valesio, Paolo. *Gabriele d'Annunzio: The Dark Flame*. New Haven : Yale University Press, 1992.

Vattimo, Gianni. *The End of Modernity: Nihilism and Hermeneutics in Postmodern Culture*. Trans. Jon R. Snyder. Baltimore: Johns Hopkins University Press, 1988.

Verlaine, Paul. *Œuvres poétiques*. Ed. Jacques Robichez. Paris: Édition Garnier Frères, 1969.

Viazzi, Glauco. 'Il futurismo come organizzazione. Tecniche e strumenti di gruppo.' *Es* 5 (1976): 36–60.

Villa, Angela Ida. *Neoidealismo e rinascenza latina tra Otto e Novecento: La cerchia di Sergio Corazzini: Poeti dimenticati e riviste del Crepuscolarismo romano (1903–1907)*. Milan: LED – Edizioni Universitarie di Lettere Economia Diritto, 1999.

Vocabolario degli Accademici della Crusca. Venice: Giouanni Alberti, 1611.

'"Vorticist Art."' *The Times* 13 June 1914. 5.

Watt, Ian. *The Rise of the Novel: Studies in Defoe, Richardson and Fielding*. Berkeley: University of California Press, 1957.

Wees, William. 'Futurismo, vorticismo e "mondo moderno."' De Felice, *Futurismo, cultura e politica*. 439–52.

– *Vorticism and the English Avant-Garde*. Toronto: University of Toronto Press, 1972.

Weir, David. *Anarchy and Culture: The Aesthetic Politics of Modernism*. Amherst: University of Massachussets Press, 1997.

– *Decadence and the Making of Modernism*. Amherst: University of Massachusetts Press, 1996.

Weisstein, Ulrich. 'Futurism in Germany and England: Two Flashes in the Pan.' *Revue des langues vivantes* 44 (1978): 467–97.

White, John J. *Literary Futurism: Aspects of the First Avant-Garde*. Oxford: Claredon Press, 1990.

Williams, Raymond. *The Politics of Modernism: Against the New Conformists*. London and New York: Verso, 1989.

Windsor, Alan. 'Wyndham Lewis's «Blast and Bless».' *Wyndham Lewis: Letteratura / Pittura*. Ed. Giovanni Cianci. Palermo: Sellerio, 1982. 86–100.

Wolfe, Don M, ed. *Leveller Manifestoes of the Puritan Revolution*. New York: Thomas Nelson, 1944.

Xavier, Louis Stan[islas] et al. *Nouveau manifeste des Princes émigrés et leur profession de foi sur la Constitution Françoise*. Coblentz and Bruxelles: Le Franc, 1791.

Yeats, W.B. *Plays and Controversies*. London: Macmillan, 1927.

Zach, Natan. 'Imagism and Vorticism.' Bradbury and McFarlane. *Modernism*. 228–42.

Index

www.ingramcontent.com/pod-product-compliance
Lightning Source LLC
LaVergne TN
LVHW090805070826
844660LV00022B/1087